Periphyseon
On the Division of Nature

*The Library
of
Liberal Arts*

JOHN THE SCOT

(JOANNES SCOTUS ERIUGENA)

TRANSLATED BY

Myra L. Uhlfelder

WITH SUMMARIES BY

Jean A. Potter

WIPF & STOCK · Eugene, Oregon

Periphyseon

On the Division of Nature

The Library of Liberal Arts

Wipf and Stock Publishers
199 W 8th Ave, Suite 3
Eugene, OR 97401

Periphyseon on the Division of Nature
By John the Scot, and Uhlfelder, Myra L.
Copyright©1976 by Uhlfelder, Myra
ISBN 13: 978-1-61097-630-5
Publication date 8/15/2011
Previously published by Bobbs Merrill, 1976

Contents

Translator's Preface

This work is an attempt to present Eriugena's *Periphyseon: On the Division of Nature* in a fuller translation than is now readily available in English. Where the text has not been translated, summaries have been inserted to give a precise and reasonably detailed idea of the content of passages deleted. The procedure ranges from a complete translation of Book 1 to a treatment of Book 2 almost entirely by summary except for the inclusion of a few brief excerpts. Books 3, 4, and 5 include fairly lengthy passages in translation joined by summaries.

The basic Latin text followed is Floss's edition, printed in volume 122 of Migne's *Patrologia Latina*. Sheldon-Williams's recent edition of Books 1 and 2 is based on earlier manuscripts and would have to be adopted by anyone concerned primarily with palaeographical and textual problems. In several passages as noted, Sheldon-Williams's readings are helpful in establishing a controversial reading or correcting a faulty one. On the whole, however, it is encouraging to see how reliable the older text is. The future availability of a complete modern edition, desirable for a number of reasons, will fortunately not invalidate scholarship based on the earlier edition. For a translator who still needs the Floss text for the later books of the *Periphyseon,* this essential soundness of the Floss text is both important and heartening.

In addition to the published partial translations of the work, I have seen several unpublished versions of Book 1, including one by Dr. Ellen Kohler of the department of archaeology at the University of Pennsylvania.

Our special thanks are gladly paid to the Pontifical Institute of Toronto and to its librarian for help in obtaining a microfilm of a most useful and scholarly dissertation by Lenke Vietorisz, *Greek Sources in the Periphyseon of John Scotus, Called Eriugena* (October 1966).

Since the text of John the Scot makes it impossible to adopt the version of any published translation of the Bible (as will be seen, the contexts in which the quotations are embedded require translations which are sometimes more literal and sometimes different in other respects from the usual versions), the translations of Biblical passages as of quotations from other sources are generally my own.

Although it is very tempting to discuss Eriugena's use of the liberal arts, the scope of this volume does not allow fruitful development of the subject. The "practical" value of the liberal arts as a whole consists, for Eriugena, in their status as a prerequisite for anyone who aspires to higher, suprarational knowledge. With this emphasis on the educational process, as in other ways, Eriugena is a proper representative of the Platonic tradition in the West. Dialectic is his chief instrument in his attempt to reconcile and harmonize Platonism and Christianity.

Myra L. Uhlfelder
Bryn Mawr College
July, 1973

Introduction

JOHN THE SCOT, AND HIS BACKGROUND

About the middle of the ninth century there appeared at the court of Charles the Bald one of the most elusive figures of the Middle Ages and certainly the most powerful philosophical intellect in Western Europe from the time of Augustine to that of Anselm. That John Scotus Eriugena's *On the Division of Nature* is acknowledged as a major speculative achievement is all the more remarkable in view of the obscurity of its author and its apparent neglect by his contemporaries and the generations that followed.

His name indicates his origin: John Scotus ("the Irishman") or John Eriugena ("born of Ireland"). What brought him to the royal court in France about 845 we do not know, and his end is as shrouded in mystery as his beginning. After what must have been a busy life as royal tutor, he probably remained in France, teaching grammar at Laon. That city, near the palace at Quierzy, was a major center of Irish influence west of the

Rhine and possessed one of the best libraries of the time. We can be quite certain, however, that William of Malmesbury's account of Eriugena's return to Britain to spend his last years is based on a confusion of names and that the bizarre tale that he was stabbed to death by the pens of his infuriated students is pure legend.

Had Eriugena never written his masterpiece, he would still have made an important contribution to the transmission of Greek learning to the West by his translations, and historians of theology would still have assigned him a secure if minor place in the formation of Christian doctrine. We first hear of him in the role of theologian when in 851–2 the Bishop of Laon mentions in a letter that he has invited Eriugena to express an expert opinion on the question of predestination. The monk Gottschalk had provoked a storm of controversy by proposing that God had predestined some men to damnation as well as others to salvation. Eriugena's *On Predestination*, while in accord with the view that finally prevailed against Gottschalk's, was sufficiently alien in its concepts to bring it condemnation. Like his contemporaries versed in the thought of Augustine and Boethius, he argues against the theory of double predestination, but where they argue from the nature of time, he begins with the nature of God as entirely simple and therefore incapable of producing two contrary effects.

As a translator Eriugena fared better in the eyes of his contemporaries. Indeed, even by modern estimates his accomplishment is considerable. Few Europeans of the time had anything beyond the most rudimentary knowledge of Greek. Two centuries earlier Irish scholars had been famous for their erudition, but it is not certain whether Eriugena's linguistic proficiency was gained in his homeland or on the continent. In any event Charles the Bald prized Eriugena's skill highly enough to entrust to him the task of translating a gift which the Emperor Michael of Byzantium had sent in 827 to Louis the Pious, the works of Dionysius the Areopagite. An earlier translation had been made under Hilduin's direction in 835, but it was a poor job, awkward, inaccurate, and unintelligible. Eriugena's version was vastly superior in rendering the meaning in Latin, and it earned him a second royal invitation to translate the *Ambigua* of Maximus the Confessor, in which Maximus had used the conceptual scheme of the Pseudo-Dionysius to unravel some of the knottier passages in the writings of Gregory Nazianzen. Perhaps he also translated Maximus' *Ad Thalassium*. A third major Greek author whom he made available to the Latin West was Gregory of Nyssa, whose allegorical commentary on Genesis, *On the Making of Man*, is quoted frequently in the *On the Division of Nature* in Eriugena's own translation under the title *On the Image*. In addition to his translations Eriugena wrote annotations on Martianus Capella and commentaries on the Pseudo-Dionysius' *Celestial Hierarchy* and the Gospel of John.

Gregory of Nyssa, Eriugena says, is the greatest of the Greek authorities, as Augustine is the greatest of the Latins. This is high praise indeed for the Cappadocian, for no authority since the age of the Apostles is held in higher esteem by Eriugena and his contemporaries than Augustine. References to Augustine outnumber all others in Eriugena's work, and where explicit acknowledgement is absent, the Augustinian parentage of key concepts is usually obvious.

The major Greek sources for Eriugena, then, are Gregory of Nyssa, the Pseudo-Dionysius, and Maximus the Confessor, and those in the Latin West are Augustine and Ambrose. But they do not teach a common doctrine. Despite their common Biblical and Platonic heritage, Eastern and Western Christian thought had by the time of Eriugena diverged steadily until each had acquired those distinctive characteristics which are evident even today. It was Eriugena, more than any other mediaeval thinker, who sought to reunite them.

Just what was the common heritage and how did the thought of East and West draw apart? Much research is yet to be done before these questions can be settled properly, but a broad sketch of the important stages in development may help to throw into relief the speculative task that confronted Eriugena.

The two traditions of Eastern and Western Christian thought had far more in common than what divided them. Both derived from the blend of Hebraic religious thought and Platonic philosophy initiated in Alexandria, the center of Hellenistic culture, first by Philo the Jew (ca.25–ca.50) and later by the Christian apologists, Clement (d. ca.215) and Origen (ca.184–ca.254). Both sought to understand Christian sacred history in the light of a metaphysics in which history is of little importance. Both also owed a heavy debt to the most powerful thinker since Aristotle, the religious philosopher and founder of Neoplatonism, Plotinus, a pagan who scorned both Jew and Christian.

When the Christians found it imperative to explain their faith to a pagan world and to themselves, Philo's works were at hand to furnish both method and concepts. There was only one truth, Philo asserted, whether revealed to the Hebrews or achieved by the speculative efforts of the Greeks. By using the categories and concepts of current Platonic thought, the so-called Middle Platonism of his day, Philo sought to get behind the crude anthropomorphism demanded by a literal reading of Scripture to reach a profounder understanding of divine revelation. Following both rabbinical and Stoic precedent, he proceeded to give allegorical interpretations of the Biblical narrative. Origen followed his example, and later Christians of the Latin West and Greek East found philosophical allegory the most effective way to comprehend, as far as it could be rationally comprehended, the revealed truth of Scripture.

With Origen began the effort to fit together two cosmic cycles of an original state of perfection, a fall, and a return, the Biblical and the Platonic. Foremost in his mind was the Christian historical drama of the creation of the world, Adam made in God's image and likeness, Adam's fall, the coming of redemption was begun and will continue until all beings, even the devil, are restored to their original state of free adoration of God, there perhaps to fall again and repeat the cycle.

Many elements of Origen's picture were discarded as fitting poorly with the Christian scheme—his description of the Trinity, the preexistence of souls, the possibility of endless cycles of fall and redemption—but much was retained, especially by the Eastern Church, whence it came to Eriugena.

Contemporary with Origen, Plotinus forged a vast and intricate metaphysics of procession and return that was to play a significant role in Christian thought of East and West. There is, he taught, nothing magical or capricious in the timeless activity of the One, the ultimate source from which all proceeds, as Jews and Christians suppose. By a universal and rational law of being, whatever exists gives of itself to the degree that it is; as the sun diffuses its light, ice its coldness, and flowers their aroma, so from the One there descends in ever increasing profusion the multiple universe, and by the same rational law, man returns to union with the One.

In the *Republic* (509b) Plato had written of the Good that it "may be said to be not only the author of knowledge to all things known, but of their being and essence, and yet the good is not essence, but far exceeds essence in dignity and power," and Plotinus asserts such transcendence of his One. It cannot be given any name, not even that of the Good, for as its cause it transcends all goodness. The One is not a being, for to be is to have a limited and determinate essence, to exclude what is other; but the One has no other. In giving itself it loses nothing and, depending on our point of view, what proceeds from it is within the One or is the manifestation of the power of the One on a lower ontological level. Each manifestation or emanation is distinguishable from its source, and yet is nothing without that source. There is perfect continuity in Plotinus' universe.

Stages or hypostases, however, can be discriminated in the procession of the One to the many. The One first produces the

the God-Man, and the consequent redemption of t
The Biblical cycle of creation, fall, and redemption
God's freedom in making the world from nothin
acting throughout human history to recall men to o
to Himself. The climax of the drama was God's free o
Himself to achieve man's salvation and blessedness. T
also the ancient Platonic tradition of the soul th
viewed the real intelligible world but through some
has fallen into the prison house of the body, here to
regain its pristine state. Following Philo's lead, but
own innovations, Origen combined the two tradition

The world came to be, Origen taught, when Go
Wisdom or Word conceived an ideal creation. Plato h
in perfect harmony with Moses it seemed, the priori
intelligible and eternal ideal over the sensuous, transit
corporeal. Succeeding generations of Platonists had i
the Good of the *Republic* with the Maker of the
while the Forms became ideas in the divine mind. The
the ideas for Philo was God's Word or Logos, and Ori
placed them in the Word, the Son of the Father, as the
Person of the Christian Trinity.

For Philo there was a double creation: first God co
an ideal blueprint of the world, and then throu
instrument, the Word, it made its appearance in the
world of space and time. For Origen the first creatior
heavenly realm of incorporeal spirits, rational intell
with the capacity of free choice. The spirits were cre
worship God, but they grew weary and fell, some a sh
to become angels, some further to become men, and
great distance to become devils. Human souls were
bodies by God, not as punishment for their sin, but as
to their instruction and a remedy for their spiritual
God, then, contrary to the *Timaeus* but in agreemen
Philo, created matter, and all that God creates is
Furthermore, as men cannot create themselves, so they d
save themselves. With the Incarnation of Christ the proc

closest unity possible, that between the mind and what it knows. A cosmic Intelligence (*Nous*) thinks the intelligible world of Platonic ideas as an articulated whole. Each object of thought or idea is itself a thinker, thinking all the others and becoming them while remaining itself. The part is the whole, the whole is in the part.

Man in his fullest reality is what he is in the Intelligence, an idea that is itself a dynamic creative intelligence. In the descending procession of the Intelligence to cosmic Soul, man is a soul, his intelligence first displaying itself as discursive thought and then, still lower, as the principle of life and motion that animates a particular body produced by the universal Soul in its guise as Nature. When the visible and mutable world of physical objects is engendered, the energy that flows from the One is too weak to proceed further. There remains only man's return to the One. By turning within himself and recalling his true home in the intelligible world, he can ascend to become again what in truth he has always been eternally and immutably.

The grand theme of all Augustine's writing is the cosmic epic of the soul of man, wandering blindly away from the immutable and eternal one God, through the many changing circumstances of mortal life until God in His grace restores him to the right path, and man becomes a pilgrim on his way home to rest in God. In writing of the descent and return, Origen had been dispassionate and Plotinus deliberately impersonal, but Augustine writes with the intensity of personal experience. The cosmic drama has been enacted in the microcosm of his own life. All along he had been seeking unwittingly for God, for it is in the nature of the soul to move toward its end, and all along in hidden ways God had brought him back from his errors. He had been saved from the materialist dualism of the Manichees, with their cosmic warfare of two ultimate principles of good and evil, by his reading of some works of Plotinus or his followers, and from these "Platonists" he had learned of the immateriality of God and the soul, the immutability of the eternal Being, and the perpetual perishing of the things of the visible world. He had then been saved from the presumption of Plotinus through the sermons of Ambrose: man cannot ascend to God unless God first descends to man. And this God has done in the Word made flesh.

The cycle of creation, fall, and return is not the result of any ineluctable natural law as Plotinus had taught. Augustine is ardently on the side of Philo and Origen: God freely created the world from nothing by His will, and chief among His creatures is man, His image, to whose nature belongs the power of free choice. Adam need not have fallen. Indeed, his sin and its consequences are strictly inexplicable, for evil is nothing positive. All that God creates is necessarily good. But Plotinus, perhaps, has given the most adequate metaphysical account: evil is a lack, an absence of good. In human beings it is to be found in expending and dispersing oneself in inordinate love of the earthly and mutable. And yet that is not all one must say. Evil is not simply an absence or privation; it is a depravation, a deliberate and conscious preference for the lower over the higher, from which no man can be released save by the grace of God in Christ.

Augustine departs further from Plotinus and from Philo as well. The divine ideas are in no way separate from God Himself. No spiritual creation precedes the actual corporeal creation of the world. Time and the empirical world began together, and Eden was a place in which human history began with Adam. As in his own life, Augustine sees the unfolding of events as the temporal movement of men to their eventual salvation or damnation. Of course, Holy Scripture is to be understood allegorically as Origen and Ambrose had shown, but the historical events must not be neglected as if they were somehow unreal or unimportant. God the eternal works in and through the temporal.

Augustine is as much a part of the Eastern legacy as he is of the West. Yet the characteristic speculation of the Eastern

Church is more akin to Origen's and perhaps Plotinus' than it is to Augustine's. This is especially true of the three Cappadocians, Gregory of Nazianzen, Basil of Caesarea, and Gregory of Nyssa, and of the Pseudo-Dionysius and Maximus, who were all to exert such a profound influence on Eriugena. Each of these thinkers made his own contribution to Eriugena's system, but since it is here necessary only to set the stage for the cosmic design of *On the Division of Nature*, the most useful light is shed by the two whom he translated and cites most often, Gregory of Nyssa (ca. 330–394) and the Pseudo-Dionysius (end of 5th century).

In Gregory's version of the cycle of creation, fall, and redemption, history is of little moment. The story of the creation in Genesis, if we interpret it aright, is an account of the subtle and complex relationship of God to man. Man is the image of God, like Him in every respect save that he is created, and the mark of all created being is its capacity for change. Man is, then, a purely intelligible, incorporeal, and immortal being, lacking no perfection. As had Philo and Origen, Gregory conceives the original creation of man as a purely spiritual one, not located in a physical garden of Eden, though, unlike Origen, Gregory holds that the soul did not exist before its entry into a body. God made everything at once; thus the priority of the soul is ontological only. Having given man free will, the power to be his own master, God knew that he would abuse it, choosing the worse in preference to the better, and so He added to the image, as eternal though accidental to it, the physical body and all that belongs to animal nature. The 'first man', man as image of God, is one; *Adam* is the name for mankind. The 'second man', the image with its additional animal nature, is multiple—all individual historical men in their countless diversity. The 'first man' was without sex, the second divisible into male and female.

In all men the image remains, for Gregory believes that the image of God is human nature itself, the immortal human essence, sullied in this temporal life by the filth of sin but incorruptible by nature. Man's task, with the help of God, is to cleanse the image, purifying it of its accretions until its original brightness is restored. In and through God's identification of Himself with fallen man in the Incarnate Word begins the journey back to that state in which at the end of time all men shall again be one man in Christ. The Christian life, then, is a progress toward perfection, a perpetual change of the soul as it is constantly renewed and transformed into the divine likeness prefigured at creation. This is the process of deification or assimilation to God, an ever increasing mirroring of the divine nature.

Deification, however, does not mean identity to Gregory. The image is always other than and less than its archetype; the distance between Creator and creature is always infinite. God forever dwells in inaccessible light, but in the desire for God is God Himself. As the soul is constantly transformed into the image, it is at every moment as completely filled with God as it is capable of being. Because God is infinite, however, the soul's desire and love for Him are insatiable. The end of man is the vision of God, but for Gregory it is neither a state of rest as for Augustine, nor an occasion for a possible further fall as for Origen, but rather a continually increasing delight in the discovery of the infinite goodness.

The Christian Platonism of the East finds its most striking expression in the unknown writer near the end of the fifth century, a Syrian perhaps, who called himself Dionysius the Areopagite. God's very nature, he taught, is His inaccessible hiddenness, His unknowability and radical otherness from the world that He wills into being from nothing. He thinks and His very ideas are creative wills, dynamic manifestations of His hidden essence, Platonic Ideas become powers. Through participation in them everything in the created world derives its being, its order, and its function. They are 'predestinations' and, as expressing God's love for the world, final causes of all things as well.

Ideas present in Gregory of Nyssa and Gregory's fellow

Cappadocians, Basil of Caesarea and Gregory Nazianzen, are amplified and modified in the light of the conceptual scheme of Proclus, the late Neoplatonist, who had elaborated the Plotinian triad of One, Intelligence, and Soul as a graded series of entities proceeding from the One according to rational law. For the Pseudo-Dionysius as for Gregory of Nyssa all beings are theophanies, ways in which, by means of His powers, the hidden God reveals His glory. To be a creature is to be a manifestation of the Divine.

God is inapprehensible and ineffable, yet we can know Him and speak of Him in terms of His creatures, for each of them is a participation of Him. Beginning with the highest created perfections—Goodness, Being, and Unity—down through all the ranks of being and perfection, all positive qualities can be ascribed to Him, not that He possesses them in the way in which creatures do but in the way appropriate to their cause. Immediately, however, we see that these affirmative ascriptions, the cataphatic way of naming God, must give rise to a negative or apophatic way, not only as corrective supplement to our thinking but also as more appropriate to the object. As the One beyond all Goodness, God is Not-good, a more accurate expression because it conveys His otherness. One can start, then, with the lowest beings in the hierarchy and ascend, negating at every step and ascribing the negation to God. At the highest level, however, when one sees that God is Not-being or Nothing, a further step must be taken: God is not an absence or lack of being, but superabundant being. He is superessential Essence, superessential Goodness, superessential Wisdom. In this last step both affirmative and negative ways combine, but the weight is on the negative.

The affirmative and negative ways are not merely modes of speaking of God but ways of coming to know Him, of returning to union with the source of one's being. At the very last in seeking Him one must go beyond the limits of intelligibility and step outside one's ordinary powers of knowing; in such ecstasy of unknowing one enters into the

divine darkness where the Incomprehensible and Unname-
able dwells, there to be united with Him.

These thinkers and others, such as Boethius and Ambrose of
the Latins and Gregory Nazianzen (whom he sometimes
confuses with Gregory of Nyssa) and Maximus the Confessor
of the Greeks, are Eriugena's acknowledged intellectual ances-
tors. Though bearing an unmistakable family resemblance,
each has his own distinctive traits. Eriugena recognizes some
of these differences clearly, but he prefers to avoid controversy whenever possible, and instead to stress their kinship.
Where differences sharpen into contradiction, however, he
states his own view unequivocally. In nearly every case he
sides with the Greeks, usually with courtesy toward the
opposing theory and an invitation to the reader to decide for
himself.

Though in fundamental agreement on both basic Christian
doctrine and some mode of Platonism as its intellectual
expression, differences in temperament and attitude perhaps
between East and West did in fact produce quite divergent
ways of viewing the universe and its relation to God. God is,
of course, for both traditions transcendent and immanent,
wholly other than the world, bringing it into being by a free
act of His will, and also in some way intimately present to it.
The Augustinian tradition expresses the otherness in terms of a
doctrine of causality in which the world is produced as
something with being in its own right, having a dependent
status to be sure, but with a character of its own. God's eternal
providence directs the course of its history and He often
bestows upon it gifts of grace which are above those that it
has by its nature. In the Eastern tradition, on the other hand,
divine transcendence is inseparable from divine immanence.
They are related as convex to concave. One is the condition of
the other, for unless God were utterly different from His
creation as a whole and from each of its parts, He could not
also be as intimately related to it as He is.

For Augustine and the Western tradition, being is the most

fundamental term to apply to God. Not that He is a being, like all other beings though preeminent among them, nor that He is an abstract being-in-general, but rather that He is Being itself. The Christian Greeks, however, following a tradition begun by Philo, prefer to place Him beyond all being: to be is to have an essence, a distinct nature; but distinctness implies limitation. As Plato taught in the *Sophist*, to be something is not to be something else. Infinity, then, as all-comprehensive boundlessness is a designation more apt than being. This is what leads Eriugena to follow the Pseudo-Dionysius and Maximus in speaking of God as Nonbeing or Nothing.

The same divergence in emphasis appears in Latin and Greek understandings of God's presence to the world. For both, of course, His creative will continually underlies the being of every creature, but the distinction between nature and grace that Augustine framed in his controversy with the Pelagians comes to occupy a prominent place in Western thought. To the fixed nature of the creature, God wills to add supernatural gifts. The point is certainly not absent from Greek thought, but the Greeks prefer to say that original man possessed most of these gifts as part of his imperishable character as God's image. So, too, drawing a clear line between God's action and man's in the work of redemption is not of importance to the Greeks, who are content to say, as Eriugena does, that though the initiative is always God's, man must cooperate freely.

Because of his changeless character as God's image, man's role in respect to history and its end takes on a different aspect in the Eastern Fathers. Actual temporal events, except that of the Incarnation, never receive the importance accorded them in the *City of God*. Yet if men like Gregory of Nyssa and Maximus do not seek God's hand in human history, they find it everywhere throughout nature in the character of all things as theophanies, God's self-manifestations, and it is by and through man that all creation is restored to its perfection at the end of time.

Eastern and Western Fathers alike hold that in this life man is journeying on a pilgrimage to God and every increase in the knowledge of God brings him a step closer to that perfect knowledge which is the Beatific Vision. Again, however, their differing conceptions of man's relation to God lead to divergent anticipations of the end. For Augustine man will rest, his desire for vision "face to face" fully satisfied. There remains only his endless enjoyment of it. For Gregory even in this life the pure may see God, but even in the life to come the progress in knowledge is never ended. The capacity of new discovery is never exhausted, for because God is infinite, and change the condition of an image, man will eternally rejoice as he ever more clearly and intensely mirrors his Creator.

On these and many other points where Eastern and Western traditions diverge, Eriugena sides with the Greek Fathers. It would be as imperceptive, however, to place him wholly within the Eastern line of development as it would be anachronistic to see him as deliberately and consciously setting himself the task of reconciliation. His intention was to construct with the materials and tools at hand a Christian understanding of the universe.

He failed, if we are to judge by the influence of the *Division of Nature* on his contemporaries or on succeeding generations of mediaeval thinkers. His translations of the Pseudo-Dionysius proved to be a much more obviously significant contribution to later mediaeval thought than his original work. He founded no school and, as far as we know, made few disciples, none of any intellectual stature. *On the Division of Nature* seems to have fallen into obscurity through indifference until the twelfth century, when Anselm of Laon, Simon of Tournai, Hugh and Richard of St. Victor, and perhaps some members of the school of Chartres show familiarity with its theological and philosophical teachings. Only Honorius Augustodunensis, the popularizer, can be said with certainty to have promulgated Eriugena's doctrines. His *Clavis physicae* is an epitome of *On the Division of Nature*, incorporating long excerpts as well as abridgements, and his other writings make use of its concepts.

About three centuries and a half passed before official notice was taken of *On the Division of Nature*, and then the result was to condemn it. The action seems to have been taken without any careful textual scrutiny by competent theologians but because of its reputed association with heretical movements and thinkers. The Cathars are said to have read it, and the Albigenses to have appealed to it. In 1210 a council of Paris ordered it burned because of its influence on Almaric of Bena. Among Eriugena's many so-called heretical doctrines that Almaric was charged with promulgating, three were singled out as examples: all things are God, the primordial causes create and are created, and at the end of the world there will be no distinction of the sexes.

In 1225 Pope Honorius III asked that the Archbishops and Bishops of France send all whole or partial copies, "swarming with worms of heretical perversity", to Rome to be burned. Whole copies did, of course, survive the burning, and more was preserved in the form of glosses on Eriugena's translations of the Pseudo-Dionysius. For example, recent scholarship has persuasive evidence that Ramon Lull (1235–1315) was significantly influenced by Eriugena's doctrines of the primordial causes and the universal elements. Nicholas of Cusa (1401–1464) mentions *On the Division of Nature* in his *De docta ignorantia* as an esoteric work to be kept from those with "weak eyes" who are incapable of understanding its teachings.

Despite the apparent neglect into which Eriugena's masterpiece fell for so many years, it is inconceivable that a work of such intellectual power, however alien to the mainstream of Latin Christian thought, should have been completely ignored. While it is true that historians' efforts to show its impact on the thought of men like Avicebron and Anselm of Canterbury have proved unconvincing, still much research remains to be done in tracing its oblique influence on scholastic metaphysics and mystical theology. The more important task for philosophers, however, is that of coming to understand and to evaluate the complex and subtle thought of this monumental achievement.

ON THE DIVISION OF NATURE

In the opening words of *On the Division of Nature*, Eriugena introduces both his subject and the conditions under which it can be treated. He will investigate the four-fold division of nature, his version of the epic theme of the procession and return of all things to God. The conditions of the inquiry are implicit in the inclusion in nature of all that is not as well as all that is, the unknowable as well as that which can be known.

By the first division, nature that creates and is not created, we are to understand God as the ultimate Beginning of things. Nature that is created and creates is God's manifestation of Himself in His creative ideas, the primordial causes of the intelligible and visible worlds. The effects of these causes are nature that is created but does not create. Finally, in the return at the end of time, God is known as the goal of all things, nature that is neither created nor creative. God, then, is the Beginning and the End, Alpha and Omega, and in the Middle is His creative power displayed in its myriad effects.

Reason is the distinctive property of man, and what he knows or senses is rightly said to be. But reason is created and its competence limited; what lies beyond it can be said not to be. God transcends all knowing whatever, whether it be human or even angelic, and in this sense He can be said not to be. The essences of all things are grounded in Him and hidden from our view, and they too must be said not to be. Both what is and what is not are found within the hierarchical order of created things, for to affirm the lower is to negate the higher, and to affirm the higher is to negate the lower. Angelic intelligences with their immediate insight into objects are not man, and human reason is not the mode of comprehension of angels. Again, what is merely potential is not yet and is known only when actualized. As we know from Plato, too, changing and corruptible things are not when compared with the eternal immutable Ideas of which they are copies. Finally, in the special case of man, as we know him now he is not what he was as the sinless being created in the image of God. Being, or what is, then, is what can be known by intellect, reason, or the senses, but nature evidently includes what lies beyond their power. Being is correlative with knowability.

To divide nature is not to take a whole and split it physically into parts. To divide in the sense intended by Eriugena is to trace the way in which God creates the cosmos and how, when it departs from His original intention, He draws it back to its perfection in Himself. God's creative activity is the expression of His rational Word, and so the order of the universe is wholly logical. The traditional division of a genus into its subordinate genera and their constituent species is not an arbitrary human invention but rather the actual structure of created being. When reason pursues the method of division in regard to nature itself, it is following the path which God took in His creation of all beings from the highest down to the least; when it retraces this path in its use of the method of collection and proceeds from the union of individuals into species and species into genera, reason follows the actual progressive unification of things as they return to rest in their source. Dialectic, then, is created in the nature of things and not by man.

Thinking is an activity, a 'motion' of the mind, and the structure of its object, reality, becomes the articulation of its thoughts. Eriugena's realism is at once a reliance on reason and a recognition of its limitations, a metaphysical doctrine of the unutterable transcendence of God and a justification of human thought and expression of Him. From the Pseudo-

Dionysius he borrows the two complementary ways in which the human mind can approach God, the affirmative or cataphatic and the negative or apophatic. Because God is the single unitary source of all, we can attribute to Him essence, goodness, truth, and the like, though only in a transferred sense, for He is their cause and thus superior to them. The Neoplatonic principle that the cause is always of a higher ontological order than the effect, is implicitly operative here. If essence, goodness, and similar terms are predicated properly of creatures, they cannot literally apply to the Creator. The negative way is therefore more appropriate. He is neither essence nor goodness nor truth nor any other thing designated. But still we have not gone far enough. To assert something is implicitly to deny its other or its negation; to deny something is to affirm what is different from that which is denied. When we speak of the essence of anything, we distinguish it, cut it off from what is not it but something other. When we attribute goodness to anything, we implicitly contrast it with evil, the lack of goodness. God is incomparable, and so neither affirmation nor negation can suffice. Since He is above all plurality and difference, the most precise terms that reason can employ are those expressing His transcendence: 'superessential', 'more than goodness', and all such words and phrases which are affirmative in their form but negative in their import and in no way definitions of God.

Definition belongs in the Aristotelian list of categories as intelligible place; to define something is to mark it off from others, to locate it by rational discrimination with respect to those others, and this one can never do with God. Not only 'place', 'essence' and 'relation' but all the rest of the categories cannot be applied literally to God but only in the way commended by the Pseudo-Dionysius. If our reason is to be faithful to the rational structure of reality, we should also be alert to the truth that the ordinary bodies of our sense experience are not *ousiai*, essences which are the subjects of accidents, but are themselves merely accidents. The true essences of visible things are the immutable ideas, as the Platonists have always taught, and these cannot be perceived by any sense or even known by reason.

Eriugena is neither a sceptic when he denies that reason can know essences nor is he a rationalist in the modern sense when he asserts that the structures of reality are logical. Reason has its divinely appointed orbit in which it functions with perfect competence, but it is never autonomous. It is a creature of God and acts (or 'moves', in his language) only under His guidance. With all the authorities on whom he relies, Eriugena attributes to knowledge an eschatological function: the search for truth is the search for the beatific vision; the end of man is to know God as perfectly as human nature permits. Reason is a motion that lifts the soul to God, but its impulse is from God. The goal to which man aspires is that intellection of God which the angels enjoy, a direct and effortless contemplation—not of God in Himself, for this is never possible for any creature, but—of the theophanies of the Divine Nature, the primordial causes of all things visible and invisible. What the intellect perceives in immediate intuition, reason must discern with effort, arguing from the effects of those causes with dialectic as its tool. The effects, however, participate in their causes and reason in intellect. What intellect sees as cause, reason receives as a law or principle.

Given this conception of reason, it is anachronistic to look for Eriugena's position on the problem of the relation between faith and reason or that of reason and revelation. Faith in the sense of divinely revealed truth accepted freely by men is presupposed, as it was for Augustine, and Eriugena could have subtitled his work *Faith Seeking Understanding* with as much right as Anselm his *Proslogion*. As for reason and revelation, the distinction does not arise: to reason is to trace discursively God's self-revelation.

Eriugena does, however, talk of the relation of reason to authority, but again the context must be noted. Authority for him connotes authorship and always refers to the written records of Scripture and the Fathers of the Church. The truth they pass on to posterity is indeed infallible, but unless it is assented to by reason it cannot be wholly effectual. Reason, on the other hand, as constituted by God in man, His image, does not need to be bolstered by the writings of authorities. It uses them as a preventive to keep itself from wandering away from truth, but it is never subservient to them. How could it be, when their common source is Truth itself?

The principal subject of the first book is God as one in His ineffable simplicity to which nothing is exterior, while in the second Eriugena considers the Godhead as a Trinity of Persons or Substances. The order is in no way intended to suggest that hidden behind Father, Son, and Holy Spirit is an undifferentiated Godhead as their foundation. Eriugena's teaching on this point is impeccably orthodox, and he is at pains to establish at some length that, though he prefers the terminology of the Eastern Church, his fidelity to the doctrine of Nicea cannot be challenged. His point is, rather, to consider the way in which God is creative, and examination of the causes of things must include the work of the Trinity as the 'Cause of causes.' The Godhead as a whole creates the world, but it is possible to distinguish the role proper to each Person, or as Eriugena prefers, each Substance. All three are identical in essence, but the Father is the ultimate principle of all creation who begets the Son, His Word, in whom all things are made as unitary ideas; these ideas are then multiplied and distributed in descending logical order by the Holy Spirit.

From at least the time of the Middle Platonists, certainly by that of Philo, the Platonic ideas had been internalized, that is, located within the divine mind. For the Christian tradition of both East and West, that locus was more precisely defined as the second Person or Substance of the Trinity, the Word of Wisdom of God. The exact status of those ideas both in their relation to God and to the empirical world came to receive, as we have seen, a different understanding in the traditions of

East and West. In the West they are identical with the Mind of the Creator, who in making the world from nothing, produces spatial and temporal copies of what is, in effect, Himself. For the Greek Christians, especially the Pseudo-Dionysius and Maximus, the divine ideas are not simply forms or paradigms according to which the world is created as an ordered whole. With the characteristic Eastern emphasis on the divine transcendence as superessential, they assert that the ideas are both in God and yet not of His essence. The divine simplicity rules out difference, but it includes distinction. While the ideas participate in that superessential essence, they are its first mode of existence outside its hidden mystery, and hence 'processions', within the Godhead and yet from the essence. They are the manifestations of that which always remains a mystery, the "manward" side of the Godhead. Moreover, the divine ideas in this tradition are more than static exemplars, for they are the divine productive powers in and through which the world is created.

Eriugena's primordial causes are obviously closer to the Greek conception of the divine ideas than to the Latin. Their nature and relation to God and the mediatorial roles that they play as theophanies in the complementary processes of creation and redemption of the world are the major topics of the second book, for they are the second division of nature, nature as created and itself creative. In their relation to God, they are ontologically dependent, hence other than He, and therefore creatures. Since they are timeless, they are eternal, although not in the sense in which the Son and Holy Spirit are coeternal with the Father as being of the same essence. In no way are they commensurable with the Trinity. God's essence is superessential, so exalted above the essence of the primordial causes as to be no essence at all, while they are essences themselves, the 'determinations' of things. They are wholly intelligible, incorporeal, and immutable. The most fundamental metaphysical distinction in Eriugena's system is between Creator and creature, cause and effect, and not between permanence and change, eternity and time, or intelligibility and visibility.

Although God is eternally Creator, Eriugena never suggests that there is any necessity in His action, not even that natural spontaneity by which the Plotinian One gives rise to the many. God's creative thinking is identical with His free willing, and yet He is present in what He has made. The creature always participates in the Creator, the lower in the higher, for in participation, as Eriugena understands it in company with the Eastern tradition, the cause remains immanent in the effect, and the effect is not so much a copy as an expression of the higher reality on a lower level. Eriugena prefers to say that since nothing is outside God, creatures are in Him and not He in them. This does not mean that Eriugena is a pantheist, for it is precisely God's transcendence that makes such language possible. He can also say that God is the substance of all things, He 'makes Himself' in the primordial causes, but this is not to deny the reality of the creature. Rather, it expresses the fact that He is their abiding principle without which they would be nothings.

Taken in themselves, the primordial causes are, as multiplied by the operation of the Holy Spirit, a hierarchy of all that is real. Created one in and by the Word, they are pluralized as the genera, species, forms, numbers, and finally individual substances that constitute the created world. In several passages Eriugena gives different lists of the primordial causes in descending order, headed by goodness in itself and essence in itself, but this order appears to be arbitrary and of little real interest to him. He does, however, distinguish occasionally between higher and lower primordial causes, calling the higher ones causes proper, while the lower, apparently the *infima species* and forms of individuals, are termed substances.

God begins to be in the primordial causes as He 'descends' into what is other than He but not outside Himself. The procession is a theophany, God's power displaying itself as a multiplicity of powers, so that every creature is a theophany, a showing forth of God in its own distinctive manner. As God is One in Three, so each creature manifests in its ontological structure a triadic character reflecting Father, Son, and Holy Spirit. Although every substance or cause is an indivisible unit, within it can be distinguished its essence *(ousia)*, its power *(dynamis)*, and its operation *(energeia)*. A being is, it is capable of something, and it is effective in what it does. As God is both Beginning and End, or in Aristotelian terminology, both efficient and final cause of the universe, so each real being is both an efficient and final cause, a center of creativity mirroring that of its Creator. Viewed in itself, it remains a wholly changeless entity; but if viewed in terms of what proceeds from it, it is the cause or principle of a multiplicity of entities of a lower degree of creative intensity. These are said to be contained in the higher, for without their principle they could not be. Just as the Source of all is Beginning and End, so there is a law of nature that the principle of each thing is also its end or goal. Number, to use a favorite example of Eriugena's, has as its principle the monad in which every member of the number series is contained, from which each derives, and to which each returns.

Chief among the primordial causes in dignity and playing the central role in creation is man, who alone of all substances is created in God's image and likeness. The resemblance lies preeminently in his capacity to know. Whatever can be attributed to the Divine Mind can be attributed to the human mind in a weaker and lesser form. In God's Mind, the Divine Word, are the ideas of all things; so too all creation is comprehended in man. God's thinking is creative, and so, in its way, is man's. Or, rather, man's is recreative, for his knowing of all things that God has made is a remaking of them in himself.

A commonplace of philosophy, with its source in the Pre-Socratics, is the concept of man as a microcosm, recapitulating in himself the entire universe, and Eriugena, following

Gregory of Nyssa, elaborates the theme. Man is the 'workshop' of all creatures, for all things are made in him. He understands like an angel, reasons like a man, senses like an animal, and lives like a plant; he is, moreover, a composite of body and soul. Man is therefore at the midpoint of the universe, a mean between the highest extreme of spirit and the lowest form of vegetative life, uniting both the spiritual and the corporeal, and perfectly situated to be the mediator both in the creation of the sensible world and in its redemption.

The way in which man mirrors God's creative knowing is to be found in the triadic ontological structure of his soul, which Eriugena identifies as its 'motions' of intellect or understanding, reason, and inner sense. Like God, the soul is a unity, and the three motions are, as it were, consubstantial with the soul itself. The unitary soul 'moves', and what it centers its attention on ('circles around') determines whether it is to be called intellect, reason, or sense. Intellect, which man shares with the angels, is the highest motion of the soul, a contemplation having as its object God, insofar as He is present in what is nearest Him. Knower and what is known are always in a sense one; the mind becomes what it knows, as Aristotle said, and since God is unknowable in Himself, so this aspect of the human soul is unknown to itself. Reason, the soul's 'middle motion', is the normal employment of man and is the meeting place and mediator of intellect and sensation. It is itself generated by the intellect above it, receiving the divine thoughts as theophanies, and it then 'descends' into inner sense, or discursive reasoning.

What we have described is not man as we know him now, under the conditions of space and time, in all his variety of races, with all his mental and physical differences. These differences belong to the corporeal creation, the accidents of those substances or ideas which are the primordial causes. Primordial man was very different from what we now find men to be. He was indeed a composite of body and soul, but his body was an incorporeal, spiritual body, the image of the soul and therefore the image of an image. His thinking seems to have been like that of the angels, 'circling around' its divine Cause, with reasoning and sensation still latent within the intellect. There was no sexual differentiation, no need of food, sleep, clothing, shelter, and all the other demands the corporeal body makes on us.

Original man was also free. He would not be a perfect image of the divine nature unless he could make his own choices without constraint. Through this freedom he fell, and the corporeal world was thereby generated. We must not conclude, however, that free will is an evil, for everything that God creates is necessarily good. Freedom was given man so that he might rejoice in the contemplation of God, but it brings with it the possibility of wrong choice, a 'perverse motion' directed toward lower goods.

In his account of the nature of evil and its origin, Eriugena follows Augustine's *De libero arbitrio* closely. Evil is nothing substantial or positive, but rather a privation, a non-being intelligible only in terms of something that is real and intrinsically good. It is a displacement of a good: ferocity in a lion is a virtue because it belongs to leonine nature, but in a man it is evil because it is not of the essence of human nature. In man it is a degradation, a taking on of a quality of being that belongs to natures of a lower rank. What appears as evil is only the part taken in isolation from the whole in which its role is that of an enriching contributory good. It is that which deceives man, an apparent good which he pursues mistakenly, for no man deliberately chooses evil. This much can be said with confidence about the nature of evil, and a careful reading of Genesis shows how it came about—through reason's attraction to a deceitful sensuous beauty, symbolized by Eve's persuasion of Adam to eat the forbidden fruit after she had herself been deceived by outward appearance.

Evil can be described, then, and reason can give an account of how it came to be in a wholly good creation, but why it occurred defies explanation. It has no cause, for how could non-being have a cause? Matter is assuredly not evil, for it is created by God in the primordial causes as a kind of spiritual potentiality to be actualized by form. Sin begins with pride. Pride, however, is not its cause but is rather itself the first manifestation of evil, the first step in the falling away from God. Like God's free creation, this 'cause' of the visible world remains a mystery. All that can be said is that its principle is the disorder and misdirection of the free will ('the perverse motion of the irrational will').

Adam does fall, and the intelligible spiritual cosmos created in his nature falls with him. The sensible world with corporeal bodies in space and time comes into being, with all the multiplicity, division, diversification, and mutability that we experience. Things in this world are generated and corrupted; everything is unstable, even the sun, moon, and stars. Mankind becomes the innumerable diversity of human beings, male and female, who reproduce as animals and perish with all visible things.

Yet the substances do not really 'fall'; their nature is immutable and eternal. Just as God their Creator remains eternally and changelessly in Himself, so the intelligible reasons of all things, the causes and substances, abide forever in His Word. Procession does not mean undergoing a change but the production of a lower degree of being while losing nothing. What we call corporeal bodies are not substances but blends of incorporeal accidents. The substance of any particular visible object is hidden in the primordial causes, and what is evident to our senses are the qualities and quantities of that immaterial substance which is intelligible in itself but unknowable to us in our present state. Again, we can know that the substances are but not what they are.

Reason can, however, delineate their creative process. Between the immaterial causes and their visible effects lies a third kind of entity, having something in common with both extremes. The universal elements—earth, air, fire, and water (not the familiar bodies with these names, but their invisible and immaterial causes)—act as intermediaries. They mix, or, rather, they remain pure and integral, but their qualities—hot, cold, wet, and dry—interpenetrate in such a way that everything we call body is a proportion of these constantly changing interminglings of the accidents. Correct analysis of the corporeal world, then, shows it to be a fusion of the incorporeal.

In this explanation Eriugena employs a device familiar to late Neoplatonic thought. Between any two things of a contrary character which are nonetheless united in such a way that the first is the cause of the second, or, what is the same thing, the second exists by way of participation in the first, there must be a mean, an intermediary, having some of the properties of the cause and some of the properties of the effect. Just as the primordial causes are intermediate between God and the empirical world, expressing His superessential will on the level of essence, so the universal elements serve to express the creative activity of the primordial causes on a lower level. Since they too are unities and cannot pass into one another but preserve their own nature, it is their accidents which mix to form the things of this world. Other instances of an intermediate entity can be found in Eriugena's thought; for example, between soul and the body which it creates, vital motion serves as a link. This introduction of a third intermediary entity is not an arbitrary expedient, invented to smooth over an embarrassing gap, but rather another expression of the triadic structure of being as essence, power, and operation. Every creative intelligence is an essence, a principle that always remains what it is, emits its power to achieve its end, and realizes its intention. The device preserves the continuity of the creative power of God, all the while stressing His radical transcendence. Between the ultimate principle and the lowest level of creation there is no distance, only difference. At the same time these differences prevent a flattening out of the hierarchy and any identification of God and creature.

The coming into existence of the empirical world is man's doing. We can give an account of the process—the primordial causes generate the universal elements—and we can know much about the nature of the original sin that triggered the process, but why the sin took place and why there is an empirical world is a mystery. Although this world is a consequence of sin, we cannot say that it is evil. Deriving ultimately from God, it is good in every detail and as a whole. It is true that Man's state would have been incomparably better had he not sinned, but there is nothing inherently evil in body, nor is there anything sinful in sex. Having entered through his sin onto the level of an animal, he now acquires over and above his changeless essence division into male and female and outer sense. Had he remained obedient, he would have reproduced as the angels presumably do, by an instantaneous spiritual multiplication. Since this is now impossible for him, God gives him companionship and enables him to reproduce his kind by means of sexual intercourse.

The account of man's coming to be in time—or, rather, with time, for time as the measure of motion originates simultaneously with generable and corruptible things—is to be found in the opening chapters of Genesis if one penetrates beyond their literal meaning. Since Philo, commentary on these three chapters had been a favorite literary device for expounding a theory of the nature and destiny of man and his status and role in the order of creation. Eriugena's innovation in the eyes of his Western readers, however, is his insistence on allegorical interpretation exclusively. Ambrose's four-fold interpretation is ignored, and the literal or historical sense on which others insist as the basic and indispensable level of exegesis is politely denied. As if to establish his orthodoxy, he uses countless details from the allegories of Augustine, Ambrose, and Gregory of Nyssa, but he is quite aware of his departure from them on the basic issue and argues effectively for his own position.

In Eriugena's allegorical interpretation of the creation narrative, temporal sequence is ignored. All events in Eden are telescoped into one timeless moment: simultaneous with his creation were man's sin and his downfall. With that mysterious act time and space began, and there came about the division and dispersal of all the primordial causal unities into the myriad things of the familiar world of empirical effects.

In the third book Eriugena gives a cosmogony, again in the guise of a commentary on Genesis, in which he presents his views on what we would call scientific matters, physics, astronomy, and biology, even here daring to present explanations counter to the accepted theories of his day. While the Platonic view of the celestial bodies—sun, moon, and stars—is conventional enough (they are not made of a superior quintessence with properties unlike those bodies composed of the four elements), Eriugena goes further and asserts that they too are mixtures of accidents which came into visible existence through man's fall. Drawing upon Martianus Capella, but going beyond even his explanations, Eriugena argues that Jupiter, Mars, Venus, and Mercury do not revolve around the earth but are satellites of the sun. Plato's world soul is invoked to show that nothing, not even a rock, is devoid of life, and from Pliny the Elder he borrows edifying details of animal behavior to show that they too have immortal souls.

God's act of creating the world is a mystery, man's fall is a mystery, and a third mystery is the redemption of the world and its return to its causes through the Incarnation of Christ. Not only does God take on that single human substance which is identical in all men, thereby uniting them all with Himself, but He also assumes the status of fallen man with all the accompanying vicissitudes. He is not only Man but a man, while remaining wholly the second Person or Substance of the Trinity. While in his Christology Eriugena successfully avoids docetism, he has no interest in the historical figure of Jesus. His is a cosmic Christ, the Redeemer of the universe, and with His Resurrection and Ascension begins the return of all things to their Source.

The return is accomplished by the grace of God, but with the cooperation of nature. God's action never abrogates or runs counter to the natural force of His creatures, for both their being and their activity are correlative expressions of His goodness. The natural force within each thing is a striving for reunion with its principle. Eriugena puts the relation between God's action by way of nature and by way of grace in the form of a distinction between the grants *(data)* and the gifts *(dona)* of the Holy Spirit. The being of any rational creature and its character as eternal being belong to the natural order; being and eternal being are grants. To them is added, when rational beings freely will the good, the gift of well-being, a perfection which is not within their nature but is rather an enhancement of their established natural goods.

Just as reason is competent to understand the way in which creation and the fall occurred, so it can trace the process of the return of all things to God. Since all things were created in man and fell into their effects with his fall, so they are redeemed in him and will rise in his resurrection to reunite with their causes. The multiplicity of individuals returns to the unity whence it derived. Eriugena marks the stages: when each man's resurrected body returns into his spirit and the parts of our divided human nature have been restored to their original unity, the mind will have regained its capacity to know all things perfectly. It will draw up into itself all that is inferior to it, for in being, known things exist in a more perfect state than they are in themselves. The soul's knowledge is then transmuted into that wisdom which is the contemplation of Truth insofar as a creature is capable. Lastly, the most purified spirits will be enabled to pass over into God, and through the grace of the Holy Spirit to receive deification.

'Deification', a term familiar enough in Eastern theology but regarded suspiciously as pantheistic in the West, is entirely a gift of grace, for it is beyond the limits established for human nature. All men are to be saved through the cooperation of nature and grace, and their salvation lies in their eternal knowing of God in theophanies hierarchically arranged so that each man sees Him to the fullest degree of his competence. Salvation is granted to all men; it is their restoration to the original natural state that would have been paradise had they not fallen in the very moment of their creation. Only those few, however, who have never wavered in their devotion to God in this life will be given the gift of the highest vision of Goodness and made as like Him as any creature can be. The deifying gift which enables the holiest men to become united with God goes beyond that rational knowing which is within the natural limit of human thought, but although it is a vision of God in "pure and immediate contemplation", it remains a knowledge of God in His theophanies and never a knowledge of Him in Himself. Eriugena calls it a "theophany of theophanies". The saint is made pure intellect and as like God as possible, but only the manhood of Christ ascends into the very Godhead itself as consubstantial with it. Thus in deification God remains transcendent of all His creation.

Eriugena has combined something of the Augustinian eschatology in which men find rest in the vision of God with Gregory of Nyssa's dynamic tension as the soul strives infinitely to close the infinite distance between itself and God. For Eriugena deification is more than a recovery of a lost state of perfection. It is the acquiring of a perfection that had never been his, a union with God in which the infinite distance is overcome while yet God in Himself remains utterly incomprehensible. Deification is, as the Pseudo-Dionysius had said, a perfect knowing which is yet a not-knowing.

All men are to be saved, for human nature is an eternal participation of the Divine Goodness. What, then, of the damned and the eternal punishment foretold by Scripture? Just as the garden of Eden was not a place in the world at the beginning of time, so heaven and hell are not situated above and below the universe, nor are the torments of hell physical punishments. How could they be when sensible matter is resolved into its causes, and space and time are no more? The substance of evil men has always been good, since it is God's creation, and so the will itself is not to be punished, but rather its perversity. The punishment will be within that will itself, forever seeking what is forbidden it, which it knows it can never possess. Just as the blessed forever rejoice in God in spiritual theophanies, so the damned punish themselves with *phantasiae* of earthly goods that can never be theirs.

The distance between hell and the heights of heaven is spiritual not spatial, and "God shall be all in all", present in every theophany granted each soul according to its capacity. When the final division of nature comes to be and union is attained, nothing that is will be lost. Just as air does not cease to be air when it is suffused with the radiance of light, so the integrity of each thing that is will be preserved in a higher state of glory. Nothing is annihilated or loses its identity, but everything comes to be—not just what it once was in a paradise that never existed—but what it is eternally intended to be. When 'well-being' is bestowed on 'being' and 'eternal being', then the creative will of God is fully realized.

There are, then, mysteries in the universe as Eriugena conceives it: God's choosing to create a world, man's choice of the lesser goods in preference to God, the redemption of the world through God's free gift of Himself, and the deification of the saints. All are grounded in that freedom which is God's will hidden forever beyond the reach of any created intelligence. We can never understand why these things should come to pass, but we can know the way in which His will is manifest. His self-disclosures are always in accord with the rational nature that he created.

If Eriugena's thought was not easily accommodated to the simpler structure of Augustinianism and was even more alien to the distinctions drawn by later mediaeval scholasticism, for those very reasons it may be appreciated more readily today. The familiar modes of mediaeval thought and their modern descendants have been widely discarded as models for understanding man's role in the universe and the relation between the Creator and the creature. If we are no longer inclined to draw the line between reason and revelation, man's action and God's, where we did until recently, Eriugena offers a new perspective worth exploring. If the conceptual tools inherited from the scholastics have failed to enable us to grasp how God can be wholly other than the universe and yet present with full immediacy in all things, Eriugena presents a quite different understanding of the divine transcendence and immanence, the legacy of another, less familiar branch of Christian religious thought. Finally, the balance he strikes in insisting that personal identity and individual worth have a timeless significance that can never be lost while avoiding appeal to the vagaries of private 'religious experience' suggests new ways of approaching many of our most urgent theological and philosophical problems. His solutions may not prove adequate, but his perspective may well yield fresh insights and approaches.

Jean A. Potter
Bryn Mawr College
July, 1973

Selected Bibliography

WORKS BY ERIUGENA

Opera omnia. Edited by J. P. Migne. *Patrologiae cursus completus, series latina,* vol. 122.
Periphyseon. Liber primus and Liber secundus. Edited and translated by I. P. Sheldon-Williams. Dublin, 1968, 1972.

STUDIES

Bett, Henry. *Johannes Scotus Erigena: A Study in Mediaeval Philosophy.* Cambridge, 1925. Reprinted, New York, 1964.
Cappuyns, Maïeul. *Jean Scot Erigène: sa vie, son oeuvre, sa pensée.* Paris, 1933. Reprinted, Brussells, 1964.
Gregory, Tullio. *Giovanni Scoto Eriugena: tre studi.* Florence, 1963.
Huber, Johannes. *Johannes Scotus Erigena.* Munich, 1861. Reprinted, Hildesheim, n. d.
O'Meara, John J. *Eriugena.* Cork, 1969.

NOTE

A complete bibliography by I. P. Sheldon-Williams is to be found in *The Journal of Ecclesiastical History,* vol. x, no. 2. 1960. *The Cambridge History of Later Greek and Early Medieval Philosophy.* Cambridge, 1967, edited by A. H. Armstrong, gives useful brief accounts of Eriugena and his Greek and Latin sources by Sheldon-Williams and H. Liebeschütz.

Periphyseon
On the Division of Nature

Book I

INTRODUCTION

Teacher: Often I investigate as carefully as I can and reflect that of all things which can either be perceived by the mind or surpass its concentrated efforts the first and highest division is into what has and what does not have being. At such times the general designation of them all occurs to me, *physis* in Greek and *natura* in Latin. Or don't you agree?

Student: Yes, I do. Although I am just entering upon the path of reasoning, I find that it is so.

T: As we have just said, then, 'nature' is a general name for all things, whether or not they have being.

S: It certainly is, for we can think of nothing at all to which such a designation does not apply.

T: Since we have agreed that this is a generic designation, I should like you to tell how it is divided into species by *differentiae.* Or if you prefer, I shall try to establish the divisions first and your task will be to judge them.

1

S: Please begin. I am eager and impatient to hear you give a true account about these matters.

[1] *T:* The division of nature seems to me to admit of four species through four differentiae. The first is the division into what creates and is not created; the second into what is created and creates; the third, into what is created and does not create; the fourth, into what neither creates nor is created. Of these four, two pairs consist of opposites. The third is the opposite of the first, the fourth of the second. But the fourth is among the things which are impossible, and its differentia is its inability to be. Does such a division seem to you correct or not?

S: It surely does, but would you please go over it to clarify the opposition of the species just mentioned?

T: Unless I'm mistaken, you see the opposition of the third species to the first. The first creates and is not created, and its opposite is that which is created and does not create. Likewise the opposition of the second to the fourth, since the second is created and creates; the fourth, which neither creates nor is created, is contrary to it in every respect.

S: I see that clearly, but I am quite perplexed about the fourth species which you added. As for the other three, I should not venture to have any misgivings; for I judge that the first is understood in the Cause of all things which have and all which do not have being, the second in the primordial causes, the third in those things known by generation in time and place. I see, therefore, that we must have a more detailed discussion about the individual species.

T: You are quite right. But I leave it to your judgment to determine our order of reasoning; i.e., to decide which species of nature should be discussed first.

S: I think that it would be proper, before dealing with the others, to say what our insight reveals to us about the first.

[2] *T:* All right, but I think that first we must talk briefly about the

highest and main division of all which, as we said, is the division into
the things which have and those which do not have being.

S: That is a very sound and judicious idea. I see that our reasoning
should begin no other way, not only because that is the first differentia
of all things, but also because it appears, and is, more obscure than the
others.

T: Well, then, the original distinguishing differentia of all things
demands clear-cut methods of interpretation.

[3] Of these, the first seems to be the one by which reason persuades
us that all things subject to corporeal sense or the perception of
intelligence can reasonably be said to have being; but all that, by the
excellence of their nature, elude not only the *hylion*, i.e., every sense,
but also intellect and reason, properly seem not to have being. They
are correctly understood only in God, matter, and the reasons and
essences of all things created by Him. And that is as it should be; for
He Himself, who alone truly has being, is the essence of all things,
according to Dionysius the Areopagite, who says: "The being of all
things is Superbeing, Divinity." [1] Gregory the Theologian too affirms
by many reasons that intellect or reason cannot grasp what any
substance or essence is, whether it belongs to visible or to invisible
creation. For just as God Himself, in Himself, beyond all creation is
grasped by no intellect, so also *ousia* considered in the innermost
recesses of the creation made by Him and existing in Him, is
incomprehensible. Besides, whatever in every creature is either
perceived by corporeal sense or considered by the intellect is simply
some accident, incomprehensible in itself, as has been said, of an
essence. By quality, quantity, form, matter, some differentia, place, or
time we know not *what* it is, but *that* it is. This, then, is the first and
highest method of division of what is said to have and what is said not
to have being. I believe, however, that that method which it seems, in a
way, possible to introduce, namely the one based on privations of states
in reference to substances, as sight and blindness in reference to the
eyes, must be utterly rejected. For if something wholly lacks being and

cannot be and does not surpass intellect because of the supernal height of its existence, I fail to see how it can fit into the divisions of things; unless, perhaps, one should say that the absences and privations of things with being are not absolutely nothing, but that they are contained by some remarkable natural power of those things of which they are the privations, absences, or opposites, so that, in a certain way, they have being.

[4]   Let us grant that the second method of being and not-being is the one considered in the orders and differentiae of created natures. Beginning from the most exalted intellectual power stationed closest to God, it descends to the extreme of rational and irrational creation. To speak more clearly, I mean from the highest angel to the lowest part of a rational or irrational soul, the vital principle of nutrition and growth (for when the soul is considered as a genus, the part of the soul which nurtures the body and causes it to grow is the lowest). Here each order, including the bottommost order of bodies with which all division is terminated, can be said in a remarkable way to have and not to have being. What is stated affirmatively of the lower is stated negatively of the higher. Likewise what is stated negatively of the lower is stated affirmatively of the higher. In the same way, what is stated affirmatively of the higher is stated negatively of the lower; and what is stated negatively of the higher will be stated affirmatively of the lower. What is stated affirmatively of a man, that he is still mortal, is stated negatively of an angel. What is stated negatively of a man is stated affirmatively of an angel, and vice versa. For example, if a man is a rational, mortal, visible animal, an angel is surely not a rational, mortal, visible animal. Similarly, if an angel is an essential motion of the intellect focussing on God and the causes of things, surely man is not an essential motion of the intellect focussing on God and the causes of things. The same rule can be observed in all celestial essences until one reaches the highest order of all which is terminated above by the Supreme Negation. Its negative definition affirms that no creature is higher than It. There are three orders called *homotageis* ("of equal

rank"). The first of these consists of Cherubim, Seraphim, and Thrones; the second of Virtues, Powers, and Dominations; the third of Principalities, Archangels, and Angels. In descending order, the lowest group of bodies merely negates or affirms what is higher than itself because it has nothing beneath itself to take away or add since it is preceded by all higher orders and does not precede anything lower than itself. Similarly for this reason, every order of rational and intellectual creature is said to have and not to have being. It has being insofar as it is known by higher creatures or by itself; it lacks being insofar as it does not allow itself to be comprehended by its inferiors.

[5] The third method is fittingly observed in the things with which the fullness of this visible world is made complete, and in their prior causes in the innermost recesses of nature. For whatever of the causes themselves is known by generation in time and place in formed matter is said, by human convention, to have being. Whatever, on the other hand, is still contained within the recesses of nature and does not appear in formed matter or in place, time, or the other accidents, is said, by the same human convention, not to have being. Clear examples of this kind abound, particularly in human nature. For God formed all men together in that single first man whom He made in His own image, but He did not bring them forth at the same time into this visible world. Rather, at set times and places in a sequence known to Himself He brings into visible essence the nature which He had formed together. Thus those who now visibly appear in the world and who have appeared are said to have being. Those who still lie hidden, but are destined to be, are said not to have being. This is the difference between the first and third methods. The first is seen generally in all things made once and together in their causes and effects. The third is seen specifically in the things which partly still lie hidden in their causes and partly are revealed in their effects; and of these the fabric of this world is properly woven. To this method belongs the reason which considers the power of seeds, whether in animals, trees, or grasses. The power of the seeds, while it lies still in the secret recesses

of nature, is said not to have being because it does not yet appear. Once it has appeared, however, in the birth and growth of animals, flowers, or the fruits of trees and grasses, it is said to be.

[6] The fourth method, according to the plausible theory of philosophers, states that only those things grasped by the intellect alone truly have being; that whatever things are varied, collected, or dissolved through generation, by the expansion or contraction of matter, and by local and temporal motions—e.g., all bodies, which can be born and destroyed—are truly said not to have being.

[7] The fifth method is the one which reason observes only in human nature. When through sin it abandoned the dignity of the divine image in which it had properly subsisted, it deservedly lost its being and therefore is said not to have being. When it is restored by the grace of God's only-begotten Son to the original condition of its substance in which it was created in God's image, it begins to have being and to be alive in Him who was created in God's image. It is evidently to this method that the following statement of the Apostle relates: "And He calls the things which have no being, just as those which do." [2] That is, God the Father calls those lost in the first man and fallen to a kind of substancelessness to have being through faith in His Son like those already reborn in Christ. This method may also be understood, however, as relating to those whom God daily calls from the hidden recesses of nature, in which they are thought not to have being, into visible appearance in form, matter, and the other things in which the hidden can appear. Perhaps a keener reason can discover something besides these methods, but I think that enough has been said about these matters for the present, unless you disagree.

S: Quite enough, except that I am somewhat disturbed by St. Augustine's statement in the *Exemeron*: "The nature of angels was created prior to all creatures in dignity, not in time." Hence the nature of angels observed the primordial causes (i.e., the archetypal examples, which the Greeks call *prototypa*) of everything except themselves first in God and next in themselves. Finally they saw the creatures in the effects of the primordial causes. Of course, angels could not know their own cause before they proceeded into their own proper species. *T:* That should not bother you. Consider more carefully what has been said. If we say that angels know primary causes of things established in God, we shall seem to be contradicting the Apostle, who declares that God Himself and the causes of all things in Him, whether or not they are the same as He, are above everything which is said and understood. We must therefore hold a straight middle course or we may appear to be contradicting the Apostle or not upholding the view of a teacher of such high and sacred authority. That both statements are true must be firmly maintained without any doubt. Reason does not allow the Cause of all things, which surpasses every intellect, to be known to any created nature. As the Apostle states it, "Who knows the Lord's mind?" [3] And in another passage, "The peace of Christ, which surpasses all understanding." [4] But if the Cause of all things is removed from all things created by It, undoubtedly the reasons of everything in It eternally and unchangeably are utterly removed from everything of which they are the reasons. In my opinion, it would be true to state that there are, in the intellects of angels, certain theophanies of these reasons—I mean divine appearances which can be grasped by the intellectual nature—but not the reasons, i.e. the archetypal examples, themselves. I believe that St. Augustine quite appropriately said that these theophanies were seen in angelic creatures before the generation of all things lower than they are. Let us not then be disturbed at our statement that angels see the causes of lower creatures first in God and then in themselves. The name *God* is applied not only to the Divine Essence, but also, as frequently in sacred Scripture, to that way in which He shows Himself, in some manner to intellectual and rational creatures, to each according to his capacity. This way is usually termed by the Greeks theophany, i.e., "an appearance of God." An example is "I saw the Lord sitting." [5] and other passages of this kind, in which man has beheld not God's essence, but something made by Him. It is not strange, then, if an angel is understood to have a threefold kind of knowledge. One is the higher knowledge of the eternal reasons of things which, in the manner just explained, is first manifested in him. Next, what he receives from things above he entrusts to himself as if depositing it in a marvelous and ineffable memory; and it is a kind of reflected image of an image. So, if he can in such a manner have knowledge of things higher than himself, who would dare to say that he has no inner knowledge of lower things? Being is correctly predicated, then, of what can be grasped by reason and intellect; and conversely, whatever surpasses all reason and intellect is likewise correctly said to have no being.

[8]   *S:*   What shall we say, then, about that future bliss promised to the saints, which we regard as simply the pure and immediate contemplation of the Divine Essence? As St. John the Evangelist expresses it, "We know that we are sons of God, but what we are to be is not yet apparent. When it is, we shall be like Him, for we shall see Him as He is." [6] Similarly the Apostle Paul: "Now we see dimly in a mirror; but then we shall see face to face." [7] So too, I believe, St. Augustine in Book 22 (ch. 29) of *The City of God* says about the future contemplation of the Divine Essence, "Through the bodies that we shall have, in every body that we shall see wherever we direct the eyes of our bodies, we shall behold the Lord Himself with perfect clarity." But if the height of the Divine Essence surpasses the purest power of angelic contemplation (for we have concluded from the reasons already stated that the Divine Essence can be grasped by no intellectual creature, and it is certain that intellectual creatures are primarily angels) and we are promised the very felicity of equality with the nature of angels, how will human nature in its felicitous state be able to contemplate the height of the Divine Essence?

T: Your observation is keen and alert, and you have good reason to be disturbed about this matter. But I should think that you would be satisfied with the general point that we established before about all creation.

S: What is that? Please repeat it.

T: Didn't we make a comprehensive statement that the Divine

Essence can be grasped in Itself by no corporeal sense, no reason, and no intellect, whether of men or of angels?

S: I remember and cannot deny that I made such an assumption. But in my opinion either that former conclusion will be completely invalidated and we shall grant the contemplation of Divine Essence in Itself to intellectual creatures; or if it cannot be invalidated because it has been established by thoroughly sound reasons, you must justify by true reasoning and plausible examples that kind of contemplation of the Divine, promised to the saints in the future, in which the angels are constantly absorbed.

T: I don't know what kind you are talking about unless it is the one which we discussed briefly a little while ago.

S: Please repeat it, since I can't recall it.

T: Do you remember what agreement we reached when we were talking about St. Augustine's *Exemeron?*

S: Yes, but I should like to hear you on the subject again.

T: If the Divine Essence with the reasons in It is essentially incomprehensible to any creature, you were disturbed, I believe, by St. Augustine's statement that angels observed first in God, then in themselves, the causes of things to be created, which are eternally in God and are God; and that they then knew the proper species and differentiae of the creatures themselves.

S: I now grasp the whole point.

T: Do you remember what answer we gave?

S: Indeed I do, unless my memory fails me. You said that angels saw not the actual causes of whatever subsists in the Divine Essence, but rather certain divine appearances which, as you say, the Greeks call *theophanies*, a name derived from the eternal causes of which they are images. You also added that the name *God* is applied not only to the Divine Essence unchangeably existing in Itself, but also to the theophanies made from and by It and made manifest in intellectual nature.

T: You have a firm grasp of the matter. That is what we said.

S: But how are those points pertinent to our subject?

T: They are very pertinent, in my opinion. I think that angels always behold God that way, that righteous men do so even in this life while experiencing ecstasy, and that in the future they will have vision like that of the angels. We shall not see God Himself in Himself; not even the angels do. Such vision exceeds the power of any creature. In the words of the Apostle, "He alone has immortality and dwells in the inaccessible light." [8] But we shall contemplate some theophanies made by Him in us. Isn't it true that everyone, in proportion to the sublimity of his holiness and wisdom, will be formed by the very same Form for which all things strive, viz., God's Word? For He says about Himself in the Gospel, "In my Father's house there are many rooms." [9] He is calling Himself "the Father's House" which, although it is one and the same, changelessly stable, will seem manifold to those granted the privilege of dwelling in It. Everyone, as we have said, will possess within himself the knowledge of God's only-begotten Word, insofar as the gift of grace is given to him. There will be as many rooms as there are elect; and the possession of the divine theophanies will correspond to the number of the souls of saints.

S: That seems likely.

T: *Likely* is the correct term, for who would boldly assert about such matters that they are eternally so, when they obviously exceed the power of human insight while we are still in this perishable flesh?

[9] S: But please give me a brief explanation of your inferences about this theophany. What is it? What is its source? Where is it? Is it formed within or without us?

T: You are asking profound questions; in fact, I can't think of any more profound inquiry for man to undertake. But I shall tell you what I have been able to find on the subject in the books of the holy fathers who have ventured to discuss such matters.

S: Please do.

T: You ask what it is, what its source, what its place.

S: Yes.

T: I find that a monk Maximus, a divine philosopher, has discussed this kind of theophany with the greatest depth and subtlety in his explanation of the Sermons of Gregory the Theologian. His words are, "Theophany originates only from God, and is brought about by the condescension of the Divine Word, i.e., the only-begotten Son, the Wisdom of the Father, toward the human nature created and purified by Him, and by the exaltation of human nature toward this Word through divine love." By *condescension* I do not here refer to that already brought about by the Incarnation, but to that resulting from *theosis*, i.e., deification of the creature. Theophany comes about, then, from the condescension of God's Wisdom to human nature through grace, and from the exaltation of the same nature to Wisdom Itself through love. St. Augustine seems to agree with this meaning in explaining the Apostle's words, "He has become our Justice and Wisdom." [10] His explanation states, "The Father's Wisdom, in which and through which all things have been made, is not created but creates. It is produced in our souls by an ineffable condescension of Its mercy, and joins to Itself our intellect, so that in some ineffable manner there is a kind of compounded wisdom made from Him as He descends to us and dwells within us, and from our intelligence, which is drawn up by Him to Himself through love and is formed in Him." Similarly he explains about justice and the other virtues that they are produced simply "from a marvelous and ineffable conformation of Divine Wisdom and our intelligence." As Maximus states, "Divine Wisdom descends through mercy as far as the human intellect ascends through love." This is the cause and substance of all virtues. Every theophany, therefore, i.e., every virtue, both in this life in which it begins to be formed in the worthy, and in the future life of the man who will receive perfect divine bliss, is produced not outside a man himself but in himself, and arises both from God and from men themselves.

S: In summary, then, theophanies are made from God in angelic and human nature enlightened, purified, and perfected by grace. They are produced by the descent of Divine Wisdom and the ascent of human and angelic intelligence.

T: Yes, and this explanation conforms to Maximus' statement, "The intellect becomes whatever it can grasp." Insofar as the mind grasps virtue, therefore, it itself becomes virtue.

[10]   If you are looking for examples of these points, they have been expressed very clearly by the same Maximus. "Just as air lighted by the sun appears to be simply light, not because it loses its own nature but because light so prevails in it that it is thought to be part of the light; so human nature joined to God is said to be wholly God, not because it ceases being human nature, but because it so participates in divinity that God alone seems to be present in it." Similarly, "When light is missing, air is dark; and sunlight subsisting by itself is not apprehended by any corporeal sense. When sunlight is mixed with air, however, it begins to be visible. So in itself it cannot be apprehended by the senses; but when mixed with air, it can." From this analogy you should understand that Divine Essence cannot be apprehended in Itself, but in a remarkable way becomes visible when joined to an intellectual creature, so that Divine Essence is the only thing visible in the intellectual creature. Its ineffable excellence so surpasses every nature which participates in It that nothing besides It makes an impression on the understanding, although in Its pure state, as we have said, It is completely invisible.

S: I see quite well what point you are trying to make, but I am not sure whether it agrees with St. Augustine's statement.

T: Well, pay closer attention, then, and let us go over this statement, which we quoted at first from Book 22 of *The City of God*, I think: "Through the bodies that we shall have, in every body that we shall see, wherever we direct the eyes of our bodies, we shall behold God Himself with perfect clarity." Examine the force of the words. He did not say, "Through the bodies that we shall have, we shall behold God Himself;" because He cannot be seen in Himself. Instead he said, "Through the bodies that we shall have, in every body that we shall see, we shall behold God Himself." He will be seen, then, through bodies and in bodies, not in Himself. Similarly the Divine Essence will appear not in Itself but through intellect in intellects, through reason in reasons. For such great excellence of Divine Power will be manifested in the future life to all worthy of contemplating It that nothing besides It will be clear either in bodies or in intellects. For God will be "all in all." [11] It is as though Scripture were openly saying,

"God alone will appear in all." Hence the holy man, Job, said, "And in my flesh I shall see God," [12] as though he had said, "In this flesh of mine, afflicted by many trials, there will be such great glory that just as only death and corruption appear in it now, so in the life to come, only God, who is truly Life, Immortality, and Incorruption, will appear in it." But if he anticipated such glory from bodily well-being, what glory must we believe would come from the nobility of his mind, especially since, as the great Gregory the Theologian says, "The bodies of the saints will be changed to reason, reason to intellect, intellect to God." Thus their whole nature will be changed to God Himself. In his interpretation of Gregory, Maximus has presented some particularly beautiful analogies to illustrate this point. We have already mentioned the one about air, but here is one about fire and iron. "When iron is melted in fire and becomes liquid, no trace of its nature remains visible to the senses, but it seems wholly converted into the nature of fire. Only by the reason is it known to preserve its own nature even though it is melted." Therefore just as air appears to be wholly light and melted iron wholly fiery, or rather fire, as we said before, even though their substances remain; so a sound intellect must realize that after the end of this world every nature, whether corporeal or not, and with its nature remaining intact, will seem to be God alone; so that God, who cannot be apprehended in Himself, is apprehended in a certain way through creation, while creation itself, by an ineffable miracle, is transformed into God. But enough of these points if they are sufficiently clear to you.

S: Yes, as clear as such matters can be to our minds. No one in this life can speak with such clarity about an ineffable subject that he can satisfy the desire of those who inquire about it, especially since the very glory promised to us in the future life is empirical knowledge of those things which here are accepted on faith, investigated by reason, and become matters of conviction as far as possible.

T: Your view is prudent and reasonable. Now I think that we should go back to the subject proposed, i.e., the division of nature.

S: Yes, we must limit our discussion for the sake of reaching some conclusion.

[11]   *T:*   Of the divisions of nature already mentioned, we thought that the first distinction marked the one that creates but is not created. And rightly so, because such a species of nature is correctly predicated only of God, who alone is understood as creating all things without a beginning (*anarchos*), since He alone is the primary Cause of all things made from and through Him; and consequently He is the End of all things which are from Him. Everything aspires to Him. He is, therefore, Beginning, Middle, and End; Beginning, because everything which participates in essence comes from Him; Middle, because in Him and through Him they subsist and move; End, because they move toward Him in their search for rest from their motion and stability for their perfection.

S: I believe very firmly and understand to the best of my ability that this is correctly predicated only of the Divine Cause of all things, because It alone creates all things which come from It, whereas It is not Itself created by any superior or prior cause. It is Itself the highest and sole Cause of all things which come from It and subsist in It.

[12]   I should like your view, however, about the disturbing statement that I often come upon in the works of the holy fathers who have tried to discuss Divine Nature. They say that It not only creates everything with being, but is also Itself created. In their words, It makes and is made, creates and is created. If they are correct, I am at a loss to explain how our reasoning can stand since we say that It only creates but is not Itself created by anything.

T: You are right in being disturbed. I too am very baffled and should like to learn from you how these evidently opposing points of view can be reconciled and how we are to pursue a valid line of reasoning.

S: Please begin, because in such matters I look to your opinion and method of reasoning, not my own.

T: Then first, if you agree, I think that we should consider the name *God*, which is most commonly used in Sacred Scripture. Although Divine Nature is designated by many names—e.g., Goodness, Essence, Truth, and others of the kind—Divine Scripture most often uses the name *God*.

S: That is clearly evident.

T: The etymology of this name is from the Greek, either from the verb *theoro*, "see", or from the verb *theo*, "run"; or, as is more likely, since one and the same meaning is inherent, it is correctly said to be derived from both. For when *Theos* is derived from *theoro*, it means "Seer", because He sees in Himself everything endowed with being; whereas He beholds nothing outside Himself since there is nothing outside Himself. When the derivation is from *theo*, *Theos* is correctly understood as "Runner", for He runs into all things and does not stand still at all, but fills everything by running. So it has been written, "His word runs quickly." [13] But yet He is wholly unmoved, since in reference to God, motion is most correctly called stable and stability mobile. He stands unchangeably in Himself, never abandoning His natural stability. Yet He moves Himself through all things to bring into being whatever essentially subsists from Him; for by His motion all things are made. Hence there is one and the same meaning in the two interpretations of the name *God*. God's running through everything is the same as His vision of everything; and everything is made by His seeing as by His running.

S: I am quite convinced about the etymology of the name and approve of it. But I do not understand very well where He, who is everywhere, can go; since nothing can be without Him and nothing extends beyond Him. In fact, He is the Place and Circumscription of all things.

T: I did not say that God moves outside Himself, but from Himself, in Himself, towards Himself. For we should not believe that there is any motion in Him except the longing of His will, by which He wishes everything to be made. Just so His stability is understood not as a coming to rest after motion, but as the unchangeable resolve of His will, by which He decrees that all things remain fixed in the unchangeable stability of their reasons. For neither stability nor motion is predicated of Him properly, since the opposition of these two is evident, especially because stability is properly the end of motion; and true reasoning forbids that opposites be conceived of or understood in Him. God does not begin to move in order to arrive at a certain stability; but these terms, like many similar ones, are metaphorically transferred from creatures to Creator by a kind of divine metaphor. And yet this metaphor has a rational basis, since God is the Cause of all things stable and in motion. From Him they set out on their course to being, since He is the Beginning of everything; and through Him they are borne toward Him by natural motion in order to stand in Him unchangeably and eternally, since He is the End and Resting Place of all things. Beyond Him they aspire to nothing; in Him they find the beginning and end of their motion. God, then, is called "Runner", not because He runs outside Himself (for He, who fills everything, always stands unchangeably in Himself); but because He makes everything take a course from non-existence to existence.

S: These statements seem reasonable. Return to the main point.

T: I wish that you would remind me of the point. In trying to discuss incidental questions, we often forget the main ones.

S: Didn't we propose to investigate as well as possible why Divine Nature is said by those who discuss It both to create and to be created? No intelligent person doubts that It creates everything; but we thought that we should not pass lightly over the sense in which Divine Nature is said to be created.

T: That is exactly right. But I think that our previous discussion has opened the door quite a bit to the solution of this problem. We concluded that the motion of the Divine Nature must be understood simply as the resolve of the Divine Will to create what is to be made. Therefore Divine Nature, which is simply Divine Will, is said to be made in all things; for in It being and will are not two different things, but one and the same in creating everything which, it seemed, ought to be made. For example, one might say that the motion of Divine Will is introduced in order for things to have being. It therefore creates all things which It brings about from nothing in order that they may pass from non-being to being; and It is created because nothing has being essentially except Itself, for It is the essence of all things. Just as there is no natural good besides Itself, but everything said to be good is good by participation in the one Highest Good, so everything said to exist exists not in itself but by participation in the Truly Existing Nature. Not only, therefore, as we observed in our previous remarks, is Divine Nature said to be made when God's Word is born, in a remarkable and ineffable manner, in those formed anew by faith, hope, love, and the other virtues; as the Apostle says in speaking of Christ: "He has been made in us wisdom from God, and justice, and redemption;" [14] but also because It appears in all things with being, It is, though invisible in Itself, fittingly said to have been made. Our intellect too, before it enters upon reflection and memory, is not unreasonably said not to have being; for it is invisible in itself and known to none except God and ourselves. But when it enters into thoughts and receives form from some *phantasiae*, it is deservedly said to be made. It is made in the memory by receiving certain forms of things, whether of sounds, colors, or other sensible things, although it was without form before it came into the memory. Then it receives a kind of second formation when it is formed by certain symbols of forms or sounds—I refer to letters as the symbols of sounds and figures as the symbols of forms—or other sensible signals for learning, by which it can insinuate itself into the senses of the perceivers. Although this analogy is far removed from Divine Nature, it can nevertheless offer a persuasive illustration, I think, of how Divine Nature, while It creates everything and cannot be created by anything, is, in a marvelous fashion, created in all things which are from It. As we have said, intelligence, resolve, judgment, or whatever term can be applied to that innermost first motion of ours when it enters into thought and receives certain forms of *phantasiae* and then proceeds into the symbols of sounds or sensible motions, is fittingly said to be made, since it is formed in the *phantasiae* though in itself it lacks all sensible form. Similarly Divine Essence, which in Its pure state surpasses all intellect, is rightly said to be created in the things made by, through, in, and directed toward Itself; so that It is recognized in Its creations through the intellect (if the creations are solely intelligible) or the senses (if they are sensibles) of those who search for It with proper zeal.

S: That point has been discussed enough, I believe.

[13] *T:* Quite enough.

S: But you must still explain why Divine Nature is called simply a Creator and not created if, as the preceding arguments have convinced me, It both creates and is created. These two statements seem contradictory.

T: You really are alert. I see that this point too deserves investigation.

S: I certainly agree.

T: Pay close attention, then, to this short answer.

S: Go ahead and I shall follow attentively.

T: You have no doubt that Divine Nature is the Creator of the universe.

S: Proceed to the other points, because it would be sinful to falter over this one.

T: You also perceive through faith and intellect that It is created by no one.

S: I perceive it completely.

T: You have no doubt, then, when you hear that It is created, that It is created by Itself and not by another nature.

S: Indeed, I have no doubt.

T: Well, then, is It not always in the process of creating either Itself or the essences created by Itself? The correct interpretation of our statement that It creates Itself is simply that It creates the natures of things. Its creation—i.e., Its manifestation in something—is surely the establishment of all existing things.

S: So far your statements seem plausible. But I should like to hear the teaching of Theology about this ineffable, incomprehensible Creator and Causal Nature of all things—i.e., whether It has being, what It is, what It is like, and how It is defined.

T: Hasn't Theology herself convinced those with clear enough insight into truth that Divine Nature, the primary or sole object of her own attention, is simply understood from Its creations to subsist essentially, but without comprehension of what Its essence is? As we have often stated, It surpasses not only the attempts of human reasoning, but even the purest intellects of celestial essences. But theologians, by true mental insight, have discovered from things endowed with being that It is; from the divisions of these things into essences, genera, species, differentiae, and numbers [i.e., particulars or individuals], that It is wise; from the stable motion and the mobile stability of all things, that It is alive. By this reasoning they have truly found the underlying Cause of all things three times. As we have said, from the essence of these things with being, It is understood to have being; from the remarkable order of things, It is known to be wise; from motion, It is discovered to be life. To sum up, Nature is the Cause and Creator of all things, is wise, and is alive. Hence searchers after truth have handed down the view that the Father is meant by Essence, the Son by Wisdom, and the Holy Spirit by Life.

S: You have quite convinced me, and I see that what you say is altogether true. One cannot arrive at a complete definition of what Divine Nature is or what It is like, for what cannot be completely understood cannot be completely defined. I should like to hear, nevertheless, by what reasoning theologians have dared to predicate Unity and Trinity of the Cause of all things.

T: This task which you have just proposed will not be too difficult, especially since the theologian St. Dionysius the Areopagite gives us a convincingly truthful and plausible account about the mysteries of the Divine Unity and Trinity. He states, "By no symbolic expression of words or names or sound articulated in any way can the Highest Essence, the Cause of all things, be signified." Unity and Trinity are not such as to be conceived of by even the most serene intellect of angels. But that the religious impulses of devout minds might be able to reflect and predicate something about an ineffable and incomprehensible matter, especially because of those who earnestly ask Catholics for a rational account of the Christian religion, whether for the sake of learning the truth, if they are good men, or for the opportunity of testing and refuting it if they are evil, these words, symbolic of the faith, have been devised and handed down by holy theologians in order that we may believe in our hearts and confess with our mouths that the Divine Goodness consists of three substances of a single essence. Nor did they come upon this formulation without searching examination by spiritual intelligence and rational inquiry. When, insofar as they were enlightened by the Divine Spirit, they gazed upon the one, ineffable Cause of all things, the one Beginning, simple, undivided, and universal, they declared the Unity. On the other hand, observing that Unity not in a barren singularity but in a remarkably fruitful multiplicity, they understood the three substances of the Unity: viz., the Unbegotten, the Begotten, and the Proceeding. They gave the name *Father* to the state of the Unbegotten substance in relation to the Begotten; *Son* to the Begotten in relation to the Unbegotten; *Holy Spirit* to the Proceeding in relation to the Unbegotten and the Begotten. But since almost the whole attention of those who expound holy Scriptures is directed toward this matter, I think that these remarks will suffice for the present.

S: Yes, indeed, but I should like to hear a clearer explanation about the state of the three Divine Substances. Some might interpret these mystic names of the Holy Trinity—Father, Son, and Holy Spirit—not as referring to relation, but as applying naturally. *Father* seems to be the name of the Father's substance, *Son* the name of the Son's substance, and *Holy Spirit* too seems simply to signify Its substance.

T: Perhaps I too would admit holding and acknowledging the same belief if it were not forbidden by the high and venerable authority of St. Gregory the Theologian and by the true and plausible argument of reason. When asked by the Eunomians, those venomous opponents of the Catholic faith, whether the name *Father* signifies nature or operation, he was marvelously enlightened by divine grace and answered: "It refers neither to nature nor to operation, but simply to the relationship to the Son." Had he answered that *Father* referred to nature, they would have kept right on and said that *Son* too is a natural designation. If this concession had been made, the necessary conclusion would have been that Father is the name of one nature, Son of another; for two different names cannot be applied to one and the same nature. Hence they would conclude that the Father and Son are *heterousion*, i.e., of different essence or nature. The same situation holds in the answer about operation. If *Father* had been acknowledged to be a name derived from operation, they would immediately have inferred that the Son is a creature since *Father* was admitted to be a name derived from operation, namely His creation.

S: His answer certainly is commendable and inspired by the truth.

But we should consider somewhat more clearly. I don't think that they could refute him at once even for saying that the name *Father* refers to nature. Can we really say that two names different in sound but not in meaning cannot be understood of one and the same nature, when we see that *Abraham* and *Isaac*—that is, *father* and *son*—signify a single nature? For Abraham is not the name of one nature and Isaac of another, but both are names of one and the same nature.

T: You would be correct if you could similarly assert in your example about Abraham and Isaac that the names *Abraham* and *Isaac* signify the very same things in them as the terms *father* and *son*. *Abraham* is Abraham's name, and father is a name denoting the same Abraham. Likewise *Isaac* is Isaac's name and *son* is a name denoting the same Isaac. But the terms *Abraham* and *father* or *Isaac* and *son* are not predicated of the same thing. Abraham refers to his substance, i.e., his individual personality; whereas no one of sound judgment would deny that he is called father from his relationship to his son Isaac. Similarly about Isaac, we must understand that by the name *Isaac* his proper and individual substance is signified, whereas his relationship to his father is recognized by the term *son*. You must admit that such names as *father* and *son* denote relationship, not substance. If such expressions in reference to us—i.e., to our nature—are predicated not of substance but of relationship, what are we to say about the highest, sacred Essence, in reference to which holy Scripture has established such names of the relationship of substances, namely *Father, Son,* and *Holy Spirit?*

S: Now I see that St. Gregory's answer was wholly supported by truth. You have convinced me that a name denoting relationship, whether in reference to divine or to human nature, cannot be applied to substance or essence. But please tell me briefly and clearly whether all ten categories can truly and properly be predicated of the single Highest Essence of Divine Goodness in three Substances and of the three Substances in one and the same Essence.

T: I don't know who can discuss this matter briefly and clearly. In a subject of this kind, one must either preserve a complete silence and put one's trust in the simplicity of the orthodox faith (for it surpasses all understanding, an idea expressed in the passage "Who alone possess immortality and dwell in inaccessible light");[15] or, if he undertakes a discussion of it, he must make his case convincingly plausible in many ways and by many proofs, using the two main theological methods, i.e., the affirmative or *kataphatiké* and the negative or *apophatiké*. The latter deries that Divine Essence or Substance is anything with being—i.e., which can be spoken of or understood. The former predicates of It everything with being, and is called 'affirmative,' not to declare that It is any of the things with being, but to convince us that all things from It can be predicated of It. For the causal agent can reasonably be signified by what it causes. This method states that Divine Essence is Truth, Goodness, Essence, Light, Justice, the Sun, a Star, Spirit, Water, a Lion, a City, a Worm, and the countless other things. Besides, this method teaches about It by drawing not only upon what has being according to nature, but also upon those which are opposed to nature when it says that Divine Nature is intoxicated, foolish, or mad. But it is not my intention to discuss these matters now, for enough has been said about them in the *Symbolic Theology* of St. Dionysius the Areopagite. We must return, therefore, to your previous question whether all the categories, or certain of them, are properly to be predicated of God.

S: We surely must return to that question. But I think that first we must consider why such names as *Essence, Goodness, Truth, Justice, Wisdom,* and the others of this kind which seem to be altogether divine and simply to signify Divine Substance or Essence have been declared by the most holy St. Gregory the Theologian to be metaphorical terms transposed from creature to Creator. We must believe that he made such a statement for some secret and mystical reason.

T: You are wide awake, and I see that we must not pass over this point either without consideration. Please tell me, then, whether you understand that anything is opposite to God or included in the concept of God. I use *opposite* to refer to privation, contrariety, relationship, or absence. By *included* I mean eternally understood with Him but not coessential with Him.

S: I see your intent clearly, and I should therefore never venture to say either that anything is opposite to Him or that anything of a different essence (*heterousion*) is included in the concept of Him. For things in a relationship of opposites are always so opposed to each other that they begin and cease together, since (1) they are of the same nature: e.g., the simple in relation to the double and $\frac{2}{3}$ in relation to $\frac{3}{2}$; or (2) they are opposite by negation, as *is, is not;* or (3) they are opposites through their natural qualities: (a) by absence, as in the case of light and darkness; (b) by privation, as in the case of life and death; or (c) by contrariety, as in the case of health and infirmity. These kinds of opposition are rightly attributed to things subject to intellect and sense, and therefore are not in God. Indeed, whatever things are at odds with themselves cannot be eternal. If they were, they would not be at odds with themselves because eternity is like itself and subsists wholly simple and undivided in itself. It is, in fact, the one Beginning and the one End of all things, in no way at odds with itself.

[14] According to the same reasoning, I don't know who would dare to assert that something is coeternal with God which is not coessential with Him. If such a thing can be conceived or discovered, it necessarily follows that there is not a single Beginning of all things, but two or more, quite different from one another, a theory which true reasoning usually rejects without hesitation. Everything properly begins from a single source; nothing from two or more sources.

T: I agree with your argument. If the divine names mentioned are in direct opposition to other names, then necessarily the things properly signified by them are understood to have contraries. Hence they cannot properly be predicated of God, to whom nothing is opposite, or with whom nothing coeternally different in nature is perceived. Of the names mentioned before and others like them, true reason can find none which does not have another name differing from it, whether in an opposite division or within the same genus. And we must necessarily recognize in things signified what we recognize in their names. But since there are countless terms designating God, which are metaphorically predicated of Him in holy Scripture by transposition from creation to Creator (if indeed anything can be rightly predicated of God, a point to be considered elsewhere), and since they cannot be discovered or collected by our poor rational power, a few designations for the Divine must be stated as an example. God, then, is called *Essence*, but He is not properly essence, for nothing is the opposite of essence. He is rather *hyperousios*, i.e., "superessential." Likewise He is called *Goodness*, but He is not properly goodness, to which evil is opposite. Instead He is *hyperagathos*, "More Than Good," and *hyperagathotes*, i.e., "More Than Goodness." He is called *God*, but He is not properly God. Blindness is the opposite of vision, and the non-seer of the seer. He is therefore *hypertheos*, "More Than Seer," if *Theos* is interpreted as "Seer." But if you resort to another etymology of this name and understand the derivation of *Theos*, "God," not from *theoro*, "see," but from *theo*, "run," the result is similar. The non-runner is opposite to the runner as slowness is to swiftness. He will then be *hypertheos*, i.e., "More Than Runner," as recorded in the passage "His word runs quickly." [16] We understand this passage as relating to God, the Word, who ineffably runs through all things with being in order that they may have being. We should have a similar kind of understanding about truth. Falsehood is the opposite of truth; hence He is not properly truth, but *hyperalethes* and *hyperaletheia*, i.e., "More Than True" and "More Than Truth." The same principle must be observed in regard to all divine names. He is not properly called *eternity*, since temporality is opposed to eternity. He is, then, *hyperaionios* and *hyperaionia*, "More Than Eternal" and "More Than Eternity." The same principle applies about wisdom also, so that it cannot be judged as properly predicated of God, since the foolish and folly are the opposite of the wise and wisdom. Accordingly, he is correctly and truly called *hypersophos*, i.e., "More Than Wise" and *hypersophia*, "More Than Wisdom." Similarly He is More Than Life, since death is opposed to life. We must have the same kind of understanding about "Light," since darkness opposes light. These illustrations of my point are sufficient, I believe.

S: I must admit that they are, because our proposed discussion, with the relevant points that must be argued, does not permit us to bring up all the necessary questions about such matters. Please go back, then, to your consideration of the ten categories.

T: I wonder about the sharpness of your concentration, which seemed so much on the alert until now.

S: What point are you making?

T: Didn't we say that the Ineffable Nature cannot properly be signified by any word, name, sensible sound, or thing denoted? And you conceded that it is called *Essence, Truth, Wisdom,* and other things of this kind not properly but metaphorically. We said that it is called *Superessential, More Than Truth, More Than Wisdom,* and other such names. But don't these terms seem virtually like proper names if *Superessential* is applied properly even though *Essence* isn't? Similarly if *More Than Truth* and *More Than Wisdom* are proper terms although *Truth* and *Wisdom* aren't? It doesn't lack proper names, then, because although these terms are not usually expressed in Latin as a single word and joined in a compound, except for the term *superessentialis* (you will rarely if ever find such Latin compounds as *superbonum, superaeternum,* or similar forms), they are expressed in Greek as compounds, every one with its single accent.

S: I wonder myself what I had in mind when I overlooked this important question. Now I am most eager to have you explain it to me. If Divine Substance can be properly expressed in any way at all, whether by simple or compound words or by words made from resolved compounds in Greek or in Latin, it will not seem ineffable. For whatever can be said in some way will not seem ineffable.

T: Now your mind is awake, I see.

S: Yes, but I still don't see any answer to this question.

T: Go back, then, to what we concluded a little while ago. We said, I believe, that there are two highest parts of theology; and our statement rested not upon ourselves but upon the authority of St. Dionysius the Areopagite. As we have said, he very clearly asserts that theology is twofold, i.e., *kataphatiké* and *apophatiké,* terms which Cicero translates as *intentio* and *repulsio,* but which we preferred to translate as "affirmation" and "negation" to disclose the force of the words more clearly.

S: I see that I do recall these points, but I don't yet understand how they contribute to our present investigation.

T: You see, don't you, that these two—i.e., affirmation and negation—are opposites?

S: Yes I do, and no things, in my judgment, could more truly be opposites.

T: Pay closer attention, then, for when you achieve the insight that comes from perfect reasoning, you will observe quite clearly that when they concentrate on Divine Nature, these two ostensible opposites are not at all opposed to each other, but are harmonious in all respects. Let us take a few examples to clarify the point; e.g., *kataphatiké* says, "It is Truth;" *apophatiké* counters, "It is not Truth." These statements seem to involve a kind of contradiction, but when you examine the matter more intently, you find no discrepancy. The statement "It is Truth" does not assert that Divine Substance is properly Truth, but that It can be called by such a name by a metaphorical transposition from creation to Creator. By such terms the *kataphatiké* clothes the Divine Essence, which is bare and lacks any proper designation. The way which asserts that "It is not Truth," clearly and appropriately recognizing Divine Nature as incomprehensible and ineffable, does not make a flat denial about It but rather denies that It is *properly* Truth or is properly so-called. The *apophatiké* knows how to strip Divinity of all the designations with which the *kataphatiké* clothes it. One clothes it by saying, for example, "It is Wisdom." The other strips it by saying "It is not Wisdom." One says, then, "It can be called this," but it does not say "It properly is this." The other says, "It is not this, although It can be given a name derived from this."

S: I believe that I see these matters very clearly. Statements which formerly appeared to me to clash now are openly revealed as harmonious and not the least discordant when they are considered in reference to God. But I admit that I still don't know how they pertain to the solution of our present problem.

T: Concentrate harder, then, and explain, insofar as you can, to what part of theology the affirmative or the negative, those designations added before—I mean *Superessential, More Than Truth, More Than Wisdom,* and the other similar ones—belong.

S: I don't dare to make the decision by myself. Since I observe that those designations lack the negative particle (*non*), I am afraid to join them to the negative part of theology; but if I join them to the affirmative, I realize that their meaning does not conform to my intention. When one says, "It is superessential," I am led to understand simply a negation of essence; for by saying that something is superessential, one is openly denying that it is essential. Consequently the negation, though not apparent in the verbal expression, does not elude those who carefully search out the meaning. I must therefore acknowledge, I believe, that these designations, though ostensibly lacking a negative, seem more in harmony with the negative than with the affirmative way insofar as one can understand them.

T: I see that you have given a very discreet and intelligent answer. I thoroughly approve of how, in expressing the affirmative part, you have quite subtly perceived the meaning of the negative. Let us then solve our present problem, if you will, by saying that all things predicated of God with the addition of the terms *Super* or *More Than*—e.g., *Superessential, More Than Truth, More Than Wisdom,* and other similar expressions—embrace both parts of theology in the fullest sense. Thus in verbal expression they possess the form of the affirmative; in meaning, however, the force of the negative. Let us conclude this matter with a brief example. *It is Essence* is an affirmation; *It is not Essence* is a denial; *It is Superessential* is at once an affirmation and a denial. On the surface, of course, it has no negative, but the negative shows its force in the meaning. By saying "It is Superessential," one is not stating what It is but what It is not, i.e., that It is not essence but More Than Essence. The statement does not, however, express what it is that is more than essence when it declares that God is not any of those things which have being, but is more than they are. It does not at all, however, define what that being is.

S: I don't think that we have to spend any more time on this problem. Now let us consider the nature of the categories, if you will.

T: Aristotle, who was reputedly the keenest of the Greeks and discovered the distinctions among natural phenomena, included in ten universal genera the countless varieties of all things which have being after God and have been created by Him. These ten genera he called 'categories' or *praedicamenta,* "things predicated." He thought that nothing can be found in the vast number of created things and the various motions of souls which cannot be included in any of these categories. These are called *ousia* (*essentia,* "essence"),[17] *posotes* (*quantitas,* "quantity"), *poiotes* (*qualitas,* "quality"), *pros ti* (*ad aliquid,* "relationship"), *keisthai* (*situs,* "position"), *hexis* (*habitus,* "state"), *topos* (*locus,* "place"), *chronos* (*tempus,* "time"), *prattein* (*agere,* "action"), *pathein* (*pati,* "being acted upon").

There are, in addition, countless subdivisions of these ten genera, but our present task does not allow us to discuss them lest we range too far afield, especially since the part of philosophy called 'Dialectic' is concerned with the divisions of these genera from the most general to the most specific, and conversely with their collections from the most specific to the most general.

[15]   But as St. Augustine says in his work *On the Trinity,* when one arrives at theology, i.e., the investigation of Divine Essence, the power of the categories is utterly destroyed. In natures created by God and in their motions, the power of any one of the categories is very strong. But in that Nature which can be neither expressed nor understood, it fails altogether. And yet, as we said before, just as virtually everything properly predicated about the nature of created things is applied to their Creator metaphorically, so the designations of the categories properly discerned in created things can fittingly be applied to the Cause of all things, not to signify properly what It is, but to persuade us metaphorically of what we may plausibly think about It when we investigate It in some manner.

S: I see clearly that the categories can by no means be predicated properly of the Ineffable Nature. If any of them could be properly predicated of God, it would necessarily follow that God is a genus. But God is not genus, species, or accident; therefore no category can properly designate God.

T: You are quite right. I believe that our energy was well expended before in our consideration of the two parts of theology. Otherwise we would not have been able to arrive so easily and almost effortlessly at our argument that the categories cannot be predicated properly of God. First we had to reach a clear conclusion that the primordial causes created in advance by the one Cause of all things—I mean essence, goodness, virtue, truth, wisdom, and the others of this kind—designate God only metaphorically. As we said, the highest created causes of all natures, which rank next in order to that Cause and which can be viewed only by the insight of the mind in its pure state, are outstripped in the excellence of their essence by the one ineffable Cause of all, so that It cannot in any way be properly designated by their names. What must we say, then, about those ten genera discerned not only in intelligible but also in sensible things? Surely we can't believe that they are predicated truly and properly of the Divine and Ineffable Nature.

S: I think that such a possibility is incredible. It is not *ousia* because It is More Than *Ousia,* but yet It is called *Ousia* because It is the Creator of all *ousion* (essences). It is not quantity because It is More Than Quantity, for every quantity has extension in three dimensions: length, width, and depth. These three dimensions, in turn, are extended to the number six, for length extends upward and downward, width to the right and to the left, and depth frontward and backward. God, however, wholly lacks dimension, and therefore lacks quantity. Likewise quantity exists in a number of parts, whether naturally joined as in the case of a line or time, or naturally disjoined as in the case of numbers, whether corporeal or intelligible. Divine Substance is not composed of continuous parts or divided by discrete parts. Hence It is not quantity. The name *quantity* is appropriately applied to It in two ways, however, either because *quantity* is used to express the magnitude of power, or because It is the Beginning and Cause of all quantity. Concerning quality, too, one must have a similar understanding. God is no quality, no quality is accidental to Him, and He participates in none. Yet quality is very often predicated of Him either because He is the Creator of all quality or because *quality* is frequently used as a designation of virtues. For goodness, justice, and the other virtues are said to be qualities, but God is Virtue and More Than Virtue.

[16] The principle (*ratio*) of relationship, however, is not so clearly apparent as the definitions of the other categories. This category alone seems to be almost properly predicated of God. I therefore think that

we must use the greatest care in investigating whether in the most sublime and sacred Trinity of the three most exalted Substances, the Father is properly spoken of in relation to the Son and likewise the Son in relation to the Father, and the Holy Spirit in relation to the Father and the Son, because He is the Spirit of both. In fact, St. Gregory the Theologian firmly asserts that these are the names of relationships. Or should we, as in the case of the other categories, believe and understand that the category of relationship too is predicated of God metaphorically?

T: I think that you are using a reasonable approach in tracking down the hidden truth. No category except that one seems properly predicated of God; but whether, in fact, it is must be examined with the most reverent care. If it is properly applied to God, virtually our whole previous line of reasoning will be nullified, since we made a generalization that nothing can be properly said or understood concerning God. Of course, the category of relationship will not be reckoned among the ten genera of categories if it is properly predicated of God, and hence the number of categories will be nine, not ten. The remaining possibility is to understand that this category, like the others, is predicated of God metaphorically. True reasoning invites and even constrains us to accept this interpretation in order not to threaten the stability of our former statements. It is surely compatible with true reasoning to say that *Father* and *Son* are names of relationship and of More Than Relationship; for we must not believe that the same kind of relationship exists in the most exalted substances of Divine Essence and in those things to which It is prior and which have been created by It. So, unless I am mistaken, It ineffably exceeds all relationship just as It surpasses all essence, wisdom, and virtue. Who, indeed, would believe that the relationship between the Father and His Word is like that which he can conceive of between Abraham and Isaac? This latter carnal relationship is to be traced to sexual reproduction resulting from the division of nature after the first man's sin. The former is believed to be the ineffable bond of the Unbegotten and the Begotten Substances, recognized by the radiance of Divine Light, insofar as such vision is granted us. The human relationship, as we have said, proceeded not from nature but from sin. The other is recognized as proceeding from the ineffable fruitfulness of Divine Goodness. But let us go on to the other categories.

S: There are six left, I believe, of which the first, *keisthai* or *iacere*, is termed by others *situs* ("position"). By *situs* is understood the position of some visible or invisible creature; e.g., the statement is made about a body that it is lying or standing. Similarly, about a soul, if it is in repose, that it is lying; if it is wide awake, that it is standing. Stability (*status*) is usually applied to this category and motion to time. Now since God neither stands nor lies, there is no principle by which this category (i.e., position) can be properly predicated of Him. Since He is, however, the cause of standing and of lying (for all things stand in Him, i.e., they remain unchangeable according to the principles of their own natures; and they lie in Him, i.e., they rest in Him, for He is the End of all things, beyond which they aspire to nothing), position may be metaphorically predicated of Him. If God truly and properly lies, sits, or stands, He is not free from position. If He is not free from position, He has a place. But He does not have a place. Therefore He is not held in any position.

[17] *T:* I understand your meaning clearly, and consequently see that we must pass to the category of state, which appears the most obscure of all categories because it encompasses so much. In fact, there is virtually no category in which some state cannot be found. Even essences or substances are associated with one another by some state. For example, we call essences *rational* and *irrational* by their state in reference to one another, since a creature would be termed *irrational* only because of its state of absence of rationality. In the same way, a being is called *rational* only because of its state of possessing rationality. Every ratio is a state, although not every state is a ratio. A ratio cannot properly be found in fewer than two, but a state is perceived even in single things. E.g., the state of a rational soul is virtue. Ratio, then, is a kind of state. If you want a clear illustration of how the state of a ratio is found in an essence, choose an example from numbers. I think that numbers are understood essentially in all things, since the essence of all things subsists in numbers. You see the ratio of two and three.

S: I see it clearly, and I think that three is half again as much as two. From this one example I can recognize the various kinds of ratio of all other substantial numbers in their relationship to one another.

T: If you pay close attention to the rest of the discussion, you will learn that there is no form of quantity, quality, relationship (*ad aliquid*), position, place, time, action, or reception of action in which some form of state is not found.

S: I have often investigated such matters and reached that conclusion. To take a few examples, in quantities the great, the small, and the medium, compared with one another, give strong evidence of state. Similarly in the quantities of numbers, lines, times, and other things like them you will clearly discover the state of ratios.

[18]   The same is true of quality. E.g., in colors, white, black, and some shade in between are joined to one another by their state. White and black, which are the extremes of colors, are related to each other by the state of extremity. On the other hand, color looks toward its extremes—i.e., white and black—from the state of the median position. In the category called 'relationship', one can clearly see the state of father in reference to son, son to father, friend to friend, double to simple, and other examples of the kind.

[19]   Concerning position too it is readily apparent how standing and lying have a certain state in relation to each other. They are, of course, diametrical opposites. The concept of standing inevitably involves the concept of lying. They always occur to the mind at the same time although they do not appear in anything at the same time.

[20]   And as for place, when higher, lower, and middle are considered, do they lack state? By no means, for all of these terms are derived not from the nature of things, but from the view of one who looks at them by parts. The upward and downward have no existence in the whole, and consequently neither do the higher, the lower, or the

middle. A consideration of the whole rejects these concepts, which are introduced by attention to parts. The same principle holds for the greater and the lesser. Nothing can be small or large in its own genus, but such concepts are produced by the thought of those who compare different quantities. The observation of places or of parts therefore gives rise to state in such matters. No nature is larger or smaller than another, just as none is higher or lower, since there subsists a single nature of all, created by the one God.

S: What about time? When the divisions of time are compared with one another, doesn't state become clearly apparent? E.g., of day in reference to hours, hour to minutes, minute to seconds, second to the lowest division of time. The result will be comparable if one considers measurements of time in their ascending order. In all of them, the state of whole in relation to parts and of parts in relation to whole is perceptible.

T: That is certainly true.

S: In the various motions of action and being acted upon, too, doesn't state appear everywhere? To love and to be loved, for example, constitute the reciprocal states of lover and beloved, whether they are present in a single person (a phenomenon which the Greeks call *autopátheia,* i.e., when action and its reception are observed in one and the same person, as expressed by the statement "I love myself") or between two persons (which the Greeks call *heteropátheia,* i.e., when one person is the lover, another the beloved, as expressed by the statement "I love you").

T: I see that this observation is true also.

S: Since this category of state appears to be naturally inherent in the other categories, why does it have a special place of its own among the ten categories as though it rested on principles properly its own?

T: Perhaps it subsists in itself precisely because it is found in everything. Whatever belongs to everything belongs properly to none, but is in all in such a way that it subsists in itself. The same principle is to be observed in the category of essence. There are ten categories, one of which is called 'essence' or 'substance', while the other nine are accidents and subsist in subsistence, for they cannot subsist by themselves. Essence, which is indispensable to their being, is evident in all of them; and yet it has its own place. For whatever belongs to everything belongs properly to nothing but is the common possession of all. While it subsists in everything, it does not cease to be in itself according to its own proper principle. The same kind of statement must be made about quantity. We speak of the quantity of essence, quality, relationship, position, state; of the size of place; of a small or large amount of time; of the extent of acting or being acted upon. You see, then, how far quantity extends through the other categories, and yet it does not lose its own status. Quality too is often predicated of all the other categories, for we speak of the kind of *ousia*, magnitude, relationship, position, state, place, time, action, and reception of action. We inquire about the quality of them all, and yet quality does not abandon the principle of its own genus. Why is it strange, then, if the category of state, while observed in all the categories, is said to have its own principle?

S: It is not at all strange. True reason convinces me that there is no other possibility.

T: You must surely see then that Divine Essence participates in no state, but that state can appropriately be predicated of It as the cause of state. If state were properly predicated of It, It would belong not to Itself but to something else. Every state, of course, is understood in some subject and is the accident of something. But it would be impious to have such a belief about God, to whom nothing is accidental and who is the accident of nothing, and who is understood in nothing just as nothing is understood in Him.

S: I believe that we have discussed this category enough.

[21]   T: Well, then, from what has already been said can't we draw brief inferences about the other categories? God is not place or time, but He is metaphorically called the "Place and Time of all" because He is the cause of all places and times. The definitions of all things, as though they were places of a sort, subsist in Him and from Him as from a kind of time, through Him as through a kind of time, and into Him as into an end of times, the motion of all things begins, moves, and stops although He is moved through time neither by Himself nor

by another. But if He were properly called "Place" and "Time," He would seem not to be outside all things by the excellence of His essence, but rather included within the number of all things with being, since place and time are reckoned among all created things. The whole world which now exists consists of these two things and cannot be without them. They are therefore called by the Greeks *hon aneu to pan*, i.e., "those things without which the universe cannot be." Everything in the world must have motion in time and limit in place. Besides, place itself is delimited and time moves. God, however, has neither motion nor limit. For the Place by which all places are delimited is the Place of Places. Since It is put in Its place by none, but places everything together within Itself, It is not Place but More Than Place. Since It is delimited by none but delimits all things, It is the Cause of all things. In the same way, the Cause of times sets times in motion, but is Itself moved by none at any time. It is More Than Time and More Than Motion. It is, therefore, neither place nor time.

S: The explanation has been so clear that I think that we have talked enough about the nature of the categories and about their metaphorical use to designate Divine Essence; for there are other matters which must be dealt with in connection with our present topic.

[22] *T:* Of these ten genera, four are stationary: viz., *ousia*, quantity, position, place; and six are in motion: viz., quality, relationship, state, time, action, and reception of action, as I believe that you are aware.

S: Yes I am, and have no further questions on the subject. But why do you bring it up?

T: To let you know clearly that the ten genera mentioned are encompassed by two higher, more general ones, namely motion and stability, which in turn are collected in the most general genus, called *to pan* in Greek and *universitas* in Latin.

S: I'm delighted by this statement because of those who think that no more general genus can be found in the universe than the ten discovered and named by Aristotle.

T: Does this division of the categories into motion and stability—
i.e., four in stability, six in motion—seem to you valid?

[23] *S:* Quite valid. But I still don't understand very well about
two of them, I mean state and relationship. These two categories seem
to me stable rather than in motion. Whatever attains to a state of
completion remains unchangeably, for if it is moved in some way, the
state obviously no longer exists. Virtue is truly the state of the soul
when it clings to it unchangeably so that it cannot be separated from it.
That is why no true state of bodies can be found, for an armed or
clothed man can be without arms or clothes. Likewise in relationship
stability is thought to be dominant, for the relationship of father to son,
of double to single and vice versa are not subject to motion. A father is
always the father of his son, as a son is always the son of his father, etc.

T: Perhaps you would not have hesitated so much if you had
observed more carefully that everything which is not perfectly and
naturally inherent in a creature but rather, through stages of growth,
advances to inseparable and unchangeable perfection, is necessarily in
motion. Every state, moreover, rises toward perfection by a certain
motion in the thing of which it is the state. And who would presume to
be certain about such perfection in this life? State, therefore, is in
motion. I wonder, too, why you hesitate about relationship when you
see that it cannot be in one and the same thing, but always appears in
two. Of course, no one could doubt that the mutual reaching out of
two things is caused by a certain motion. Another principle too very
clearly separates what is in motion from what is stable. To express it
briefly, this most general principle shows that everything created by
God and subordinate to Him is in motion—for all things move from
the non-existent to existence by generation when the Divine Goodness summons them out of nothingness from non-being into being so
that they may be. Thus every single thing endowed with being is
moved by a natural reaching out to its essence, genus, species, and
number. What we properly say is stable subsists in itself and needs no
subject in order to have being. Whatever things exist in something,
however, because they cannot subsist by themselves, are not unfit-

tingly judged to be in motion. Thus state and relationship are in some
subject in which, by a natural motion, they always long to be because
they cannot be without it. They are, therefore, in motion.

[24] *S:* What about place, quantity, and position, which you put
among stable things? No one, of course, has any doubts that *ousia,* i.e.,
essence, needs nothing else in order to subsist. In fact, everything else
is believed to be supported by it. On the other hand, place, quantity,
and position are counted among the accidents of essence. And through
the subject in which they are and without which they cannot be, they
are moved by longing. If this theory is true, everything is in motion
except *ousia,* which alone lacks motion, except the motion by which all
things long to have being; for it alone subsists by itself.

T: Your point is not wholly absurd because you are following the
common opinion. If you consider more carefully, though, you will find
that place is contained by nothing but contains everything placed in it.
For if place is merely the boundary and limit of each finite nature,
surely place does not long to be in anything, but all things in it always
rightly long for the boundary and limit in which they are naturally
contained and without which they seem to flow on to infinity. Hence
place is not in motion since all things in it are moved toward it while it
stands still. Reason teaches us the same thing about quantity and
position. Each and every sensible or intelligible participant in quantity
or position longs only to reach its perfect quantity or position in order
to rest in it. They (quantity and position) therefore do not themselves
have longing, but are longed for. They are not, therefore, in motion
but are stationary.

S: Are these three—quantity, position, place—to be called accidents of *ousia* or independent subsistences?

[25] *T:* I see that this point too deserves investigation. According
to the opinion of dialecticians, everything endowed with being either is
a subject or concerns a subject or is in a subject. True reasoning
counters, however, that being a subject and concerning a subject mean

one and the same thing and differ in no respect. For if, as they say, "Cicero" is a subject and primary substance but "man" concerns a subject and is a secondary substance, what difference is there according to nature except that one is in an individual, the other in a species? A species is simply the unity of individuals and individuals are simply the plurality of the species. If, then, the species is a single, undivided whole in individuals and individuals are an undivided one in a species, I fail to see the natural difference between a subject and what concerns a subject. We must have a similar understanding about accidents of a primary substance. For what is said to be in a subject is the very same thing as what is said to be at once in a subject and concerning a subject. For example, a discipline is one and the same in itself and in its species and individuals. The proper discipline of each and every thing, then, which dialecticians refer to as merely 'in the subject,' is the very same as the general discipline which they call 'in the subject and concerning the subject,' as though, subsisting in the subject—i.e., in the primary substance—it is predicated of the subject—i.e., the proper discipline of something. In fact, it is one and the same as a whole and in its parts. So there remain the subject and what is in the subject.

If you now closely follow the tracks of St. Gregory the Theologian and his wise interpreter, Maximus, you will discover that *ousia* in itself in all things endowed with being cannot be grasped at all by either sense or intellect. Its existence is therefore inferred from what may be called its attendant circumstances, viz., place, quantity, and position. Time also is added to these circumstances. Within these, as though encompassed within certain boundaries, essence is known to be enclosed, so that accidents do not appear to be subsisting in it, for they are outside. Neither, on the other hand, do they seem able to exist without it, because it is the center around which times revolve, and on all sides of which are stationed places, quantities, and positions. Some categories, then, are predicated about *ousia*, and they are said to be *periochai*, i.e., "standing around" because they are observed around it. Some categories in *ousia* are given the Greek name *symbamata*, i.e., accidents, and they are quality, relationship, state, action, and reception of action. These categories are also understood outside being in other categories, e.g., quality in quantity, as color in body. Likewise quality in *ousia*, as invisibility and incomprehensibility in genera. Similarly relationship outside *ousia*, as father to son, son to father; for they do not come from nature, but from the accidental, corruptible generation of bodies. A father, of course, is not the father of his son's nature or a son the son of his father's nature; but father and son are of one and the same nature. No nature, moreover, either begets itself or is begotten by itself. Relationship is present in *ousia* itself when genus is related to species and species to genus; for a genus is the genus of a species, and a species is a species of a genus. State, too, is found both without and within *ousia*, as we say "armed" or "dressed" in reference to the body. The state of *ousia*, genus, or species is the immovable power through which genus, when divided by species, always remains one and undivided in itself and whole in the individual species, while every one of the individual species is a unit in it. The same power is perceived also in species which, though divided by individuals, preserves the whole strength of its undivided unity. All individuals into which it seems divided to infinity are limited in the species itself, with every individual an undivided one. Concerning action and reception of action no one has any doubt, since we see that bodies, related as they are to quantity, both act and are acted upon. Also the genera and species of *ousia* itself are seen to act when they multiply themselves into different species and individuals. Whenever anyone, by the power of reason, practices the discipline of analytics by collecting individuals into species, species into genera, and genera into *ousia*, they are said to be acted upon, not because he collects them (for they are collected by nature, just as they are divided), but because he is seen to collect them by an act of reason. Also when he divides them, he is similarly said to act and they to be acted upon.

[26]   *S:*   Although these matters seem obscure, they do not elude me so completely that I have no clear and distinct idea of them. Now, since I note that virtually all categories are so bound together that they

can hardly be distinguished from one another with certainty (for I see that they are all intertwined with one another), please reveal to me the distinguishing property by which each of them can be discovered.

T: Don't you think that *ousia* is universally and properly contained in the most general and the more general genera, in the genera themselves and their species, and also in the most specific species called "atoms", i.e., individuals?

S: I see that *ousia* can be naturally inherent only in genera and species, from the highest downward, from the most general to the most specific, i.e., individuals. Or conversely upward from individuals to the most general. Universal *ousia* subsists in these which are, so to speak, its natural parts.

T: Take up the other categories then. Doesn't the property of quantity seem to lie in the number, spaces, and measurements of parts, whether those parts are continuous, as in the case of lines, times, and other things consisting of continuous quantity; or separate, marked off by fixed natural boundaries, as in numbers and every multitude in which separate quantity obviously exists?

S: This point too is clearly apparent.

T: Doesn't quality find its proper place in figures and surfaces, whether in natural bodies or in geometrical ones, such as planes, triangles, squares, polygons, circles, and the surfaces of such solid figures as cubes, cones, and spheres? I say "surfaces" because when the inside of solid bodies, whether natural or geometrical, is considered, they are referred to quantity because of their three dimensions of length, width, and depth. When their surface is examined, though, they are connected with quality. Similarly in incorporeal things it surely has the biggest place since all disciplines and powers, whether rational or irrational, not having yet arrived at the unchangeable state of mind, are referred to it.

S: Go right on with the other categories, because I see clearly and agree with what you have said.

T: Doesn't relationship possess its proper place in the universe in the ratios of things or of numbers and in their reciprocals, which are related by inseparable conversions? So what one thing is called is understood to receive its name not from itself, but from its opposite.

Examples of this firm friendship and inseparable bond are the multiple numbers joined to one another, viz., of the double, triple, quadruple, and other relationships of this kind to infinity. Similarly the fractions, as $\frac{3}{2}$, $\frac{4}{3}$, $\frac{5}{4}$, and the others of this kind. In all of these examples, not only do the whole numbers, compared with one another, show their force in different ratios, but also the parts of individual numbers, joined to one another, are inseparably linked by systems of ratios. You will find this not only in the terms of numbers, but also in the ratios of ratios, which arithmeticians call proportions.

S: I'm quite aware of that too, because these matters are very familiar to those versed in the Liberal Arts.

T: What are we to say about position? Surely it has its proper place in the natural orders of things or the artificial positions of corporeal or spiritual things. When I say "first", "second", "third", etc., whether about wholes or parts, genera or species, am I not considering a certain position of the individual components? Similarly if I say "to the right", "to the left", "upward", "downward", "in front", "behind", am I not simply pointing out a certain position, whether of the whole world in general or of its parts? When anyone says of a body that it is lying, sitting, or standing, he merely implies that it is reclining in a low position or is raised up or is in a kind of state of suspense between upward and downward. Likewise if one makes such statements about the soul, the meaning seems to be simply that it is still lying in the passions of sins, or is trying in some way to leave them behind, or is raising itself perfectly to virtues.

S: This point too seems easy to understand. Go on with the rest.

T: The category of state is left, I believe. It is most clearly perceived in the firm possession of virtues or vices. The term *state* is applied to every discipline, i.e., to every rational motion of the mind or to every irrational motion when it attains such great stability that it cannot be moved from the mind in any way or under any circumstances, but always clings to it so that it seems to be the very same thing as the mind. So every perfect virtue, inseparably clinging to the mind, is truly and properly called a state. Accordingly in bodies, in which nothing appears stable, state in the proper sense is seldom or never found. For whatever is not always possessed, even though it seems to be possessed for a time, is called *state* only by an abusive extension of the term.

S: Go right on. No one would deny the plausibility of your point.

[27]   *T:* Next comes place, which, as we said a little while ago, is established in the limitations of things which can be delimited. Place is simply the circuit by which everything is enclosed within definite boundaries. There are many kinds of places, for there are as many places as there are things, whether corporeal or incorporeal, which can be circumscribed. E.g., body is a certain compound of four elements with qualities, made into a whole under a certain species. By this definition, a general description, all bodies consisting of matter and form are included. Similarly spirit is an incorporeal nature which, of itself, lacks form and matter; for all spirit, whether rational or intellectual, is formless in itself. But if it turns to its Cause, the Word by which everything has been made, then it receives form. God's Word, then, is the one Form of all spirits, rational and intellectual. If the spirit is irrational, it is likewise formless in itself, but receives form from the *phantasiae* of sensible things. In other words, the *phantasia* of corporeal things, fixed in the memory through the physical senses, is the form of all irrational spirits.

In the Liberal Arts too, many places are found, for no art is without its own *loci*. There are, for instance, the *loci* of dialecticians, from genus, from species, from name, from antecedents, from consequents, from contraries, and the others of the kind which we don't have the time to discuss now. Dialectical *loci* are so widespread that a dialectician, whatever source he discovers to confer credibility upon something doubtful, describes it as the *locus* or "seat" (*sedes*, "resting place", "abode") of the argument. You will find a similar situation in the other arts, which are encompassed by their own *loci*, i.e., their proper definitions. Here are some examples. Grammar is the discipline that guards and controls articulated sound. Rhetoric is the discipline which copiously and ornately discusses a limited subject in respect to person, material, occasion, quality, place, time, and faculty. Rhetoric can be defined briefly as the keen and ample discipline that deals with a limited subject in seven sections. Dialectic is the discipline which carefully investigates the common rational conceptions of the mind. Arithmetic is the valid and pure discipline of the numbers subject to the contemplation of the mind.[18] Geometry is the discipline which, by keen mental insight, considers the spaces and surfaces of plane and solid figures. Music is the discipline which, through natural ratios, discerns by the light of reason the harmony of all things endowed with being, whether they are in motion or in a knowable state of stability. Astrology [i.e., Astronomy] is the discipline which investigates the spaces, motions, and returns at set times of celestial bodies. These are the general *loci* of the Liberal Arts. They are contained within these boundaries, within which there are countless other arts.

[28] *S:* From these arguments I must admit that place is only in the mind. If every definition is in a discipline and every discipline in the mind, every place, because it is a definition, will necessarily be only in the mind.

[29] *T:* You are quite correct.

S: What about those, then, who call the dwellings of men and other animals *places?* They similarly regard the common air and the earth as the places of all who dwell in them. They call water the place of fish, and consider ether the place of planets, and the celestial sphere the place of stars.

T: We have no course except to persuade them, if they can learn and wish to be taught, or to dismiss them entirely if they are uncooperative. Of course, true reasoning scoffs at those who make such comments; for if body is one thing and place another, it follows that place is not body. Air, moreover, is a fourth part of this corporeal, visible world. Hence it is not place. It is well established that this visible world is composed of four elements, as though of four general parts. It is something like a body made up of its parts. From these universal parts, of course, the proper and individual [literally, "most specific"] bodies of all animals, trees, and grasses are compounded by a remarkable and ineffable mixture; and at the time of their dissolution, they return to these parts. [30] As the whole universe which appears to our senses revolves around its axis with continual motion (I mean around the earth, around which, as a kind of center, the three other elements, water, air, and fire, revolve in ceaseless rotation) so with invisible motion and without a pause the universal bodies, i.e., the four elements, come together and form the proper bodies of individual things. When broken up again, these bodies return from their distinctive properties to the universal elements; for there always unchangeably endures as a kind of center of individual things the proper, natural essence which cannot be moved, increased, or diminished. Accidents, of course, are in motion, but essences are not. In fact, even the accidents themselves are not in motion, whether in growth or decay; but a participation in accidents by essence involves such changes. True reasoning allows of no other possibility, for every nature, whether of essences or of their accidents, is unchangeable. On the other hand, as we have said, participation by accidents in essences or by essences in accidents is always in motion. Participation can be begun, increased, and diminished until this world reaches the end of its stability in all things. After that, no essence, accident, or participation of those two in each other will endure any motion. All things will be one and immovable, since all things will return to their changeless reasons. But I think that we must discuss this return at another point.

[31]   But the question of why only the center of the world, the earth, is always stationary while the other elements revolve around it with eternal motion, demands no little consideration. We are familiar with the views on this subject of both the secular philosophers and the Catholic Fathers. Plato, the greatest of the philosophers on the subject of the world, declares in his *Timaeus* with many rational arguments that this visible world, as though it were a large animate creature, is compounded of body and soul. The body of this animate creature, he

says, is made up of the four very well known general elements and of various bodies compounded from them. Its soul is the generic principle of life, which gives vigor and motion to all things moving and stationary. Hence the poet says: "First of all, a spirit within feeds heaven and earth, the fluid plains of water, the bright globe of the moon, and the Titanic stars." [19] But although, as Plato says, soul itself moves eternally toward its body, i.e., to endow with life, govern, and move the whole world by the unions and dissolutions, according to various principles, of different individual bodies, it yet remains in its natural and motionless state. Therefore, since it always moves and stands, its body—i.e., the universe of visible things—partly stands in eternal stability, as the earth does, partly moves with eternal swiftness, as does the expanse of ether, partly neither stands nor moves swiftly, as is the case with water, and partly moves swiftly but not with the greatest swiftness, as air does. This account of the greatest philosopher is not utterly to be despised, in my judgment, for it appears acute and in conformity with nature. But since the great Bishop Gregory of Nyssa expounds this same matter very subtly in his sermon *On the Image*, I see that we must rather follow his statement when he says: "The Creator of the universe established this visible world between two extremes, i.e., heaviness and lightness, which are diametrically opposed to each other." Hence, since earth is established in heaviness, it always remains motionless; for heaviness is incapable of motion and is established in the middle of the world and has an outermost and a middle boundary. The expanses of ether, on the other hand, always revolve about the middle part with ineffable speed because they are established in the nature of lightness, which cannot stand still and has the outermost part of the visible world as a boundary. The two elements established in the middle, namely water and air, move constantly in proportioned measure between heaviness and lightness. Both of them rather follow the outermost boundary nearer to them than the one far away. Water moves more slowly than air because it clings to the heaviness of earth. Air is hurried along more rapidly than water because it is joined to the lightness of ether. But although the extreme parts of the world seem at odds with one another because of their different qualities, they do not altogether differ from one another.

Although the expanses of ether always revolve at the highest rate of speed, the chorus of stars keeps its changeless seat, so that it both revolves with ether and, like the stable earth, holds fast to its natural place. Although earth, on the contrary, is eternally at rest, yet all things which arise from it are, like the ethereal lightness, always in motion, being born through generation, growing into the number of places and times, and diminishing again and arriving at dissolution of form and matter.

[32] *S:* You seem to me to have made quite a long digression. Although we had intended to examine place, you abandoned that subject to deal with the world, and I still don't see the point of the discussion.

[33] *T:* Simply to distinguish by careful reasoning between the nature of bodies and the nature of places. Confusion about these matters is the greatest if not the only cause of error to virtually all who think that this visible world and its universal and special parts are places. If, through valid reasoning, they made sharp and accurate distinctions among the genera of all things, they would by no means include body and place in one and the same genus. No one who correctly observes and distinguishes the natures of things mixes places and bodies in a single genus, but separates them by a reasonable distinction. Bodies are contained in the category of quantity, which is naturally far removed from the category of place. Body, then, is not place, because locality is not quantity. As we previously stated, quantity is simply the fixed measurement of parts separated either by reason alone or by a natural difference, and the systematic progression to fixed boundaries of those things which have extension through the natural dimensions of length, width, and depth. Place is simply the circuit and boundary of things marked off by a definite limit. If, then, this visible world is a body, it necessarily follows that its parts also are bodies. But if they are bodies, they come under the genus of quantity, not of place. Moreover, they are bodies; therefore, they are not places.

Don't you see, therefore, how we reached the conclusion from our former reasoning that this world with its parts is not place but is contained in place, i.e., within a definite circuit of its outer limit? The container is one thing, the contained another. Bodies are contained within their places. Hence body is one thing and place another, just as the quantity of parts is one thing and their delimitation another. Consequently those four most familiar elements are not places, but are circumscribed in place because they are the main parts by which the whole of the sensible world is filled.

S: These statements of yours about the difference between places and bodies seem plausible. But please go over them in greater detail. I don't see why this world is not a place since many things are placed in it.

T: You are quite aware, I believe, that none of the ten categories defined by Aristotle falls within the province of our corporeal senses when it is rationally considered in itself, i.e., in its own nature. *Ousia* is incorporeal and subject to no bodily sense; and the other nine categories are related to *ousia* or are in it. But since *ousia* is incorporeal, doesn't it seem to you that all things which cling to it or subsist in it and cannot be without it are incorporeal? [34] All categories, then, are incorporeal when understood in themselves. But as Gregory states, some of them by coming together in a remarkable union produce visible matter, whereas others do not appear in anything and always come into being as incorporeal. E.g., *ousia*, relationship, place, time, action, and reception of action are touched by no corporeal sense. On the other hand, as we have said, when quantity, quality, position, and state produce matter by their union, they are customarily perceived by corporeal sense. If place, then, is numbered among things not subject to corporeal senses in any way, but bodies are not bodies if they are not perceptible to the senses, must we not grant that place is not body? By *bodies* I now mean things made up by the coming together of the four cosmic elements; for although these four elements are bodies even in their unmixed state, they elude all mortal sense because of their ineffable natural subtlety and purity. To sum up, then, place is one thing and body another. Or don't you agree?

S: I certainly do. The last conclusion from our reasoning forbids the admission that place and body belong to a single genus. But I am considerably perplexed by the statement you included that visible matter joined to form—for whatever appears does so through form—is simply the coming together of certain accidents.

T: Don't be perplexed. As I stated, the great Gregory of Nyssa in his sermon *On the Image* (24) argues convincingly and with sound reasons that this is so. His words are: "Matter is simply a compound of accidents proceeding from invisible causes to visible matter." This is as it should be, because if there were a simple, changeless, and wholly indestructible essence of this corporeal, destructible matter, it would not be subject to destruction at all by any means or any action. But since it is, in fact, destroyed, it obviously has no indestructible substratum. Genera, species, and irreducible individuals (*atoma*) always have being and endure because they have within them something indivisible that cannot be broken up or destroyed. Accidents, too, remain unchangeably in their own natures because they all have a certain indivisible substratum in which all subsist naturally as one.

[35]   *S:*   Quite true, in my opinion; and so I am waiting for you to bring our present investigation to a close.

T: It simply remains to say by way of illustration that when we see our bodies established on this earth or surrounded by this air, they are merely bodies within bodies. The same holds for fish in water, planets in the ether, stars in the firmament; they are bodies in bodies, smaller ones in larger, grosser in more subtle, light in lighter, pure in purer. True reasoning teaches that all of these sensibles, like intelligibles, are contained within their own places, i.e., within their natural limitations.

[36]   *S:*   I agree to this conclusion too, since I see that it is valid. I do wonder, though, how it became a common human practice to call all these bodies—whether of heavens, the air, water, or earth—the places

of the smaller bodies within them; just as *ousia* is judged to be simply this visible and tangible body. Please, then, don't object to satisfying my request that you speak at greater length about this difficulty.

T: Well, then, we agreed some time ago that everything known by corporeal sense, reason, or intellect can appropriately be predicated of God, the Creator of all things, although the pure contemplation of truth proves that He is none of the things predicated about Him.

S: Reason tells me that that conclusion stands firm and that it is as clear as can be.

[37] *T:* If all things with being are duly predicated of God, not indeed properly but by a kind of transposition, because they are from Him (since we observe that things contained are named by metonymy from what contains them), why is it strange if all things in place, when they seem wholly encompassed on all sides by bigger things, can be called *places,* although none of them is properly a place but is contained in the place of its own nature? And yet the smaller bodies are not contained by the larger in such a way that they cannot subsist without them within their own natural limits. Common human usage designates a wife or family as "home" although they differ in nature. A home does not confer substantial being upon a wife or a family, but their natural place does. But since they are held by it, they are customarily called by its name. Similarly things which contain are named from what is contained. For instance, air contains light; hence, lighted air is called *light.* The eye is called *sight* or *vision,* although it is neither according to its proper nature. Everyone knows that the eye is a corporeal part of the head, that it is humid, and that through it sight, like rays, is poured out from the meninx, a membrane of the brain. The meninges receives the nature of light from the heart, the seat of fire. Sight is the outpouring in rays of the natural light which dwells in the visual sense. When this outpouring is encompassed by the colors and forms of external, sensible bodies, it becomes conformable with remarkable speed to those colored visible forms. The vision of corporeal forms and colors is a certain conformed image in the rays of

the eyes, which is received without delay by the sense and is fixed in the memory of the perceiver. The same principle prevails also in the auditory sense. The part of the head properly called *ear* (*auris*) is named from hearing (*ex auditu*), since it is an instrument of hearing. And there are a thousand examples of this kind.

[38] *S:* I perceive this point clearly too.

T: And so do you see how mankind, since he is impelled by the necessity of signifying things and lacks the power to distinguish their true nature, customarily has devised these faulty designations, as when he names the lowest, central part of the visible world—I mean earth—"the place of creatures that walk." Similarly man calls the part inseparably joined to earth and closest to it in the quality of coldness—namely, water—"the place of swimming creatures." Next in the natural order he judges that the third part of the world is "the place of the winged genus." In the same way, he usually names the vast stretches of ether "the places of celestial bodies which revolve in it in a circle." But if one considers the truly valid principle of distinguishing natures, all of these are seen to be not places, but parts of the world circumscribed by their own places.

[39] Besides, in order that you may clearly recognize that the general parts of the world which we have mentioned, and the parts of those parts down to the very smallest subdivisions, are not places but parts of the world circumscribed by their own places. The nature of place itself must be considered more carefully, if you approve.

S: I certainly do, and am extremely eager to hear about the subject.

T: Well, then, listen to the beginning of this reasoning, which I have drawn from the holy fathers, Gregory the Theologian and Maximus, the distinguished interpreter of his sermons. Everything endowed with being except God, who alone properly subsists above being itself, is understood in place. Always and in every respect time is understood jointly with place. It is impossible for place to be understood without time, just as time cannot be defined without involving the coexisting idea of place. These things (time and place) are put among those which always exist together inseparably. Without them no essence which receives its being through generation can, in any way, exist or be known. The essence of all existing things, therefore, is subject to place and time. Hence, it is not known in any way except in place and time and under place and under time. But the whole universe is not under itself or within itself. For it is irrational and impossible to decide that the universe itself is above itself, since it has as a limit the supremely Causal Power which, beyond all things, circumscribes everything beneath and within Itself. And so the outer bound is the place of the universe. In fact, some define place as "the circuit outside the universe," or "the position outside the universe," or "the embracing limit in which the embraced is embraced." The universe is also proved to be subject to time, since everything beneath God has qualified, not simple, being and so has a beginning. For although everything susceptible to a rational account has a certain kind of essence, it did not formerly have it. It therefore has qualified being, i.e., being in place, and a kind of beginning of being, i.e., being in time. Hence all things except God, since they subsist with qualification and began to subsist through generation, are necessarily limited by place and time. When we say that God has being, we do not say it with any qualification. He is and was, and we refer to Him simply, without limit, and absolutely in Himself. The Divine is incomprehensible to all reason and intellect; and therefore in predicating His being, we do not call Him Being Itself; for being is from Him, but He is not being Itself. He is, in a way, above being itself, above being and in general above whatever is said and understood. Moreover, if things endowed with being have qualified but not universal being, they will surely be shown to be under place through position and the limit of the reasons in which they have being according to nature, and completely under time through a beginning. Don't you see, then, that place and time are understood as prior to all things with being? The number of places and times, as St. Augustine says in Book 6 *On Music*, precedes everything in them. Limit, i.e., the measure of all created things, naturally precedes their formation as a reason. This limit and measure is said to be, and is, the place of every single thing. Similarly, the starting point of birth and the beginning are perceived to precede, as a reason, everything that is born and begins. Everything, therefore, which formerly had no being but now has, has begun to be from a starting point of time. Thus God alone is infinite; everything else is limited by a "where" and a "when", i.e., time and place; not because place and time are not in the number of things created by God, but because they preceded everything in the universe not by intervals of time, but by the sole reason of creation. Whatever contains is necessarily understood as prior to whatever is contained, as cause precedes effect, fire a conflagration, voice a word, and the other similar examples. We therefore believe that the very bliss promised to the worthy and the very end of this world will be that all who are to receive the glory of deification will rise beyond places and times. Whoever is constrained by place and time is finite, but eternal bliss is infinite. Participants in eternal and infinite bliss will therefore not be circumscribed by place or time.

[40] I think that we must understand generally about all who will participate in future bliss what has been written only about Melchisedech[20]—namely, that he had no father and mother, no beginning of his term of life through generation into essence, and no end in time. All who are to return to their eternal reasons (which have neither beginning of time through generation in place or time nor end through dissolution, and which are not circumscribed by any position in place), so as to have being only in them and to be nothing but them, will surely lack all limit in place and time. They will be infinite and will cling for infinity to the Cause of all things, which is free from all circumscription since It is infinite. Only God will appear in them when they transcend the limits of their own nature, not in such a way that their nature will perish, but so that only He who truly has being will appear in them. The transcendence of nature is the non-appearance of nature, just as, to take our frequent former example, air when

filled with light is not apparent, since only the light is dominant. What is understood about the general place and the general time of universal creation will necessarily be understood about the specific and proper places and times of its parts from the highest downward. General time and place logically precede everything within them. Hence knowledge of specific and proper places and times precedes the things specifically and properly understood in them. Thus we deduce that place is simply the natural definition, measure, and position of every single creature, whether general or specific; just as time is simply the movements of things through generation from non-being to being by a beginning, and the definite measurements of the motion of changeable things until the arrival of that fixed end where all things will stand firm without change.

S: The point of your reasoning is beginning to be clear, I believe; for insofar as I can understand it, it is trying to convince me that place is simply the natural definition of every single creature, that within it the whole is contained, and that beyond it there is no extension of any kind. My inference is that whether one says *place, end, boundary, definition,* or *circumscription,* the meaning is one and the same: viz., the circuit of finite nature.

[41] Although some think that there are many kinds of definitions, the only one that may truly be given that name is the definition called *ousiodes* in Greek, "essential" in our language. The others are either enumerations of the intelligible parts of *ousia,* or arguments from outside by accidents or some kind of statements. Only the *ousiodes* deals exclusively with what completes and perfects the wholeness of the nature which it is defining. As St. Augustine says, "A definition contains nothing greater or less than what it has undertaken to explain. Otherwise it is utterly faulty."

T: Your perception is clear, for our previous argument tries to make the very point that you have stated.

S: But I do wonder, and I do not see very well, how the definition of each essence is said to be without and not within it; i.e., how it cannot be called either the whole or a part of it.

T: If you pay closer attention, you will understand this clearly too.

S: As far as my intelligence allows.

T: Please answer this question. Everything is divided into two genera: what is visible and is or can be perceived by the corporeal senses, or what is invisible and is or can be regarded by the mind's eye, either through itself or through something attached to it. To which of these genera do definitions belong, in your judgment?

[42] *S:* That is a ridiculous question. No one with sound reason would put place, end, definition, or any kind of circumscription by which the substance of anything is encompassed among the things subject to the bodily senses, when he sees that the limits of a line, a triangle, or any plane or solid figure are incorporeal. E.g., a point from which a line begins and in which it ends is neither a line nor part of one, but the limit of a line. Hence its place is not perceived by sense but conceived of by reason alone. A sensible point is part of a line, but not its beginning or end. Similarly the line itself is shown by the counsel of reason to be incorporeal and the beginning of a surface. The surface, too, is incorporeal and the end of a line but the beginning of solidity. Solidity too is incorporeal and is the end of all perfection. Whatever among these—i.e., visible point, line, surface, or solidity— the corporeal sense touches are the figures of the incorporeal things, not their true substance, which is incorporeal. Similarly the natural bounds of natural bodies, whether they are sensible through a blending of the elements of which they subsist or whether, by their subtlety, they elude human gaze, are perceived by the intellect alone. Of course form, which contains all the matter of bodies, is incorporeal. If one looks closely, even matter itself is composed of a union of incorporeal qualities.

T: You believe, then, that definitions, which we have called "the places of circumscribed things," are included within the genus of invisible things?

S: I do, and I am certain of it.

[43] *T:* You are quite right. But the genus of invisible things in turn undergoes division into many species; for some are understood and understand; some are understood but do not understand; some neither are understood nor understand. In which species do you think that the definitions of invisibles should be numbered?

S: Obviously in the one that understands and is understood; for the action of definition is the action of a nature which reasons and understands.

T: That seems necessarily true. No nature which does not understand that it itself has being can define what is equal to or lower than itself. It obviously cannot recognize what is above itself since it cannot attain to knowledge of it.

S: Skill in forming definitions, then, belongs solely to the intellectual nature established in man and angel. But whether an angel or a man can define himself, or a man an angel, or an angel a man is a weighty question. I should like to know what you think about the subject.

T: I think that they can define neither themselves nor one another. If a man defines himself or an angel, he is greater than himself and the angel since what defines is greater than what is defined. The same reasoning holds true about an angel. I therefore think that they can be defined only by Him who created them in His own image.

S: My deduction from this reasoning is that the only natures defined by the rational soul are those, whether visible of invisible, which are lower than itself.

T: This statement is on the right track. Consequently, where there are definitions of things defined, there also are surely the places of what is circumscribed since our former reasoning led us to the conclusion that place is definition and definition is place.

S: It certainly did.

T: Definitions of bodies and of things without reason exist only in the rational mind. There too, consequently, are the places of all things comprehended in place. But if the rational mind is incorporeal—a point unchallenged by anyone with sound judgment—obviously everything understood in it is necessarily incorporeal. Because place is understood as in the mind, as was previously granted, it too is therefore incorporeal.

S: I see that this conclusion too is correct. The argument is not refuted whether the nature of angels contains the definitions of things lower than itself, as Augustine apparently believes (for angels too are thought to govern what is beneath themselves), or whether it always fixes its gaze on what is higher than itself, i.e., on the eternal causes of things. One would not stray from the truth, I believe, in thinking that the human mind, though still weighted down by earthly *phantasiae*, can comprehend the created causes of natures inferior to itself if it lives a pure life; and that the mind of angels aspires to the eternal reasons of all things and, moved by love,[21] always attracts human nature to this goal.

T: Your perception is sound. You see, then, don't you, that place is simply the action of one understanding and comprehending by the power of intelligence what he can comprehend, whether these objects are sensible or comprehended by the intellect? Now, if this is so, what is defined is different from its definition.

S: I see that it is different. But since intellect, which understands itself, also defines itself, it seems to be its own place.

T: That would be a reasonable statement if any intellect lower than God, who is called the Intellect of all things, can understand itself. If every intellect except God is circumscribed not by itself but by what is superior to itself, however, no intellect will be its own place but will be placed within what is superior to itself. Didn't we agree about this very matter a little while ago?

S: I think that we must discuss it more fully at another point.

[44]   But now I should like to know whether the nature of the mind which defines (i.e., which encompasses in the place of knowledge everything understood by it) is one thing and the place itself (i.e., the definition of what is placed or defined) something else.

T: I see that this matter too deserves investigation, because many are uncertain about it. But we see that the Liberal Arts established in the soul are one thing and soul itself, which is a kind of subject of the arts, is something else; while the arts appear to be, in effect, inseparable and natural accidents of soul. Surely, then, we may put the discipline of defining among the arts by adding it to dialectic, the property of which is to divide, join, distinguish, and assign the proper places to every one of those things which can be understood. Hence philosophers usually call it 'the true contemplation of things.' In every rational and intellectual nature, we may regard three things as inseparable and abiding unimpaired—viz., *ousia (essentia,* "essence"), *dynamis (virtus,* "power"), and *energeia (operatio,* "operation"). St. Dionysius attests that these three cling inseparably to one another just as they are and can be neither increased nor diminished, since they are immortal and unchangeable. Don't you think it plausible and reasonable that all the Liberal Arts should be judged as being in the part called *energeia,* i.e., the operation of the soul? Philosophers have investigated truly and discovered that the arts are eternal and always cling to the soul without change, so that they seem to be not among its accidents but rather its natural powers and actions which do not and cannot withdraw from it in any way. They do not come from another source, either, but are naturally implanted in the soul so that it is unclear whether they confer eternity upon it, since they are eternal, and whether they always cling to it in order that it may be eternal; or whether, by reason of the subject, namely the soul, eternity is conferred upon the arts (for the *ousia* and power and action of the soul are eternal); or whether they so cling to one another, since all are eternal, that they cannot be separated.

[45] *S:* Since this reasoning is true, I don't think that anyone would venture to argue against it. Any of these possibilities is reasonable, but the last is clearly the most plausible. But to return to the same matter, I don't see very plainly how *ousia* can be defined among genera, species, or individuals, since we previously deduced that it can be comprehended by no corporeal sense and no intellect.

T: No one can define *ousia* in itself and say what it is. It can be defined only from those things which cling to it inseparably and which are indispensable to it—I mean time and place. All *ousia* created from nothing has being in place and time. It is in place because it has qualified being, since it is not infinite. It is in time because that which was not, begins to be. No definition can be given in any way of what *ousia* is, but the fact of its existence is defined; for from place, time, and other accidents understood either in or outside it, we may infer simply *that* it is, not *what* it is. The same statement might suitably be made generally about all *ousia*, whether the most general or the most specific or in a middle classification. The Cause of all things, God, is also merely known, from what He has created, to be; but by no proof derived from creatures can we understand what He is. Hence the sole definition predicated of God is that He is the One who is More Than Being.

S: No one of sound intelligence will oppose this reasoning either, in my opinion.

[46] *T:* You now have the clearest possible perception of how to deal with those who believe that the parts of this visible world are the natural places of the other bodies established within them. They are to be scoffed at, or rather pitied and so recalled to valid judgment if they are willing; or they are to be utterly abandoned if they prefer to follow their usual path, which diverges completely from the truth. To speak about my body, for example (because it is completely shameless to think that soul is contained within the corporeal spaces of this world), if air is its place, it follows that a fourth part of itself is its place. As everyone knows, every visible body consists of four parts: fire, air, earth, and water; and it is the height of irrationality to think that the whole body is located in a part of itself. Of course, it is correctly believed that the whole embraces all its parts, but not that any part encompasses the whole. Also, if I say that my body is in the air as if in its place, the result is that it can have no definite place there. Since the air is always revolving about the earth, a body set in it must have countless places in one and the same period of time. But that concession may not be rationally granted, since our former arguments convinced us that place is stationary and not altered by any motion. Whoever stands, sits, or swims in a river cannot hold fast to that part

of the river so that he can claim to be in possession of a definite place of the river since, as is generally agreed, it flows on ceaselessly. Similarly, no one should state that the place of his body is this air, which moves ceaselessly and does not stand still for a single instant. If anyone counters this argument by saying that earth, since it is always stationary, is rightly termed the place of bodies, he should observe in the same way that earth is the matter of bodies, not their place. No rational person would dare to say that the matter of bodies is their place, especially since matter, considered by itself, is neither in motion nor stationary. It is not in motion because it has not yet begun to be contained in a definite form; for matter is moved by form, without which, according to the Greeks, it is motionless. But by what will it be moved when it is not yet bound by any definite time or place? Nor is it stationary, since it does not yet possess the end of its perfection. Stability is, of course, the end of motion. But how can something be stable when it has not yet begun to move? How, then, can the matter of body be the place of the body made from it when matter itself is circumscribed by no definite place, limit, or form, and is defined in no certain way except by negation? It is said not to be any of those things endowed with being, since from it all created things are believed to have been formed. Likewise, if parts of this visible world are places of our bodies or of other things, our places cannot always exist. Once the body of some animal is dissolved and its parts separately return to their natural habitations from which the body was taken, its place—e.g., air, water, earth, or fire—will not exist. But the individual parts of a single body are so commingled with the individual elements whose nature they share that they are one with them and are not virtually one body in another. What is restored to air will be air, and will not, so to speak, be set in a certain place of air. There will not be a resulting confusion of bodies, but in a remarkable natural way, every individual will have his own proper part in the individual elements, whole through the whole element, not a part in a part. So at the time of resurrection everyone will receive only his own, just as the light of many lamps is joined in such a way that there is no commingling in it and no separation. While it seems to be one and the same light, yet each lamp has its own light not commingled with the light of another; but whole lights are marvelously formed in wholes and produce a single light. Our conclusion, then, is that air is one thing and its place another. We must, I think, realize that the same holds true for the other elements and the parts of dissolved bodies restored to them. If this is so, it must be granted that those general parts of the world are not the places of bodies which are filled with and compounded of them; or that bodies themselves have no fixed place; or that bodies are altogether without place. The nature of things and true contemplation about it do not allow such a concession; for no creature, whether corporeal or incorporeal, can lack its definite, unchangeable place and definite intervals and limits of times. These two things, place and time, are therefore, as we have often said, called 'indispensable' (*hon aneu*) by philosophers. Without them no creature beginning by generation and subsisting in some way can exist. To adopt a very closely related argument, if the place of a body is everything which envelops it, color will be the place of body since there is no visible body which is not enveloped by color. But if color is the place of a colored body, it must be granted that quality is the place of body. But no one is so appallingly stupid as to admit that the quality of a body is its place. Although color is an incorporeal quality of body and encompasses body from without on all sides, no philosopher considers color the place of body. According to this reasoning, one must refuse to grant that either air or any other cosmic element, even though it encompasses the bodies set within it, can in any way be their places.

[47]   *S:*   We have discussed this subject enough. But I think that we must make some brief comments in opposition to those who do not realize that body is one thing and the essence of body something else. They are led so far astray that they firmly believe that substance itself is corporeal, visible, and tactile. Many persons—in fact, almost all—suffer from such a delusion through ignorance of the natural differentiae of things.

T: Nothing is harder than to oppose stupidity, because it does not acknowledge its defeat by any authority and is not persuaded by any reason. But since the stupidity of men varies and their minds are not equally obscured by the same mist of error, I see that we must use a few arguments against them.

S: Indeed we must. If it helps them, that will be a gain; but in any case, by our zeal in discussion we will strengthen our own convictions about such distinctions among natures.

T: Well, then, give your thoughtful attention to these few dialectical syllogisms about a number of matters. Every body compounded of matter and form is corruptible since it can be dissolved. Mortal body is compounded of matter and form. It is therefore corruptible. Next: all *ousia* is simple and unsusceptible to composition from matter and form since it is one and inseparable. No *ousia*, therefore, is reasonably admitted to be mortal body. This point has been made, because even though all *ousia* is understood as a compound of essence and essential differentia (and no incorporeal essence can fail to have this compound, since even Divine *Ousia* itself, which is believed to be not only simple but More Than Simple, has an essential differentia; for It contains within It the Unbegotten, the Begotten, and the Proceeding substance), the compound itself, recognized by reason alone and not acknowledged as the product of any act or operation, must reasonably be judged as a simple state. To acquire a sounder knowledge about the incorruptibility of *ousia*, read the book of St. Dionysius the Areopagite *On Divine Names* in the passage where he argues that the nature of demons and their wickedness can corrupt no essence, either their own or that of others. You will find him arguing very subtly that nothing endowed with being can be corrupted in any way insofar as it is essence and nature.

[48] These three things in every creature, whether a corporeal or an incorporeal one—i.e., essence, power, and natural operation—are incorruptible and inseparable, as he shows by the most cogent arguments.

S: I should like an example of these three things.

T: There is no nature, whether rational or intellectual, which is unaware of its being, even though it does not know what it is.

S: I have no doubt on that score.

T: When I say, "I understand that I have being," don't I, by the single verb "understand", signify three inseparable things? I point out that I have being, that I can understand that I have being, and that I *do* understand that I have being. You see, then, that by the one verb I indicate my *ousia*, my power, and my action; for I would not have understanding unless I had being; I would not have understanding if I lacked the power of understanding; and that power is not dormant in me, but results in the operation of understanding.

S: Both true and plausible.

T: Won't those who call material body *ousia* either have to admit that their body has not been compounded of form and matter but is incorruptible *ousia*, or else be forced by truth to concede that their body is corruptible and material and hence is not *ousia?*

S: They surely will. But you do not appear to be denying that all body in general, but merely that all body compounded of form and matter, is *ousia*.

T: Consider this point carefully, then. Don't suppose that I was talking only about a certain kind of bodies, but generally about every body, although I specifically mentioned body composed of form and matter because of its usefulness for our present debate against those who say that their mortal, transitory bodies are the same as their *ousia*, and that their *ousia* is the same as their material body, compounded of different species, namely form, matter, and various accidents. [49] Listen to the following kind of argument in order to understand clearly that *ousia* generically speaking is no body.

S: I shall listen, but I see that first a kind of formulation of our previous argument must be made. Our former reasoning appears to be an argument from the contrary rather than a dialectical syllogism.

T: Let the chief proposition, then, be put as follows: Is *ousia* corruptible body? Every *ousia* is incorruptible. Every incorruptible body is non-material. Therefore every *ousia* is a non-material body. And conversely, every material body is not an *ousia*. Likewise, every body compounded of form and matter is not simple. Every *ousia*, however, is simple. Therefore no body compounded of form and matter is an *ousia*. Likewise, the *ousia* of all men is one and the same, for all participate in one essence; hence, since it is common to all, it is proper to none. A body, however, is not common to all men, for every man has his own body. *Ousia* is therefore not both common and a body. But it is common. Hence it is not a body.[22] The same reasoning comes through with striking clarity in regard to other things, animate and inanimate.

S: This is a suitable formulation. Please go back to the general kind of argument which you promised, from which the inference is drawn that no body is an *ousia*.

T: Everything comprehended by length, width, and depth, since it is enclosed by different dimensions, is a body. Whatever has none of these dimensions, however, since it is one and simple and can receive no movement of its nature through the dimensions, is necessarily incorporeal. *Ousia*, moreover, has no extension in length, width, or depth; and since it remains undivided in the simplicity of its nature, it is incorporeal. Therefore no *ousia*, lacking dimension as it does, is corporeal; just as no body, because it has extension in the (three) dimensions, is an *ousia*.

S: I should like this point, too, to be represented in a definite dialectical formulation.

T: Let it take the formulation of a conditional syllogism, with the chief proposition as follows: Is *ousia* body? If it is, it has the dimensions of length, width, and depth. But *ousia* does not have length, width, and depth. Therefore it is not body. If you wish also to hear a syllogism in the form of an enthymeme (i.e., a common conception of the mind, which holds the dominant position among all conclusions because it is drawn from things which cannot exist simultaneously), then hear a formulation such as the following: "Something cannot at once be *ousia* and not be incorporeal. But it is *ousia*. Therefore it is incorporeal, since it cannot at the same time be *ousia* and not be incorporeal." Similarly, "Something cannot at once be *ousia* and body. But it is *ousia*. Therefore it is not body." Likewise, "Something cannot at once not be both *ousia* and incorporeal; but it is *ousia*; it is therefore incorporeal."[23] The chief argument, in sum, establishes the distinction that body is one thing, *ousia* another. *Ousia* is divided into genera and species, but body as a whole is separated into parts. Also, body is not whole in any of its parts; for example, the whole body is not included in the head, hands, or feet. Also the body is larger in all of its parts together, and smaller in the individual parts considered separately. On the contrary, though, *ousia* is whole in its individual forms and species. It is not greater when they are all collected together, or smaller in individual ones separated from one another. It is no larger in the most general genus than in the most specific species; nor is it smaller in the most specific species than in the most general genus. To take some examples, *ousia* is no greater in all men than in a single man, and no smaller in a single man than in all men. It is no greater in the genus made up of all species of animals than in man alone, or ox, or horse. Nor is it smaller in these individual species than in all of them taken together. Another argument is that body can be cut into parts so that the whole of it dies. E.g., when it is resolved into the elements from the union of which it is made up when form is added, the whole perishes. When the parts are not all together and held in their proper form, the whole cannot actually be together in anything, even though the parts seem to be together in the thought of one considering the nature of things. But it is one thing to be together in the rational consideration of nature, for such consideration always collects everything by the intellect and inseparably encompasses the universe; it is something else which is achieved visibly in the separation or collection of sensible parts by what the agent does and what the object of the action experiences. For instance, the reason of all numbers in unity is firm-set and cannot be either increased or diminished. Numbers which are corporeal or imaginary, however, can be increased to infinity and so reduced as not to exist at all. But although *ousia* is divided by reason alone into its genera, species, and numbers, it remains undivided in its natural power and is not separated by any visible act or operation. It always subsists eternally and unchangeably whole in its subdivisions, all of which are always together as an inseparable unity in it. That is why body, which is simply the quantity of *ousia*—or, to speak more accurately not the quantity but the *quantum*—is separated into different parts by action or by the passive experience of its inevitable frailty; while *ousia* in itself, of which body is the *quantum*, endures immortal and inseparable by its own natural power. [50] My point in adding that body is more correctly called quantum than quantity is that accidents called 'natural' because they are naturally perceived in themselves, are incorporeal and invisible, and are viewed only by the eye of reason in reference to *ousia* itself or in it. These accidents are, as it were, causes of their effects, as quantity and quality are the causes of the *quantum* and the *quale.* The same point holds true for the other kinds of accidents, about which I think that we have said enough. Although invisible, they produce visible effects. Body is not, therefore, the quantity of *ousia* but its *quantum;* just as visible color, perceived around a body, is not a quality of *ousia,* but a *quale* fixed in the *quantum.* And so it is for the other examples of this kind. I have decided to add to our discussions the following statement from St. Augustine's book on Aristotle's *Categories* (71–72).

[51]   "Now that *ousia* has been described, since it could not be defined for the reasons given above, the necessary sequence demanded the definition of accidents. The first of these is *quantum,* and rightly so; for when we see something, we must judge how big *(quantum)* it is. But how big something is can be discovered only by inference through the application of measure. If one wishes to overlook width and measure only length, length subjected to measure without width is called *grammé* ("line"). Not that there is any length without width, but that anyone measuring length alone is said to be measuring a line. Width measured with length is called *epiphániea* ("surface"). If depth is also joined to the measurement, all three dimensions together produce body. But we do not mean the same thing by this term as natural body, as I point out to avoid the appearance of returning to the subject of *ousia.*"

The purpose of this statement is to teach us that individual rules are established in geometric bodies, in which these three dimensions can be discerned separately. In natural bodies, however, where they are inseparably bound, quantity is separated from *ousia* only by the intellect. For when someone is evidently discussing quantity as though he were saying something about *ousia,* he is thought to be confusing them. Do you see what pronouncement this most authoritative teacher is making? When someone is evidently discussing quantity, he says, i.e., the dimensions of which a body is composed, those who regard *ousia* as simply visible body think that he is saying something about *ousia* itself. Geometric bodies are observed by us only with the mind's eye, and we take care to fashion them only by the imagistic representations stored in the memory. If these bodies subsisted in *ousia*, they would undoubtedly be natural; and there would be no difference between natural and geometrical bodies. Actually, though, since we observe geometric bodies only with the mind and they do not subsist in any *ousia* and are therefore correctly termed 'imaginary', whereas bodies are natural and real for the very reason that they subsist in their natural essences, without which they can have no being (for otherwise they would merely be conceived of rationally without subsisting in natural entities); we may surely deduce that body is one thing and *ousia* another. Body sometimes lacks *ousia* and sometimes adheres to it to achieve reality (for without *ousia* it cannot be real, but only formed by a certain imagination); whereas *ousia* does not need body at all in order to have being, since it subsists by itself. I think that we have said enough on this subject.

S: Quite enough. But I see that you must still give a brief explanation about matter itself and form, of which you affirm that material things are compounded. In my judgment, this topic must not be overlooked, since I am not quite clear about whether it is the same form which is subordinate to genus and which is joined to matter in order that it may be body.

[52]   *T:* Some forms are understood in *ousia*, others in quality; but those in *ousia* are the substantial species of genus. The genus is predicated of them because it subsists in them. As we have often stated, genus is whole in its individual forms, just as individual forms are one in their genus. All of these, genera and forms, flow from a single fountain of *ousia* and return to it by a natural circuit. The forms attributed to quality are properly called 'forms' in natural bodies, but 'figures' in geometrical bodies. Every geometrical body consists only of dimensions and figure, not of any substance. Of course, every body produced by *phantasia* is made up of the three universal dimensions,

length, width, and depth; but not all geometrical bodies are circumscribed by a single figure. Some rise from a triangular figure, others
from a tetragon, others from a pentagon, and from the other polygons
to infinity; whereas others have a circular surface. In proportion to the
increase in the number of lines from three, therefore, the multiple
order of figures and surfaces is varied. Thus the number of dimensions
and lines in geometrical bodies is put to the account of quantity. The
order and position of sides and angles, and the relations (*habitudines*) of
surfaces are the property of quality and called geometrical 'form' or
properly, 'figure'. The observation in natural bodies of the number of
members and the distinction whether they are disjoined by natural
separations or whether they are naturally joined to one another is, as
everyone concedes, proper to quantity; while the order and position of
the natural parts or members is referred to quality and properly called
'form'. We say, for example, that the form of a man is erect, turning
upward, while that of other animals is prone, turning downward.
Hence those who lack fitting harmony of members are called
'deformed', as are those who lack beautiful color, which is born in
bodies from a fiery quality, which is *calor* ("heat"). In fact, the word
color is derived from *calor* with a single letter changed. *Forma* too is
named from *formum*, i.e., "hot", with the syllable *-mum* changed to
-ma; for the ancients used the term *formum* to mean "hot". Hence the
word *forcipes* ("tongs") for *formum capientes* ("what takes hold of
something hot"). We also use the term *innormes* for those who exceed
the natural rule of members, as though they were "without norm", i.e.,
without rule. You see, don't you, that this concept does not depend
upon the number or size of members, but upon the position of the parts
of the body and the coloring. Or don't you agree?

S: Yes, I agree, but I'm waiting to find out how this distinction is
relevant to our question.

T: We admitted in our former arguments that body is one thing
and *ousia* another, didn't we?

S: We came to the most complete agreement on that subject.

[53] *T:* If, then, quantity of body is separated from the concept

(*intellectus*) of *ousia* by a natural distinction, even though they are interconnected so that *ousia* is the subject of quantity and *quantum*, while quantity and *quantum* are accidents of *ousia*; is it not crystal clear that there is one kind of form observed in *ousia*, not as an accident, but as the very same thing; another which, arising from quality and joined to quantity, produces a perfect body?

S: Now I see what your point is.

T: Do you think I mean that essential form joined to matter produces a natural body?

S: No, in fact, I see that that is not your meaning.

T: Tell me, please, how you reach this conclusion.

S: From our previous differentiation of forms into those belonging to *ousia* and those belonging to quality, you appear to me simply to be arguing that the form which is a species of quality, when added to matter, produces the body of which *ousia* is the subsistence. These three things noted in all natural bodies are *ousia*, quantity, and quality. But *ousia* is perceived only by the intellect, and does not appear visibly in anything. Quantity and quality, however, are invisibly present in *ousia* in such a way that they emerge visibly into the *quantum* and the *quale* when, by their union, they compose a sensible body. If geometrical body, which has no underlying *ousia*, is reasonably proved to consist solely of the quantity of dimensions and lines and of the form of quality called 'figure', what is to prevent us from saying that natural body, which the power of *ousia* supports to make it endure insofar as it can, is made up of the form which comes from quality joined to quantity taken from matter? I think that you are simply trying to give a persuasive argument to show that by the meeting and blending of the four elements of this world the matter of bodies is made; and that when form is added to the matter from any quality whatsoever, a perfect body is produced. I am not bothered by what is an obstacle to many, who think that we are contradicting ourselves and strengthening the opposing side when we say sometimes that the union of the four elements engenders matter, and at other times that the coming together of the quality and quantity of *ousia* is the cause of matter. Their reaction is not strange, since they are unaware that the elements of this world are compounded solely by the meeting of those accidents of *ousia*. Of course, heat joined to dryness produces fire; heat joined to moisture, air; moisture joined to cold, water; cold joined to dryness, earth. Since these qualities which come together cannot appear by themselves, quantity supplies them with the *quantum* in which they may be clearly visible to the senses. Quantity is, in effect, a second subject after *ousia*, and therefore follows it immediately in the order of categories; since without quantity, quality cannot become manifest. Thus if the elements are made by quantity and quality and bodies are made from elements, then bodies are made from quantity and quality.

T: Since I see that you have perceived my intention clearly, tell me, please, whether this division of forms into two species of different genus, viz., of *ousia* and of quality, appears valid or not.

S: It does seem valid and plausible, although I should not concede that it is reasonable without mental reservation. I should more readily be persuaded that substantial rather than qualitative form constitutes natural body when added to matter since it seems more likely to me that *ousia*, not quality, is the cause of the constitution of body. From our previous reasoning I infer that quality is the cause not only of matter, but also of form. When mixed with quantity, it produces matter; but it imposes form upon matter by itself. Not that I am unaware that a single cause produces many effects, since I see that heat and light emerge together from a single fire, and that the light is the cause of brightness and of shadows. Not to mention how many different bodies are fashioned of one and the same matter, or into how many numbers [i.e., individuals] a single form [i.e., species] is multiplied, and other examples of the same kind. I should therefore have thought that *ousia* itself, not its accidents, becomes the form of matter.

T: I'm very much surprised at how quickly you have forgotten what we clearly deduced a little while ago. Consider more carefully while we repeat the arguments briefly.

S: I'm ready; repeat them.

T: Didn't we reach a firm agreement that *ousia* is incorporeal?

S: Yes, we did.

T: I should have thought you would remember that quantities and qualities, insofar as they are conceived of in themselves, are incorporeal; that *ousia* is the only subject in which they subsist as accidents, and that they remain inseparably in it.

S: I have a sure grasp on this point too.

T: The most plausible statement, then, would be that everything composed of quantity and quality, i.e., of the *quantum* and the *quale*, have *ousia* as the only source of their constitution, since quantity and quality are acknowledged as the first and greatest natural accidents of *ousia* and cannot be without it. I don't know why anything which issues from something in a source should not be referred to the source itself; especially since *ousia* itself, insofar as it is *ousia*, cannot be evident at all to the sight or touch and has no extension in space. The meeting of accidents which are in it or are understood in reference to it can, by generation, create something sensible with extension in space. Now quantity and quality join the *quantum* and the *quale* to each other; and these two joined together, receiving generation in a certain way and time, produce a complete body. The other accidents seem added secondarily to these two. In regard to our own bodies and the bodies of other animate and inanimate things, we inquire mainly about the following four points: (1) How big is it? Of what parts does it consist? Does it have extension in length, width, and depth? (2) Of what kind is it? Does it have an upright human form or a prone bestial form? (3) When was it generated? (4) How is it defined? Thus it is put in its place so that it may not be infinite, but a single limited thing in its own genus. These matters, as we have said, are considered first in regard to our bodies. Beyond them, however, we contemplate *ousia* with deeper consideration, for it is the origin of substantial forms; and we inquire about a given body what its substantial form is. Is it that of man or horse or some irrational animal included within *ousia?* By these names, of course, we are referring not to the bodies of the animals but to their substantial forms.

[54] We should have distinct awareness of three factors whether reflecting about ourselves or about other animals: What are we? What is ours? What is related to us? We are our substance, which is vital and intelligible, above body and all its senses and visible form. Ours, but

not ourselves, is body, which adheres to us. It is compounded of *quantum, quale,* and the other accidents; and it is sensible, changeable, soluble, corruptible. One can most truly say that it is simply the instrument or seat of the senses, the Greek term for which is *aistheteria,* i.e. *aistheseon teria,* "the guards of the senses." Since the soul is incorporeal and cannot reveal its operations by itself without the senses, and the senses can be guarded only in some seats, the Creator of nature fashioned body for the use of the soul in which it might guard its vehicles, so to speak—i.e., the senses. Related to us are all sensible things which we use: e.g., the four elements of this world and the bodies compounded of them. Without these, our mortal bodies cannot endure, since they are given food by earth, drink by moisture, breath by air, and heat by fire. They grow and are nourished by two, earth and water; they are served by two, air and fire, in order that they may have life. Two elements, earth and water, are acted upon by passing into the body; two, air and fire, cause the workshop of the body to function by their joint action. The power of fire, with its seat in the heart, distributes the subtle vapor of food and drink through hidden pores to various parts of the body, and separates the waste matter. But fire itself, unless suffused by the breath of air and nourished by food and drink as fuel, is quickly extinguished. Then the whole structure of the body immediately collapses in dissolution and grows stiff as cold overcomes the force of heat. But this is not the place to discuss these topics.

[55] *S:* I consider these points well taken. But I keep going over in my mind how these theories can be reconciled—i.e., how things incorporeal and invisible in themselves produce visible bodies by coming together, so that matter simply is and has as the sole cause of its constitution the blended union of and in themselves and not in anything else of those things which are regarded solely by the gaze of wisdom. My doubt is strengthened especially by the following statement from the book *On Arithmetic* of Boethius, the best philosopher of all who wrote in Greek and Latin: "Wisdom is the comprehension of truth concerning things endowed with being, which

have their own allotted unchangeable substance. I refer to those things which are not increased or diminished, which undergo no change, but always preserve themselves with their own force, supported by the aid of their own nature. These things are qualities, quantities, forms, magnitudes, smallnesses [*parvitates*], equalities, states, acts, arrangements, places, times, and whatever is found united to bodies in some way. They are themselves of incorporeal nature and thrive in the principle of their unchangeable substance, but they are changed by participation in body; and by contact with what is variable they pass over to changeable inconstancy. Since, then, nature has allotted them unchangeable substance and force, they are truly and properly said to have being."

[56]   May we not clearly understand from this statement that matter and body made from it are different from quantity, quality, and the other things which are contemplated by wisdom alone, and which always preserve the unchangeable power of their nature? But matter and body, of which those things are accidents, are different and inconstant with variable change. Doesn't it seem plausible that if matter subsisted of quantity, quality, and the other natural accidents bound to one another, it too would necessarily be unchangeable? Why should we not understand about effects what is understood about their causes, so that just as quantities, qualities, and the rest are beheld only by the mind's eye, matter and body also would be subject to the intellect but not to the corporeal senses? But we now perceive formed matter, by which body is produced (for formless matter is wholly intelligible), by corporeal sense; but we see quantity and quality by the intellect alone. How, then, can quantity and quality produce matter, which differs from them so greatly?

   T: You are seriously deceived by a false argument, or else you wish to deceive others. I still don't know, however, whether you yourself are in doubt about these matters or whether you are assuming the role of others who are in doubt.

   S: I see myself in both positions. Assuming the role of others who appropriately feel uncertainty or are completely ignorant about such matters, I have carefully proposed these questions. But I see that I myself am not so clear about them yet that I don't have to make further inquiries.

T: I believe that we must use reason and authority so that you may discern these matters clearly, for from them comes the whole power of discovering the truth about things.

S: You are quite right. These matters have been investigated by many but found by few.

T: Tell me, then, do you think that matter itself, from which formed bodies are made, is observed by sense or by reason as long as it is in a pure state and formless?

S: By reason, surely. I should not venture to say "by sense," for matter without form cannot be touched by any corporeal sense.

T: You have given the right answer, but don't inquire again at greater length about what you have just assumed. We are spending too much time on such matters when deeper questions invite our consideration.

S: I don't think that I shall bother you further about what we have just defined with such clear understanding. I am amazed, though, at your comment that deeper questions invite our consideration. I do not see what deeper subject is to be considered by reason after God than formless matter, because it involves the questions: What is matter? What is form? What is made up of matter and form? What is the source of matter? Is it to be counted among the primordial causes created in the beginning by God, or among the secondary causes born from the primordial? Is it to be reckoned among things impressed upon the senses or upon the intellect? Can it be defined while it is still infinite? Or can even infinite matter be defined? This possibility seems opposed to reason since the holy fathers clearly deduced that there are only two things which cannot be defined in any way, viz., God and matter. God, of course, is infinite and formless, since He is formed by none but is Himself the Form of all things. Formless matter is similarly infinite. It must be formed and limited by something else, since in itself it is not form but is receptive to form. An opposite interpretation is given to this likeness of the Cause of all things from which, in which, through which, and in reference to which all things have being; and to the formless cause, I mean matter, which was created in order that things which, by themselves, could not be touched by the senses could, in a certain way, appear sensibly in it. The highest Cause of all things is formless and infinite by surpassing all forms and ends. Not only is It the principal Form of all things, but It is More Than Form, exceeding all form, and forming everything formable and unformable. It is the Form of things which can be formed, since they either aspire to It or turn toward It. It is also the Formlessness of things which, because of the excellence of their nature and their close resemblance to the Cause, cannot be formed. Of course, the Formlessness of the unformable is not called 'Formlessness' as lacking all form, but as surpassing all sensible and intelligible form. Therefore it it usually both affirmed and denied as the Cause of all things, so that statements like the following are made about It: "It is Form; It is not Form. It is Formlessness; It is not Formlessness." Whatever is predicated of It can be both affirmed and denied, because It is above everything which is said and understood and not understood. Matter, on the other hand, is called formless because it is deprived of forms. Nothing is formed by it, but it receives countless different forms.

T: You are close to the truth. Doesn't it necessarily follow, then, since formless matter is perceived only by the mind's eye—i.e., reason—that it is incorporeal?

S: I should not dare to deny it.

T: It is incorporeal, then.

S: Yes, and I see that I am hedged in by my own judgment.

T: Would you like me to confirm this point by authority?

S: Very much, and I beg you to do so.

[57]   *T:*   We find that many of those skilled in both worldly and divine wisdom have discussed matter, but it will suffice to use the testimony of a few. St. Augustine asserts in the *Confessions*: "Formless matter is the changeability of changeable things, and is receptive of all forms." Plato expresses a similar view in the *Timaeus* by saying: "Formless matter is receptivity to forms." Their compatible view can be expressed and defined as follows: "Formless matter is the

changeability of changeable things which is receptive of all forms." St.
Dionysius the Areopagite in his book *On Divine Names* (4.28) says
that matter is "participation in ornament, form, and species, without
which, by itself, matter is formless and cannot be understood in
anything." We may infer, then, from Dionysius that if matter is
participation in ornament, form, and species, whatever lacks such
participation is not matter but a kind of formlessness. Whether
formless matter is changeability receptive of forms, as Augustine and
Plato say, or a kind of formlessness without participation in species,
form, and ornament, as Dionysius states, I don't think you will deny
that if it can be understood at all, it is perceived only by the intellect.

S: I have already made a firm concession on this point.

T: As for that species, form, and ornament by participation in
which formlessness or changeability is turned into matter, do you
think that it is observed in any other way than by mental insight?

S: Not at all. We have established sufficiently by our former
reasoning that form and species, without which no ornament can be
made, are wholly incorporeal.

T: So now you see that something corporeal—I mean matter and
body—is created from incorporeal things, viz., from a changeable
formlessness receptive of forms and from form itself.

S: I see that clearly.

T: You grant, then, that bodies can be made from the union of
incorporeal things.

S: Reason forces me to grant it.

[58] *T:* You must confess, therefore, that bodies can so be resolved
into incorporeal things as to be not bodies[24] but completely dissolved.
By their natural coming together and by a marvelous harmony,
incorporeal things produce bodies without at all losing their natural
stability and their motionless force. Just as, to use an analogy, a shadow
arises from light and body, but neither light nor body changes into the
shadow. But when the shadow is dissolved, it is understood as
returning to its causes, namely body and light. True reason teaches
that the cause of shadows is body and light, in which the shadows are

naturally in repose since they can appear nowhere because of the brightness of light everywhere poured about bodies. For it is an error to think that shadow perishes when it does not appear to the senses. Shadow is not nothing, but something. Otherwise Scripture would not say, "God called light 'day', and darkness 'night'." [25] For God names only what comes from Himself; and in that passage the sublimity of the speculation does not destroy the truth of the account. There, from our observation of what was made, we understand darkness and night simply as the shadow of the earth always opposite the globe of light and made like a cone by the pouring of the sun's rays around the earth. The same principle obtains for smaller shadows, projected by any kind of light and bodies, whether the shadows are finite or infinite, and whatever their form. And so you should not be surprised that bodies are created from incorporeal causes and are resolved into them again; and that the causes themselves are created and proceed from one and the same creative Cause of all things.

[59]   For from the Form of all things, God's only-begotten Word, every form has been created, whether it is substantial or whether it is a form which, taken from quality and added to matter, generates body. From It, too, comes all formlessness. Nor is it strange that formlessness, the privation of all forms, has been created from the Form which is formless because of its excellence. For not only things of a single genus but also those of different genus, and not only what are said to have or not to have being because of excellence but also what are said to have or not to have being because of privation, flow from the same source of all things. Don't you see very clearly, then, that reason supported us when we said, following the authority of St. Gregory of Nyssa, that bodies are made from a coming together of accidents? You note that other Greek and Latin authors, too, affirm that bodies are made from incorporeal things. I therefore think that it is a good idea to quote here in our discussion St. Gregory's statement in *On the Image* (24) against those who say that matter is coeternal with God: "The assumption which posits that matter has subsistence from the intellec-

tual and the immaterial is not inconsistent with later findings. We have found that all matter consists of certain qualities; and if it is stripped of them, it will not be comprehended in any way by itself. But every single species of quality is separated by reason from its subject. Reason, moreover, is a certain intellectual and incorporeal speculation. For instance, if some animal or tree or anything else with a material constitution is proposed as the object of speculation, we understand many things about the subject according to an intellectual process by division. The reason of every one of these things is considered by itself in reference to what is being observed. There is one reason of color, for example, another of heaviness, still another of quantity, and another of the understanding of the tactile property of the subject. Softness, a length of two cubits, and the other things mentioned are not mixed by the reason either with one another or with the body. In each one of these is understood the specific cause according to which it is interpreted, and none of these qualities speculated about in reference to a subject is mixed with another quality. If color is intelligible, then so is solidity and quantity and the other such specific qualities. If any one of these is removed from the subject, the whole reason of the body will be destroyed at once. Consequently we must assume that material nature is created by the coming together of these things the absence of which we have found to be the cause of the body's dissolution. For there is no body without the presence of *ousia*, figure, solidity, extension, heaviness, and other specific qualities; yet none of these is body but is found to be something besides body when it is separate. Conversely, whenever these things have come together, they produce corporeal substance. But if the understanding of specific qualities is intelligible and God too is called intelligible by nature, it follows reasonably that from incorporeal nature these intellectual occasions have been set in place for the generation of bodies by intellectual nature, which establishes intelligible powers; and that their coming together brings material nature to generation."

[60] You see then, don't you, that the great and very strong argument of this teacher is sufficient? If body were anything except

the coming together of the accidents of *ousia*, it would subsist in itself by itself when those accidents were withdrawn. Of course, every subject subsisting by itself, e.g., *ousia* itself, has no need of accidents in order to have being. Whether or not it has accidents; whether what cannot exist without it is in it or what can be separated from it departs from it; whether only in thought or actually, it always subsists unchangeably by its own natural resources. Body, however, cannot subsist by itself at all when its accidents are withdrawn, because it is supported by no substance. For if you remove quantity from body, it will not be body, since it is held together by the dimensions of limbs and by number. Similarly if you remove quality from it, it will remain bereft of form and will be nothing. The same principle is to be observed in the other accidents by which body is evidently held together. Whatever cannot subsist by itself without accidents must be understood as simply the coming together of those same accidents.

[61] It isn't strange or contrary to reason, therefore, when we hear in the same vein that the great Boethius understood something variable as simply material body which, as he says, "is constituted from a coming together of those things which truly have being." [26] And while they are considered in it (i.e., in body), they necessarily undergo a certain change. Nor is it strange if things unchangeable in themselves are perceived one way in their simplicity by pure mental insight and differently by corporeal sense when they are compounded in some matter made from their coming together. For we see that things simple and incorruptible in themselves produce something compound and corruptible when they come together. Everyone knows that this mass of the terrestrial sphere is made up of four simple elements; and that although the earth is corruptible and soluble, the elements of which it is composed endure in their insoluble simplicity. This same principle is commonly observed in virtually all bodies. And now I think that we have discussed this subject enough.

S: We surely have. I see that we must now go back to speculate about the other categories. To have any further hesitation on these points would undoubtedly be appropriate only to those who had not devoted much thought to the nature of things. I'm sorry and embarrassed about my slowness in many matters.

T: Don't be sorry or embarrassed. Although wise men find these subjects so clear that they present no difficulty, I am sure that they are useful to novices making their way from below to the heights of reason.

S: That is quite certain, and I see that I am in that very situation. Go on, then, with the other points.

[62] *T:* Two categories remain to be considered, if I am not mistaken: action and reception of action. When we talked about place, we made some observations about time that satisfied the needs of our present discussion.

S: I won't ask you anything further now about time and place, since our former statements are adequate. Whoever said everything about all points which reason is eager to consider would hardly, if ever, finish his discussion.

T: Consider, then, whether action and reception of action are properly predicated of God or, like the other categories, should be regarded as attributed to Him metaphorically.

S: Metaphorically, of course. We must not think that these two categories go beyond the rules of the others, since they appear to have less power.

T: Tell me, please, are not moving and being moved the same as acting and being acted upon?

S: I don't see any other possibility.

T: That identity holds, I believe, for loving and being loved.

S: They come under the same rule. These words and others like them are active and passive, as everyone skilled in the Liberal Arts is aware.

T: If these words, then, whether active or passive in meaning, are predicated metaphorically rather than properly of God, and if everything metaphorically predicated is said of Him not in accordance with reality but with qualification, God does not really act and is not acted upon, does not move and is not moved, does not love and is not loved.

S: This last conclusion demands considerable thought, for I believe that the authority of the whole sacred Scripture and of the holy fathers appears to oppose it. As you know, sacred Scripture often explicitly states that God acts and is acted upon, loves and is loved, cherishes and is cherished, sees and is seen, moves and is moved, and so on. Since there are countless examples and one can find them by searching at random, I have decided to skip them in order to avoid a long discussion now. Let this one example from the Gospel suffice: "Whoever loves me will be loved by my Father, and I shall love him and shall reveal myself to him." [27] In his *Exemeron*, St. Augustine, too, makes the following statement about divine motion: "The creating Spirit moves Itself without time and place, moves created spirit through time without place, and moves body through time and place." If action and reception of action, as we have said, are predicated of God not truly, i.e., not properly, it follows that He neither moves nor is moved; for to move is to act and to be moved is to be acted upon. Then, too, if He neither acts nor is acted upon, how can He be said to love everything and to be loved by everything made by Him? Love is a certain motion of one acting, and being loved is a motion of one being acted upon. Motion is both the cause and the end. But I am following popular usage in making this statement. Whoever examines the nature of things quite carefully will find that many words which seem active when only their external vocal form is considered, nevertheless have a passive meaning; just as, conversely, a passive form can signify an action. E.g., whoever "loves or cherishes" is acted upon, and whoever "is loved or cherished" acts. If God loves what He has made, He surely is seen to be moved, for He is moved by His own love. Also, if He is loved by whatever can love, whether or not they know what they love, isn't it obvious that He moves? Of course, the love of His beauty moves them. I cannot see by myself, therefore, how, in order to prevent His appearing to act and be acted upon, He can be said neither to move nor to be moved. I therefore beg you to solve this knotty problem.

T: Do you think that, in those who act, the agent is one thing, the ability to act another, and the action a third; or are they all one and the same?

S: In my opinion they are not one, but three different things. E.g., the lover—i.e., the one who loves—is the substance of a clearly defined person who has, as an accident, a certain power by which he can act, whether he does so or not. If, in fact, the substance moves itself to do something through that power, it is said to act. Hence there appear to be three things, viz.: substance, with an inherent ability to act. The effect of this ability, as of a cause, is to act in something, whether the action is reflexive—i.e., returns to the same person—or passes to another person.

T: Your distinction is correct. Well, then, must we not observe the same distinction in one acted upon, so that the recipient of the action is one thing, the capacity for being acted upon another, and being acted upon a third, whether one is acted upon by himself or by another?

S: Yes indeed, the very same distinction.

T: These three things, then, both in those who love and in those who are loved, are not of the same nature.

S: No, I don't think that they are. There is one nature of substances, another of accidents. The one who acts or is acted upon is a substance. The ability to act or to be acted upon and the actual acting and being acted upon are accidents.

T: I'm surprised at how you have forgotten what we looked for and found, I believe, and defined in our earlier reasoning.

S: Please remind me and help me recall what these arguments are. I admit that I have a faulty memory and am forgetful.

T: Do you recall that we inferred and concluded that essence, power, and operation are a kind of inseparable and incorruptible trinity of our nature, joined by a marvelous harmony of nature, so that the three are one and the one is three; that they are of one and the same nature, not of a different one; and that they are not like a substance and its accidents, but that there is a certain essential unity and a substantial differentia of the three in one?

S: I remember, and I shall never forget it again. To forget the very clear image of the Creator is exceedingly foolish and wretched. But I don't see the point yet unless it is, perhaps, that I answered your question about three things differing from one another by saying that one was subject and the other two accidents. These three things seem quite remote from the three mentioned earlier. Hence perhaps those three which we said are of one and the same substance, viz., essence, power, and operation, are the only real ones; and what I now added—i.e., substance with its accidents, viz., potentiality of action and the effect of that potentiality, which is action—must be considered superfluous and discovered without reason. Or perhaps the opposite is true. Or again, as I think may more correctly be said, both sets of threes really are in the nature of things, and are distinguished by their natural differentiae. But I leave it to your judgment whether we must make such a concession.

T: Your last statement seems correct. Whoever says that the essential trinity—viz., essence, power, and operation—is firmly and incorruptibly inherent in all things, and especially in rational and intellectual natures, is not far from the truth in my opinion. This trinity can be neither increased nor diminished in anything in which it inheres. The second trinity, however, is understood as a kind of effect of the preceding trinity. It would not be false, I believe, to say that from essence itself (which has been created one and universal in everything and is common to everything, and therefore is not said to be proper to any because it belongs to all that participate in it) there emanates by a natural progression a certain proper substance of the individuals participating in it, which belongs to none except that one whose substance it is. Inherent in this substance is its own potentiality, taken from the universal power of the universal essence and power. Similarly in regard to the proper operation of the most specific substance and potentiality we should say that it descends from the universal operation of the same universal essence and power. Nor is it strange if these three things observed in individuals are said to be accidents and first appearances of that universal trinity; for it by itself is one, and remains unchangeably in everything which exists from it and in it. It cannot be increased or diminished; it cannot be corrupted or perish. What we observe most specifically in individuals, however, can be increased, diminished, and varied in many ways. Not all participate similarly in universal essence, power, and operation; but some more, others less. None, however, is wholly deprived of participation in it. Of itself it remains one and the same in all that participate in it, and it is no more or less available to any for participation. An analogy would be light for the eyes, which is whole in individuals and in itself. Increase or diminution, however, is a certain loss or gain of participation. Hence it is not unreasonably judged to be an accident.

[63] What is always the same thing is correctly termed true substance. What varies, however, proceeds either from the changeability of unstable substance or from participation in accidents, whether natural or not. Don't be surprised that certain accidents are called substances, because they are the substances of other accidents. For example, you see that quantity, which undoubtedly is an accident of substance, receives other accidents, such as color, which appears around (*circa*) quantity, and times, which are understood in the lingering motions of things. For time is the definite and systematic measurement of the rest and the motion of changeable things.

S: The conclusion drawn from our investigation does not conflict with this point, I believe. But I should like you to define this last observation briefly and clearly.

T: Let us posit, if you will, the threefold intelligence of things, i.e., the unchangeable subsistence and the firm foundation established by the universal Creator of all things, namely essence, power, and operation.

S: I think that we should.

T: Next that trinity which can be observed in individuals and which proceeds from the first essential trinity as the effect of a foregoing cause must be weighed along with its primordial motions and certain primordial accidents, I see.

S: I admit this point also.

T: Whatever belongs to that second trinity as an accident, whether from inside or from outside, whether naturally or by circumstance, seems to be an accident of accidents.

S: I agree with this conclusion also. According to Aristotle, there are ten genera of things called 'categories', i.e. "things predicated"; and we find that no philosophers who wrote in Greek or Latin object to this division of things into genera, but we see that there have been included under one genus all the prime essences which the Greeks rightly call *ousiae* because they have being in themselves and have no need of anything in order to be. They have been established in this way as unchangeable foundations by the Creator of all things. Like the chief Cause of all, they subsist in their remarkable and unchangeable trinity: i.e., as we have often said, essence, power, and operation. The other nine categories, however, are said to be accidents, and rightly so; for they subsist not in themselves, but in the essential trinity of which we have just spoken. Now, although the Greeks call time and place "indispensable" (*hon aneu*), i.e., categories without which the others cannot exist, we must not understand that the substantial trinity of things should be reckoned among the things which cannot subsist without place and time. It does not need the assistance of place and time in order to subsist, since in itself, before and above time and place, it exists by the dignity of its own condition. But the nine genera assigned only to accidents have been so divided by the authors that the accidents themselves, originally seen in essences, are soon converted into substances, since they are the substances of other accidents. The first division of all things is into essences and accidents, the second of accidents into substances. This division extends virtually to infinity, since what is now an accident of something prior to itself soon becomes the substance of what is subsequent to it. But we should discuss these matters elsewhere. Now let us pursue our proposed subject if you agree.

T: Do you think that accidents exist only as belonging to some essence or accident?

S: Anyone skilled in the Liberal Arts would say so. The only reason that it deserves the name of accident is that it has fallen to the lot of an essence, a substance, or some accident.

T: Are acting and being acted upon contained within the number of accidents?

S: Yes.

T: To what substance do they belong, then? They occur as accidents to their own proper substances, for general essences have no accidents.

S: I agree.

T: Tell me, please, does the highest, simple Divine Nature have any accident?

S: Far from it.

T: Does It belong as an accident to anything?

S: I should not say so. Otherwise It would seem capable of being acted upon, changeable, and receptive of another nature.

T: It receives no accident, then, and is not Itself an accident to anything.

S: Quite true.

T: Are acting and being acted upon accidents?

S: This too has been granted.

T: Then the highest Cause and Principle of all, God, does not act and cannot be acted upon.

S: I am hard-pressed by this line of reasoning. If I say that it is false, perhaps reason itself will mock me and expose all my previous concessions to attack. If I say that it is true, however, I shall have to make the same concession about active and passive verbs of all kinds that I have made about acting and being acted upon: i.e., I shall have to say that God does not love, is not loved, does not move, is not moved, and a thousand similar examples. And even more, that He neither has being nor subsists. But if I make such an admission, you see with how many formidable shafts of sacred Scripture I shall be overwhelmed. The Scriptural passages seem to shout on all sides and to declare that this view is false. And you are quite aware, I believe, how difficult it is to persuade simple souls of such a point; for even the ears of the sophisticated seem to be horrified when they hear this statement.

T: Don't be alarmed. Now we must follow reason, which tracks down truth and is not overwhelmed by any authority or prevented in any way from openly revealing and proclaiming what has been investigated and laboriously discovered by those who zealously apply themselves to reasoning.

[64]   Of course, the authority of sacred Scripture must be followed in all matters since truth resides in it as in its secret dwelling place. We must not, however, believe that it always uses words or names as proper symbols in communicating Divine Nature to us. Instead it adopts certain analogies and various kinds of metaphorical words or names in condescension to our weakness; and by simple teaching it raises up our senses, which are still childlike and untrained. The Apostle says: "I have given you milk to drink, not solid food." [28] By such means the divine words try to coax us and to give us something to reflect upon about the Ineffable, the Incomprehensible, and the Invisible in order to nurture our faith. In fact, nothing should be said or thought about God by those who live purely and piously, and zealously seek the truth except what is found in sacred Scripture; nor should those who have a belief about God or are discussing Him use any designations and metaphors except the Scriptural ones. Who would presume to say anything of his own devising about the Ineffable Nature beyond what It Itself has attuned Its sacred instruments, the theologians, to say about It? But to give you stronger faith and a firmer grasp on this point, I think that the testimony of St. Dionysius the Theologian should be inserted here, if you are willing.

S: Indeed I am. There is nothing which I would rather hear than reason supported by the strongest authority.

T: In the first chapter of the book *On Divine Names* (1.1), he commends the authority of sacred Scripture with high praise. But because, in his customary fashion, he discusses the matter in an involved way and in unusual word order, he appears to many quite abstruse and difficult to understand. I have therefore decided to draw from his statement on this subject, but to express it as follows in easier word order than his: "Generally one should not dare to say or to understand anything about superessential Divinity except what has been expressed for us by divine revelation in Scripture. Knowledge of the Superessential which surpasses reason, intellect, and essence must be referred to the higher sources of enlightenment gathered closely about the Divine with moderation and holiness, which look up as far as the ray of divine Scripture presents itself."

[65] You see, then, how he makes a general prohibition against daring to say anything about hidden Divinity except what has been said in holy Scripture. Using a name that is glorious and altogether appropriate, he calls Scripture the "higher sources of enlightenment gathered closely about the Divine with moderation and holiness." A little later in the same work he says: "Just as invisible things elude comprehension and observation by sensibles, simple things which have no likeness elude whatever is in an image and likeness, and the untouched, unshaped formlessness of incorporeal things eludes what has been formed according to corporeal shapes; so, according to the same principle of truth, superessential Magnitude surpasses essences and Unity above soul surpasses souls. What surpasses the sense cannot be attained by any powers; and secret from all reason are the Good above reason, the Unity which unifies all unity, the Superessential Essence, the Invisible Intellect, the Secret Word, Nonrationality, Invisibility, and Namelessness, which does not exist according to the principle of anything endowed with being. It is the Cause of being for all, though It Itself is not something endowed with being *(on),* since It is the summit of all essence; and yet in some way It knowingly and properly makes a revelation about Itself. Concerning this superessential, hidden Divinity, as we have said, we must not dare to say or to understand anything except what has been expressed for us from the Divine Source; for It has given to us a splendid account of Itself in sacred Scripture. But the knowledge and contemplation of what It is like is inaccessible to everything endowed with being, since It is essentially separated from everything." These words suffice on the subject of following the sole authority of sacred Scripture, particularly in discussions about the Divine. [66] In this matter, reason generally strives to persuade us and to prove by sound investigations of truth that nothing can be stated properly about God since He surpasses every intellect and all sensible and intelligible designations. He is known

better by an absence of knowledge; for ignorance of Him is true wisdom. He is more truly and faithfully spoken of negatively than affirmatively in all respects. Whatever you deny about Him, you deny truly; but you do not affirm truly all that you affirm. If, in fact, you grant that He is one thing or another, you are charged with falseness because He is not among the things which can be stated or understood. If you declare, though, that He is not one thing or another or anything at all, you will appear truthful, because He is none of the things endowed or not endowed with being. No one can approach Him without first fortifying his mind and abandoning all the senses, intellectual operations, sensibles, and everything with and without being; and, in his ignorance, being restored, insofar as it is possible, to unity with Him who is above all essence and intelligence. No reason or understanding applies to Him. He cannot be spoken of or understood; and no name or word is proper to Him. But, as we have often said, everything from the highest down can reasonably be said about Him because of a certain similarity or dissimilarity or contrariety or opposition; since He is the source of being of all things which can be predicated of Him. But He did not create only what is like Himself, but also the unlike, since He Himself is like and unlike. He is also the cause of contraries; for true reason affirms that within the power of what was truly created by Him are also contained the things which appear contrary and which, because of privation of essence, have no being. No imperfection is found which is not the shadow of some virtue, either by a specious similarity or by clear contrariety. Examples of similarity are arrogance clothed in the shadow of true power, luxury of repose, rage of valor, wrath of uprightness and justice, etc. An example of contrariety is wickedness in contrast to goodness. Just as Goodness brings the non-existent into existence so that it may have being, so wickedness seeks to corrupt all things endowed with being and to destroy them utterly so that they may not have being. If this should happen—i.e., if everything should perish—wickedness too would perish at the same time; for if nature were to perish, so too would all imperfection. But by the power of Goodness all nature is held together to keep it from perishing. Wickedness is still permitted in nature, though, to redound to the praise of its direct opposite, goodness, through comparison and through the exercise of virtues by rational activity. Wickedness also exists to purify nature itself when death will be swallowed up in victory and only goodness will appear and rule in all, and wickedness will utterly perish. But these topics will be discussed more fully in Book V. Don't let any authority deter you, then, from what the reasonable persuasion of right contemplation teaches. True authority is no obstacle to right reason or right reason to true authority, since both undoubtedly flow from a single source, Divine Wisdom. [67] The one (i.e., reason) has made many concessions to those who reverently inquire about the Incomprehensible and Ineffable Nature, and has given them the means to reflect and speak in order to prevent the zeal for true religion from being inarticulate in all. It also strives to nurture with doctrine those who are still novices of simple faith. Finally, equipped with armor and defended by divine bulwarks, it aims at countering the rivals of the Catholic faith. The other, however, aspires to correct with chaste sanctity those who are still simple nurselings in the cradle of the Church, in order to keep them from having any unworthy belief or thought about God, or from regarding everything predicated by the authority of sacred Scripture about the Cause of all things as applicable in a proper sense. These predications include the most glorious and the highest of all things, such as life, virtue, and the names of the other virtues; the things that come in the middle, such as sun, light, star, and all the things from the higher regions of this visible world which are predicated of God; and what comes from the lower movements of visible creation, such as wind, the splendor of a cloud, sunrise, thunder, dew, storm, rain; also water, river, earth, rock, tree, vine, olive, cedar, hyssop, lily, man, lion, ox, horse, bear, leopard, worm; also eagle, dove, fish, sea monsters, and the countless other things referred by transposed figurative meaning from created nature to Nature the Creator. Even more remarkably, the artful Scriptures have made transpositions not only from creation to Creator, but also from things contrary to nature, viz., madness, drunkenness, gluttony, forgetfulness, wrath, rage, hatred, concupiscence, and the like, by which the minds of the simple are less deceived than they are by the higher metaphorical figures derived from nature. For a rational soul, even though it is quite simple and would be deceived upon hearing the names of natural things predicated of God and would think that they are intended in their proper sense, is not completely led astray. Upon hearing the names of things contrary to nature predicated about the Creator, therefore, it would either judge them to be utterly false and reject them, or else grant and believe that they are predicated figuratively.

S: I am not so intimidated by authority or by the attack of the narrow-minded that I am embarrassed to declare openly what true reason clearly deduces and defines with certainty; especially since such matters are to be dealt with only among the wise, to whom no words are sweeter than true reason, nothing more pleasant to track down when it is hunted, nothing lovelier to behold when it is found. But I am eager to know the purpose of your reasoning.

[68]   *T:* Why, I was merely trying to make you understand that just as nouns signifying things, whether substances, accidents, or essences, can be predicated metaphorically but not properly of Creating Nature, so too in the case of verbs signifying natural or unnatural motions of created nature the same situation prevails. If the names of essences, substances, or accidents are attributed to God not truly, but by a certain necessity of expressing the Ineffable Nature, doesn't it necessarily follow that neither can the verbs which signify the motions of essences, substances, and accidents be predicated properly of God who, by the incomprehensible and ineffable excellence of His nature, surpasses all essence, substance, accident, motion (both active and passive), and whatever is said and understood, or not said and understood about such things, and yet is present in them? For example, if God is metaphorically called Love, although He is More Than Love and surpasses all love, why would He not similarly be said to love, although He surpasses all motion of love since He aspires to nothing besides Himself, since He alone is all in all? Similarly, if He is described as acting and Actor, doing and Doer, not properly but by a kind of metaphor, why should the same kind of figure of speech not predicate that He acts and does, is acted upon and has something done

to Him? I believe that we must have a similar understanding about the other verbs which signify the motions of all changeable creation, whether those motions are natural, unnatural, intellectual, rational, irrational, corporeal, incorporeal, local, temporal, straight, oblique, angular, circular, or spherical.

S: You press me hard to admit these points according to reason. But I wish that you would fortify your argument by the authority of the holy fathers.

[69]   *T:* You are aware, I think, that what is prior by nature is of greater dignity than what is prior in time.

S: Almost everyone knows that.

T: We have learned that reason is prior by nature, authority in time; for although nature was created together with time, authority did not have its inception from the beginning of time and of nature. Reason, however, arose at the very outset along with nature and time.

S: Reason itself teaches us this point also. Authority, of course, proceeded from true reason, but reason did not at all proceed from authority. All authority not approved by true reason seems weak. Since true reason, however, holds an impregnable position as valid and unchangeable by its own powers, it does not have to be strengthened by the assent of any authority. True authority seems to me simply the truth discovered by the power of reason and entrusted to writing by the holy fathers for the edification of posterity. But perhaps you have another view.

T: Not at all. First we must use reason in our discussion, then, and authority afterwards.

[70]   *S:* Start in whatever order you like, and I shall follow you.

T: Do you think that acting and being acted upon are possible without some motion of the agent or the one acted upon?

S: I have no doubt about the agent, since I don't see that the agent can act without some motion. But I don't yet clearly understand how the object of the action is moved in itself.

T: Don't you see that everything that acts moves itself or is moved for the purpose of moving the object of its action from what it was not to what it is? Nothing can pass from what it was not to what it is without motion of its own and of another agent, whether or not it is aware of those motions. I am not now speaking of that general motion naturally common to all creatures, by which they are moved from nothing into being, but rather that customary motion in time by which every day changeable matter, whether nature or art moves it, receives forms endowed with qualities.

S: Now I understand, and I admit that I was quite slow in not realizing that every object of action receives motions, whether its own, or those of other agents, or both.

T: Both actor and acted upon, then, experience their own motions. Whatever acts, experiences its own motion for the purpose of acting. What is acted upon undergoes its own motion and that of another; its own motion by passing from what it was not to what it is; that of another, since the cause of its own motion is not itself, but the natural motion or free will or a certain necessity of what acts upon it. What is acted upon, then, as we have said, experiences both its own motion and that of another; what acts, experiences only its own motion. And yet it often happens that the agent is moved to action by some other cause, so that both the actor and the recipient of the action seem one and the same. But although the actor's motion arises from various causes—natural, voluntary, or involuntary—it is said to be within its own province since it is understood as internal rather than external in origin.

S: I won't deny that you have convinced me, and so I am waiting for the rest of the argument.

T: I think that no motion can lack beginning and end. Reason demands that every motion begin from a certain starting point and direct itself toward a certain end where, upon its arrival, it will rest. The venerable Maximus states this point as follows very clearly in chapter 3 of *The Ambiguities* (7): "If God is unchangeable, as the fullness of all things, and all non-existents which receive being are moved, He is correctly referred to as a kind of cause." For as Maximus teaches elsewhere, "The Cause of all things is the same as their End."

God is the Beginning of all creatures—i.e., their Cause—and the End, since from Him they receive being and begin to be; and they are moved toward Him in order to rest in Him. He also says a little later in the same chapter, "There is a motion of things which have been made, intelligible for intelligibles and sensible for sensibles. Nothing which has been made is wholly immobile." And a little later: "Those who, in sacred manner, have introduced to us the sacred knowledge of divine mysteries designate as 'natural power' the motion hastening toward its end, or 'passivity', i.e., motion going from one thing to another, with impassivity as its end, or 'active operation' with perfection in itself as its end. Nothing made is its own end, since it is not its own cause. Otherwise it would be ungenerated, without beginning, and unchangeable, deservedly not having to be moved toward anything in any way. It would transcend the nature of things with being, since it would be for the sake of none, if the definition, although from an alien source, is true in stating that the end is that for the sake of which all things exist, whereas it exists for the sake of none. Neither is anything which has been made perfection in itself. Otherwise it would not be brought to a state of true fullness, and likewise it would not have its being from anything; for it would be perfect in itself and also without cause. Nor is it impassivity, for otherwise it would be enduring, infinite, and uncircumscribed. Receptivity to action is not naturally present in what is naturally impassive, because it is not loved by another or moved by love toward anything else. It is characteristic only of God to be the End, Perfection, and Impassivity since He is properly unchangeable, full, and impassive. On the other hand, whatever has been made is moved toward an End which has no beginning. Everything that has been made undergoes motion, just as whatever lacks being is motion in itself or power in itself. If, then, the things which have been generated subsist as rational beings, they also are moved in every respect, since they are moved from beginning to end according to nature through being, and according to knowledge through well-being. The end of motion of things which are moved is well-being in that which always has being. Likewise the beginning is the very being which is God, who grants being and gives well-being as a gift, and is truly the Beginning and the End. From Him come our absolute motion as from a beginning, and our being moved in a certain way toward Him as toward our end. If the intellectual is moved intellectually according to the principle of its nature, it wholly understands. If it wholly understands, it wholly loves what it understands. If it loves, it wholly experiences a movement of departure toward the object of its love. If it does, it certainly also hastens. If it hastens, it wholly strives for energetic motion. But if it strives for energetic motion, it does not stand still until it is wholly in the whole object of its love, and is wholly embraced by it, freely and willingly as a whole receiving a salutary embrace so that, as a whole, it is affected by the embracing whole; and so that, able to know that it is wholly embraced, it has nothing at all left to wish from itself, but from its embracer; just as air is wholly illuminated by light and iron wholly liquefied by fire." You see how the venerable teacher instructs us that all motion is present only in things which have a beginning and, through natural motion, make their way toward their end. He defines natural motion in the following three ways: "Motion is natural power hastening toward its end." Or "Motion is passivity going from one thing to another, with impassivity as its end." Or "Motion is active operation, the end of which is perfection in itself." When the second definition is understood in reference to natural motion, one should not understand that the beginning from which passive motion—i.e., motion experiencing its own motion—sets out is different from the end which it seeks. All things which move naturally have a single Beginning and End, God, from whom, through whom, and toward whom all things are moved. But since the concept (*intellectus*) of beginning is different from that of end, the two concepts are spoken of as two different things, although they focus on a single Beginning and End of all things. It is as though one were to say, "from the concept of beginning to the concept of end in God."

[71]   Consider, then, that everything which lacks beginning and end necessarily lacks all motion as well. God, moreover, is without beginning (*anarchos*), because nothing precedes Him and brings Him

into being. Neither does He have an end, since He is infinite. Nothing is understood after Him, since He is the Limit of everything, beyond which nothing advances. He therefore receives no motion. He has no place to which He may move Himself, since He is Fullness, Place, Perfection, Station, and the Whole of everything. In fact, He is More Than Fullness and Perfection, More Than Place and Station, More Than the Whole of everything. He is more than what is stated and understood about Him, however it may be stated and understood.

S: I have a clear idea of these matters, I think.

T: If you assign all motion to creatures, then, and make God free from all motion, are you so slow-witted as to attribute action or reception of action to Him from whom you withdraw all motion? For surely before, when we were drawing logical conclusions, you wholeheartedly admitted after due consideration, I believe, that action and reception of action can be produced only in things in which motion is inherent.

S: There is no question about reception of action, for I both believe and understand that God is wholly impassive. By *passivity* I mean "being acted upon," the opposite of action. Who would dare to say or believe, much less understand, that God is subject to being acted upon when He is Creator, not creature? A long time ago we concluded that when God is said to be acted upon, the expression is obviously figurative. He is universally thought to be acted upon in His creatures, since He is not only understood as being in them (for they cannot have being without Him), but He is also their essence. "For the being of all things is Superbeing, Divinity," as St. Dionysius says. He is also said to be acted upon in the souls of the faithful when He is either conceived in them by faith and virtue or begins to be understood in some way by faith (for, in my opinion, faith is simply a beginning from which knowledge of the Creator begins to be made in a rational nature). But as for action, I am not yet sure, because I hear the entire sacred Scripture and the Catholic faith acknowledging God as the Maker of all.

T: You have already granted that action is impossible without the motion of the actor.

S: Yes, I have.

T: Then you will either grant God the motion without which He cannot be understood to act, or you will take motion and action away from Him at the same time. [72] For these two things are reckoned among those which exist, begin, and end at the same time.

S: I cannot grant motion to God, who alone is unchangeable and has no place or object to which to move, since everything is in Him; or rather, since He Himself is everything. But I cannot take action away from Him, since He is the Maker of all.

T: Then you will separate motion and action.

S: No, I won't; I see that they are inseparable.

T: What will you do in that case?

S: I don't know, and I therefore beg you to clear some path for me and free me from this great confusion.

T: Well, then, take this way of advancing in your course of reasoning. Do you think that God had being before He made all things?

S: Yes.

T: Then making was accidental to Him; for whatever is not coeternal and coessential with Him is either outside Him or accidental to Him.

S: I should not believe that anything is beyond Him and outside Him; for everything is in Him and nothing is outside Him; and I should not rashly grant that anything is accidental to Him. Otherwise He is not simple, but a compound of essence and accidents. If anything besides Himself is understood with Him, or if He has any accident, He is surely neither infinite nor simple, but the Catholic faith and true reason most vigorously denounce such ideas. They acknowledge that God is infinite and More Than Infinite, for He is the Infinity of the infinite, and that He is simple and More Than Simple, for He is the Simplicity of all simple things. And they believe and understand that nothing is with Him, since He is the Circuit of all things which have or do not have being, which can be and which cannot be, and which seem contrary or opposite to Him, not to say like and unlike. He Himself is the Likeness of the like, the Unlikeness of the unlike, the Opposition of opposites, the Contrariety of contraries. He collects and composes them all with an ineffably beautiful harmony into a single concord. For the things in the parts of the universe which appear opposed to one another, contrary, and dissonant, are compatible and consonant when they are considered in the general harmony of the universe itself.

T: Your understanding is correct. Take care not to regret in the future any of these concessions which you have now made.

S: Go on in any order you like. I shall follow you and not withdraw what I have already admitted.

T: Well, then, God did not have being before He made everything.

S: No, because otherwise making everything would be accidental to Him. If it were, then motion and time would be understood in reference to Him. For He would have moved Himself to make what He had not already made, and He would be prior in time to His action, which was not coessential or coeternal with Himself.

T: God's making [action, *facere*], then, is coeternal and coessential with Himself.

S: So I believe and understand.

T: Are God and His making, then, two things or one simple and undivided thing?

S: I see that they are one. God does not receive number in Himself, since He alone is unnumberable, Number without number, and above all number the Cause of all numbers.

T: God's being and making, then, are not two different things, but the very same.

S: I don't dare to resist this conclusion.

T: When we hear, then, that God makes all·things, we should simply understand that God is in all things, i.e., that He subsists as their essence. He alone by Himself truly has being, and He alone is everything which is truly said to be in things endowed with being. None of those things with being really has being naturally inherent in itself. Whatever is truly understood in it, receives being by participation in Him who, by Himself, alone truly has being.

S: I should not wish to deny this point either.

T: Do you see, then, how true reason completely separates the category of acting from the Divine Nature and assigns it to changeable and temporal things, which cannot lack beginning and end?

S: I see this clearly too, and now I understand without reservations that no category applies to God.

[73]   *T:* Shouldn't we examine in the same way the power of all words which sacred Scripture predicates of Divine Nature, so that we may judge that they signify only the Divine Essence and More Than Essence, which is simple, unchangeable, and incapable of being grasped by any intellect or any designation? E.g., when we hear that God wishes, loves, cherishes, sees, hears, and the other verbs which can be predicated of Him, we should think only that His ineffable essence and power are being spoken of persuasively in designations suited to our own nature. Such speech is to prevent the true and holy Christian religion from keeping such silence about the Creator of all that it dare say nothing about Him to instruct simple souls and to refute the guile of heretics, who always lie in ambush for the truth and struggle to overthrow it and to deceive those not well versed in it. We must understand, therefore, that for God, being, willing, doing, loving, cherishing, seeing, and the other actions of the kind which, as we said, can be predicated of Him, are not different, but are all one and the same thing in Him; and they subtly convey His ineffable essence to us in the way in which It allows Itself to be symbolized.

S: Indeed they are not different, for where there is true, eternal, and indestructible simplicity in itself, it is impossible for anything else, manifold and different, to come into being.

[74]   I wish that you would tell me more plainly, though, to make me see clearly that when I hear that God loves or is loved, I should understand simply His nature without any motion of lover or beloved. When I am convinced on this point, I won't have any hesitation when I read or hear that He wishes or desires and is desired, cherishes and is cherished, sees and is seen, longs and is longed for, and also moves and

is moved. All of these must be grasped by one and the same concept. Just as will, love, affection, vision, longing, and motion, when predicated of Him, implant one and the same idea within us; so the verbs, whether active, passive, or intransitive and whatever their mood have no difference of meaning, in my opinion.

T: You are quite right. First, then, hear this definition of love: "Love is the connection and bond by which the whole universe is joined together with ineffable friendship and insoluble unity." It can also be defined as "the natural motion of all things in motion, and the end and resting place beyond which no motion of created things advances." St. Dionysius openly assents to these definitions in his "Amatory Hymns" when he says: "Let us understand love, whether we are speaking of the divine, angelic, intellectual, spiritual, or natural kind, as a unifying and blending power which moves higher things to forethought for the lower, joins equals in a reciprocal bond of communion, and turns the lowest and subordinate toward their betters, placed above them." [29] In the same work he says: "Since we have arranged in order the many loves from the one, let us now join them all together again and gather them from the many into a single, combined love, the father of them all. First let us draw them together into the two universal powers of love, over which complete dominion and primacy are held by the immeasurable Cause of all love, which transcends all things. Toward It universal love reaches out in accordance with the nature of each and every existing thing." [30] Again in the same work he says: "Come now, and let us gather these powers of love again into one, and say that it is a single, simple power which moves itself to a unifying mixture, from the best to the least of existing things, and from it again in order through all things to the best. Its circular motion is from itself, through itself, and toward itself; and it always returns to itself in the same way." [31] God is deservedly called "Love", therefore, since He is the Cause of all love and is diffused through everything and gathers everything together, and revolves toward Himself with an ineffable motion of return, and limits the motions of love in all creation in Himself. The very diffusion of Divine Nature into everything in and from It is said to love everything, not that It really is diffused in any way (for It lacks all motion and fills everything at the same time), but that It diffuses and moves the sight of the rational mind through everything (since It is the cause of the mind's diffusion and motion) to search out and find It and, insofar as possible, to understand that It fills all things in order that they may have being; and that, as though by a pacifying bond of universal love, It collects and inseparably comprehends everything in an inseparable unity which is Itself. God is likewise said to be loved by all things that are from Him, not because He is acted upon by them in any way (for He alone is incapable of being acted upon), but because they all long for Him, and His beauty attracts all things to itself. He alone is truly lovable, because He alone is the highest and the true Goodness and Beauty. Indeed, everything in creatures which is understood as truly good, beautiful, and lovable is Himself. As there is nothing essentially good besides Him alone, so there is nothing essentially beautiful or lovable besides Him.

[75]   Just as a magnet by its natural power attracts iron near it without moving itself to do so, and without being acted upon by the iron which it attracts, so the Cause of all things leads everything from It back to Itself without any motion of Its own, but by the sole power of Its beauty. Hence the same St. Dionysius says, among other things: "Why do the theologians sometimes call God *Amor*, sometimes *Dilectio*, sometimes *amabile* and *dilectabile?*" [32] And he concludes his sermon as follows: "Because He is moved by the one and moves by the other." The venerable Maximus explains this conclusion more clearly by saying: "Subsisting as *Amor* and *Dilectio*, God is moved; but as *amabile* and *dilectum* He moves toward Himself everything receptive of *amor* and *dilectio*." [33] And again, in an even plainer statement: "He is moved as though bringing an inseparable union of *amor* and *dilectio* to things receptive of them; but He moves as though drawing desire through the nature of those things which are moved to Him; He moves and is moved as though thirsting to be thirsted for, loving to be loved, and cherishing to be cherished." For even the sensible light which fills the whole visible world is always motionless, although its chariot, which we call the body of the sun, revolves about the earth through the

spaces of ether with eternal motion. The light itself, however, flowing from its chariot as from an inexhaustible source, so permeates the whole world by the immeasurable diffusion of its rays that it leaves no place to which it may move and it remains always motionless. Everywhere in the world it is always full and whole, not abandoning or seeking any place except a small part of this lower air around the earth, which it leaves in order to take up the shadow of the earth, which is called night. Yet it moves the sight of all animals which can perceive light, and it attracts them to itself in order that through it they may see as much as they can and what they can. It is regarded as being moved because it stimulates the rays of the eyes to move toward it; i.e., it is the cause of the motion of the eyes for the purpose of seeing. Now don't be surprised when you hear that the nature of light, which is fire, fills the whole sensible world and is everywhere, immune from change. St. Dionysius teaches us in the book *On the Celestial Hierarchy* (and St. Basil makes the same affirmation in the *Exemeron*): "The substance of light is everywhere; and in the bodies that illuminate the world, whether they are large or small, it breaks forth by a certain natural operation so that it not only gives light but also distinguishes all time by the motions of celestial bodies." There is hardly need to mention the Liberal Arts, which remain full, whole, and unchangeable in and by themselves, but are said to be moved since they stimulate the sight of the rational mind to seek and find them. They so draw the mind to consider them, although they are, as we have said, unchangeable in themselves, that they seem to be moved in the minds of the wise when they move them. There are many other illustrations, too, in which a dim likeness of Divine Power is beheld; for It Itself is above all likeness and surpasses every example. Though It remains unchangeably and eternally by and in Itself, It is said to move all things since through It and in It they subsist and have been brought from non-being into being. Its being is Its own source [literally, "it is by being"], but everything else proceeds from nothing to being. It also attracts everything to Itself; It is also said to be moved because It moves Itself toward Itself, and hence It moves Itself and is, so to speak, moved by Itself. God in Himself, then, is Love, Vision, Motion; and yet He is not Motion, Vision, or Love, but More Than Love, More Than

Vision, More Than Motion. And He is in Himself Loving, Seeing, Moving; and yet He is not in Himself Loving, Seeing, and Moving because He is More Than Loving, Seeing, and Moving. Likewise in Himself He is Being Loved, Being Seen, Being Moved; and yet He is not in Himself Being Moved, Being Seen, or Being Loved since He is More Than What Can Be Loved, Seen, and Moved. He therefore loves Himself and is loved by Himself, in us and in Himself. And yet He does not love Himself and is not loved by Himself in us and in Himself, but He more than loves and is more than loved in us and in Himself. He sees Himself and is seen by Himself in Himself and in us; and yet He does not see Himself and is not seen by Himself in Himself and in us, but more than sees and is more than seen in Himself and in us. He moves Himself and is moved by Himself in Himself and in us; and yet He does not move Himself and is not moved by Himself in Himself and in us, because He more than moves and is more than moved in Himself and in us.

[76]   According to the careful, salutary Catholic profession to be made about God, we should first predicate all nouns and verbs of Him affirmatively, not properly but metaphorically. Next we should deny by the negative way, not metaphorically but properly, everything predicated of Him by affirmation. For the denial that God is any of the things predicated of Him is truer than the affirmation that He is. Then, above everything predicated of Him, Superessential Nature, which creates everything and is not created, must be more than praised superessentially. What God, the Word made flesh, said to His disciples: "It is not you who speak, but it is the Spirit of your Father speaking in you," [34] true reason compels us similarly to believe, to say, to understand about other similar things. It is not you who love, who see, who move, but the Spirit of your Father who speaks in you the truth about Me and My Father and Itself. It loves and sees Me and My Father and Itself in you, and It moves Itself in you to cherish Me and My Father. If, then, the holy Trinity loves Itself in us and in Itself, it also sees and moves Itself. It surely is loved, seen, and moved by Itself, according to the most excellent way, known to no creature, in which

It loves, sees, and moves Itself, and is loved, seen, and moved by Itself, in Itself, and in Its creatures, although It is above all things predicated of It. Who or what can speak of the Ineffable, for whom no proper name or word or expression is found, exists, or can be made, "Who alone possesses immortality and dwells in the inaccessible light?" [35] For who knows the intellect of the Lord? But before we finish our present discussion, I thought that, if you are willing, we should quote here the chapter of St. Dionysius about divine stability and motion.

[77] *S:* I am quite willing, and I see that this last reasoning has cleared away all my uncertainty.

T: In the book *On Divine Names,* he says (9.8–9): "We have yet to speak of the divine standing or sitting. What is it except God's remaining in Himself, and being steadfastly fixed in immovable natural unchangeability and being established firmly on high and acting in the same way according to the same conditions and in reference to the same object; also, in accordance with His utter stability, subsisting altogether from Himself, unchangeable and completely immovable and this in a superessential way? He is the cause of all standing and sitting, He who is above all sitting and standing, and He has established all things in Himself, immovable and protected in the stability of their own goods. Moreover, when the theologians say that the Unchangeable goes forth into all things and is changeable, must not this expression be interpreted in a manner appropriate to God? We must think reverently about God's being moved, and not believe that it refers to His being borne or estranged or altered or turned or moved in place, whether straight or in a circle or a combination of both; nor must we believe that it is intelligible or spiritual or natural motion. We must rather think that God brings all things into essence and keeps them, and that He completely provides for them, and that He is present to them by His immeasurable envelopment of all things and by His provident advances toward them and His operations on their behalf. We must also be willing to praise the motions of God, the Unmoved, in words that befit Him. *Straight* must be understood as signifying the inflexible and irrevocable going-forth of His operations, and the generation of all things from Him. The spiral motion, i.e., the oblique, refers to steady issuing forth and fruitful stability. The circular motion refers to His sameness; and to His embracing what is in the middle and at the extremes, which embrace and are embraced; and to the turning toward Him of what has proceeded from Him."

S: I see that order demands a brief summary about the fact that no one can properly predicate of God acting and reception of action; and with such a conclusion you may end this book.

T: Long ago, I believe, you granted that being and acting are not different in reference to God, but one and the same thing; for a simple nature is not susceptible to the concept of substance and accidents.

[78] *S:* I did make that firm concession.

T: As being is predicated of Him, then, although He is not properly Being since He is More Than Being, and the Cause of all being, essence, and substance, so acting is also predicated of Him, although He is More Than Acting, and the Cause of the acting of all things, without any motion which can be understood accidentally, above all motion. He is the Cause and Beginning of all motions and of all accidents, as of all essences.

S: I should grant this point too without hesitation.

T: The only thing remaining, then, is for you to understand that just as being and acting are properly separated from Him, so reception of action should also be separated. I do not see how anything which cannot act can be acted upon.

S: Set an end to the book. It includes enough.

Notes

1. *Celestial Hierarchy* 4.1.
2. Romans 4:17.
3. 1 Cor. 2:16.
4. Phil. 4:7.
5. Isaiah 6:1.
6. John 3:2.

7. 1 Cor. 13:12.
8. 1 Tim. 6:16.
9. John 14:2.
10. 1 Cor. 1:30.
11. 1 Cor. 12:6.
12. Job 19:26.
13. Psalm 147:15.
14. 1 Cor. 1:30.
15. 1 Tim. 6:16.
16. Psalm 147:15.
17. The transliterations of the Greek terms are given first, with the Latin and English translations in parentheses.
18. Translator's Note: The second of the Latin terms used to describe Arithmetic, *intemerata* (which literally means "unviolated", "undefiled"), may seem to the modern reader to be strangely moralizing in tone. Perhaps our term *pure* (as opposed to *applied*) conveys some of the idea. Probably the freedom of Arithmetic from contact with matter (since it properly deals with intelligible numbers) is at least partly responsible for the use of a morally tinged adjective (participle).
19. Vergil, *Aeneid* 6.724–26.
20. Heb. 7:3.
21. This version presupposes *motum*, not the *motus* of the MSS.
22. The translation here follows the superior reading of the Sheldon-Williams text.
23. The Sheldon-Williams text here corrects the earlier faulty reading.
24. Reading *corpora* with Sheldon-Williams.
25. Gen. 1:5.
26. *De Inst. Arith.*, pp. 7–8, ed. Friedlein.
27. John 14:21.
28. 1 Cor. 3:2.
29. *On Divine Names* 4.15.
30. *Ibid.* 4.16.
31. *Ibid.* 4.17.
32. Both *amor* and *dilectio* are usually translated as "love" and often used interchangeably. The verb *diligere* in this translation is sometimes rendered as "cherish". When the two words, whether in nominal, verbal, or adjectival form, are to be distinguished, *amor* is more generic. It sometimes, though not here, indicates love in a lower as well as a higher sense. *Dilectio* is always positive in connotation, and carries the specific implication of value and esteem.
33. *The Ambiguities* 23.
34. Matthew 10:20.
35. 1 Tim. 6:16.

Book II

The second of the four 'divisions' of nature is the focus of Book II, but consideration of "nature which creates and is created" leads to additional inquiry into God as the uncreated Creator of all and into man as created after God's image and himself a subordinate creator.

Book II begins with a restatement of the four-fold division, emphasizing the unity of the first and last. Since all proceeds from God and returns to Him, the distinction between nature which creates and is uncreated and nature which is neither created nor creative is one of human reason alone. There is a difference between God and His invisible and visible creatures: the One causes the many and effects their return to ultimate unity. Only the Creator truly is, however, for the things that are from Him exist only insofar as they participate in Him. In this sense there is a unity of Creator and creature (523D–528B). Whether we investigate the descent into the multiplicity of created things, proceeding from the most general to the most specific, or whether we trace their return by uniting individuals into species, species into genera, and

107

genera into still higher unities is of little importance. The two methods, division and collection or analysis, are complementary ways of understanding what is in fact the same process. It is the method of division that Eriugena employs in Book II, postponing the use of collection until Book IV (525D–526C). In an excursus Eriugena likens his division of nature to the five-fold division of Maximus the Confessor. The order of the stages in the procession for Maximus is: the uncreated and the created, the intelligible and the sensible, heaven and earth, paradise and the world, and male and female. This, says Eriugena, is fundamentally identical with his own, except that Maximus has subdivided into three parts his third division, nature which is created and does not create, and does not distinguish the fourth from the first.

The first stage in creation is the formation in the Word of God of the primordial causes. Mediating between God the one and the many creatures of the invisible and visible world, like God they create and like the world they are created. Eriugena summarizes their function toward the end of the second book in this way:

Chapter 36 (Columns 615–617A)

T: And so the primordial causes, as I have said in the preceding discussion, are what the Greeks call 'ideas', i.e., eternal species or forms and unchangeable reasons, according to which and in which the visible and invisible world is formed and ruled. They have therefore merited the name, given them by Greek philosophers, of *prototypa*, i.e., "archetypal examples", which the Father made in the Son and, through the Holy Spirit, divides and multiplies into their effects. They are also called *proorismata*, i.e., "predestinations"; for in them whatever things are, have been, and will be made by Divine Providence were unchangeably predestined at once and together. Nothing arises naturally in visible and invisible creation except what has been preordained and given prior definition in them before all times and places. They are likewise commonly designated by philosophers as *theia thelemata*, i.e., "divine wills", since whatever God wished to make, He made in them primordially and causally; and whatever is to be, was made in them before the ages. Hence they are said to be the beginnings of all things, since everything sensed or understood in visible or invisible creation subsists by participation in them. They themselves are participations in the single Cause of universal creation, viz., the sublime and holy Trinity; and they are said to have being in themselves because no creature mediates between them and the single Cause of all things. And while they subsist unchangeably in It, they are the primordial causes of other causes which follow them, as far as the extreme limits of all nature created and multiplied to infinity. I speak of infinity from the point of view of creation, not of the Creator; for the end of the multiplication of creatures is known to the Creator alone, because it is He Himself and no other. The primordial causes, then, which divine philosophers call the beginnings of all things, are goodness in itself, essence in itself, life in itself, wisdom in itself, truth in itself, intellect in itself, reason in itself, virtue in itself, justice in itself, salvation (*salus*) in itself, magnitude in itself, omnipotence in itself, eternity in itself, peace in itself, and all the virtues and reasons which the Father made in the Son at once and together, and according to which the fabric of universal order is woven from the highest things downward, i.e., from intellectual creatures, who are closest to God after God, to the lowest order of all things in which bodies are contained. Whatever is good is good by participation in the good in itself; whatever subsists essentially and substantially, subsists by participation in essence in itself; whatever is alive possesses life by participation in life in itself. Similarly whatever things are wise and endowed with understanding and reason, are wise and endowed with understanding and reason by participation in wisdom in itself, understanding in itself, and reason in itself. The same kind of statement must be made about everything else. In fact, no general or specific power (*virtus*) is found in the nature of things which does not proceed from the primordial causes by an ineffable participation in them.

In the course of the argument further characteristics of the primordial causes are specified. In Chapter 15 Eriugena embarks on an interpretation of the opening verses of Genesis, designed to give Scriptural support to his understanding of creation. Although recognizing alternate interpretations of many Biblical passages, he insists that his is best supported by reason. The most probable or likely interpretation of "In the beginning God created heaven and earth" is that in His Word, the second Person of the Trinity, the Father created the primordial causes, for God's Word is the Beginning of all (546–547). *Heaven* means the prototypes of all things intelligible and spiritual, while *earth* stands for the primordial causes of all those sensible things which compose the visible world. The Student tries to reconcile this view with the more familiar theory that God's first creation was formless matter by identifying the primordial causes with a primordial matter. He is reminded, however, that Augustine has said that nothing is nearer to non-being than formless matter, and since being and non-being are contraries, that which is nearest true being or God must be the created causes of all creatures (547–548). Neither prime matter nor space nor time is identifiable with these creative Ideas; instead, they are themselves created by the primordial causes.

The preferred sense, then, of the verse, "And the earth was without form and void" is that *earth* stands for the primordial causes of corporeal nature. An immaterial creation is founded in the Word prior to the appearance of the visible world. Such immaterial 'earth' is said to be void because when it is considered as existing prior to its effects, it is *empty* of all sensible things. It is *formless* since it is without quantity, bodily mass, place, and time—that is, all that determines physical shape. Later (Chapter 19), Eriugena makes clear that the priority is logical and metaphysical, not temporal, for time is simultaneous with the visible world.

The primordial causes are the source of the intelligible world as well, and *heaven* refers to these causes. They are also indicated by the phrase, "And darkness was on the face of the deep", for the exemplars of the intelligible world are too "deep" for any human mind to comprehend.

From Chapter 17 (Columns 550C–551A)

T: They are called *the abyss* because of their incomprehensible depth and their infinite diffusion through all things, which is perceived by no sense and comprehended by no intellect. In accord with the excellence of their ineffable purity, they have deserved to be called by the name of *darkness*. Of course, even our sensible sun often brings darkness upon those who gaze at it without being able to endure its excessive brilliance. And so there was darkness over the abyss of the primordial causes. Before their procession into the number of spiritual essences, no created intellect could know what they were. And even now there is darkness over this abyss because it is perceived by no intellect except the One which fashioned it in the beginning. Moreover, from its effects—i.e., its processions into intelligible forms—there is only knowledge that it is, but there is no understanding of what it is.

To be sure, there is a sense in which the creative ideas are knowable in their effects. Just as our knowledge remains in our minds but is attested to by external signs, so the primordial causes proceed or flow into their effects while remaining in themselves unchangeable and incomprehensibly other. God, of course, knows them since it is He that has caused them in Himself; indeed, His knowing is His causing and His causing is His knowing (559B).

The primordial causes of both invisible and visible things are eternal, but it would be incorrect to say that they are coeternal with the Father and the Son. Only the Son, the Word, is strictly coeternal with the Father, for only He is of the same essence as the Father. The primordial causes, on the other hand, are caused in the Son and therefore are subordinate and secondary. The eternality ascribed to the primordial causes must therefore be distinguished from that accorded the Trinity. A maker precedes his product, but since without a product he is not a maker, the Word and the primordial causes must be simultaneous. In the strict sense the only real eternity is one without any beginning or source whatever, and this is true of the Trinity only. If, then, we say that the primordial causes are eternal or coeternal with God, we mean that they are always in Him without any temporal beginning, although they do have a "Beginning" in the sense of a principle or cause on which they depend (561B–562C).

The primordial causes, then, are God's creative ideas. Their locus is His mind, the Word, but they are not identical with Him. In distinguishing creature from Creator, Eriugena makes clear that they are neither begotten like the Son nor do they proceed as does the Holy Spirit. In Genesis he also professes to find some further understanding of the doctrine of the Trinity, for the whole Biblical account of creation is, he says, not only about the causes of things—that is, the primordial causes—but also about the Trinity as the Cause of causes. *God* stands for the Father, *Beginning* for the Son, the Word, and the *Spirit of God* who "moved above the waters" is the Holy Spirit, described here as more ultimate than those primordial causes which are the well-springs from which all the universe flows.

Again Eriugena stresses the transcendence of God. He is not to be identified with His first creatures, exalted as they are. If they can be called eternal, He is more properly termed eternal. If they are beyond the comprehension of any intellectual power, what He is is totally unknown, even to Himself. God does not know what He is, because He is not a what (589B). Since He is not a substance but as infinite transcends all the categories and all higher determinations, He is not being (*esse*). God's supreme ignorance of Himself is the highest wisdom—or, rather, ignorance must be denied Him (593C). While we say correctly that He does not Himself know what

He is, He does know Himself to be in all other things that are and He knows Himself not to be any of them. He knows that He exceeds the categories. We can, moreover, specify three kinds of what might be called the divine ignorance.

From Chapter 28 (*Columns 596A–C*)

T: The first is the one by which He does not know evil, because His knowledge is simple and formed by the only substantial Good, i.e., Himself. He alone is substantial Good in Himself, but everything else good is good by participation in Him. God therefore is ignorant of evil, for if He knew evil, evil would necessarily be in the nature of things. Divine knowledge, of course, is the Cause of all things with being. God does not know the things which have being because they subsist, but they subsist because God knows them. Divine knowledge is the cause of their essence; and hence, if God knew evil, it would be understood substantially in something and evil would be a participant in good; and vice and wickedness would proceed from Virtue and Goodness; but true reason teaches that this is impossible. The second kind is that by which God is said to be ignorant of anything except the things of which He made and knows the reasons eternally in Himself. He essentially possesses knowledge of those things over which He naturally has power. The third is that by which, as we have previously stated, God is said to be ignorant of those things which are not yet manifestly apparent in their effects as the result of action. But He does possess their invisible reasons, created in Himself by Himself and known to Himself.

The cause of all is a Trinity, and Eriugena uses both Greek and Latin formulations to express the Godhead as One in Three and Three in One: we may speak indifferently of one essence in three substances or of one substance in three persons (598C–D). Eriugena himself prefers the Greek. While the whole Trinity is known (from its effects) to be, to be wise, and to be living (Ch. 19) and to be essence, power, and operation, still we may rightly say that there is distinction as well as community of being. The Father begets the Son and establishes the primordial causes in Him. The Holy Spirit, proceeding from the Father, multiplies and distributes the primordial causes in their effects. That is, the primordial causes are one and simple in the Word, and through the operation of the Holy Spirit they are divided into the various genera, species, forms, numbers and individuals that constitute the world of invisible and visible creatures. Eriugena stresses that the Spirit not only endows those who participate in the life of the Church with the seven supernatural gifts of which St. Paul speaks: the third Person of the Godhead is also active in creation, distributing as grants all those goods with which natural things are endowed. No created nature possesses anything but what it has received; if it is, it has received being; if it lives, it has received its life. All goods, then, whether of the order of grace or that of nature have their origin in the Father, their archetypes in the Son, and their multiplication and distribution through the work of the Holy Spirit (562C–566D).

The Father is the cause of the Son in the sense of logical precedence of begetter over begotten. This is not to say that the nature of the Father is to be the begetter of the Son, for both are one nature or one essence. The relation of the Holy Spirit to Father and Son is not so clear, however, as the dispute between the Eastern and Western Church attests. The Eastern theologians propose "from the Father," a phrase that suggests the single causality of the Father. The formula of the Latin Doctors ("proceeding from the Father and the Son") and that of some of the Greeks ("proceeding from the Father through the Son") seem to indicate dual causality. But Eriugena, implicitly invoking the Neoplatonic principle that unity is always prior to duality, argues that reason forbids us to say that a single and simple cause can have two causes (602A). The unity of essence of Father and Son does not solve the problem, because the question concerns the roles of the two distinguishable Persons (607C). The answer lies in understanding the Spirit as the Spirit of both, the love of the Father for the Son and the Son for the Father. The formula "from the Father through the Son" expresses this most adequately. Creation provides some helpful analogies, and Eriugena exchanges the apophatic for the cataphatic method (599B–D). Augustine has taught us of the trinity of mind (*mens*), knowledge (*notitia*), and love (*amor*) which is the essence of the human being made in the image of God. The mind, engendering its knowledge of itself, produces its love of itself, and this is a likeness of the divine Trinity (603A). An even better example is that of the process whereby a ray of light continually arises from the presence of fire, from which brightness can also be said to proceed. Although the brightness seems to come from the ray, it does so not because the ray is something in itself apart from the fire but only because of the fiery power within the ray. Similarly, the Holy Spirit proceeds from the Father through the Son because the Father is entirely in the Son and the Son entirely in the Father, and both are entirely in the Spirit and it in them (608B–609D). The Substance or Person of the Father, like fire, is the "principle and sole cause" of Son and Spirit; yet there is an identity of essence of all three. It does not matter, therefore, which of the three formulas is employed as long as priority of Substance or Person is given to the Father.

But finally we must confess that our thought about the Trinity goes beyond what words permit, and our understanding goes beyond our rational thought, while the Trinity itself is exalted beyond all understanding. Anything that can be said, thought, or understood about the mystery of the Persons of the Godhead is merely an image or theophany of the truth itself.

Chief among those creatures that God has made "in" the primordial causes is man. Man's soul is made in God's image and likeness, and since all that is is found in the archetype, so the whole created universe must also be found in the image. If

God is the creator of all, His image is also creative. Man is the microcosm who in a sense recapitulates in himself all of nature. He therefore occupies a crucial place in the universal scheme of procession and return.

From Chapters 4–5 (Columns 531A–C)

T: Man . . . was made in such an honorable position in created nature that there is no creature, whether visible or invisible, which cannot be found in him. By a marvelous union, he was compounded from the two universal parts of created nature, the sensible and the intelligible; i.e., he was joined from the extremes of all creation. Nothing in the nature of things is lower than body, and nothing higher than intellect, as St. Augustine attests in the following passage of his book *On True Religion:* "Between our minds, by which we understand the Father Himself, and the truth, through which we understand Him, there is no creature as intermediary . . ."

S: I see this plainly and I marvel greatly at the dignity of our nature among all the things which have been made for . . . I perceive in it a kind of remarkable compound of all created substances.

As originally created by God, man was a single spiritual entity, Adam. His soul was made in God's image, and, as Gregory of Nyssa says in the *De imagine* (*On the Making of Man*), his body is the soul's image. This does not mean that the prototypical man created his own body. Soul and body were created by God simultaneously, although the soul precedes the body in dignity and excellence (582). Man's original body, however, is not his present physical body, but a spiritual one. His corruptible earthly body is the result of his sin and consequent fall. When Adam in his pride turned away from God, he introduced division and multiplicity into the world. First came sexual division: man was separated into male and female (532A). Then followed his multiplication both quantitatively and qualitatively into all the races of the earth (533A–C).

Had he not sinned, he would have reproduced as the angels are said to do. Had he not sinned, there would be no separation of the visible world from heaven; everything earthly would remain eternally in its proper non-spatial 'place' in the primordial causes. There would be only the spiritual earth, without time, place, or motion. The physical or material world, then, is the result of man's fall (536).

Man's corporeal body is his own creation. When he fell, he made a dwelling place for himself in which he does penance and seeks to return to his pristine state (583B). The Biblical account of Adam and Eve taking fig leaves to make themselves loincloths is interpreted as man's making of his physical body (583C–584D). The leaves symbolize its frail, perishable condition: just as leaves of a tree give shade and keep out sunlight, so the body covers the soul with the darkness of ignorance and keeps out knowledge of the truth. Because our physical bodies are perishable, they cannot have been made by God. Everything that God makes is as immortal as Himself. Nor are they made from nothing, for God creates all things in His Word. Only God creates from nothing; man must use incorporeal qualities as his material (580). The physical body, then, is not ours by nature (571A–B), and after our resurrection we shall be restored to our immortal spiritual bodies which remain forever in the primordial causes. We are essentially, then, not what we appear to be but what we are eternally in the Word of God.

Anticipating what he discusses at greater length in Books IV and V, Eriugena explains that man's return to his primordial unity, and through man, the reunion of the rest of visible creation, takes place through the Incarnation and Resurrection of the Word. Christ took upon Himself not only human nature but also this earthly body, and by transfiguring it into the heavenly spiritual body of His Resurrection, He has begun the work of restoration, return, and reunion (571D–572A).

Because Eriugena is concerned at this stage of the argument with the causes of things, consideration of man in this mortal life is postponed. It is sufficient for him to note here that God in His mercy gives the soul power to care for its corporeal body—that is, the capacity to give it life, and to direct, nourish, and unite it into a whole—but this vital activity of the soul is not an essential part of human nature (570A–D). Essential to man and not lost even in his fall is his soul fashioned in God's image. Itself among the causes of things, the soul's nature and activity throw light upon the nature and activity of the triune principal Cause. The Student asks what in us is the image of the Trinity so that we can know what to ascribe to Him (566D). Repeating the triad of essence, power, and operation as that in which all being subsists, the Teacher argues that man like God is a unity of the three factors. Man's essence is an image of the Father, his power an image of the Son, and his operation an image of the Holy Spirit (568). Just as each of the three Persons is distinct and yet there is unity in being and essence, so our soul is a trinity of diverse activities, though one and indivisible (570A). Corresponding to this triad of essence, power, and operation is the triad of intellect, reason, and inner sense.

From Chapter 23 (Columns 570A–C)

S: For *nous* and *ousia*, i.e., intellect and essence, signify the loftiest part of our nature, or rather the loftiest motion. Of course, as you understand, the being of our nature is the same as its motion; for its essence is stable motion around God and creation, and mobile stability. But while it moves around God, who surpasses everything, the highest motion is granted to it; when it turns, however, about the primordial causes, which are immediately next after God, it is understood as moving in a middle course; but when it tries to perceive the visible or invisible effects of the primordial causes, it is discernibly undergoing its lowest motion; not because the same substantial motion can be increased or diminished in itself, but because it is judged least, moderate, or greatest according to the dignity of the things around which it revolves. Thus the essence of our soul is intellect, which presides over the whole (*universitas*) of human nature and revolves unknowingly around God above all nature. Reason (*logos*) or power (*dynamis*) makes its way into what is, in effect, the second part; and this is reasonable, since it is borne around the beginnings of things which are first after God. The third part is called by the names of sense (*dianoia*) and operation (*energeia*). It holds what is virtually the lowest place of the human soul, and rightly so, since it revolves around the visible or invisible effects of the primordial causes.

Acknowledging a debt to Maximus for the doctrine, he discusses each of the motions in turn. Little can be said about the intellect, directed as it is toward the unknowable God. The Student asks how the intellect can ascend above all created things to know God. It is, after all, confined within the limits of human nature; indeed, it *is* human nature. The Teacher's answer is that grace alone makes it possible, for nothing created has the power to surpass its own nature. Consequently, this movement of the soul is unknowable and ineffable by the soul itself (572A–576B).

Somewhat more can be said about the activity of reason. It is, as we saw, that activity whereby the soul defines God as the cause of all things in seeing that the primordial causes are grounded eternally in something more than themselves and are themselves the grounds of all things. As the "middle motion" of the soul, reason's function is to be understood in terms of its relation both to the intellect and to the inner sense. Just as the Father begets His Word in which the primordial causes are established, so the intellect generates reason from itself and in itself. The relation is like that of an artist who first expresses his art within his own mind and fashions there archetypes of his creation before they appear externally and in actuality. Reason is like this art, born within the soul, in which all the things that the soul is to make are foreknown and "pre-caused" (577A). This is why reason is sometimes called the form of the soul: if the soul as intellect is unknown to itself, in reason it begins to be evident to itself and others. Again we are to recall the analogy with God, who knows Himself only in His creation of the primordial causes and in His theophanies (577B–C).

If this is how the soul knows itself, how does reason know God? From the primordial causes it receives thoughts which are themselves theophanies—that is, its knowledge of God as principal cause of all is an apprehension through the primordial causes. Not that it understands what these causes are, for that surpasses all motions of the soul, but it apprehends that they are and that they pour forth a procession of effects (577A).

The relation of reason to inner sense can best be understood if we begin with the function of the latter, the lowest motion of the soul which, as we have seen, circles around the invisible and visible effects of the primordial causes. First, it is important to note the difference between inner and outer sense. Outer sense is the result of the conjunction of soul and corporeal body. It is not essential to the soul, for when the body is dissolved, its action ceases. As Augustine says, sensation is a passion of the body which does not lie in the soul as such; it is a *phantasia,* an image of sensible things received through the instrumentality of the body. Thus it functions as a mediator between body and soul. This outer sense is what the Greeks call *aisthesis* (feeling), and its instruments are the five senses. Its location is in the heart, and what we call the five senses are like the gates of a city through which the likenesses of all sensible things enter from the external world. Then outer sense presents the likenesses to the inner sense (569–570A).

Inner sense, in contrast, does belong to the soul as its third and "lowest" motion. It is what the Greek philosophers called *dianoia,* discursive thinking, the operation of the soul. Although really just as simple as the first and second motions, inner sense can be called composite in that its activity is dependent on both reason and outer sense: by itself it cannot begin to know the reasons of sensible things (573A).

Let us begin with its dependence on outer sense. It first receives from outer sense the *phantasiae* or likenesses of external things which have been received through the instrumentality of the five bodily senses. It then collects, separates, and arranges them in an order that proceeds from the most general essences and higher genera down to the most specialized species, finally arriving at finite individuals. The principles that guide its classificatory activity are given it by reason. In short, it is inner sense that performs the discursive function of the collection of individual things into classes and the division of classes into subclasses and the myriad particulars that are their members. What intellect knows of God and what reason knows of the primordial causes is known by inner sense as the multiplicity of effects—forms and individual things. The changeless, simple entities of reason are subject neither to accidents nor to spatial and temporal distinctions. It is inner sense that grasps the innumerable things of the corporeal world as changing and in space and time. To function it must depend both on the data of the outside world presented it by outer sense and on the principles of order given it from above by reason (573B, 577C–578D).

It must not be forgotten that because the soul is in the image of the divine Trinity, it is not a collection of three faculties working together harmoniously; it is a unity of essence, with logical priority given to the intellect. The triune motion of the soul is summarized in this passage:

From Chapter 24 (Columns 579B–580A)

T: Just as we call the Son the Art of the omnipotent Artificer,— and not undeservedly, since in Him, His Wisdom, the omnipotent Artificer, the Father Himself, has made everything He wished and guards it eternally and changelessly—so whatever human intellect, too, most clearly and readily perceives about God and about the beginnings of all things, it creates in a kind of art of its own, I mean reason, by a remarkable operation of knowledge through cognition, and stores it through the memory in its most secret recesses. Moreover, whatever the Father, the omnipotent Craftsman of all things, created at once and together primordially, causally, uniformly, and universally in His Art—i.e., His Wisdom and Power, His Word, His only-begotten Son—through the Holy Spirit proceeding from Himself and His Son, He divides among the innumerable effects of the primordial causes, whether they have come down into intelligible essences and differentiae which surpass all corporeal sense, or whether they have streamed into the various and manifold adornments of this sensible world, marked by differences of places and times. In the same way intellect, i.e., the principal motion of the soul formed from the contemplation of intelligible things by supernatural knowledge, divides into the distinct and unconfused cognition of individual things, whether intelligible or sensible, whatever it creates in the art of reason and stores through the inner sense of the soul. Everything which intellect considers universally in the reason, it divides into parts by sense into the distinct cognitions and definitions of all things. You therefore see that the Father universally created in His Son everything that He wished, and that through His Holy Spirit He distributed, is distributing, and will distribute it in parts. And according to the likeness of the three Persons of Divinity, know that our intellect universally creates—i.e., forms—in the reason through cognition by the act of knowledge whatever it can understand about God and the causes of things; and through the sense which is consubstantial with itself, by the power of unconfused contemplation, it divides these things by parts into the individual definitions of things, which it collects in the reason.

The primary activity of the human soul, then, is a creative knowing, not indeed that creation from nothing which only the Godhead can effect, but a subordinate creation of the sensible world. All that is in the universe is recreated in the mind of man.

Book III

[1] In the second book our rational inquiry was directed almost wholly to recording, in reference to the second aspect of universal nature and to its form or species, whatever seemed to us probable and, I believe, clearly deduced and firmly supported by the conclusions of true reason. The second aspect of universal nature, moreover, consists of that part which both is created and creates, and in which the beginnings of all things—i.e., the primordial causes or, as has often been said, the predestinations of things to be created, or the divine wills—are to be considered, as we are taught by the authority of the holy fathers and by truth counselled by right reason. The discussion there necessarily caused us to introduce some treatment of incidental questions in order to clarify the primary question. In my opinion, every primary question involves incidental questions when it is carefully examined. Otherwise it cannot be solved, especially since it would become necessary and inevitable, while discussing the beginnings of things—i.e., the primordial causes—to add one's thoughts about the single Beginning of all things, viz., God, who is unique and

the sole and first Cause of all causes, a Cause above causes, Superessential Goodness. All beginnings and all causes of all things subsist by participating in Him, whereas He participates in none because He wholly lacks all beginning superior to Himself or existing with Him but not coessential with Him. Who could make a correct statement about created causes without first clearly perceiving the unique, independently subsisting Cause of all, created by nothing before Itself—that is, insofar as it is possible to speak about the Ineffable, to comprehend the Incomprehensible, to understand what surpasses all understanding? Along with these matters, we also gave a brief preliminary account about the return of things that are changeable and separated throughout the various divisions and parts of nature, i.e., the things of which this world is made up, into their beginnings, from which they proceed and in which they subsist without change until the coming of the end of all things and the stabilizing of what is in motion, after which nothing will be moved. As I have said, the order of our second discussion is woven of these and other strands of discourse. Next, unless I am mistaken, the sequence demands that the third book, under God's guidance, should deal with whatever the eternal Light has revealed to our minds about the Third aspect of universal nature, i.e., the part of creation which is created but does not create.

S: That is exactly how we must proceed, in my opinion. Since the first book is about the Nature that creates everything and is created by none, and is understood in reference to God alone; and the second, by a reasonable progression, deals with that which both is created and creates and is recognized in the first beginnings of things; surely the third would, according to proper sequence, take as its subject the third nature which is created and does not create. But before we turn to an explanation of this part of nature, I should like to know why you chose to posit as the first part of the universe itself that Nature which is removed from the universe of all natures by Its excellence and Its infinity. The universe is filled with the numbers of its forms and parts, and hence does not proceed to infinity. It is limited above and below by its own boundaries. Beginning from intellectual creation, consisting of angels, or, to go higher, from the primordial causes, above which true reason finds nothing higher except God alone, it descends through the natural orders of intelligible and celestial essences and the visible things which comprise this world, and is borne to the lowermost order of all creation, which is filled with bodies and the growth and decay of bodies, and with the various disappearances and successions through the coming together of the universal elements into particulars and their dissolution again into universals. Since Nature, the Creator of the whole universe, is infinite, It is confined by no limits above or below. It encompasses everything Itself, and is encompassed by nothing. No wonder, since It may not be encompassed even by Itself because It cannot be encompassed at all. How it can be embraced at all by Itself, not to say by anything else, either in something limited or in something supernaturally definable, eludes the understanding. Unless perhaps one should say that It encompasses Itself solely in realizing that It cannot be encompassed; It comprehends Itself in realizing that It cannot be comprehended; It understands Itself in realizing that It cannot be understood in anything because It surpasses all that is and can be. Since this is the case and no true philosopher rashly counters these arguments, I do not clearly see why It is established by you among the divisions of the universe.

T: I should by no means set It among the divisions of the created universe; but I judged for many reasons, not just one, that It should be set among the divisions of the universe itself, which is comprehended by the single designation of universal nature. By that name *Nature,* not only the created universe but also its Creator is usually signified. In fact, the first and greatest division of universal nature is into the Creator of the founded universe and the nature created in that founded universe itself; for surely that natural division is uniformly preserved to infinity in all universals. For example, the first division of universal good is into that one highest, inherently unchangeable and substantial good from which all good flows, and that good which is good by participation in the highest, unchangeable good. Similarly there is the same primary division of universal essence, universal life, universal wisdom, and universal virtue. In these and the other things like them, that Nature which by Itself, from Itself, and in Itself is truly and unchangeably Essence, Life, Wisdom, and Virtue is first distinguished from that nature which, by participation in the highest good, either merely has being; or has being and life; or has being and life and feels and reasons; or has being and life, feels, reasons, and is wise. Do you see how the Founder of the whole universe holds the first place in divisions? Rightly so, since He is the beginning of all, and inseparable from all the diversity which He founded and without which He cannot subsist as a founder. In Him all things have being unchangeably and essentially, and He Himself is the Division and the Collection of universal creation, and is Genus, Species, Whole, and Part; although He is not genus, species, whole, or part of anything; but they all are from Him, in Him, and related to Him. The monad too is the beginning of numbers and the first progression. From it the plurality of all numbers begins, and their return and collection is consummated in it. Indeed, all numbers universally and unchangeably subsist in the monad, and it is whole and part in them all, and the beginning of all division, although in itself it is neither number nor a part of number. The same principle is true of the center in a circle or sphere, of the point of inception of a plane figure, of a point in a line. Although, then, the division of the whole universe begins from its Cause and Creator, we should not understand It as a first part or species, but we should understand that all division and separation into parts begin from It since It is the Beginning, Middle, and End of the whole universe. Although these statements are both predicated and understood about It—i.e., although It holds first place among the divisions of universals —every devout believer and understander of the truth constantly and unhesitatingly declares that the Creating Cause of the founded universe is supernatural, superessential, and above all life, wisdom, virtue, and everything stated, understood, and perceived by every sense; for it is the causal Beginning of them all, the essential Middle which gives fullness, the End which consummates, stabilizing all motion and producing quiet; and the Circuit bounding all things that have and all that do not have being.

S: I willingly yield to these analogies produced by deep and careful reasoning, and I approve them as plausible. But before you turn to consider the effects of primordial causes, from which especially the first and only Creative Cause of all is usually designated, it seems appropriate to know their natural order. Up to this point, I think that they have been introduced in a confused and indistinct manner. In my opinion, it will be very helpful to those who seek a perfect knowledge of them and of their effects if first there is a lucid explanation of the natural order in which they were founded by the Creator.

T: St. Dionysius the Areopagite, that zealous investigator of Divine Providence, has arranged the series of primordial causes very clearly in his book *On Divine Names.* He declares that the first gift and participation in the Highest Good, which participates in nothing else since it is goodness in itself, is goodness in itself, by participation in which anything at all is good. It is called goodness in itself because by itself it participates in the Highest Good. The other goods, on the other hand, participate in the highest, substantial Good not by themselves, but by it, which is, in itself, the first participation in the Highest Good. This rule is uniformly observed in all primordial causes; i.e., that in themselves they are the primary participations in the single Cause of all, namely God. Since indeed the first aspect of the highest and true Nature is that by which the highest and true Good is understood, and the second is that by which the highest and true Essence is understood, essence in itself deservedly holds the second place among primordial causes; for since it is the first participation in the highest and true Essence, all things after it receive being through participating in it; and consequently are not only good but also existent. The third examination of Divine Nature is that by which the highest and true Life is understood. Life in itself is reckoned as third among primordial causes because it was created as the first participation in the highest and true Life in order that all living creatures after it might be alive by participating in it. As a result, the good and existent and living have being. The fourth speculation about this same Nature is that by which the highest and true Reason is recognized. Hence reason in itself is perceived to have the fourth place among primordial causes, and the first participation in the highest and true Reason; and to hold in its possession the origins of all rational creatures after itself, i.e., of those that participate in reason. The fifth speculation about Divine Nature deals with the highest and true Intelligence; for it is the Intellect which understands all things before they are made. Hence intelligence in itself is recognized as fifth in the order of primordial causes, for by participation in it other things have understanding and are intellects; but it itself was created as the first participation in the highest and true Intelligence. The sixth contemplation of Divine Nature is devoted to the true and highest Wisdom. Hence wisdom in itself is deservedly set in the sixth place among the primordial causes, for it is the first participation in the highest and true Wisdom, and by participating in it the cause of being wise was created for all wise things after it. The seventh contemplation of the true and highest Nature is that which considers its highest and true Virtue. Hence virtue in itself occupies the seventh place among the primordial causes, and is the first participation in the highest and true Virtue. The other species of virtues after it are participations in it. The eighth step of speculation is that in which the highest part of mind, pure and true, beholds the bliss of Divine Nature. The first participation in it is bliss in itself, which all blessed things after it participate in as the eighth of the primordial causes, and the source of their own bliss. Ninth in order is speculation about the divine and highest Truth, the first participation in which is truth in itself, after which and through which, as the ninth of the primordial causes, all things are true which are, indeed, true. In tenth place is eternity in itself, which is the first participation in the highest and true Eternity, after which and through which all eternal things are eternal. The same principle is true about greatness, love, peace, unity, and perfection. Through these primordial causes from the highest Cause of all descend whatever things participate in greatness, love, peace, unity, and perfection. These examples suffice, I believe, to demonstrate our point. This speculation everywhere casts its gracious, godlike beam uniformly upon our mental vision in regard to all the first principles of all things as they proceed to infinity, whether in those which can be understood and named; or in those which are perceived by intellect alone but lack designations; or in those which are neither grasped by intellect nor expressed by names, for they elude every sense and every mental insight, obscured by the excessive brilliance of their sublimity. They are in Him of whom the Apostle said: "Who alone possesses immortality and dwells in the inaccessible light." [1] Nor is it strange if the primordial causes should extend to infinity. As the First Cause of all from which, in which, through which, and in relation to which they were created is infinite, so they too know no end by which they may be bounded except the will of their Creator. You must note that the order of primordial causes which you demand of me in order to distinguish clearly a sure method of proceeding has been established not in the causes themselves, but in speculation, i.e., in the insight of a mind that seeks them out and takes up the knowledge of them in itself, insofar as it can, and orders that knowledge in a certain way, so that it can make some sure statement about them defined by pure intelligence. The first causes themselves are, in themselves, one, simple, defined by no known order and unseparated from one another. Their separation is what happens to them in their effects. In the monad, while all numbers subsist in their reason alone, no number is distinguished from another; for all are one and a simple one, and not a one compounded from many. Indeed, the whole multiplicity of numbers proceeds from the monad to infinity, but the monad is not made up of the manifold numbers proceeding from it and, as it were, gathered into one. Similarly the primordial causes, while they are understood as stationed in the Beginning of all things, viz., the only-begotten Word of God, are a simple and undivided one; but when they proceed into their effects, which are multiplied to infinity, they receive their numerous and ordered plurality. Not that the Cause of all things is not Order or Setting in Order or that setting in order in itself is not numbered among the beginnings of things, since everything ordered has been set in order by participating in it; but all order in the highest Cause of all and in the first participation in it is one and simple, distinguished by no differentiae; for there all orders are indistinguishable since they are an inseparable one, from which the multiple order of all things descends. Thus the order of primordial causes is established according to the judgment of the contemplating mind, insofar as knowledge of them is granted to those who discuss divine causes. Devout and pure philosophers may begin with any of them that they wish, and turn the mind's eye, true reason, to the other causes in a certain order of contemplation, perceiving them all, as far as possible, and setting any of them as the limit of speculation. For example, the weak force of my examination began to reckon the number of primordial causes as though they were set in a certain order, beginning with goodness; and it gave perfection in itself as the final example as if in the fifteenth place, since it chose these primary causes as examples in proportion to its powers and ordered them as seemed best to it. Not that they have been so set by their nature, where they are all one, together, and in a simple state; but when anyone investigates them and wishes to make some illustrative statement about them, they usually appear in their theophanies, in the light of the divine radiance, in particular aspects, multiple, and infinite. To clarify this point by an example from the world of sensibles, consider carefully a center and the circle circumscribed around it and the straight lines beginning from the center and reaching the circumference and ending there.

S: I have often seen it, whether internally in my mind through a *phantasia* or externally, subjected to the senses in a visible and corporeal figure.

T: Haven't you obsepved how all the lines are united at the center so that none of them can be distinguished from others; since all of them are one at the center and are not at all separate? So a center is reasonably defined not as the junction of lines into one, but as the simple and undivided source and beginning from which, whether by nature or by art, the manifold number of lines proceeds. For the center is the universal beginning of lines, in which all are one.

S: This point has been very clearly and convincingly demonstrated to me by the reasoning of geometers. But these matters are all perceived more by mind than by sense, whether one wishes to discuss such things as are perceived internally by a *phantasia* or externally through sense.

T: You are quite right. These matters and others of the kind are discerned by pure mental vision. You see, I believe, in the first progression of lines from unity itself, which is in the center, how closely they are joined to one another so that they can scarcely be distinguished from one another. As they extend farther from the center, the spaces separating them begin to grow a little wider until they reach the circumference, by which they are bounded. There is the widest extent of their intervals—i.e., the spaces between lines equal to one another so that none of them is found to be wider or narrower than others. Similarly the length of all the lines is the same so that none are longer or shorter than others, and a natural and systematic equality is preserved in both, I mean the width of the spaces and the length of the lines.

S: That is so, and I understand it plainly.

T: What if you should wish to determine the number of spaces and lines and to reduce them to a certain order? You couldn't find a particular space or line, could you, from which you would naturally and properly begin?

S: It doesn't occur to me that I would. There is such equality among them that no space and no line can be distinguished from another by any differentia or property. Even that circle, within the orbit of which everything is encompassed, is so like itself in itself that no part of it may be distinguished from another, whether by nature or by art. It has continuous quantity, so that it does not begin from any definite starting point and is not bounded by any established limit, but subsists wholly for itself in the whole as both starting point and limit. That is why circular motion is correctly named *anarchos* by the Greeks, i.e., "without beginning," and it holds first place over other motions, i.e., straight and oblique.

T: Your statements are all correct, I believe, for true reason so indicates. You see then, don't you, that no governing principle of figures bars or inhibits you from beginning to arrange and calculate about the whole figure starting with any space or line? So reason dictates, and hence there can be as many beginnings and ends of arranging and calculating as there are spaces and lines.

S: I grant this conclusion too, but I'm waiting to learn the point of it.

T: It is simply that we may recognize as clearly as possible that the greatest theologians and their followers can, in full conformity with reason, take any of the primordial causes as the starting point of their contemplation and set any as the limit, as they see fit. Thus, as many as are the primordial causes—or, to speak more cautiously, as many as are or can be formed in the intellects of the contemplators—so many orders and numbers, by a marvelous arrangement of Divine

Providence, spontaneously present themselves to the speculation of true philosophers according to the capacity and will of each. While these processes are occurring in various remarkable ways in the minds of those who speculate about divine discipline and divine theophanies, the primordial principles in themselves of all things with being subsist eternally, uniformly, and unchangeably in God's Word, in which they were made, as one and the same, beyond all orders and all number.

S: Now I clearly see the goal of your examination and reasoning. I believe that you are merely trying to persuade me that no specific natural order is to be sought in the beginnings of things. And rightly so, for who would reasonably seek order or number in things which the Creator of all has made above all number and all order by the sublimity of their nature? They are themselves the beginnings of all number and order, united in themselves and with one another, and not to be distinguished by the sight of any lower nature. Only their Creator's power of knowledge is fittingly believed capable of numbering, distinguishing, multiplying, arranging, and dividing them. In some unknown, supernatural way, in their theophanies they are made conformable to the minds of those who contemplate; and in them also they are discerned as subject to multiplication, division, and enumeration in proportion to their intellectual power of contemplation. Hence it happens that these primordial causes in themselves receive no order known to intellect or sense, but that in the mind which speculates about and contemplates them there arise different and manifold orders as a certain conception of the understanding proceeds to arise in reason through certain plausible formations of images. But although this is the case, I should not suppose that you began your consideration of primary causes with goodness in itself without some special reason; for those who discuss properly do not say anything at random or without a cause.

T: Perhaps you would be right if you recognized me as one of those who discuss devoutly and perfectly, without swerving at all from the path of true reasoning. Since, however, I scarcely find a place among the lowliest followers of great philosophers, one must not make rash promises about my advances over the highest slopes of speculation. Often even those of better and incomparably purer natural ability, after beginning to set foot upon the slopes, have wandered astray or, unable to ascend higher, have returned to lower ground; or paying homage to those heights by silence, have said nothing since, with reasonable caution, they have not presumed to undertake the greater heights. It is given to those who are closest to perfection and illumined by the splendors of divine radiance and hence led by a hidden hand to the most sacred of the celestial mysteries to scale the highest steps of divine speculation and unerringly to behold the sight of truth most openly revealed and enshrouded by no mist. These achievements surpass my aspirations, for I, who am still oppressed by the weight of the corporeal senses, cannot attain them. But lest I seem sluggish in performing God's tasks by burying the Lord's talent in the earth and neglecting His coin without gaining interest, and so incurring the sentence of the wicked servant,[2] I shall say what seems rather probable about the matters under discussion, insofar as the innermost light presents itself to me in the inquiry. At the same time I shall everywhere observe the rule of humility and not judge myself to be what I am not; for it has been written, "Do not have an arrogant mind, but be reverent." [3]

[2] I was led to put goodness in itself as the beginning of the first principles specifically because I observed, with the authority of the holy fathers, especially of Dionysius the Areopagite, that goodness in itself is the most general of the divine gifts and that it in some way precedes others. The Cause of all, the creative Goodness which is God, first of all created the cause called "goodness in itself" in order, through it, to bring into being from nonexistence everything that has being. It is, indeed, the property of Divine Goodness to call into essence what previously had no being; for the Divine Goodness and More Than Goodness is the essential and superessential Cause of the created universe which has been brought into essence. If, then, the Creator through His goodness derived everything from nothing so that it might have being, the understanding of goodness in itself must necessarily precede the understanding of essence in itself; for goodness was not brought about by essence, but essence by goodness. This point

is made very clearly by Scripture in the statement, "And God saw everything, and it was very good." [4] It does not say, "And God saw everything and indeed it really had being." What advantage would mere being offer without well-being? Everything with being *has* being insofar as it is good. Insofar as it is not good or is, so to speak, of relatively slight good, it lacks being. Hence if goodness is completely removed, no essence remains. The designations of 'being' or 'eternal being' are improperly applied to simple being and eternal being without well-being and eternal well-being. Thus when goodness is taken away, one cannot properly speak of essence or eternal essence. And lest you perhaps respond that we can similarly declare that when essence is wholly removed, no goodness remains (for when existence is gone no good thing will subsist), listen to this more powerful argument. Not only things with being but also those without it are called good. Furthermore, things without being are termed better than those with it; for insofar as they surpass essence by excellence, they approach the Superessential Good, namely God. To the extent that they participate in essence, they are removed from the Superessential Good. Non-being, I believe, is predicated of those things which, because of their supernal excellence, their indivisible unity, and their simplicity cannot be perceived by sense or intellect. Those, on the other hand, are judged as having being which are objects of intellects or senses and, in a certain definite substance, are circumscribed by differentiae and properties, are subject to accidents, and are varied and dispersed in place and time so that they are unable to be together at one and the same time. Do you see, then, how much more general goodness is than essence? One species of the goodness of good things is in things which have being, the other in those which do not. Hence, beginning with the more general gifts of divine bounty and proceeding through the more specific, under Theology's guidance I established a certain order of primordial causes.

[3]   *S:*   Now I understand that you adopted a reasonable method in beginning your consideration of first principles. Whoever divides correctly should begin with the most general, proceed through the

more general, and so, aided by the power of contemplation, arrive at the most specific. As I examine the matter in my own mind, I believe that I understand this point also in relation to the first principles which you first established. As goodness is, so to speak, a kind of genus of essence and essence is believed to be a kind of species of goodness, so essence is a genus of life; for everything that has being is divided into what has life in itself and what does not. Not all essence is alive in itself or is life. So of things with being, one species consists of those which are alive in themselves or are life; the other, of those which in themselves neither participate in life nor are life. This principle can be noted in what follows also. Life is a kind of genus of reason, for all living things are either rational or irrational. Consequently one species of life is rational, the other irrational. Likewise there is a twofold species of reason, the one wisdom, the other knowledge. The name *wisdom* is properly given to that power by which the contemplative mind, whether of man or of angel, considers the divine, eternal, and unchangeable, whether it is concerned with the First Cause of all or with the primordial causes of things which the Father created in His Word at once and together. This species of reasoning is called *theology* by wise men. Knowledge, however, is the power by which the speculative mind, whether of man or of angel, deals in terms of differentiae and properties with the nature of things which proceed by generation from the primordial causes and are divided into genera and species. It does not matter whether that nature is subject to or free from accidents, joined to bodies or wholly liberated from them, distributed in places and times or, beyond places and times, united and inseparable in its simplicity. This latter kind of reasoning is called *physics,* which is the natural science of natures subject to senses and intellects. It is always followed by the discipline of ethics.

Whoever looks intently will find the same rule in all or many of the primordial causes. Not that I believe that some of the primordial causes are more general, others more specific. Such inequality is impossible, I believe, in what is endowed with the highest unity and the highest equality. It is rather that the mind of the contemplator and the manifold division of things find among their effects more numerous participations in some than in others. Participations in goodness in itself occur more often than in essence in itself; for the former is participated in by things which have and those which do not have being, while the latter is participated in only by those which have being. It would not be wrong to have a similar understanding about the other first principles. Both things which are alive and those which are not participate in essence; but only those which are alive participate in life. Both rational and irrational creatures participate in life, but only rational in reason. Wisdom and knowledge participate in reason; but wisdom is participated in only by those intellects which, with an eternal, ineffable motion, revolve around God beyond all nature of visible and invisible things and outside themselves and around the first principles of things. Hence genera or species, plurality and paucity are to be observed not in the first principles of things but in their participations, i.e., not in the causes made uniformly, changelessly, and equally in the Word of God, but in their effects, with which the world, visible and invisible, is filled. In the causes there is the greatest equality and no diversity, but in the effects there is a manifold and infinite variety of differences. But I do not yet understand what *participation* means, and without such understanding no one, in my opinion, can clearly discern what we have already said.

   T: Everything which is either participates or is participated in or is participation or simultaneously is participated in and participates. That is merely participated in which participates in nothing above itself, a situation rightly understood about the highest and only First Principle of all, namely God. All things from Him participate in Him, some of them directly by themselves, others through intermediaries. That merely participates which participates in what is naturally established above it, while it is not participated in by anything lower because no natural order is below it. Bodies are an example, for nothing subsists by participating in them; for we do not reckon shadows among subsisting things. By *bodies* I do not now mean those which are simple, invisible, and universal, but the ones compounded from them and subject to the senses and to corruption, i.e., dissolution. Everything else, set in the middle and ranging downward by natural degrees and by the steps established by Divine Wisdom from the single First Principle of all to the lowest point of all nature, where bodies are contained, both is and is called participator and participated in. The most excellent of these, between which and the highest Good there is no intermediate creature above, directly participate in God and are the first principles, i.e., the primordial causes, of all things, established around and after the one universal First Principle. The essences which come after them subsist by participating in them. Do you see how the first order of the created universe participates in the single First Principle of all and is participated in by creatures which come after itself? Similarly we must understand about the other orders. Every order set in the middle from the highest downward—i.e., from God to visible bodies—participates in the order above itself and is participated in by that below itself; hence it both participates and is participated in, but participation is understood in reference to all. For as between the terms of numbers— i.e., the numbers themselves—that are arranged according to a single system, the ratios are similar; so among all natural orders from the highest down, the participations by which they are joined are similar. And just as among the ratios of numbers there are proportions—i.e., similar systems of ratios—in the same way in the participations in the natural orderings, the creative Wisdom of all things has established marvelous and ineffable harmonies by which all things come together in a concord or friendship or peace or love or however else the union of all things can be designated. Just as the concord of numbers has received the name of *ratio* and the bringing together of ratios the name of *proportion*, so the distribution of natural orders has received the name of *participation* and the bond of distributions the name of *love* in general, which binds everything together in an ineffable friendship. Participation, then, is not the taking of a certain part, but the distribution of divine grants and gifts from the highest to the lowest, through the higher orders to the lower. First a grant and a gift are made to the first order directly by the Highest Good of all. To clarify the terms, it is granted being; it is given the gift of well-being. The first order then distributes being and well-being to the next. So the distribution of being and well-being flows down gradually from the highest Source of all good grants or gifts, through the higher to the lower until it reaches the lowest orders. We must observe here that *well-being* is understood in two ways. One is that all things with being are called good because they were made by the Highest Good, and they are good in proportion to their participation in goodness. The other refers to the adornment with the gifts of virtues of all things which naturally subsist as good, so that their natural goodness is more evident. Although the gifts of grace, usually designated by the term *virtue,* are especially and chiefly assigned to rational and intellectual creatures, none even of the lowest natures must be regarded as deprived of a proportionate participation in divine grace. As all things participate in goodness, so they participate in grace, in goodness that they may have being, in grace that they may be good and beautiful. We must have a similar understanding about life, sense, reason, wisdom, and the other divine grants and gifts. They are distributed in the same way through the higher to the lower as far as they extend, for not all grants descend to the lowest level. For example, being and well-being are naturally distributed even to the lowest part of the created universe, but life does not reach the lowest order; for bodies are not in themselves alive or life, but receive life through an order above them. This order is established in the nutritive and active life, and flourishes in seeds. As for sense, reason, and intellect, everyone clearly perceives that sense goes as far down as irrational creatures, while reason and intellect do not go beyond the rational and the intellectual.

The difference between "grants" (*dationes*) and "gifts" (*donationes*) is that the proper distributions by which every nature subsists are, and are called, grants; but gifts are the distributions assigned by grace, by which every subsisting nature is adorned. Thus a grant is made by nature, a gift by grace, for every perfect creature is made up of nature and grace. Hence every essence is properly called a grant and every virtue a gift. So *Theologia* (the Divine Word) says: "Every good grant and every perfect gift is from above, descending from the Father of lights." [5] Yet often Holy Scripture puts *grant* for *gift* and *gift* for *grant.* We should know, too, that *virtue* (*virtus*) is to be understood in three ways. There is a substantial *virtus;* for everything which subsists does so through a kind of natural trinity, viz., essence, *virtus,* and operation, a subject which we have discussed sufficiently in the first book.[6] The second kind of *virtus* is that which fights against the corruption of nature, as health against illness, knowledge and wisdom against ignorance and folly. The third is the one opposed to wickedness, as humility to arrogance, chastity to lust. This kind is evident insofar as the irrational movement of free will extends to intellectual nature. Proportionately as wickedness multiplies the kinds of vices, goodness sets up in opposition the ramparts of virtues. It is also noteworthy that *participation* is designated in Greek more meaningfully, explicitly, and comprehensibly by the words *metoche* or *metousia*. *Metoche* is named as though it were *metaechousa*, i.e., "having afterwards" or "having secondarily"; *metousia* is named as though *metaousia*, i.e., "after-essence" or "second essence." Thus one can understand very readily that participation is simply the derivation from higher essence to the essence following after it, and the distribution from that which first has being to what follows, so that it may be. We can demonstrate this point by examples taken from nature. [4] A whole river flows from its source as point of origin, and through its channel the water, after rising in the source, pours out constantly and without stopping throughout the river's whole length, however great. So Divine Goodness, Essence, Life, Wisdom, and all things which are in the Source of all things, first flow down into the primordial causes and give them being; then, in some ineffable way, they course down through the primordial causes into their effects through the appropriate orders of the universe, always flowing down through the higher to the lower; and, through hidden natural passages by a carefully concealed path, they return to their source. That is the origin of all good, all essence, all life, all reason, all wisdom, every genus, every species, all beauty, all order, all unity, all equality, all difference, all place, all time, all that has being, all that has no being, all that is understood, all that is sensed, and all that surpasses sense and intellect. The changeless motion and the simple multiplication and the inexhaustible diffusion from Itself, in Itself, toward Itself of the highest, threefold, and only true Goodness in Itself is the Cause of—or rather is—everything. If the Intellect of all things is all things and It alone understands all things, then It alone is all things since It is the only power of knowledge (*gnostica virtus*) which recognized all things before they had being. It did not recognize all things outside Itself, because nothing is outside It but It contains everything. It encompasses everything, and nothing within It truly has being except Itself, because It alone truly has being. The other things which are said to have being are Its theophanies, which also truly subsist in It. So God is all that truly has being, for He makes everything and is made in everything, as Saint Dionysius the Areopagite says. Everything understood and sensed is merely the appearance of the Non-appearing, the manifestation of the Hidden, the affirmation of the Denied, the comprehension of the Incomprehensible, the expression of the Ineffable, the approach to the Inaccessible, the understanding of the Unintelligible, the body of the Incorporeal, the essence of the Superessential, the form of the Formless, the measure of the Immeasurable, the number of the Unnumberable, the weight of the Weightless, the turning into flesh of the Spiritual, the visibility of the Invisible, the setting in place of the Unplaceable, the setting in time of the Timeless, the definition of the Infinite, the circumscription of the Uncircumscribed, and the other things which are reflected about and perceived by pure intellect, but which cannot be grasped within the limits of memory and which elude mental insight. We can complete this illustration by examples drawn from our own nature. Our intellect too, although invisible and incomprehensible in itself, is both manifested and comprehended by certain signs when it is, as it were, embodied in sounds or letters or gestures. Although it thus becomes apparent without, it always remains invisible within; and while it bursts out into various forms comprehensible to the senses, it does not abandon the always incomprehensible condition of its nature; and before it is revealed outside, it moves itself within. Hence it both is silent and it shouts, and it shouts while it is silent, and while it shouts it is silent; and though invisible, it is seen, and while seen it is invisible; and though uncircumscribed it is circumscribed, and while circumscribed it remains uncircumscribed. When it wishes, it is incorporated in words and letters; and when incorporated, it remains incorporeal in itself. When it, as it were, fashions for itself from air or from sensible figures chariots in which it can be drawn to the senses of others, as soon as it reaches their outer senses, it leaves the chariots and, absolutely alone, enters the inmost heart and mixes itself with other intellects and becomes one with those to which it is joined. And while accomplishing this, it always remains in itself. While it moves, it stands still; while it stands still, it moves. It is a mobile state and a stable motion. When joined to others, it does not abandon its simplicity. There are many other marvelous and ineffable thoughts which can be framed about the nature made in God's image. These examples suffice, however, to give an idea of the ineffable diffusion of Divine Goodness through all things from the highest down—i.e., through the universe created by It. This ineffable diffusion makes everything and is made in everything and is everything.

S: The examples are, indeed, quite ample insofar as the Ineffable can be expressed by likenesses, although It is actually removed from all likeness. But the likeness of our intellect which you used as an example differs, in my view, from what it is to illustrate in that intellect, using matter created outside itself, forms and adapts those chariots in which, as you say, it is conveyed to the senses of others. Divine Goodness, however, outside of which nothing has being, did not take the matter for Its appearance from anything, but from nothing. [5] But when I hear or say that the Divine Goodness created everything from nothing, I do not understand the meaning of *nothing*; i.e., whether it is privation of all essence or substance or accident, or whether it is the excellence of the Divine Superessentiality.

T: I should not readily concede that the Divine Superessentiality is nothing, or that it can be designated by such a term of privation. Although It is, indeed, said by theologians not to be, they do not mean that It is nothing, but that It is more than being. How would the Cause of all things with being be understood to be no essence, when all things with being demonstrate that It truly is? And yet an understanding of what It is is not achieved by any evidence derived from things with being. If, then, because of Its ineffable excellence and incomprehensible infinity Divine Nature is said not to be, it does not follow that It is absolutely nothing; for the very cause of calling It not *Being* but *Superessential* is that true reason does not allow It to be reckoned among the number of the things with being because It is understood to be above all things with being and without it.

S: How, then, should I interpret your statement that God made from nothing all things with being?

T: Understand that existing things were made from the non-existent by the power of Divine Goodness. Those things which had no being received it from nothing. For they were made because they had no being before they were made. By the term *nothing* no matter is thought of, no cause of existing things, no procession or occasion followed by the creation of those things with being followed, no thing coessential or coeternal with God, no thing outside God subsisting by itself or derived from some source from which God, so to speak, took some matter for fashioning the world. But rather it was the name of complete privation of essence or, to speak more accurately, it is the term for the absence of all essence; for privation is the removal of a condition. How, someone might ask, could there be privation before the state was brought into being? Of course, there was no state before all things with being received the condition of subsistence.

S: That name *nothing,* then, implies the negation and absence of all essence or substance—or rather of everything in universal creation.

T: That is true, I believe. Almost all expounders of sacred Scripture agree that the Founder of universal creation made from absolutely nothing, not from something, everything that He wished to be made.

S: I feel myself enveloped by the dark mists of my reflections. In such matters I have nothing left except faith handed down by the authority of the holy fathers. When I try to reach a clear state of understanding about these matters to which I cling by faith alone, I am thrust back, struck by the extreme dimness, or rather blinded by the excessive brightness of the subtle reasons which elude me.

T: Please tell me what causes your impasse and what disturbs you so much that, as you say, you cannot arrive at a state of clear understanding. Where does our reasoning falter, as I infer that it does, since it cannot lead you to a certain definition and knowledge of these matters?

S: I ask you to be generous and to bear patiently the delays which my slowness causes. I should think that these very finespun investigations would not be so clear to the inner eyes even of those closer to perfection than I am that they would quickly fix themselves in their minds; especially since these obscurities appear to be assailing me although they arise from matters about which we had seemed to arrive at a clear understanding long ago. We concluded about the primordial causes of all things that they were made eternally at once and together by the Father in His inborn Word—i.e., in His Wisdom—so that, just as the Father's Wisdom Itself is eternal and coeternal with Its Father, so all things made in It are eternal; except that all things have been made in It, whereas It Itself was begotten, not made, and is the Maker. Just as in the foundation of universal creation the will of the Father and of the Son is one and the same, so the operation is one and the same. Thus in their primordial causes, all things are eternal in the Wisdom of the Father, but not coeternal with Him; for a cause precedes its effects. As the understanding (*intellectus*) of the artificer precedes the understanding of the art, and the understanding of the art precedes the understanding of what is in it and made by it, so the understanding of the Father, the Artificer, precedes the understanding of His Art, i.e., His Wisdom, in which He created all things. Next the knowledge of everything made in and by that Art follows the understanding of the Art Itself. Whatever true reasoning finds prior in any sense must precede according to natural sequence. Hence God the Father, Artificer of all, precedes His Art causally; since the Artificer is the cause of His Art, but the Art is not the cause of the Artificer. The Art Itself, in turn, precedes all things that subsist in, through, and by It, for It is their cause. That is why I conclude that all things in the Wisdom of the Father are eternal, but not coeternal with It.

T: We discussed these matters some time ago and arrived at a sound view about them by true reason and the testimony of the holy fathers, who agree about them.

S: Don't you see, then, that I have reason to be agitated and lashed, as it were, by the opposing waves of different thoughts? How can these points be reconciled? If all things with being are eternal in the creative Wisdom, how can they have been made from nothing? How, indeed, can anything be eternal which had no being before it was made? And how can something be in eternity which begins to be in time and with time? For whatever participates in eternity neither begins to be nor ceases. Moreover, what had no being and begins to be, will necessarily cease to be what it is. Whatever has a beginning must have an end. I therefore do not see how these two points can fail to be in conflict, and how all things are both eternal in God's Wisdom and also made from nothing—i.e., how they had no being before they were made. Perhaps someone might say that the primordial causes of everything always are eternal in God's Wisdom, but that formless matter, in which and through which they proceed to their effects by generation into the genera and species with which the world is filled, is not eternal. But whoever says this will be compelled to confess that matter, made from nothing, is not to be reckoned causally among the eternal causes of things. When this concession is made, one must deduce and grant that not everything, but some things, are eternal in the Wisdom of the Father. No true philosopher would deny that formless matter is reckoned among all things made by God in His Wisdom. I do not see at all how anyone can say that the causes of all things have been eternally created in the Word of God, but that formless matter lacks its own cause. If matter is included in the sum of universal creation, then, it necessarily follows that its cause is not excluded from the number of causes eternally created in the Wisdom of God.

T: Concerning formless matter, which the Greeks call *hyle*, no one versed in sacred Scripture who rightly considers the creation of natures doubts that it was created by the Creator of everything both causally among causal things and proportionately among the effects of causes. He who made the world from formless matter also made formless matter from absolutely nothing, since the Creator of the world made from formless matter is one and the same as the Creator of matter previously made from absolutely nothing; for all things with being, whether formless or formed, proceed from a single First Principle. The universe has been created from One just as all numbers are created from the monad and all lines emerge from the center. On this point in particular one can refute the error of secular philosophers who have dared to deal with the making of this world. They have said that formless matter is coeternal with God, and that God undertook His constructive work using it, as though it subsisted outside Him and were coeternal with Him. They considered it unfitting for formless matter to have been created by God. How, they ask, blinded by the mists of their own false reasoning, would the formless come into being from the Form of all things; the variable and changeable from the Immovable and altogether inherently Invariable; that which is subject to various accidents from Him who has no accident; that which receives intervals of places, times, and quantities from what is not extended through spaces of times and places? How could what is receptive of different qualities and shapes be made by what is subject to no quality; the corruptible by the incorruptible; the compound by the simple; and so on? We, on the other hand, perceiving the truth of Scripture and following in the footsteps of its godly interpreters, believe by faith and observe, insofar as our intellect permits, that everything—the formlessness of all things, the forms and everything in them, whether essential or accidental—has been created by the single Cause of all.

[6] For the omnipotent Founder of the universe, free from all defects and reaching to infinity, was able to create, and actually created, not only what is like Himself but also what is unlike. Had He created only what is like Himself—i.e., the truly existing, eternal, unchangeable, simple, inseparably united, incorruptible, immortal, rational, intellectual, knowing, wise, and [things endowed with] the other virtues—He would seem to have been deficient in the creation of the unlike and of opposites, and would not be judged the Craftsman of absolutely everything which reason teaches us can be made. By *unlike Himself* and *opposite* are meant all things opposed to the virtues just named, not by negation or privation, but by an unlikeness and opposition of their nature. For example, to perfect essence similarly drawn up in genera and species by differentiae and properties and uniformly arranged in individual species without any confusion, there are opposed mobility and the imperfection of still formless matter. So the temporal are opposed to the eternal, the changeable to the changeless, the compound to the simple, and the other diametrical opposites. Of all of these, then, I mean like and unlike, there is one and the same Artificer, whose omnipotence does not fail in the operation of any nature. Hence the beauty of the whole created universe, of like and unlike, was

established with marvelous harmony from different genera and various species, from differing orders of substances and accidents, and was joined together in an ineffable unity. A musical melody, for instance, is made up of different qualities and quantities of sounds which, when heard by different persons and separately, are far removed from one another by discordant proportions of tautness and relaxation. When they are joined together, however, according to fixed and systematic rules of the musical art in individual modes, they produce a certain natural sweetness. So too the harmony of the universe has been made one according to the uniform will of the Creator from different subdivisions of one nature which, when perceived singly, are dissonant. Since these matters have been so defined, it is no wonder that, as you say, you are lashed by different, opposing waves of thoughts. We have concluded and firmly established that all things with and without being flow from a single First Principle of all, whether they are in the primordial causes made eternally at once and together in the only-begotten Word of God, or in formless matter, from which the primordial causes of visible creation have received the occasions of manifesting themselves by generation, or in their effects, by which this world is brought to completion from beginning to end by a natural order under the guidance of Divine Providence. As the Lord says, "My Father is still working, and so am I." [7] But how these ostensibly contradictory ideas can be reconciled in a single connecting bond of understanding—i.e., how everything is at once eternal and made— seems to me as well as to you worthy of the most careful rational inquiry.

[7]   S: Indeed it is. I believe that no problem to be investigated by those who search for truth is more profound than this one. As we said before, things made are opposed to the eternal. Hence, if they were made, they are not eternal; if they are eternal, they were not made. I can't conceive of how the same things may be shown to be at once both eternal and made. The only remaining course, therefore, in my judgment, is either to pay due respect to the depth of the problem by preserving an absolute silence or, if you see any point about it that should be investigated, that you begin to investigate it.

T: I believe that we should adopt both of your suggestions. We should not weary of investigating the problem insofar as our mental insight, enlightened by God, is not turned back by the excessive brilliance of its subtlety. Otherwise we might incur the charge of indolence or sloth. But when the problem exceeds the power of our concentrated gaze and refuses to be clearly discerned and fully perceived by minds still weighted down by their earthly dwelling, then it must be honored by the silence of heart and mouth lest we make some rash pronouncement about it.

S: Very well, set foot right away on this path of inquiry.

[8]   *T:* In my judgment, we must talk first about the fact that everything in the only-begotten Word of God is eternal.

S: I agree completely, for reasoning must begin from what comes first. Since eternity precedes creation, we must begin with it.

T: Pay close attention, then, and be careful not to make any unwary concessions which you will regret.

S: Begin. I'm on guard against rash concessions.

T: Do you think that God can be receptive of accidents?

S: Far be it from those who have sound feelings about the truth to say or to think such a thing. His nature is simple and more than simple, free from all accidents and more than free.

T: Doesn't God have any accident then?

S: None at all.

T: In that case the creation of the universe is not accidental to Him. That He did create it is not passed over by sacred Scripture, but openly proclaimed in the passage, "In the beginning God created the heavens and the earth," [8] and the other words which are read about the works of the first six days.

S: God did create the universe of creatures, and its creation is not accidental to Him.

T: He did not subsist, then, before He created the universe. Otherwise, the creation of things would be accidental to Him.

S: We believe that God precedes the universe not in time, but only in the sense that He is understood as the Cause of everything. If He were prior in time, the creation of the universe would be accidental to Him according to time. Since, however, He is prior only as Cause, it follows that the creation of the universe is not accidental to God but conforms to an ineffable principle according to which participants in a cause always subsist in their cause.

T: If God precedes the universe founded by Him simply in the sense of being its Cause—and this and every other participant in a cause always subsist in their cause (otherwise the cause is not a cause and the participant in a cause is not a participant in a cause); and if God is not accidentally causal, but always is, was, and will be a cause; and participants in a cause always subsist, subsisted, and will subsist in their cause—then the universe is eternal in its Cause since it participates in its Cause. It is obvious, therefore, that the universe of all creation is eternal in the Word of God.

S: I cannot counter this conclusion when I observe, without any uncertainty, that all numbers subsist eternally and uniformly in the monad and that all lines so subsist in the center. Although they are formed by the act and function of those who deal with numbers and lines into various kinds of numbers and various shapes, yet in their first principles—i.e., in the monad and the center—they remain the same in form. Their first principles are not understood as ever having been without them, and they did not begin to be made in their first principles; and though they flow out from them in many forms, yet they do not cease to be in them uniformly and in an eternal and changeless state.

T: Your example is extremely close and as close to true as possible. Also, the testimony of sacred Scripture and of the holy fathers declares that all things are eternal in God. The Apostle says: "In Him we live and move and have being." [9] We are in God through the excellent reason of our essence, which has prior existence in Him. We move in God by the powers of good action according to the reason of well-being which is prior in Him. Finally, we live in God according to the reason of always living and existing, which is prior in Him. Moreover, lest anyone think that we are one thing and our reasons something else, the Apostle did not say "In Him our reasons live and move and have being," but "in Him *we* live and move and have being." Insofar as we have being, we are merely our reasons eternally stationed in God. St. Augustine too, expounding in his short books the fourfold reason of divine operation, declares that the second things in the arrangement of God's Word were not made but are eternal. By this statement he meant not only the ages but also everything with which the ages are completed and filled. His words are: "Divine operation, which has created and governs the ages, is distinguished by a fourfold reason. First of all, because they are eternal, not made, in the dispensation of the Word of God who, before the times of this world, according to the witness of the Apostle, predestined us for the kingdom." Similarly, when writing elsewhere *On the Trinity*, he says: ". . . the Word of God, through which all things were made and where they all live immune to change; not only those things which have been, but also those which are to be. They were not in It then, and they will not be in It in the future. Rather, they merely are. All things are one; or rather only the One has being." Likewise in the *Exemeron*[10] he says about God the Word: "Those things made by It are under It in one way, and those which are Itself are in It in another way." It is as though he were openly saying: "They are under It in one way when, made by generation, they become visibly manifest through matter in genera, species, places, and times. They are in it in another way when they are understood eternally in the primordial causes of things, which not only are in God but actually are God." That is why he says "those which are Itself;" not that there are some things which are in God and are learned to be God because of unity of nature, and others which come into the world by generation; but that one and the same nature of things is observed one way in the eternity of God's Word, another way in the established temporality of the world. Saint Dionysius the Areopagite too, in his chapter on the one and perfect God, says: "He is called the One because He is all things universally; for there is nothing in existence which does not participate in the One." [11] And a little later: "And so we must recognize this too, that the species of each and every thing is predetermined in thought according to the One and, itself united, is said to unite. It is the single exemplar of everything. If you were to destroy the One, there would be no universe or anything else in existence; for the One uniformly surrounds and encompasses everything in Itself." [12] By collecting examples and testimonies of this kind, one may very clearly understand that all things in God's Word are not only eternal, but are actually the very Word Itself. Since it is very plainly declared by the testimony of sacred Scripture that all things were made at once and are eternal in God's Word, John the Evangelist says: "Through Him all things were made, and nothing was made without Him." [13] You can see that he says as openly as possible that all things were made in the Word. But lest anyone think that they were merely made and are not eternal, he adds: "What was made in Him was life." [14] It is as if he had said, "Whatever was made, whether in the primal causes or in their effects, was life in the Word Itself, in which the reasons of all things are eternal." So the Apostle said: "For in Him were created all things in heaven and on earth: everything whether visible or invisible: Thrones, Dominations, Sovereignties, Powers; all things were created from Him, through Him, and in Him." [15] As the blessed Maximus says: "Having, by good will, stationed there before the ages the causes of those things which have been made, according to those causes He established visible and invisible creation from the non-existent. By reason and wisdom at the seasonable time He made, and makes, all things that have being both universally and singly—for in creating the cause of angels, we believe that He produced the cause of each and every essence and power which fills the world above us as well as the reason of men and of everything which receives being from God. He recapitulates it all in Himself, i.e., He brings it to fulfillment; for through Him are being and enduring and from Him and in relation to Him what has been generated, insofar as it has been generated, remaining firm or moved, participates in God. All things, because made from God, participate proportionally in the Lord, whether by intellect, reason, sense, vital motion, or essential and acquired opportunity, as the great and godly exegete Dionysius the Areopagite believes. No one, therefore, who is faithful and devoutly investigates sacred Scripture should doubt that everything in God's Word is at once eternal and made. Both true reasoning and the authority of sacred Scripture are in complete agreement on this point, that things eternal are not different from those made, but that the same things are at once both eternal and made. How we can understand eternal things as made or the made as eternal you properly ask me to explain. Of course, the subsisting as eternal and made seems to you logically incompatible; and perhaps I myself do not yet clearly discern how the two conditions can be reconciled.

S: Please begin, then, to investigate and reveal whatever must be said about this matter.

[9] *T:* The reasons of all things, as long as they are understood in the nature of the Word, which is superessential, I judge to be eternal. Whatever has substantial being in God the Word must be eternal, since it is simply the Word Itself. My inference, therefore, is that the Word Itself and the manifold and primal Reason of universal creation are one and the same. We can also express ourselves this way: The simple and manifold primal Reason of all things is God the Word. By the Greeks It is called *Logos*, i.e., "Word, Reason, or Cause." Hence the words of the Greek Gospel *"En arche en ho logos"* can be interpreted *"In principio erat Verbum"* ("In the beginning was the Word," or "In the beginning was the Reason," or "In the beginning was the Cause"). Whoever offers any of these versions will not be deviating from the truth; for the only-begotten Son of God is the Word, the Reason, and the Cause. He is the Word because through Him God, the Father, said that all things were being made. Or rather He Himself *is* the Father's speech, word, and discourse; as He Himself says in the Gospel: "And the discourse which I have spoken to you is not my own, but it is the discourse of Him who sent me." [16] It is as though He were openly saying: "I, the Discourse of the Father, who have spoken to you, am not my own but belong to the Father who speaks in Me and begets Me from the hidden recesses of His substance and makes everything through me, i.e., by begetting Me." He is the Reason since He is the Archetypal Exemplar of everything visible and invisible; and He is therefore called *Idea*, i.e., "species" or "form", in Greek. In Him before creation the Father saw all things to be created which He (viz., the Father) wished to be created. He is also the Cause since the occasions of all things subsist eternally and unchangeably in Him. Since the Son of God is, then, Word, Reason, and Cause, it is

not incongruous to say that the simple and, in itself, infinitely manifold creative Reason and Cause of universal creation is God's Word. And so the statement would recur that God's Word is the simple and, in Itself, infinitely manifold creative Reason and Cause of universal creation. He is simple because the universe of all things in Him is one undivided and inseparable whole. Surely the undivided and inseparable unity of all things is God's Word, for It is all things. It is deservedly understood as manifold because It is diffused to infinity through everything; and the diffusion itself is the subsistence of all things. It reaches in full force from one end to the other and beneficently arranges everything. So in the Psalm, "His word runs quickly," [17] the prophet designates as *Sermo* the Father's Word which runs quickly through all things in order that they may have being. His course through all things is the multiple, infinite subsistence of all. Hence St. Dionysius in his chapter on the Perfect and the One says: "It is, indeed, perfect not only as perfect in itself and uniformly separated from Itself and according to Itself, whole through the whole and the most complete state of perfection; but It is also more than perfect according to the excellence of all things, and sets a limit to all multitude. It is expanded above any highest point and placed or encompassed by none, but extended at once into all things and above all things with unfailing increases and endless operations. Moreover, It is called *perfect* as not increased, *always perfect* as undiminished. It surpasses everything in Itself, overflowing in a single, ceaseless bounty which is inherently beyond fullness and inexhaustible." [18] It remains, then, universally and simply in Itself since all things are one in It. It reaches from one end to the other and runs swiftly through everything, i.e., without delay It makes everything and becomes everything in everything. While in Itself It subsists as One, perfect and more than perfect and separate from all, It extends Itself into everything and the extension itself *is* everything. This is the apparent meaning of *Cherubim*, the name of the celestial essence itself. The sages of the Hebrews have passed down the tradition that *Cherubim* means "the diffusion of wisdom." One must subtly understand by this diffusion or extension or course of wisdom, or however else one may express the infinite multiplication of the Word, not a movement into things which had being before the Word and Wisdom of the Father was diffused or extended or ran Its course. Rather Its diffusion, extension, or course precedes all things and is the Cause of their existence; and is, in fact, all things. What man who considers the truth would believe or think that God had prepared for Himself places through which He might diffuse Himself, when He is contained in no place but is the common place of all things? Hence the Place of Places is held fast in no place. Or can He be believed to have prepared for Himself spaces in place or time through which He might extend Himself or run His course, when He is free from all space and surpasses all times by His eternity? Or would anyone say, as is even more incredible, that another first principle prepared for God spaces of place and time or intervals of any quantities of whatever kind which He might fill by His diffusion or go through in His course or solidify by His extension? For not only to say such things, but even to think them and to fashion them in false imaginings about the Ineffable and Superessential Nature is thoroughly ridiculous and harmful. No other death of the rational soul is worse or more shameful than to contrive such monstrous and abominable images about the Creator of all things when truth itself in the intellects of those who devoutly seek and love their Creator generally proclaims in an intelligible voice about all things that have and do not have being—i.e., those which can be comprehended by sense or intellect and those which surpass sense and intellect, whose being it is to lack all comprehensible essence—that nothing else subsists except the participation in the one and only Cause of all things. Moreover, everything participated in is prior to the participation in it and to its participants. God therefore precedes all things which participate in Him, whose essence is their participation in Him. Hence the great Dionysius the Areopagite in chapter four of the book *On the Celestial Hierarchy* (i.e., the episcopacy) says: "First of all, it is true to say that by universal goodness the Superessential Divinity, establishing the essences of those things which are, has brought them into being. For it is the property of the Cause of all and of the Goodness which surpasses all to call the things with being to a communion in Itself, as the proper proportion is set for each of them. All things, then, participate in the Providence which flows from

Superessential Divinity, the Cause of all. They would not have being unless they partook in the Essence and First Principle of those things which have being. Everything in existence, then, participates in being; and the being of all things is Superbeing, Divinity. Living creatures participate in the same life-producing Power, which is above all life. Rational and intellectual creatures participate in the same inherently and previously perfect Wisdom, which is above all reason and intellect." [19] You have heard the statement of that best of theologians, Dionysius the Areopagite, the most illustrious bishop of Athens, about participation in the Divine Essence. In it he most clearly reveals that all things with and without being are to be understood simply as participation in Divine Essence, and the participation itself is simply the partaking in that Essence. They would not have being, he says, except by partaking in the Essence and Principle of those things which have being. Participation is, then, partaking in Divine Essence. The partaking is the diffusion of this Divine Wisdom, which is the substance and essence of all things and whatever is naturally understood in them.

Now hear what St. Dionysius said about the procession of God through all things and about His remaining in Himself. The following words are in the letter written in response to the bishop Titus, who asked what was the house of wisdom, what its crater, what its food and drink. "Divine Wisdom sets out two kinds of food; one solid and to be chewed; the other liquid and to be poured. It providently offers Its goods in a crater, round and turned up, which symbolizes the Providence of all things, at once spreading out and going about into all things without beginning or end. While penetrating everything, It remains in Itself and stands in the unchangeable likeness of Its nature; and, altogether perfect, It has irreversibly stationed Itself firmly and immovably in one place, even as a crater stands. Wisdom is said, moreover, to build a house for Itself and to put there the solid foods and the drinks and the crater; that so it may be clear to those who make divine symbols by divine inspiration that perfect Providence is the very cause of the being and well-being of all things, that It proceeds into all, is made in each one and contains all. But, on the other hand, because of Its excellence, It in Itself is nothing in or through anything else, but Itself in Itself is exalted by all, existing, standing, and remaining in the same way eternally, always in the same state, in no way made outside Itself, not deserted by Its own weight or unchangeable stability or goodness. In Itself too, in the best way bringing into operation whole and perfect providences, It proceeds into everything, remains in Itself, and always moves though standing still." [20] Note that he says "proceeds into all things and is made in each one." He says the same thing elsewhere in these words: "One must dare to say this too about the Truth, that the very Cause of all, by His surpassing love for all, is, through the excellence of His loving goodness, made outside Himself by His providential acts into all things which have being. And just as by goodness, affection, and love He fosters and surpasses them all though removed from all things, He is drawn toward them by His superessential and unchangeable ecstatic power." [21] These views are also supported by the statement which Dionysius took from the theological commentaries of St. Hierotheus. "The deity of Jesus, the Cause which fills all things, is the salvation of the parts which are harmonious with the whole. It is neither part nor whole and both whole and part, as encompassing all, both part and whole, in Itself and rising above and excelling. It is, indeed, perfect in the imperfect, as the primal Perfection. It is, however, imperfect in the perfect as the More Than Perfect and previously perfect Form, producing form in the unformed as the Archetypal Form. It is unformed in the forms themselves as More Than Formed, the uncontaminated Essence of all essence on a higher plane, superessentially removed from all essence, determining all beginnings and ranks, but placed above all beginning and rank. It is the Measure[22] of things which have being, and of the ages, and beyond the ages. Before the ages It was full in those that lacked and more than full in the multitudes. It is mysterious, ineffable above soul, above life, above essence. It possesses the supernatural supernaturally and the superessential superessentially." [23]

These passages suffice, I think, to teach those of good understanding that the steadfastness of the Divine Goodness in Itself is the unchangeable Cause of all things. Its procession and ineffable movement produce the effects of all things. Moreover, the participation in and partaking of It are simply the essence of all things. Note carefully his statement that the Providence of all things is the perfect Cause of the being and well-being of all things. Hence the Providence of all things is not different from their Cause, but one and the same God is the perfect Providence of all and the Cause of their being and their well-being. What follows next—that He proceeds into all things and is made in everything (i.e., in the universe which He makes) and contains all things—is so effective in resolving our present problem that I do not believe that a solution can be reached in any other way by the power of reason. If He Himself, who is the Causal Force of the being and well-being of everything, proceeds into everything and is made in every creature and contains everything, we are inevitably led to understand that the Wisdom of God the Father, about which such things are predicated, is the creative Cause of everything and is created and made in everything which It creates, and contains everything in which It is created and made. In all things, whatever is truly understood to have being is simply the manifold power of creative Wisdom which subsists in all things. If you mentally remove creative Wisdom from all things which It creates, they will be utterly reduced to nothing; and no essence, no life, no sense, no reason, no intellect, and no good whatever will remain. St. Augustine in his *Confessions* (7.11) appears to understand this point when he directs the following words to Truth Itself, viz., to the Divine Wisdom: "And I beheld the other things within You, and I saw that they neither wholly have nor wholly lack being. They do not wholly have being because they are not what You are, and they do not wholly lack being because they are from you." By these words he implies that all creation considered entirely by itself is nothing. Whatever is understood as subsisting in it, subsists through participation in the creative Truth. If everything true is true as a result of Truth and only Truth remains firm while all else moves, only Truth subsists in all true things. I said, moreover, that they move because they do not subsist in themselves but decline to nothing. They stand and are prevented from falling away to nothing by the power of provident Truth which subsists in them. If, then, God's Word both makes everything and is made in everything, and this point can be proved from the words of Dionysius and of others, why is it strange if all things understood as subsisting in the Word Itself are believed and known to be at once eternal and made? I do not see why what is predicated of a cause cannot also be predicated about what participates in the cause. All things with being, then, are fittingly said to be at once eternal and made since in them their Maker, Wisdom Itself, is made; and the Cause in which and through which they are both eternal and made is eternal and made in them.

S: I am completely amazed, and virtually paralyzed in thought. These arguments attract me since they are plausible and strengthened by the testimony of the holy fathers and of sacred Scripture. But then I waver and draw back and soon slip again into the deepest shadows of my reflections. My mind is not keen enough to perceive and thoroughly fathom the depth of this question. When I heard the words: "You who have made the world from formless matter," [24] I merely thought that the visible and invisible world were being described as made from formless matter, which God created from absolutely nothing as a kind of beginning of His work of construction, and that there was a time when the universe of this whole world did not exist. Hence in the first beginnings of its creation it proceeded from absolutely nothing into formless matter, and subsequently through genera and species and the other natural numbers it reached a certain perfection known only to the Creator. St. Augustine in his *Exemeron* showed convincingly that this creation did not occur at different periods of time; for formlessness does not precede form in time, but in the natural order by which cause is prior to effect. Of course, voice and a word proceed at the same time from a speaker's mouth, but yet sound comes before the word, not in time but as its cause. A word is produced from voice but voice is not in any way produced from a word. So the formlessness of all things, the bestowal of form, and the perfection were clearly brought at once and together by the will of the Creator from nothing into essence, and this was accomplished in a certain natural order of priority and sequence, though not in intervals of time. Such was my faith and my understanding, meager as it is. But now I hear from you a different explanation which moves me deeply and makes me abandon, against my will, the view which, until now, I thought I held firmly. The present reasoning, I believe, seems to aim simply at showing that the things which I thought were made from nothing and were eternal in no sense—for there was, I thought, a time when they did not exist, and hence that they had received what they had not had—are at once eternal and made. I consider this very contradictory, and rightly so, for these two things seem opposites, the eternal to the made and the made to the eternal. Eternal things never begin to be and never cease subsisting; and there was never a time when they had no being. They always had it. Whatever things have been made, however, have received a beginning of their making. They have begun tó be because there was a time when they had no being; and they will cease to be because they have had a beginning. Right reason, of course, tells us that whatever has a temporal beginning is not allowed to endure forever. Whatever begins to be in time must turn toward that final end where it must perish. No one should think that I am trying to argue for a return to nothing of those things which are made in the world in time from matter through generation. Such a view would be thoroughly evil. I am rather talking about a dissolution of those things into the elements from which they are compounded and in which they subsist. Human bodies, too, and the bodies of other animals are said to perish when they are dissolved. Yet they are not reduced to nothing, but return to the universal elements. Such a view is generally held, and fittingly so, about this whole visible universe. Since it has received a beginning of being, it will inevitably receive an end of its essence. As there was a time when it was not, so there will be a time when it no longer will be. The Psalmist bears witness when he proclaims in these words the eternal Creator of the universe: "The heavens are the work of Your hands; they will perish, but You will remain; all will grow old like a garment and You will change them like clothes; but You Yourself are the same, and Your years will never fail." [25] The Creator of all things even said Himself, "Heaven and earth will pass away, but not My words." [26] If, then, the part of the world which is greatest in expanse, most beautifully bedecked by the sublime splendor of the constellations, most pure in the subtlety of its nature, strewn with the stars that are stationed there, harmonious because of the course of the planets, and always full of light—if this part, I say, will perish according to the testimony of Scripture, surely we must not think that the parts within, much inferior to it, will endure. When the better passes away, it is impossible for the worse not also to pass away; and true reason does not grant that what is contained can endure when what contains it is taken away. Such is my statement to distinguish the eternal from the made. There is no slight difference between what neither begins nor ceases to be and what begins and cannot always endure. It is with cause, therefore, that the minds of those with imperfect understanding of such matters are shaken when an attempt is made to persuade them that the eternal are made and the made are eternal. I should not think that you would readily agree with those who mean that many—or rather all—of the things which have been made will always endure and so be eternal. As they say, for example, that universe consisting of heaven and earth, shaped by the four elements into the form of a perfect sphere and called by the name *world*, has been made from nothing and yet will endure eternally except for some small parts of itself, i.e., corruptible bodies subject to generation and corruption, which they cannot deny will perish. The heaven with its constellations, however, they say will last forever, whether it revolves or ceases to move. On this point, indeed, their opinions differ, for some declare that there will be a stability of what is now changeable, while others argue that the natural motion of the elements will never cease. The former follow the passage "All things will be quiet," [27] and interpret it in reference to the stability of the changeable. The latter, citing "Who will cause the harmony of the heavens to sleep?" [28] understand it as referring to the eternal motion of the changeable. How, indeed, will celestial harmony be possible without the motion of the ethereal sphere and of all the constellations, since music always involves motion as geometry involves stability? They follow the passage "A generation comes, a generation goes, but the earth stands firm forever"; [29] and unhesitatingly affirm that the mass of earth will always have its proper quantity, except that its surface will everywhere be made smooth so that it will be rendered more beautiful than it now is and like new. The evenness of its parts will be renewed, so as to bring about not the end of what now exists, but the endurance of its quantity and its evenness, which will be changed for the better. They have the same interpretation about the heaven, namely that the beauty with which it now graces the corporeal senses will, at the end of the world, be increased without any loss of its spherical form or of its starry adornment. Their authority is the passage "There will be a new heaven and a new earth." [30] They understand that the heavens which will perish are not those of the higher parts of the world, but those of the spaces of our sublunar atmosphere; so that just as those heavens were turned into water at the time of the deluge, so they will be turned to flame at the end of the world. They not only do not deny, but they even affirm that change will put an end to the generation of all animals, shrubs, and trees, and to the growth and decline of everything contained within the circuit of the moon. They believe, moreover, that the spaces of air and ether are to be divided, with ether as the eternal possession of the blessed angels and of men like them, and the lower air, diffused on all sides around the earth, as an eternal prison, and eternal flames, which will burn visibly in their appointed place, torturing the Devil and his members— i.e., the apostate angels and impious men like him. Hence, since they think that all creation is and will be in place and time, they do not doubt that places and times, i.e., the spaces of the world and its movement marked by intervals of periods, will always endure. Through these and other such false opinions they try to assert that things which had no being and began to be can be called at once made and eternal, on the grounds that they will always remain in the same state in which they were created in time. They think that things which have a beginning will have no end; so that they have both been made, since they began to have being, and they are eternal, because they will not cease to subsist. But I should not expect you to agree with such views, which true reason mocks; or to have tried to persuade me by your reasoning of such eternity—or, to speak more accurately, "semi-eternity"; or to have taught in this sense that things are at once made and eternal. I realize rather that with a deeper insight into natures that goes beyond human opinions, in some manner still unknown to me, you are penetrating the inmost shrines of divine mysteries by following in the deep-set footsteps of the fathers who have investigated such matters. [10] They say that the nature of this world will always endure, for it is incorporeal and incorruptible; but that everything else of which it consists—i.e., everything compounded in it—will perish. Since there is no body in it which is not a compound, and every compound will be dissolved into the elements from which it is compounded, this whole visible, corporeal, compounded world will be dissolved and only simple nature will remain.

T: I cannot deny that I was formerly deceived by the false reasonings of human opinions far removed from the truth. When I was still untrained, I gave assent to all or nearly all of them, for I was led astray by a certain likeness of truth and by the carnal senses, as has happened to many. Now, however, I follow in the footsteps of the holy fathers and retreat somewhat, because the ray of Divine Light calls me back from my own errors and the errors of others and leads me to the straight path. Divine mercy does not allow those who seek truth devoutly and humbly to go astray in the shadows of ignorance and to fall into the pits of false opinions and to perish in them. There is no worse death than ignorance of truth, no deeper chasm than the approval of the false instead of the true, which is characteristic of error. From these sources the most shameful and abominable monsters are usually fashioned in human thoughts; and when the carnal soul loves and pursues them as though they were truths, it turns its back to the true light and desires to embrace the fleeting shadows. Since it cannot do so, it usually falls into the abyss of wretchedness. We should therefore constantly utter the prayer, "O God, our Salvation and Redemption, You who have granted us nature, lavish upon us grace also; and cast Your light ahead for those struggling in the shadows of ignorance and seeking You. Call us back from our errors; stretch forth Your right hand to the infirm, who are unable to reach You without Your help. Show Yourself to those who seek nothing but You. Dissolve the clouds of vain fantasies, which do not allow the mind's eye

to behold You in the way that You, though invisible, permit Yourself
to be seen by those desiring to see Your face, their Repose, their Goal,
beyond which they seek nothing because there is no other highest
superessential Good." But go on to the rest of your statement.

S: All that is left is to bring up what perplexes me deeply—i.e.,
how everything is eternal and made, and how what lacks beginning
and end is circumscribed by beginning and end. These concepts are at
odds with each other, and I do not know how they can be reconciled
unless you persuade me. I believed that God alone is *anarchos* (i.e.,
without beginning), since He Himself is the Beginning and End of
everything, starting from no beginning and bounded by no end; that
all other things begin and incline each toward its own end, and hence
are not eternal but made. But the assertion you make on the authority
of St. Dionysius the Areopagite seems to me incomparably deeper and
more remarkable, viz., that God Himself is both the Maker of all
things and is made in all things. Like almost everyone else, I was
unfamiliar with this view before and had not even heard of it. If it is
true, anyone would immediately shout and proclaim: "And so God is
all things and all things are God." Such a judgment will be regarded as
monstrous even by those who are thought wise when they consider the
manifold variety of things visible and invisible, whereas God is one.
Unless you can make your arguments plausible by comprehensible
examples, they will inevitably be dismissed after being merely set in
motion but not thoroughly examined. I should be very sad about that,
for even in the midst of the thickest shadows, those who hope for the
rise of a coming light are not altogether overwhelmed by sorrow. But
if the light which they hope for should be taken away from them, they
are left not only in darkness, but also in great torment, having lost the
good for which they had hoped. The result would be that all your
statements about these matters would be judged as altogether false by
those of lesser understanding; and, scorning these views, they would
slip back into their original opinions as true; for they are not yet
willing to abandon them. At first, therefore, the way of reasoning must
be entered upon with examples drawn from nature, which no one
resists unless he is blinded by excessive stupidity.

[11]   *T:*   Are you skilled in the art of Arithmetic?
  S: I am, unless I'm mistaken. I have studied it from early childhood.
  T: Well, then, define it clearly and briefly.
  S: Arithmetic is the science of numbers, not those which, but those according to which, we count.
  T: You have defined Arithmetic carefully and alertly. If you were to define Arithmetic simply as the science of numbers, you would include all numbers in general, and so your definition would not hold. The art does not deal with every kind of number, but considers only those numbers which it knows are solely in knowledge and intellect, according to which the other kinds of numbers are counted. Wise men, indeed, do not say that the numbers of animals, shrubs, grasses, and other bodies or things are related to the knowledge of the arithmetical art; but they assign to arithmetic only the intellectual, invisible, incorporeal numbers established in knowledge alone and not placed substantially in any other subject. Of course, these numbers are not so perceived in knowledge, intellect, reason, memory, the senses, or figures that they are substantially one with the things in which they are seen. They possess themselves as their proper substance. If they were of the same substance (as the things in which they are seen), knowledge, intellect, and reason would judge about them, not according to them. Moreover, an art and its judge cannot be the same thing. Such an identification can be correctly made only in reference to God the Word, who is both the Judge and the Art of His Father. You were alert, then, as I said, when you added that they are not those which, but those according to which, we count. We do not see them in any subject, whether corporeal or incorporeal; but they are perceived by the intellect alone in wisdom and knowledge beyond every subject, freed by the excellence of their divine nature from everything which is counted according to them.
  S: I have often thought of this matter and perceived it clearly, I believe.
  T: Is it, then, a natural art?
  S: Yes, and none is more so, since not only does it subsist as the immovable foundation and the primordial cause and beginning of the

other three parts of mathematics which follow—namely Geometry, Music, and Astrology—but also the infinite host of all things visible and invisible receives its substance according to the rules of numbers which Arithmetic contemplates. Our first witness is the discoverer of the art, Pythagoras, a superlative philosopher who declares with sure reasoning that intelligible numbers are the substances of all things visible and invisible. Nor does sacred Scripture deny it, for it says that everything was made in measure, number, and weight.[31]

T: If you are looking for natural examples of this art, or rather of the numbers which it contains, then, examine the nature and rules of the art carefully in order to arrive, under God's guidance, at a knowledge of those things which you regard as incompatible and at odds with one another.

S: I willingly accept examples drawn from Arithmetic, since it neither deceives nor is deceived. Although relatively unintelligent persons are often deceived about it, the fault should be ascribed not to the art but to the dullness of those who treat it carelessly.

T: You have no doubt, I believe, that the monad is the beginning of numbers, with which the science of Arithmetic deals.

S: Whoever is uncertain about this point is no arithmetician. The monad, i.e. unity, is the beginning, middle, and end of all numbers, and the whole, part, and every quantity of all terms.

T: Tell me, then, are not all numbers, which reason can multiply as it will, causally and eternally in the monad?

S: That is exactly what true reason teaches us. The cause is in it, and they are causally in it because it subsists as the beginning of all numbers. In it all numbers are simply, i.e. all together, an undivided one, and they are multiple only in reason but not in act and in function. Nor is that one accumulated from many, but it is one endowed with a simple and multiple singularity; so that all numbers are in it at once and simply as their cause, and it is understood multiply as substance in all of them by an ineffable distribution. It is the cause and substance of all numbers; and although it does not give up the changeless state of its nature, it diffuses itself in multiple fashion into all of them. They subsist in it eternally, since their being in it has no temporal beginning. Unity never lacked the multiple reasons in which all numbers subsist. No one of clear intelligence, realizing that the monad extends to infinity, would say that it had a beginning. How, indeed, can an infinite progression be made from a finite beginning? The infinite proceeds from the infinite, but nothing infinite from the finite. Someone may ask how this point can be maintained when even in numbers themselves we see many infinites beginning from the finite. For example, from the finite number two, all doubles are born and extend to infinity. Similarly from the finite three, all triples take their beginning and know no end of their multiplication. To state the point briefly, no number is limited by its own quantities or by monads alone so that multiples do not flow from it to infinity. To such a questioner one must reply that all those numbers are limited by their parts, from which the multiples proceed to infinity; but in the monad itself, where all are one, they are infinite. Accordingly he will deny that all numbers are in the monad and will declare that they are limited in their multiples outside it; or, if he is unable to make such a statement because true reason resists it, he will have to admit that all numbers subsist as finite in their parts, but infinite and uniformly eternal in the monad. Of course, water does not begin where its source appears, but it flows from other places through hidden passages undefined by the senses long before it appears in its source. As the name of *source* is improperly applied to the place where water first visibly rises (for long before, it was in the hidden places of earth, ocean, or elsewhere where it hid [*latebat*] from sight, for *latex* ["liquid", "water"] is so named from hiding [*latendo*] in the veins of the earth), so numbers too, whose multiplication or other arithmetical relations proceed to infinity, derive their origin not from the finite numbers which first appear to the mind of the contemplator, but from the eternal and infinite reasons in which they causally subsist. They are in the monad, and so they are infinite in the monad, from which every infinite series of numbers proceeds and in which it ends. If unity, called *monad* in Greek, is the beginning, middle, and end of all numbers—for they proceed from it, move through it, make their way toward it, and end in it—and every wise man is quite sure that that is so, then the unity from which numbers proceed and through which they move will be the same as the one toward which they make their way and in which they end; for it is beginning, middle, and end. Thus numbers, proceeding from their beginning, proceed from no other source than their end; for one and the same unity is their beginning and end. The necessary conclusion is that, if they extend toward an infinite end, they begin the extension from an infinite beginning. Moreover, the same unity is the infinite end of all numbers; it is therefore also the infinite beginning of all numbers. If all numbers subsist eternally and independently[32] in their beginning, they must subsist eternally and independently in their end. In addition, just as there will be no end without things terminating in it, so there will be no beginning without things setting out from it by the act and operation of intelligence. All numbers, then, subsist eternally in the monad; and when they flow from it, they do not cease to be in it since they cannot abandon their natural state. If they are multiplied or completely reduced, they come from it and return to it according to the rules of the discipline which oversees their reasons. But if such is the case, only a shameless man will deny that numbers subsist eternally in unity through their reasons. Whoever examines the matter attentively, moreover, will have no doubt that the reasons themselves are everlasting.

T: I perceive that you are well versed in the art of arithmetic. Everything that you have said about it so far is declared and confirmed by true reason to be exactly right. But to strengthen your point about the eternity of numbers in the monad, give a brief and clear explanation of their reasons, which, as you state, are eternal and unchangeable.

S: The first progression of numbers is from the monad, and the beginning of multiplication is the dyad, i.e., two; the second is the triad, three; and the third the tetrad, four; and then all the terms established within their places. Two is the origin of all evenness which occurs to the intellect, and three of the oddness. From these two, I mean evenness and oddness, all kinds of numbers, whether simple or compound, are generated. The simple are even and odd; the compound, established by these two, are the evenly even, the evenly odd, and the oddly even. Do you see how impossible it is for this order of numerical progression to be brought about differently or to move some other way? No other number established by natural order except two holds the place of first procession from unity; nor of second procession except three; nor of third procession except four. Each number has its natural position which no number beside itself, to which that place belongs, is allowed to occupy. In unity itself, however, all numbers are together and none precedes or follows another since they are all one. Yet they would not unchangeably possess the natural order in which they are contained in their multiples unless their eternally changeless cause in unity had precedence. We must have a similar understanding about doubles, the first of which is two; and triples, of which three comes first; and quadruples, which begin from four; and all kinds of multiples. Each of them starts from its own beginning and extends to infinity. The relationship of double, triple, quadruple, or any other such relationships are not understood specifically and distinctly in unity, since in it all multiples are together and are one, and a one that is multiple and simple; simple in nature, multiple in the reasons according to which they receive their changeless order in multiplication. What shall I say about the remarkable, even divine, arrangement and relationship of numbers as improper fractions,[33] which the species receive singly from unity? What about the proportions which we observe in ratios and in the differences of terms, in which there is the constancy of ineffable, divine power, so that no one penetrating the secrets of wisdom maintains that they are not eternal? Moreover, if that definition of truth is correct which states that truth is what always remains, and if what always remains is eternal, then the reasons of numbers are true because they remain always and unchangeably and hence are eternal. Anyone who wants to be well informed on these matters should read carefully the books *On Mathematics* of the great Boethius. Now hear a similar, very brief argument about the eternity of numbers in their beginning, i.e., the monad. If unity is unity of numbers, then unity never was without numbers, of which it is the unity. Likewise, numbers flow from the monad as from an unexhausted fountain, and they end in it however much they are multiplied; but they would not flow from it unless, before their flowing, they subsisted in it causally; nor would they seek to end in it unless they recognized by a natural motion that their causes eternally remain in it. They never cease to return to these causes by the same steps by which they had flowed from it according to the rules of analytics by which all inequality is called back to equality. Everyone interested in a remarkable investigation of such natures will find the rules of analytics at the beginning of the great Boethius' second treatise *On Mathematics.*[34]

Perhaps someone will say, moreover, that the unity of numbers and the fact that numbers themselves are together inseparably (since they are appropriately reckoned among things which are together inseparably) must rather be admitted than denied; but that one must not, on that account, believe or understand that they are eternal and lack a beginning. Many things begin together to have being but are not therefore compelled to subsist together eternally. E.g., matter and form, voice and word begin together and stop together, but are not eternal; for if they were, they would neither begin nor stop. And the same point holds for many things of the kind. To such an argument we must answer that the number six is not separated from unity and from the multiplicity of other numbers, especially since it alone in the cardinal numbers, i.e., in the first series of numbers from one to ten, is perfect. It is made up of its parts, i.e., a sixth, a third, and a half. A sixth of it is one, a third two, and a half three, which, when put together, make up the quantity of six; for $1 + 2 + 3 = 6$. There is another way, too, which remarkably communicates the perfection of the number six, which completes the first series of numbers by its parts set in order. One, a sixth of it, holds the first place among numbers; two, a third of it, holds the second place; three, a half of it, holds the third place; $3 + 1$, a half plus a sixth of it, hold fourth place; $3 + 2$, a half plus a third of it, hold fifth place; all its parts together—$1 + 2 + 3$—make up the sixth place, namely itself; the whole $+ \frac{1}{6}$ of it, i.e., $6 + 1$, hold seventh place; the whole plus $\frac{1}{3}$ of it, i.e., $6 + 2$, hold eighth place; the whole $+ \frac{1}{2}$ of it, i.e., $6 + 3$, hold ninth place; and if to them you add one, in which the end of all numbers is established, you fill the quantity of ten. If, then, the perfect number six is established in the unity of numbers, let him take notice who denies its eternity, since in it the Creator of all things completed His works. Here we must note that the number six is not perfect because in it God brought to fulfillment all that He wished to create, but that He created all His works so as to signify perfection by the perfection of the number. It is incredible and implausible, therefore, that this very great and divine exemplar, in which God made His works, had a beginning in time, since in it not only things which have being in time but also times themselves and what subsists beyond times have been established by the Artificer of all. No one of sound mind, then, even if he depends on the evidence of the number six alone, will be in doubt about the eternity of numbers. What is understood about its eternity is to be understood likewise about the perennial nature of others. Of course, it was not only about the number six, but about all numbers in general that it was said: "God made all things in measure number, and weight." [35] But if places and times are reckoned among all things which God has made, necessarily intelligible numbers, established in knowledge alone, precede places and times by the perpetuity of their nature and are counted among things which are at once eternal and made. They are eternal in the monad, but made in their multiples.

T: We have had enough discussion about the eternity of numbers in the monad. It is quite necessary, though, to investigate how, where, and from what source they are made; for by using them as evidence, we are trying to make our point that everything from God is at once eternal and made.

S: I have explained, as far as I can, the eternity of the monad and of all numbers in it. It is your task, however, to explain how, where, and from what source intelligible numbers—i.e., those according to which all things that can be numbered actually are numbered—are made. I speak with awareness that it is easier to inveitgate, find, and argue persuasively about their eternity than about their creation.

T: I see that you have a high opinion of me, since you entrust to me the task of investigating, finding, and arguing persuasively about the more difficult subject. It is my duty to investigate, but the finding belongs only to Him "who lightens what is hidden in the shadows." [36] It is His function, too, to persuade, for He alone can open the sense and the intellect. What good is outer persuasion without inner illumination? What you said a little while ago, that things are eternal in the monad but made in their multiples, I regard as a foretaste of this investigation. If you understood what you said, you are asking superfluously what you already understand. Otherwise, we must take up the question.

[12] *S:* I see completely that numbers can be made only in their multiples, for they are eternal in the monad. But I do not yet see how, where, or from what source they are made; and I therefore ask you to inform me about these matters.

T: We have no doubt that all numbers always have being causally—i.e., potentially—in the monad.

S: To doubt that is a sign of inferior intelligence.

T: You understand also, I believe, that the monad subsists eternally in wisdom and knowledge.

S: If I have any other view, I am far from true recognition of the monad itself.

T: You realize, I presume, that the numbers established potentially in the monad are the same as, not different from, those which actually flow out into the genera and species of intelligible numbers.

S: Yes, they are the same, not different; but they are seen in different aspects.

T: In what way?

S: In the monad they are drawn up potentially, but in the genera and species, actually and functionally.

T: Your answer is correct. Don't you see, then, that the same numbers are eternal where their being is potential and causal, viz., in the monad; but where they are understood actually and functionally, they have been made?

S: You are going too fast. We must begin our reasoning gradually to avoid making any careless or rash assumptions. First we must ask what the force and potentiality of numbers are in the monad, and what their activity and function are in the genera and species.

T: The force, I believe, is the substantial power of things which subsist eternally and unchangeably in the monad. Their potentiality is the inherent possibility by which they can be multiplied into genera and species and become manifest to intellects by definite distinctions of terms, by diversity of quantities, by intervals of differences, and by a remarkable equality and insoluble harmony of ratios and proportions. The activity is the motion of the mind contemplating, in itself and in themselves, the multiplication of numbers proceeding from the monad into different genera and species, before they reach the *phantasiae* of thought—i.e., simply in an incorporeal nature, free from any image, when the pure eye of the intellect considers the numbers themselves above all quantity, quality, places, and times. To give a brief definition, the activity is the motion of the mind observing pure numbers in their own nature without any representation. The function is the motion of the same mind which, in itself, considers pure numbers and, after incorporating them, as it were, in *phantasiae*, entrusts them to memory. There it orders them and deals more easily with their reasons; and when they have been designated by symbols that touch the corporeal senses, it transmits them outward to the awareness of others. Do not interpret me as trying to persuade you that the numbers themselves are multiplied and created by the intellect or reason and not by the Creator, Multiplier, and Orderer of all things. For if numbers first underwent their multiplication by any created intellect, they would not have within them a divine and ineffable changelessness and harmony of their reasons. Therefore intellect must not be considered as creating intelligible numbers because it contemplates them in themselves. We must believe, rather, that they are made in intellects, whether of men or of angels, by the single Creator of all, by whom they have also been eternally stationed in the monad; and that, through the intellect, they descend from it to the awareness of reason. For example, a plan or any kind of natural art, while contained in the inmost recesses of intellectual nature, is all together and a single, simple thing, without parts or divisions, without quantity, quality, place, or time, and altogether free from all accidents, and known scarcely to the intellect alone—for the intellect is not the maker, but the discoverer, of natural arts, but it finds them within, not outside, itself. When that art, however, by an intelligible progression begins to descend into the reason from its secret hiding places, where it is all together in the mind in which it has being, it soon begins to disclose its hidden rules gradually by open divisions and differentiae; but these rules are still quite pure and devoid of any representation. This first procession of the art from knowledge itself, in which it first subsists, through the intellect into the reason is achieved by the activity of the intellect itself. Of course, everything which arrives at reason from the secret recesses of nature approaches through the action of intellect. Then that same art, as though in a second descent, goes from reason to memory and gradually reveals itself more clearly in *phantasiae* as though in certain forms. By a third descent it is next diffused to the corporeal senses where, by sensible symbols, it divulges its power through genera, species, and all its divisions, subdivisions, and distributions. Thus intelligible numbers are so poured out from the monad that in some way they become clear in the mind; next, flowing out from mind to reason, they reveal themselves more openly; soon, rushing down from reason to memory, from the nature of memory itself they receive appearances in *phantasiae*, in which they clearly disclose the powers of their manifold forms to those in search of them; next they enter the senses, and finally figures. Don't you see, then, the three points about which you asked—viz., how, where, and from what source? From what source? From the monad. Where? In the intellect. How? They descend by various steps, first from themselves into intellect, from intellect into reason, from reason into memory, from memory into corporeal senses: and, if it is necessary for the benefit of students, in their last step from the senses to visible figures.

S: I see it plainly and very clearly.

T: You are well aware then, I believe, that numbers are both eternal and made. They are eternal in the monad, but made in many forms in their steps of descent. First they are made in the intellect of those who contemplate them in themselves. This method of making is far removed from the senses; for the numbers are said to be made in the awareness of those who understand them. While they are in the monad, by their ineffable unity they surpass every intellect except the divine, which nothing anywhere eludes. It Itself is the Intellect of all things—or rather, It *is* all things. We are not now dealing with that Monad which is sole Cause and Creator of all things visible and invisible, but with that created monad in which all numbers always subsist causally, uniformly, and according to their reasons, and from which they emerge in many forms. Secondly they are made in the reason, where they are said to be made because they reveal themselves more openly there. Yet they are still by themselves, without any coloring of *phantasiae.* Next they are produced in memory and senses in certain *phantasiae.* The *phantasiae* themselves are taken either from the nature of memory—i.e., from the part of the soul assigned to the formation of images—or, through the external senses, from without from the surface of bodies. Those which come from without are properly called *phantasiae,* but those from memory *phantasmata.* A *phantasia* is an image which I fix in my memory when I have taken it by the sense of sight from some body, color, or space which I have seen. A *phantasma* is an image which I shape from something that I have never seen. The latter is rightly termed a false image since the object of my thought either has no being at all or, if it does, is different from the way that I imagine it. Here we should observe, if we follow St. Augustine, that a *phantasma* arises only from a *phantasia.* As he says, it is the image of an image—i.e., an image born from another image. E.g., I have the *phantasia* of the sun which rises daily, and I have received this *phantasia* from the appearance of the circular body itself. Next, according to the likeness of that *phantasia,* I fashion in my memory a thousand images of the sun, greater or smaller, as my thought determines; and so they are false because they are not an imitation of anything real. The Greeks have another understanding of the word *phantasma.* They say that it is the awareness in the mind of sensible natures, an awareness received through their *phantasiae.*

S: I believe that you are stating, then, that numbers made in two ways are eternally stationed in the monad. They are either made pure in themselves, appearing free from any representation, in the mind, in reason alone, and in the simple intelligence; or in the memory and the corporeal sense when embodied in some representations and, as it were, made from and in some matter.

T: That is correct, but your addition "made from and in some matter" does not show clear enough perception. *Phantasiae,* which receive the capacity from memory or the sensible to appear in the memory or sense, are not made from any matter, but are incorporeal and derived from the incorporeal. They are not made from the matter of corporeal things, but from their likeness, which is undoubtedly incorporeal, and from colors, which are not bodies but are understood in reference to (*circa*) bodies. Hence nothing is more fitting and natural than that intelligible numbers should show their power in things that are incorporeal and taken from the incorporeal; and that in some ineffable way they should, when made, proceed into sensible generation. After perceiving the reasons of things, anyone would be justified in saying that the *phantasiae* themselves, in which numbers reveal themselves to the inner eyes of counters, come simply from intelligible numbers. For if there is a vast number of sensible forms in which matter is contained so as to be perceptible to the senses (for it is invisible in itself and derives its origin in forms from intelligible numbers) and if, from that vast number of forms, memory is conformed to *phantasiae* through the corporeal senses, then we must inevitably understand that intelligible numbers flow from the monad in a twofold way and, when made in the memory by the mind's eye, are multiplied, divided, compared, collected, and united. Either, as we said before, they descend through the intellect into the reason, and from the reason into the memory; or, through the likenesses (*species*) of visible things they flow together into the bodily senses, and again from them into the memory in which, when they receive the forms of *phantasiae*, they are made and become subject to the inner senses. So however numbers allow themselves to be perceived, they are themselves the only source from which they grasp the occasion of their appearance. They are eternal, therefore, both in the monad and by themselves in whatever part of nature they appear as made—i.e., in the intellect or in the reason without any representations; or in the memory formed from the likenesses of sensible things when, as though made, they make from themselves certain *phantasiae* in which they may appear.

S: We have dealt sufficiently with numbers, for from these arguments we have reached a conclusion and a clear understanding about where they are eternal, and where and how they undergo creation, so that we correctly perceive that they are both eternal and made. But I am waiting eagerly to learn the point of this proof; for the subject was brought up not for its own sake, but to make something else more plausible.

T: I am surprised that you have forgotten your own words so quickly. A little while ago you asked me for natural examples by which I could introduce you to an understanding of the matters which we were discussing—i.e., how everything from God is at once eternal and made; and especially how God Himself is both the Maker of everything and made in everything. That is the sum and substance of our whole present course of reasoning.

S: Now I am recovering myself. As happens to many persons, I was dumbfounded by the difficulty of the subject and by speculation about matters still unknown to me; and so I was lifted outside myself. What neophyte or person who had not yet scaled the loftiest height of wisdom would not suffer a mental lapse when reflecting about such things and hearing about the eternal creation of all numbers in the monad by the Creator? and of their procession into genera and species, in which they are said to be made, since in them they allow themselves to be understood by intellects; then of their virtual second generation in rational nature, for they more obviously increase their powers there; and next of how they are, in some way, made not from some other matter, but from themselves when, in the memory and the senses, they receive *phantasiae*, or rather theophanies; for we can be sure that anything from the nature of things formed in the memory has its occasions in God. But now I am awakened, so to speak, and, returning to myself and so, perceiving the ray of the inner light more clearly, I am beginning to recognize what you have said. You are trying to convince me, I think, that all numbers, streaming from the monad as from a source, flow out like two rivers rising from a single vein of earth; and that they are separated into two channels, one of which runs through the inner passages of nature (i.e., the intellect and reason), the other through the external species of visible things and through the senses, until they flow together into the memory, in which they are formed in many ways.

[13]   But I do not see very well how things that are incorporeal and, because of the supernal excellence of their nature, removed not only from the senses but even from memory and all representation—I do not see, I say, how such things can appear in the memory or senses—i.e., in images and visible figures as though in bodies.

T: By this single example I realize that you understand the whole matter. Just as you said, numbers flow out from the monad and stream together into the memory. But listen to my opinion about the point which you do not see clearly enough. The nature of spiritual things is not so subject to the contemplation of the mind that we may give an account, in individual cases, about what is brought about concerning it, in it, or through it. Many things customarily appear in it, brought about in a remarkable and ineffable way not according to its laws, known or unknown, but beyond all law by divine will, which is limited by no law, for it is the law of laws and the reason of reasons. For example, who, if questioned, can give an account of how Moses appeared visibly when the apostles were carried away to the mountain (i.e., the height) of spiritual vision when the Lord's Transfiguration occurred? [37] Surely we must not listen to those who think that He arose for the time in the flesh so as to appear visibly on the mountain with Elijah, not in soul but in body, and that He returned again to the grave. Who is to say how an incorporeal and invisible soul was seen by the invisible spirits of the apostles as though in the body, although He appeared neither in His body nor in any matter sensible or taken from another source; but by some ineffable power known only to God His invisible spirit was made visible in itself? What are you to say about how the soul of the prophet Samuel, as though visible while invisible, spoke with Saul? [38] He too, carried off in spirit like the apostles, saw such sights. Of course, we must not believe those who say that not he but some wraith in his likeness appeared. They judge it unfitting for a holy soul to be recalled from the depths by the incantations of a sorceress, for they do not note that Divine Providence governs the universe as much by unclean as by clean spirits. It is certain, moreover, that Samuel's soul visibly in itself, as it were, and not in the flesh or in any likeness prophesied to the soul of the king who was consulting it.

If this seems incredible or doubtful to anyone, let him read St. Augustine in the book *On the Care of the Dead* (18). But let us return to some very clear examples of nature, against which no true philosopher contends.
S: Tell me, please, what they are.

[14] *T:* Wise men say that the forms of things are incorporeal. They express the same opinion about colors, declaring that true reasoning shows them to be incorporeal.
S: Whoever is in doubt on that point has no place among philosophers.

T: If forms and colors are reckoned, then, among the number of incorporeal things, tell me, if you can, in what way they are subject to the corporeal senses. For everything sensed by the eyes can be sensed only in a form endowed with color.
S: I think that forms and colors cannot appear by themselves, but in some matter subject to them.

T: I am surprised that you are so far off the track of philosophy.
S: At what point?

T: Don't you realize that you went astray in saying that forms and colors in themselves can be subject to the senses only in some matter, although matter itself, devoid of form and color, is wholly invisible and incorporeal? You must therefore give an account of how forms and colors, although of incorporeal nature, can be subject to the senses in matter which is incorporeal when considered by itself, i.e., without form and color. It would therefore be more reasonable to say that formless matter becomes sensibly apparent in colors and forms than that forms and colors do so in matter.

S: I don't deny that I went astray, because I was deceived by the habit of false reasoning. Now I am thoroughly at a loss about what I should do.

T: Do you recall what conclusion we reached about matter in the first book, where we argued that it is made by the coming together of intelligibles? Quantities and qualities, indeed, though incorporeal in themselves, produce formless matter when they come together. This matter, with incorporeal forms and colors added, is changed into various bodies.

S: I certainly do recall.

T: And so bodies are born from incorporeal things.

S: I can't deny it, since that is the deduction from our former reasoning.

T: Bodies, then, are made not from nothing but from something. No one would say, of course, that their occasions—viz., quantities and qualities, forms or species, colors, intervals of length, width, and height and, together with these, places and times—are nothing. If you take them away, there will be no bodies; if you add them, bodies are soon produced, whether universal ones such as the four largest bodies of the world or particular bodies assigned to individuals. You will not deny, I believe, that they are all compounded of the four simple elements since they are resolved into them.

S: No, I shall not deny it; but I should say that those elements, simple in themselves, which produce all bodies when compounded, have been made from nothing.

T: What will you say, then, about the primordial causes, about which we have had a great deal to say? We must ask why they are called *causes* if they do not proceed into their effects. Of course, if all bodies come from elements and the elements from nothing, then their cause will seem to be nothing rather than the primordial causes which God the Father made in His Word. If that is so, then nothing will not be nothing, but it will be a cause. But if it is a cause, it will be better than the things of which it is the cause. The necessary consequence will be that either the Word of God, in which the Father made all things, is nothing—and to say "nothing" in the privative sense is impious, for the negation of the Word is found in theology because of the excellence of Its nature, not because of privation of substance—or some cause outside the Word and called *nothing* will be posited, from which God has made everything and in which He stationed everything before it was made. Otherwise there is no cause. And if that is so, I do not see why it is called *nothing*. I should have said that it is everything rather than nothing; for in a cause everything of which it is the cause subsists causally and primordially.

S: I must confess that the four elements of this world subsist in the primordial causes. They are not merely the causes of certain things, but universally of all things visible and invisible; and nothing in the order of all natural things is perceived by sense, reason, or intellect except what proceeds from them and subsists causally in them.

T: Your understanding is sound. You will not deny then, I believe, that all compound and destructible bodies, which hold the last place in the universe, come from something, not from nothing.

S: I shall not deny it. They are produced from the qualities and quantitites of bodies which are simple, invisible, and beyond the grasp of the senses. These bodies are called *elements* because from their coming together, as investigators of natures say, all bodies are compounded; and all bodies are resolved into them and conserved in them. They are usually called *universal* since the particular bodies of individuals are made from them. I admit also that the elements are not made from nothing, but proceed from primordial causes. That these primordial causes were made at once and together in God's Word, none of the faithful doubts; for he hears the prophet saying to God: "You have made everything in wisdom;" [39] and he looks at the beginning of sacred Scripture, where it is written, "In the beginning God created heaven and earth." [40]

T: We must still inquire whether the primordial causes themselves were made from nothing in God's Word, or whether they were always in It. If they were always in It, there was no time when they had no being, just as there was no time when the Word, in which they were, had no being. And if they were always in the Word, how were they made in It from nothing? For surely it is not consistent with reason for what always had being to have begun to be made from nothing. If anyone should say that that nothing from which they were made always had being and that they were always made from it, he will be asked where that nothing always was. Was it in God's Word, in which all things subsist, or by itself outside the Word? If he answers, "It was always in the Word," the opposing argument will be offered that it was not, then, nothing, but something great; for everything that subsists in God's Word, subsists truly and naturally; and what was considered nothing and the source from which everything is believed to have been made, is reckoned in the order of primordial causes. On the other hand, if he expresses the view that the *nothing* is by itself outside the Word, he will be judged as fashioning, like a Manichaean, two opposing principles. Of course, many of the secular philosophers have thought that formless matter is coeternal with God, and that He created all His works from it. They called this matter *nothing* because, before it received forms and species from God, it did not appear in anything and was, as it were, complete nothingness. In fact, it is not unjustifiable to give the name of *nothing* to whatever is wholly lacking in form and species. But the light of truth banished all these delusions by declaring that all things come from a single First Principle, and that nothing is found in the nature of things visible and invisible, by whatever kind of generation it emerges into its own species, which is not stationed eternally in the only-begotten Word of God, in which all things are one. It also proclaimed that God Himself had not received from outside any matter or cause for the universe founded by Him in His Wisdom (for outside Him there is nothing), and had not found within Himself anything coessential from which He might, in His Wisdom, make whatever He wished to create. [15] No place is assigned to nothing, therefore, either without or within God. And yet He is not vainly believed to have made everything from nothing. Hence the only possible meaning of the statement that all things are created from nothing is that there was a time when all things had no being. It is therefore not incongruous when we say, "They always had being; they did not always have being. There was no time when they had no being; there was a time when they had no being." They always had being in God's Word causally and potentially beyond all places and times, beyond all generation that occurs in place and time, beyond all form and species known by sense and intellect, beyond all quality and quantity and the other accidents by which the substance of every creature is understood to have being although its nature is not known. And yet they did not always have being; for before they flowed by generation into forms and species, places and times, and all the accidents which befall their eternal substance incommunicably stationed in God's Word, they had no being in generation, place, time, or in their proper forms and species, which receive the accidents. Hence it is reasonable to predicate of them that there was no time when they had no being, [they began in time, through generation, to be what they were not; whereas in God's Word they always subsist and have no beginning] since eternity is infinite. And yet there was a time when they were not; for they began in time through generation to be what they were not, i.e., to appear in forms and species. Accordingly, if anyone intently examines the nature of things, no creature will be found subject to senses or intellects of which it cannot be truly said that it always had, has, and will have being; and that it always did not, does not, and will not have being. Of course, that first establishment in God's Wisdom through the primordial causes unchangeably had, has, and will have being. But because that establishment is known only to God and surpasses all sense and intellect of creation as a whole, and its nature cannot be recognized by any intellect yet created, it begins by generation in time to receive quantities and qualities in which, as though cloaked in garments, it can reveal *that* it is but not *what* it is. In a sense, then, it begins to be, not insofar as it subsists in primordial causes, but insofar as it begins to appear from temporal causes. By *temporal causes* I mean qualities, quantities, and the other things accidental to substances in time through generation. It is therefore said that there was a time when these things had no being because they did not always appear in accidents. For the same reason they are now said to be; and they have and will truly always have being insofar as they subsist in their causes. To the extent, however, that they are said to be in their accidents, which come to them from outside, they do not have true or everlasting being. They will be dissolved into the things from which they were taken, in which they truly and always have being, since all substance will be cleansed of all corruptible accidents and freed from everything extraneous to the state of its proper nature. It will be of indestructible simplicity, made beautiful only by natural virtues. Adorned by the gifts of grace in those who are good, by the contemplation of eternal bliss it will be glorified beyond all nature, even its own, and turned into God, made God not by nature but by grace. After considering these reasons, who but a very slow-witted or contentious man would not grant that everything from God is at once eternal and made?

S: You have thoroughly convinced me, but not yet dispelled my whole sense of ambiguity. I see quite unambiguously your point that all things from God are both eternal and made because they are eternal in God's Word. As St. Augustine says, "Existing things were not made in substance, but in time through generation in form, species, and accidents." Since it has been written, "In the beginning God created heaven and earth" and "You made everything in wisdom," [41] I am forced to admit that everything in God's Word is both eternal and made. By *everything* I mean the visible and the invisible, the temporal and the eternal, all the primordial causes with all their effects, with which the order of ages is completed in place and time and this visible world is filled. But how this can conform to reason, I cannot clearly perceive.

T: Do you think that I wanted to show that all things, insofar as they are eternal, are eternal in God's only-begotten Word, but that insofar as they are made, they are made outside the Word? You do not believe, I know, that it conforms with principles of truth for the universe of created nature to be at once eternal and made in the Word.

S: No, I did not think that that was your point. In fact, I don't believe that any true philosopher thinks that part of the universe subsists as eternal in God's Word and that part, outside the Word, is made in time. Sacred Scripture forbids such thoughts when it says in the Psalm: "You have made everything in wisdom;" in *Genesis:* "In the beginning God created heaven and earth;" through the Apostle: "In Him were created all things in heaven and on earth, whether visible or invisible, whether Thrones, Dominations, Sovereignties, or Powers. All were created from Him, through Him, and in Him;" [42] in the Gospel: "All things were made through Him and without Him nothing was made." [43] Reason, too, forbids such a belief. Nothing outside the Word can perish in substance or in accident. Reason proclaims that all things which have and all which do not have being (and I am using the term in reference not to privation but to excellence) are encompassed in the Word and have or do not have being in It. What is taken in by intellect or sense has being, but what surpasses all sense and intellect has no being. That all things in God's Word are at once eternal and made is attested in these words of the theologian John, who draws the eternal and truthful waters of understanding from the heart of Wisdom: "Whatever was made in Him was life." [44] Or someone may follow St. Augustine's punctuation in breaking the sentence down to mean: "What was made in place and time, in Him was life." [45] We must not believe or judge in any way about that expert investigator of truth that he wanted to punctuate the Gospel that way to imply that what was made in place and time was made not in, but outside, the Word; for that same St. Augustine teaches us very clearly that both places and times, along with what was made in them, were made eternally in God's Word. He correctly understood the Apostle who said about the Word: "In Him were created all things in heaven and on earth, whether visible or invisible." [46] Hence if places and times with all things contained in them are in the number of visible, i.e., of sensible things; and if all visible things, according to the Apostle's testimony, were created in the Word; then places, times, and everything in them were created in the Word. Or one may read the previous sentence of the Evangelist simply as others do by saying: *Quod factum est in Ipso* ("What was made in Him"), as if dividing so as to begin another clause with *vita erat* ("was life"). We find many Greek manuscripts punctuated that way to give the meaning that what was made in Him in time and place by generation was eternally life through its reason [*ratio*, principle], i.e., through creation in the primordial causes of all things.

T: You do not doubt, then, that all the causes of everything and all the effects of the causes are eternal in the Word and made; and you do not think that I am trying to show anything else.

S: I have no doubt about the eternity of all things and about their creation in the Word, and I do not think that you are trying to show anything else. My only question is how everything is at once eternal and made in the Word, which is coeternal with the Father. I do not regard it as reasonable for the made to be eternal and the eternal made. In fact, there will seem to be no difference between creation and the eternity of the universe in the Word if eternity is created and creation eternal.

T: I am amazed and deeply disturbed that you are looking for reason in what lacks all reason, or understanding in what surpasses all understanding. Surely you do not believe that the plan of Divine Wisdom can become manifest to intellects, either of men or of angels, when you read that those mystic spirits veil their faces and their feet with their wings, fearing to gaze upon the height of Divine Power over all created nature, and Its depth in the things made through, in, and from It. And yet they do not cease flying upward, for they are always searching, insofar as they can; and raised up by the vehicle, so to speak, of divine grace and by the subtlety of their own nature, they strive to infinity for what is above them. When they fail, however, they reverently hide their faces (i.e., the eye of contemplation), recoiling at the divine radiance; and from the entrance of the incomprehensible mysteries they draw back their feet [their intellectual steps] from their theological quest, to avoid rash, unwary presumption about the Ineffable which surpasses all understanding. The symbols of the purest intellects, between whom and the Word there is no intermediary except the primordial causes of everything, are set by theology before these spiritual creatures. These intellects are afraid to gaze upon the loftiness of Divine Brilliance over everything and of Power diffused in all things and of Wisdom reaching from the highest down, from end to end; i.e., from the beginning of intellectual creation to the lowly worm. They realize that the capacity of their nature is not equal to beholding such things. Why, therefore, do we, who are still weighted down by the flesh, try to give an account about Divine Providence and operation? We must think only of the Divine Will, which performs all works as It wishes, because It is omnipotent; and It implants in all things the natural reasons which are hidden and subject to investigation, because It is the supernatural Reason of all. Nothing is more hidden, nothing more present. It is difficult to determine where It is, but more difficult to determine where It is not. It is an ineffable light always present to all eyes of the intellect, but unknown in nature to any intellect. It is diffused through everything to infinity, made as everything in everything and as nothing in nothing.

When I said that there was no intermediary between those intellects
and the Word, I added "except the causes of all things" lest anyone
think that celestial essences are immediate—i.e., that there is no
intermediary between them and the Cause of everything. For although
they are called *angeli* as though *eggigi*—i.e., "established next to God
Himself" (for *eggis* is Greek for "next to"), yet they must not be
believed to have been so made that their causes were not created in the
Word. Indeed, there is no creature without a prior cause created in the
Word, according to which it is established in order that it may have
being, and is arranged in order that it may have being in beautiful
form, and is guarded, that it may have eternal being, and is made
manifest either to the senses or to the intellects as the basis (*materiam*)
for praising the single Cause from which, in which, through which,
and in relation to which it was created. And so if we believe and, as far
as is granted, behold with the mind's eye all things visible and invisible,
eternal and unbounded by time, and eternity itself, time, places,
spaces, and everything named according to substance and accident, we
must generally state that all things which the whole universe of
creation contains are at once eternal and made in God's only-begotten
Word; and that in them eternity does not precede making, and making
does not precede eternity. Their eternity was created and their
creation is eternal in the dispensation of the Word. All things which
are seen to arise in the order of the ages in times and places through
generation were made eternally at once and together·in God's Word.
For we must not believe that they have just begun to be made at the
time when they are seen arising in the world. They always had being
substantially in God's Word, and their rising and setting in the order
of times and places by generation—i.e., by their taking on of
accidents—always was in God's Word, where things which are to be
have already been made. Divine Wisdom encompasses times, and all
things which arise in time in the nature of things have prior and eternal
subsistence in It. It is Itself the measureless Measure of all things, the
numberless Number, and the Weight (i.e., Order) without weight. It
is Itself time and age; It is past, present, and future. The Greeks call it
Epekeina ["Beyond"] because it creates and circumscribes all times in
Itself, while It is above all times in Its eternity, preceding, encompass-

ing, and limiting all intervals. No one can give an account even about the things which we see produced every year in the course of nature in the order of seasons. Who, for example, in reflection upon the force of seeds and how they burst forth through the numbers of places and times and the various species of animals, shrubs, and grasses, would presume to say why and how it happens or would be able to discern their occasions clearly, and would not at once proclaim that they must all be assigned to divine laws which surpass all sense and intellect? And one should not conjecture why and how things are this way and not obliged to fill the order of times another way; and why, though from invisible causes once established in the force of seeds, they proceed into sensible forms not at once but at intervals of times and places. One should not conjecture, I say, as though they could not be made otherwise if that seemed best to the Divine Will, which is bound by no law. Often, in fact, many things happen contrary to the usual course of nature to show us that Divine Providence can govern all things not only in one way, but in infinitely many. If, then, the government of the universe by divine laws is not known to any intellect, by what rational or intellectual creature can the eternal creation of that same universe in God's Word be clearly seen? But none of the faithful should be unaware that all things are at once eternal and made in God's Word, even though he does not understand how the eternal are made and the made are eternal; for this is known only to the Word, in which they are both made and eternal.

S: I am not seeking a rational explanation about the creation of the universe in the Word and about its eternity. No one can say how the eternal have also been made. No rational or intellectual creature can know the way that things were created in the Word, for that is revealed only to the power of true knowledge (*gnosticae virtuti*). I am asking, rather, whether we can find out why we must admit that the eternal have been made in God's Word. We are not dealing now with the multiple effects of the primordial causes in things visible and invisible; for every wise man is certain that everything in those causes has been made. It would seem possible to solve our present question if anyone could show by valid reasoning that all things, insofar as they subsist in their first principles in God's Word, are to be understood as eternal; that insofar as they proceed in the order of times through generation into their effects, whether intelligible or sensible, they are made. Thus their eternity in God's Word would precede their creation in the order of ages, whether they fill the invisible world above us or the world visible to us. But now true reason does not permit us to acknowledge such theories, for it proclaims most truthfully that not only primordial causes but also their effects, places, times, essences, substances (i.e., the most general genera and general species and the most specific species down to individuals with all their natural accidents), and to put it simply, everything in universal creation, whether grasped by the sense or intellect of man or angel or whether it exceeds all sense and all keenness of mind but yet has been created—all, I say, are at once eternal and made in God's Word. They were never eternal and not made, or made and not eternal. The only thing left is to ask not how they are eternal and made, but why they are said to be both made and eternal.

T: The statement about their being made rests on the authority of sacred Scripture which proclaims, to use the same examples: "In the beginning God created heaven and earth;" "You have made everything in wisdom;" "All things were made through Him;" "In Him were created all things in heaven and on earth, whether visible or invisible;" and many passages of this kind. Let him who can speak about the method and reason of the creation of everything in God's Word. I confess that I do not know them. Nor am I ashamed of my ignorance, for I hear these words of the Apostle: "Who alone has immortality and dwells in the inaccessible light," [47] especially as though viewing from afar the end of our present task. For our present course of reasoning—or rather reason itself—will lead us to understand with simple mental insight that not only in God's Word are all things eternal and made, but that He Himself makes everything and is made in everything. As St. Maximus says: "Bringing the intellect through the reasons in existing things to the causal Word, and binding the intellect to It alone since It gathers together and attracts all things from It, and using the reasons through the individual existing things in order, and no longer in confusion, but clearly believing from the careful examination of things with being that only God is properly left as the Essence of existing things, the Motion, the Distinction of the different, the insoluble Binding Force of the mixed, the unchangeable Foundation of what has been placed, and simply the Cause of any essence, however understood, and of motion, difference, mixture, and position . . ." [48]

Hence if only God's Word is left as the Essence of existing things, their Motion, the Distinction of the different, the insoluble Binding Force of the mixed, i.e. of the compounded, and the unchangeable Foundation of what has been placed, i.e., come to a changeless state, and the Cause of any essence, however understood, and of motion, difference, composition, and state, must we not understand that He Himself becomes all things in all things? But how and according to what principle God's Word is made in everything made in Him eludes our mental insight. Nor is that strange, since in sensible things no one can say how the incorporeal force of the seed, bursting out into visible species and forms, into various colors, into different fragrant odors, becomes manifest to the senses and is made in things, although it does not stop being hidden even while it becomes manifest. And whether manifest or hidden, it is never deserted by its natural powers, wholly present in whole things, whole in itself. It neither increases when it seems to be multiplied, nor is diminished when it is thought to be contracted into a small number; but it remains unchangeably in the same state of its nature. For example, it is no smaller in a single grain of wheat than in abundant harvests of the same grain; and, what is even more remarkable, it is no larger in a single whole grain than in a part of the same grain. It is manifold in one and one in the manifold. But if anyone should say that the force of seeds is revealed not by itself but in some matter, i.e., moisture, and that it is made through what appears, but in something that it causes to appear in order that it itself may appear, performing its operations not from itself but from some matter,[49] we must answer with questions. If it appears and is made in form (*species*), is form matter? Clear reason proclaims that whatever remains in matter does so through form since matter by itself is unstable, formless, and virtually nothing. If it appears in colors, is color matter? It is generally agreed that colors are understood in reference to (*circa*) matter, or rather in reference to form. If it appears in sweet odors, is odor matter? Odor is said by those who treat such topics to be the quality of affecting the sense of smell, and quality is incorporeal. We should make similar comments about the other qualities in which the power of seeds usually appears. If, however, all the things that we have mentioned are incorporeal and adhere to bodies but are, in themselves, understood as outside bodies, who but a fool would say that the incorporeal force of seeds needs corporeal matter in order to make itself appear? Of course, if you take away form and all quality and quantity, the power of seeds in bare matter cannot be brought into being or felt in any way. But if the matter itself in which it is thought to appear and act is proved to derive its origin from qualities in corporeal things, may we not conclude that those things in which the force of seeds operates, derive it simply from itself and in itself, i.e., in its natural powers; so that in a marvelous way it is made and makes and is its own matter, operation and operator?

[16] Thus the firm authority of divine Scripture compels us to believe that universal creation was founded in the Word of God, and that the Reason for the actual creation surpasses all intellects and is known only to the Word, in which all things were founded. But if you wish to hear my view about the eternity of the universe in the Word of God, pay close attention to what follows.

S: I am ready.

T: Do you think that the Word of God in which all things were made, made all things which were made in It?

S: Yes, I do. For although the divine operation by which all things were created is regarded by theologians in three ways, according to sacred Scripture—for the Father makes them; they are made in the Son; they are distributed by the Holy Spirit—it is yet one and the same operation of the supreme Holy Trinity. What the Father makes, the Son and the Holy Spirit also make; and what was made in the Son was also made in the Father and the Holy Spirit. Indeed, if the Son is in the Father, everything made in the Son must necessarily be in the Father. It is unreasonable to understand that the Son alone is in the Father, but that what the Father makes in the Son is not in the Father.

Similarly, whatever the Holy Spirit nourishes and distributes is nourished and distributed by the Father and the Son.

T: If, then, the Son makes what is made in Him, are we to believe that He made what He did not see?

S: I think that He saw what He made and what was made in Him.

T: You are correct. Tell me, then, how did He see it? Was it by corporeal sense or by intellect?

S: I should not say that God saw what He made either by sense or by intellect. Of course, He lacks corporeal sense since He is incorporeal. Nor is He properly called Intellect who surpasses all intellect. Yet He is metaphorically called *Intellect*, just as He is called *Mind* by transposition from creation to Creator; since He is the Cause and Creator of intellect and mind as a whole. He does not, therefore, see through creation, whether corporeal or incorporeal, for He needs no creation as an instrument for seeing what He wishes to make. As Maximus says (7): "It is impossible, as reason shows, for Him who is above existing things to apprehend existing things through existing things." [50] But we say that He knows the things which are as His will, and we add reasoning from the cause. If He made everything by His will and no reason opposes, and if it is devout and just to say that God always knows His will, then He voluntarily made every single thing that has been made. Hence God recognizes the things which have being as His wills, since He voluntarily made what has being.

T: Does God see what He has made as He sees His wills?

S: Yes, in the very same way. He does not, as fools declare, see the sensible through sense or the intelligible through intellect, but He sees the sensible and the intelligible as He sees His wills.

T: Your understanding is plain and clear. But tell me, please, whether the divine wills which God sees are different from the things made, which He sees as His wills.

S: I am not fit to give a satisfactory and correct answer to this problem. I am pressed in on all sides. If I say that they are different, you will soon say that God does not then see what He made as His wills, for in things diverse and different in nature, there cannot be produced one simple vision. You will then conclude that divine vision is simple, one, and uniform. Hence, if God's will is one thing and what

He made is something else, He does not see what He has made as His will. But if I say that they are not different, the necessary consequence will be that the will of God is what He has made, and that He has made His wills, and that what He has made are His wills. The single, same, simple divine vision forces everything that it sees to be one and the same thing. Moreover, it sees as its wills whatever It has made. Therefore, the divine wills and what God has made are one and the same thing. The simple divine vision, which sees all things as one and one as all things, unites them. If such a concession were made, I am afraid that you would force me to one of two admissions: either that God's will is separated from God and joined to creation, so that God is one thing and His will something else—i.e., that God is the Maker and His will is made; or, if true reason forbids such a statement, that God and His wills and everything which He has made are one and the same thing. Immediately then the force of argument will lead to the conclusion that God has made Himself if His wills are not outside His nature, and He does not see His wills differently from the way that He sees what He has made, but He sees what He has made as His wills. If that is so, who would be in doubt about the eternity of all things made in God, since they are understood to be not only made and eternal, but also to be God?

T: You are entering upon the path of reason very cautiously and alertly. If you understand clearly and without ambiguity, therefore, that what you have said is so and not otherwise, I see no need of further effort to persuade you about the eternity of everything made in God's Word.

S: You are mocking me, I think, in dealing with me freely—i.e., in allowing my free judgment to choose and to hold on to whatever it wishes; and in not forcing me to deduce by true reasons what must be believed and understood about such matters when all falsehood has been set aside. If I clearly understood by myself what I have said, perhaps I would not be afraid to express an open opinion about whether divine wills are one and the same thing as whatever has been made. I am afraid, though, because I know that I am not qualified to enter upon such an investigation.

T: Approach it gradually then, to avoid making a misstep, and hold steadfastly to whatever you have conceded as true.

S: Go ahead and I shall follow you.

T: Although you are in doubt, I believe, about the will or wills of God or about the ineffable multiplicity of the divine Unity—for God in Himself is a manifold One—that is, about whether or not they belong to the simple nature of the Highest Good, so that they are simply His very self; you do not, on the other hand, think that He lacked His wills.

S: To be in doubt on that point is very stupid. Everything which He has, He has always and unchangeably, since nothing is accidental to Him. Therefore, either He never had His wills or, if He did, there can be no doubt that He always had them.

T: So God always had His wills, and He always saw them; for whatever He had could not elude His notice.

S: He both had them and saw them. Only madmen would think that God lacked His wills or did not always have them or did not see them.

T: Then the divine wills are eternal since He whose wills they are is eternal.

S: I should grant this point completely.

T: Well, then, did He not always have and always see what He wished? You clearly understand, I believe, that nothing is future in reference to God since He encompasses within Himself all times and everything in them. He is, in fact, Beginning, Middle, and End of everything, and Circuit and Course and Backward Course.

S: I have no doubt that nothing is future in reference to God.

T: He therefore always had in His wills what He wished to make; for in Him wishing is not prior to what He wishes to be made, since it is coeternal with His will. He certainly does not anticipate whatever He wishes as though it were yet to be, because all things are present to Him whose will is the Cause of all things, and whose vision brings them about and perfects them. Whatever He sees to be made is made without delay. But if His will is His vision and His vision His will, everything that He wishes to be made is made instantly. But if everything that He wishes to be made and sees should be made is not outside Himself but within, and there is nothing in Him except His very self, it follows that everything that He sees and wishes is understood to be coeternal with Him, if His will and vision and essence are one.

S: Now you are compelling me to admit that everything that is called eternal and made is God. If divine will and divine vision are essential and eternal, and God's being is not different from His wishing and seeing, but one and the very same superessential thing; and if reason does not allow us to understand whatever He embraces within His will and His vision as anything but Himself—for a simple nature does not allow anything alien to be in itself—then we must unconditionally admit that one God is all things in all things. If that is the case, no devout philosopher should be unaware of the eternity of all things which are in God, or rather which *are* God. But I still do not see very well how Divine Nature, outside of which there is nothing and within which all things subsist, allows nothing to be within It that is not coessential with It.

T: You have no doubt, I believe, that no nature subsists except God and creation. In fact, I am quite aware that you see the point. I think that in speaking of Divine Nature outside of which there is nothing, you mean that Creative Nature allows nothing outside Itself because nothing can be outside It; that It contains within Itself the whole of what It has created and creates; and yet that It is one thing Itself, because It is superessential, and what It creates in Itself is something else. Self-creation does not seem to you plausible.

S: You have thoroughly perceived the whole tenor of my thought about God and creation. I firmly and steadfastly maintain that no nature, created or uncreated, subsists or has being in any way outside God; but that everything which subsists, whether created or uncreated, is contained within Him. Hence I held until now that the fullness of the whole universe is contained, as it were, in these two parts, i.e., God and creation. But now my conviction is weakened by our previous arguments and seems to be wavering again.

T: I see that your faith has been made firm and fortified by true reason, at least in believing that there is nothing outside God.

S: You are quite correct, for I see that point very clearly.

T: Focus your mental vision more clearly and sharply, then, on what you believe is inside God.

S: I perceive that there is nothing in God except Himself and the creation established by Him.

T: Then you see in God what is not God.

S: I see it, but it is created from God.

T: What do you think? Did God see all things which He made before they were made?

S: I should judge that He saw all things that He wanted to make before they were made.

T: Then He saw what He wanted to make and He saw only what He made, and He saw what He made before He made it.

S: That is what I maintain.

T: Tell me, please, what are those things which God saw before they were made? How did He see creation which had not yet been made? And if He saw only creation and if everything which has being is either God or creation, what did He see? He must either have seen Himself before He made everything that He made, or He saw creation, which had not yet been created. But how did He see what did not yet exist? If it had being and was seen for that reason, then surely there was, before creation, something which was not creation. If, however, only God and what is coessential with Him is granted as being before all creation, then nothing else which God might see preceded creation before He made creation, except either God Himself or the Eternal Nature in Him which is coeternal with Him. But we concluded that God had seen what was to be made; for He did not make in ignorance or without foresight what He wanted to make.

S: I see that I am hedged in on all sides and that no way of escape is left. If I say that God saw in Himself what was to be made, I am forced to admit that He saw Himself, because there was not yet any creation which He might see, and there was nothing else before all creation except Himself which He could see. Hence if He saw in Himself everything which was to be made before it was made, true reason will necessarily show that He saw Himself, and He Himself will be everything which He made. If He made in Himself the things which He saw, He will be both the Maker and the made. But if I say that He saw the creation to be made before it was made, you will say that then there was a creation before it was made. For if God saw it before it was made, what God saw in it really had substantial being before it was made. Surely God did not see falsehood, because He is changeless Truth, and in that Truth everything is true and changeless. If God saw creation in Himself before it was made, He always saw what He saw. Seeing what He sees is not accidental to Him, since for Him being is the same as seeing because His nature is simple. Moreover, if He always saw what He saw, then what He saw always had being and hence must be eternal. If He saw creation, which did not yet have being, and if what He saw actually had being (for everything that God sees is true and eternal), the only possible conclusion is that creation was in God before it was made in itself. Then we shall arrive at a twofold concept about creation: one regards its eternity in Divine Knowledge, in which everything endures truly and substantially; the other regards its creation in time, as it later existed in itself. In that case, the consequence of our reasoning compels us to choose between calling the same creation either better than itself or worse. It is better insofar as it subsists eternally in God. It is worse insofar as it is created in itself. Then its creation will be judged not in God but as though outside God in itself, and it will be contrary to Scripture, which says, "You have made everything in wisdom." [51] Or else it is not the same nature which was eternally in the Knowledge of God and which later, so to speak, was created in itself. Hence He did not see what was made before it was made, but He saw in Himself only what is eternal. Yet whoever makes such a concession will seem in opposition to the profession of the Catholic faith. Holy wisdom does not profess that God saw some things in Himself before they were made and that He later made other things in themselves; but that the same things were eternally seen and eternally made, and that this whole is in God and nothing is outside Him. Moreover, if the nature of Divine Goodness is one thing and what He saw to be made and actually made was something else, and He saw and made it in Himself, then the simplicity of the Divine Nature will be broken since something other than Itself is understood in It; and that is altogether impossible. But if Divine Goodness is not different from what He saw to be made in Himself, but if there is one and the same Nature whose simplicity is inviolable and whose unity is inseparable, then surely it will be granted that God is Everything everywhere, Whole in the whole, Maker and made, Seer and seen, Time and Place, Essence and Substance of all, Accident, and, to put it simply Everything That Truly Is and Is Not, superessential in essences, supersubstantial in substances, Creator above all creation, created within all creation, subsisting below all creation, beginning to be from Himself, moving Himself through Himself, moved toward Himself, resting in Himself, infinitely multiplied in Himself through genera and species, not deserting the simplicity of His nature, and recalling the infinity of His manifoldness to Himself. For in Him all things are one.

T: Now I see that you perceive very clearly what you seemed uncertain about; and I do not think that you will falter any more in admitting that all things are both made and eternal, and that whatever in them is truly understood to subsist is simply the Ineffable Nature of Divine Goodness. It is the substantial Good, and no one is good except God alone. What remains, then, is to deal with the eternal creation of all things in God, insofar as the ray of Divine Truth allows our mental vision to rise to the divine mysteries.

S: You are right, and now the order of our discussion demands it. But first I should like you to summarize briefly all that we have agreed to so far about the question at hand.

T: We have clearly deduced, I believe, that Divine Goodness saw, and always saw, what was to be made.

S: Yes, we have.

T: And It did not see some things and make others, but It made what, as It had always seen, had to be made.

S: Yes, we admitted that too.

T: And It always made everything that It always saw, for in It sight does not precede operation, since operation is coeternal with sight, especially since Its seeing and operating are not different things, but Its sight is Its operation. It sees by operating and operates by seeing.

S: We made this assumption too.

T: In regard to the simplicity of the Divine Nature, we discussed the fact that anything alien and not coessential with It is not truly and properly understood in It, and that everything is truly and properly understood to be within It; for nothing subsists outside It. The conclusion was that It alone truly and properly has being in everything, and that nothing except Itself truly and properly has being.

S: That was our conclusion.

T: We should not therefore understand God and creation as two different things, but as one and the same. For creation subsists in God, and God is created in creation in a remarkable and ineffable way, manifesting Himself and, though invisible, making Himself visible, and though incomprehensible, making Himself comprehensible, and though hidden, revealing Himself, and, though unknown, making Himself known; though lacking form and species, endowing Himself with form and species; though superessential, making Himself essential; though supernatural, making Himself natural; though simple, making Himself compound; though free from accidents, making Himself subject to accidents and an accident; and, though infinite, making Himself finite; though uncircumscribed, making Himself circumscribed; though above time, making Himself temporal; though above place, making Himself local; though creating everything, making Himself created in everything. The Maker of all, made in all, begins to be eternal and, though motionless, moves into everything and becomes all things in all things. Nor am I talking about the incarnation of the Word and Its becoming Man, but about the ineffable condescension of the Highest Good, which is Unity and Trinity, to things with being in order that they may have being or rather that It Itself may be in everything from the highest down, always eternal, always made by Itself in Itself, eternal by Itself, made in Itself; and while It is eternal, It does not cease to be made; and though made, It does not cease to be eternal, and makes Itself from Itself. It has no need of other matter besides Itself, in which It makes Itself. Otherwise It would seem impotent and imperfect in Itself, if It received from another source any assistance toward Its appearance and perfection. From Himself, then, God receives the occasions for His theophanies, i.e., His divine appearances, since "all things are from Him, through

Him, in Him, and directed toward Him." [52] Hence matter itself, from
which, as we read, He made the world, is from Him and in Him and
He is in it insofar as it is understood to have being. Nor is this strange,
since Scriptural examples provide instruction about such matters. The
souls of Moses and Samuel, though invisible and incorporeal by nature,
in order to perform mysteries appeared to the minds of others
(namely, of the Apostles and Saul) not in *phantasiae,* but as really
visible and corporeal. They did not make their appearance in matter
taken from outside, but by themselves and without mediation. What,
then, prevents us, led by such a miracle, from scaling the greater
heights of Divine Power in order to understand that It is both above
everything and made in everything? As we said, it does not receive
from elsewhere or make from nothing the matter in which It is made
and makes Itself manifest.

We have had enough discussion about the power of seeds which,
though invisible and incomprehensible in itself, multiplies itself into
infinite forms and species and is subject to the corporeal senses. When
it is sought, it eludes all the keenness of the mind. Thus no place is
yielded to that nothing—i.e., to the privation of all state and essence
from which those of inferior understanding think that all things have
been made; for they do not know what sacred Theology means by the
term.

Chapters 18–40 (697–742B)

Teacher and Student continue to explore the creation of the
world as God's self-creation. The world is the intelligible and
visible theophany of the unintelligible and invisible Creator.
How God produces Himself in the plurality of things while
remaining eternally beyond them in His indivisible simplicity
is, of course, a mystery. Yet because the visible things of this
world participate in the invisible, some understanding can be
gained from observing the relation of the sun of our visible
world to everything on earth (680 A–B). Without losing its own
nature as simple fire, it embraces the nature of all sensible

things as their cause. Through its light and its warmth it has created all the visible bodies that it surrounds, bringing them to birth and enabling them to live. This hidden power, coursing through the world and animating every being, is the same everywhere, and after its diffusion in all things, it returns to its source.

Though the sun is a useful analogy, the relation of the divine transcendence and otherness to the divine self-creation finds better expression in saying that God is the Nothing from which all things are made (680 C–681 C). By *Nothing* is meant here, of course, God as superessential, that Divine Goodness which is ineffable, incomprehensible, and inaccessible to every human and angelic intelligence. When Goodness begins to appear in its theophanies, it proceeds from nothing into something, and what is beyond every essence is then known in every essence. Every creature, whether visible or invisible, can be called an appearance of the divine.

The first stage of its procession is that of the primordial causes, where it establishes what Scripture calls a "formless matter": *matter,* because it is the beginning of the essence of things and *formless* because it is nearest the formlessness of the divine Wisdom itself, the infinite exemplar of all forms. Thence it descends to become every essence, substance, genus, species, quality, quantity, and relation of the whole universe. Therefore, when the divine Goodness is considered as beyond all thought, it is said not to be, but when it proceeds through the primordial causes, it is all that is in every creature. From the negation of all that is and is not comes the affirmation of all that is and is not. This Nothing is a negation, not a privation. Privation presupposes an essence and a relation to that essence; therefore, it cannot precede essence and relation. The absolute negation of all essence and relation, indeed, the negation of all that is, is necessarily God Himself (686).

Of the four divisions of nature distinguished at the beginning, the first two have now been explored. God, both uncreated and creating, creates Himself in the primordial causes, His created and creating theophanies. We have next to investigate the third division, the divine nature as created but not creating, and its procession from the primordial causes (688A–690B).

This investigation takes the form of an allegorical gloss on the account in Genesis of the six days of creation. As in Book II, "the darkness over the deep" is taken to refer to the primordial causes in their initial state as invisible and simple in the hidden Wisdom of God. God's utterance, "Let there be light", is the sign of their appearance in their visible effects (691–693). It is as if God had commanded that the invisible, inaccessible causes should manifest themselves in forms, genera, and visible creatures. God's division of the light from the darkness represents His separation of the intellect's knowledge of effects from the obscurity in which the causes are hidden from men and angels (692D). Yet the words, "Evening came and morning came: the first day", indicate that there is only one creation, obscure to us in its first state as cause in God's thought but lucid and intelligible as effects when pronounced by His utterance (693A–C).

On the second day, when Scripture recounts the creation of the firmament or vault separating the waters, we are not to understand the literal creation of waters or of a place dividing them. Eriugena consciously departs from earlier interpretations: nothing spatial is intended (693C–695A). "Above the firmament" is the purely spiritual realm of the reasons or primordial causes, while beneath is the corporeal world. Everything "above" is simple and eternal, everything "below" composite and thus subject to generation and corruption. What, then, is the "firmament", the connection between the invisible, spiritual world and the visible and corporeal? There is a third kind of entity participating in both spirit and body that acts as intermediary—the universal elements of earth, air, fire and water. Like their causes among the eternal reasons, these elements are in themselves immutable and simple, exempt from corruption and mixture; but they resemble the visible effects since every corporeal body is generated from their qualities and in turn is resolved again into them (695A). The primordial causes "descend" into the universal elements, and these in turn "descend" into bodies. When the bodies are corrupted, they ascend into the primordial causes through the medium of the elements (696B).

Though bearing the same names, these elements are not the earth, air, fire, and water that we perceive (701B). These four greatest bodies of our visible universe are the results of their mysterious and incomprehensible diffusion and compenetration, and the causes are named after the effects (712). Nor should we suppose that the universal elements produce only the greatest bodies; all four elements, or rather their qualities of hot, cold, wet, and dry, are in varying proportions in all things, whether celestial, aerial, aquatic or terrestrial. While those bodies that we call celestial and ethereal—the sun, moon, and stars—seem to us to be spiritual and incorruptible, they are neither, and the day will come when they too are dissolved and destroyed, to return by means of the universal elements to their sources in the primordial causes (701B, 712). Corporeal bodies, then, are formed by the coming together of incorporeal realities.

A second mode of analysis yields the same result. Every particular body can be analyzed into three intelligible factors: matter, species or qualitative form, and essence or substantial form. Considered in itself, matter is formless, and only when the species is added to it is a body produced that is visible to the senses and undergoes generation and corruption. The substantial form is, as it were, the changeless ground supporting and containing the formed matter. Matter is the principle of mutability in things, the capacity to receive qualitative forms. While the qualitative form, a combination of the accidents of quantity and quality, is sensuously perceptible, the substantial form is known only by the intellect. By participation in the substantial form every individual species is formed. It is wholly in every one of its species. The form of man, for example, is wholly in every human being (701A–703C).

The work of the third day of creation is an allegorical account of the coming to be of the two inferior elements, water and earth. When God said, "Let the waters under heaven come together in a single mass, and let dry land appear," we are to understand by *waters* the material universe of composite beings, while *dry land* symbolizes the stable, imperishable essence or substance that remains unchanged throughout its multiple appearances (701–702). "Let the earth produce vegetation: seed-bearing plants, and fruit trees bearing fruit with their seeds inside, on the earth" means that the nature common to all beings gives rise to the individual distinctions of each—that is, universals produce genera, genera species, and species individuals (704C–715A).

The account of the fourth day, the creation of the sun, moon, and stars, affords Eriugena opportunity not only to consider the two superior elements, air and fire, as the causes of these celestial beings but also to develop his astronomical views at some length. Earlier, when denying that the waters above the firmament are to be understood literally, he had challenged a prevalent theory: those who argue from the paleness of the stars to their entering into a cold and watery sphere are mistaken. A semi-heliocentric theory of planetary motion is proposed in explanation. Jupiter, Mars, Venus, and Mercury revolve around the sun, although the earth is, of course, taken to be the center of the universe. The changing color of the sun's satellites is due to their position in relation to the sun; when they orbit above it, they move in a cold area and are pale; when they are below it, they take on the redness of hot bodies (697–698).

No one, he holds, has given a completely adequate theory of the celestial spheres and the distances between them (715D–716A), but Eratosthenes has measured the earth's circumference as 252,000 stades, which divided by two (sic) yields its diameter. Taking this diameter as the astronomical unit of measure, we find by observation of lunar eclipses that the distance from the earth's surface to the moon's center is one unit, to the sun's center is three units, and to the fixed stars six units. These ratios are also those of the musical scale, and thus the harmony of the spheres is produced. The diameter of the earth represents one tone, so that an octave of seven tones is represented by the space from the earth to the fixed stars, with the addition of the earth's diameter. The radii of the lunar orbit, the solar orbit, and that of the stars are respectively three times, seven times, and thirteen times that of the earth's radius (716C–723B).

Not until the fifth day of creation is life mentioned, a fact that has misled some commentators on Scripture to think that the work of the first four days was devoid of all life. Plato, however, the greatest of the philosophers, recognized a world soul—that is, that the world itself is alive. So too is each individual being in the world, however dead or lifeless it appears to us. Just as matter without species does not make a body, and species cannot subsist without its proper substance, so no substance can exist without a vital motion. Everything that moves naturally is moved by some kind of life (727D–728).

Even when a body undergoes dissolution, life does not desert it entirely. Life or soul is spiritual and nearer in nature to the higher, simple incorporeal universal elements into which the body is dissolved than it is to the corporeality of the body. Thus even when a body returns to its elements, life or soul continues to govern it, though to be sure in a non-corporeal way (732B).

The general life of the world is divided into two classes of rational and irrational creatures, and each class is subdivided into two subclasses. Angels and men form the class of rational living beings, and animals and plants that of the irrational. The kind of life manifested at each level is then examined (732B–742B).

Rational life is displayed in angels and men, and wherever it is found, there is the image of God. Strictly speaking, angelic life is intellectual life, while the term 'rational' is reserved for human beings. Although intellectual life is superior to rational, there is a most important sense in which man's nature entitles him to a more exalted role in creation than that of the angels. Anticipating the thorough examination of man's unique nature in Book IV, the Teacher describes him as a microcosm: understanding like an angel, reasoning like a man, sensing like an animal, and living like a plant. Such a claim cannot be made for angels; as pure intelligences they lack bodily sensation and a fortiori the senseless life of the lowest creatures. Men, however, cannot only sense; the lowest life is evinced in their bones, fingernails, and hair. For this reason, that all things are contained in man, the explicit creation of man is reserved for the last day as a climax (733A–734A).

Below the level of rational life the general life of the world is exhibited in the sentience of animals, then in the life of vegetation. Plants, then, in manifesting a power of life, are ensouled bodies. Even the lowliest body—a stone, for example is not wholly devoid of life, although we cannot discern it. The nature of things demands that this be so, for body is composed of matter and form, and form always participates in the power of life. Every creature, then, is either living in itself or participating in life in some fashion (734–736).

Along with a few tales from Pliny the Elder, illustrating the remarkable talents of animals, the question of the immortality of animals is considered. Eriugena argues that they must be immortal. If a genus were to perish, so must all its constituent species: conversely, if all the species were to perish, the genus would also disappear. If animal is the genus of everything composed of body and soul—for example, man, lion, cow, horse—and all these species are substantially one in it, how could all the species perish and only man remain? The genus would itself be destroyed, for a single species cannot constitute a genus. A genus is a substantial union of many forms and classes, and it cannot subsist if this union is destroyed

(737A–738A). Further, if at death the body of an animal is not annihilated but transformed into the qualities of the four elements, it is inconceivable that the soul, the higher nature, should perish while the lower and less powerful continue to be. The life or soul, therefore, which governs the bodies of animals is not derived from the earth, and through its participation in that common life which had no beginning, it can never be extinguished entirely (738A–B).

Notes

1. *Tim.* 6:16.
2. Matthew 25:24–30.
3. Romans 11:20.
4. Gen. 1:31.
5. James 1:17.
6. Most often in this translation *virtus* is rendered as *power*, except where the meaning *virtue* seems indicated by the context, as in the third kind mentioned here in the text.
7. John 5:17.
8. Gen. 1:1.
9. Acts 17:28.
10. Augustine, *De Genesi ad Litteram* 2.6, ed. Zycha (*C.S.E.L.* 28, Pt. 1).
11. *On Divine Names* 13.2.
12. *Ibid.* 13.3.
13. John 1:3.
14. John 1:13–4.
15. Colos. 1:16.
16. John 14:24.
17. Psalm 147:15.
18. *On Divine Names* 13.1.
19. *On the Celestial Hierarchy* 4.1.
20. *Epistle* 9.3 [Migne *P.G.* 1109B–C].
21. *On Divine Names* 4.13.
22. The *mansura* is simply a printing error for *mensura*, as the text of Pseudo-Dion. and John the Scot's translation of the text (col. 1125A Migne: *mensura*) show. (Cf. The Greek:

23. On Divine Names 2.10.
24. Wisdom 11:18.
25. Psalm 102:25–27.
26. Matthew 24:35.
27. 1 Chronicles 14.7.

28. Job 38:37.
29. Ecclesiastes 1:4.
30. Revelation 21:1.
31. Wisdom 11:21.
32. The Latin word is *incommunicabiliter*, "incommunicably", i.e., "without sharing in one another."
33. The text refers to four kinds of numbers:
  1. the *superparticularis*, in which the larger number contains the smaller + 1 part of it, as $\frac{3}{2}$, $\frac{4}{3}$, $\frac{5}{4}$, etc.
  2. the *superpartiens*, in which the larger number contains the whole of the lesser number plus 2 or more parts of it.
  3. the *multiplex superparticularis*, in which the larger number contains a multiple of the lesser number + 1 part of it, as $\frac{5}{2}$, $\frac{7}{4}$, etc.
  4. the *multiplex superpartiens*, in which the larger number contains a multiple of the lesser number + 2 or more parts of it.
34. *De. Inst. Arith.* 2.1.
35. Wisdom 11:21.
36. 1 Cor. 4:5.
37. Matthew 17:3; Mark 9:3; Luke 9:30.
38. 1 Samuel 28:7–19.
39. Psalm 104:24.
40. Gen. 1:1.
41. Psalm 104:24.
42. Colos. 1:16.
43. John 1:3.
44. John 1:4.
45. *In Joan. Ev.*, Tract I, 16.
46. Colos. 1:16.
47. 1 Tim. 6:16.
48. Amb. 10,19.
49. There are textual problems in this passage.
50. This version follows the reading of A, the *Editio Princeps*, which corresponds to John the Scot's translation of Maximus (col. 1207A).
51. Psalm 104:24.
52. Romans 11:36.

Book IV

[1] *T:* The first point and the main topic of our discourse on nature was that *hyperousiotes,* i.e., Superessential Nature, is the creative Cause of all things existing and not existing, that It is created by none, that It is the one Beginning, the one Starting Point, the one and universal Source of all, derived from none but from which all are derived, the Trinity coessential in three Substances, without beginning (*anarchos*), the Beginning and End, the single Goodness, the one God, *homoousios* and *hyperousios,* i.e., coessential and superessential. As St. Epiphanius, Bishop of Constantia in Cyprus, says in his sermon *Ancoratus,* "On Faith": "Three holy things, three jointly holy, three acting, three acting together, three forming, three conforming, three operating, three co-operating, three subsisting, three subsisting together, coexisting with one another. This is called the Holy Trinity, three things existing, one harmony, one Deity of the same essence, power, and subsistence, like in like ways. They put into operation the equality of grace of the Father, the Son, and the Holy Spirit. But in what manner They have being it is left for Them to teach; for no one

knows the Father except the Son, or the Son except the Father and any to whom the Son has revealed Himself; and He is revealed through the Holy Spirit. These three existing things, then, are not worthily understood in anything as existing from it, through it, or in relation to it as *phos, pyr, pneuma*—i.e., light, fire, and breath—reveal them." As I have said, these words have been handed down by Epiphanius so that anyone, if asked what Three and what One he should believe to be in the Holy Trinity, may reply with sound faith, or approaching faith, may be so instructed. I believe that he put *breath* ("spirit") for *heat,* as though he had said in a simile, "light," "fire," and "heat." But it is no wonder that he mentioned light first. The Father is light, fire, and heat; the Son is light, fire, and heat; and the Holy Spirit is light, fire, and heat. The Father enlightens, the Son enlightens, the Holy Spirit enlightens; for from Them all knowledge and wisdom are given. The Father burns, the Son burns, the Holy Spirit burns, because They consume our sins together and by *theosis,* i.e., "deification", They convert us, as though we were a holocaust, into Their Unity. The Father heats, the Son heats, the Holy Spirit heats because with one and the same surging tide of love They foster and nourish us and, as though from the deformity of our imperfection after the fall of the first man, They bring us up to be the perfect man, and train us for the fullness of Christ's time. Moreover, the perfect man is Christ, in whom all things have been fulfilled, and the fullness of whose time is the fulfillment of the universal salvation of the Church, which is composed of angels and men.

In the second book we discussed nature which is created and creates, and we said that it subsists in the beginnings of things, i.e., in the primordial causes. It is created by the One Cause of all, which is the Highest Good, whose property it is to lead all things from non-existence to existence by Its ineffable power. It does not cease creating, by participation in Itself, the other things which come after It. The third book discusses nature which is created but does not create, i.e., the last effects of the primordial causes, which hold the outermost share of all things. The motion of progressions of the universe ends in them, since it has nowhere lower to go because it is established in bodies. In this book we also considered many points about the primordial causes; and about God and His image in the mind, reason, and sense; and about the quality of the nothing from which everything was made; and how the only-begotten Word of God both makes everything and is made in everything. We also dealt briefly with the works of the first intelligible week until the sixth day.

[2] Let this fourth book, which begins from the works of the sixth prophetic contemplation about the creation of the universe and will consider the return of everything to that Nature which neither creates nor is created, mark the end. The difficulty of this task and the confrontation and struggle of different senses strikes such terror into us that, compared with it, the three preceding books seem to offer a safe course to readers who are like sailors coasting in a smooth sea, navigable with calm waves and without danger of shipwreck. This book, however, is impassable because of its sinuous bends, steep with the obliquity of its statements, dangerous with the expanses of the Syrtes, i.e., the guidance of unfamiliar learning of most subtle intellects, like hidden rocks which suddenly shatter ships, exposed to shipwreck because of fogginess, and extending to the fifth book as its prolixity necessitates. But under the guidance and helm of Divine Mercy, with the favorable breath of the Holy Spirit filling the canvas of our ship, we shall make a safe, straight course among these dangers and, free and unscathed, shall arrive by a gentle course at the harbor toward which we are making.

S: We must spread our sails and set out, for reason, well acquainted with this sea, hastens us on. It does not fear any threats of waves or bends or Syrtes or rocks. It takes greater delight in exercising its power in the hidden waters of the divine ocean than in resting at ease in smooth and open waters, where it cannot reveal its force. It (reason) was bidden "with sweat on its brow to eat its bread," [1] i.e., the word of God, and to cultivate the ground of sacred Scripture, which produces thorns and thistles, i.e., the thin density of divine intellects; and with the constant steps of speculation to track the land which is impassable to those who scorn zeal for wisdom, "until it finds a place for the Lord, a tabernacle for the God of Jacob" [2]—i.e., until, with the guidance, help, and co-operation of frequent and laborious study of God's words, and with divine grace advancing it toward this goal, turning back it may arrive, arriving it may love, loving it may remain, remaining it may rest in the contemplation of Truth, which it had lost by the fall of the first man.

[3]   *T:*   God also said, "Let the earth produce every kind of living soul: cattle, reptiles, and every kind of wild beast," etc. He said "Let the earth produce a living soul" as if He were openly saying, "Let the earth produce a living animal." That trope, which is called *synekdoche* (i.e., *conceptio*), is very widely used in Biblical speech. It is the form of speech which takes the whole from a part and a part from the whole. Thus sacred Scripture usually designates the whole animal merely by the term *soul.* In the *Acts of the Apostles* it says: "We were in all two hundred and seventy-six souls on board that ship;" [3] but of course the souls were not without the bodies. Likewise in *Genesis:* "All the souls of the house of Jacob who entered Egypt were seventy." [4] In the Gospel the whole man is designated by the flesh: "The Word was made flesh," [5] i.e., the Word was made the whole Man, consisting of flesh, soul, and mind. Elsewhere too in the passage "The spirit is willing, but the flesh is weak," [6] by the term *flesh* He signifies His whole human nature, but by *spirit* He means the Holy Spirit which is ready and strengthens Itself for the redemption of mankind by the trial of the passion. This Spirit, when fixed to the cross, He committed to the Father by saying, "Father, into Your hands I commit My Spirit." [7] It is as if He had said, "Into Your hands I commit the Spirit which proceeds from You and from Me, since It is not subject to suffering, while I alone suffer in the flesh; for I alone took on flesh and was made flesh. Not that He Himself is subject to suffering in His divinity, but the capacity for suffering and the suffering and the death of human nature, which He alone had taken on, fall to Him and He suffered with the human nature which He had taken into the unity of His substance. Since, then, He is deservedly said to have suffered with it [i.e., His human nature], He is correctly said to have suffered. In the Passion, the single substance of Word and Man was not separated. To

help you understand this point better when it is corroborated by authority, listen to Epiphanius in his sermon "On Faith" (92,5–94,1) "Once He died for us, enduring to suffer for our sufferings; once He tasted death, death even to the cross. The Word willingly entered upon death for us, that He might destroy death. The Word was made flesh, not suffering in Godhead, but suffering with His human nature in His unsusceptibility to suffering. The suffering was attributed to Him, moreover, although He remained unsusceptible to suffering. Death was ascribed to Him, but He remained immortal. For He said, 'I am Life.' [8] Life, moreover, never dies; but He came to produce life by accepting death for us. We did not have life through man or hope through flesh. He said, 'Accursed is he who hopes in man;' and 'Whoever hopes in man will be like the tamarisk of the field.' Shall we infer from these words that Christ was not man? It is clear to everyone that we unambiguously acknowledge the Lord God, the Word, made Man, not according to opinion but in very truth. But the Man did not come for the advantage of Godhead. In man we had no hope of salvation, for no man from Adam on could produce salvation. But God the Word was made Man that our hope might be not in man but in the true and living God made Man. Every priest accepted from among men is established for men, as it has been written. Hence the Lord came and received flesh from our human nature, and God the Word was made Man for us, that salvation might be granted to us in Godhead and that, in His humanity, He might suffer for us men, paying for suffering by suffering, and putting death to death by His death. Moreover, suffering was attributed to Godhead even though Godhead did not suffer; and suffering was ascribed to Godhead because that was the will of the Holy Word, exempt from suffering, that came to us. An analogous example would be the case of a man clad in a garment, if some blood were sprinkled and defiled the garment without touching his body. Yet the pollution of the blood on the garment would be ascribed to the man wearing the garment. So Christ suffered in the flesh, that is in the God-Man. So coming from heaven, the holy God Himself reformed the Word into Himself. As the blessed Peter says, 'In the flesh He was put to death, but in the spirit He was raised to life;' [9] and elsewhere 'Christ suffered for us in the flesh, and we should arm ourselves with the same resolve.' [10] Thus as the blood on the garment is ascribed to the wearer, so the suffering of the flesh was ascribed to Godhead, although Godhead did not suffer at all. The purpose was that the world might not have hope in man, but that when the God-Man had taken on Godhead, suffering might be ascribed to It in order that salvation might be brought about for the world from the Godhead which is unsusceptible to suffering; and that when suffering was brought about in the flesh, even though Godhead underwent and sustained no suffering, the suffering might be attributed to It, in fulfillment of the Scriptural passage: 'If they had known, they would never have crucified the Lord of glory.' [11] He was crucified, then, the Lord was crucified, and we adore Him crucified, buried, and rising again on the third day and ascending to heaven."

That you may recognize, moreover, that the passage "Father, into Your hands I commit my spirit" refers specifically to the Holy Spirit, hear Epiphanius in the same work (69,7–8): " 'If you hear that, raised to the heights by God's right hand and receiving from the Father the Holy Spirit who was promised . . . ;' [12] or 'to wait for the promise of My Father, which you have heard;' [13] or 'The Spirit sent Him into the desert;' [14] or, in His own words, 'Do not think of what you are to say . . . because it is the Spirit of My Father who speaks in you;' [15] or 'But if I cast out devils, it is through the Spirit of God;' [16] or 'He who blasphemes against the Holy Spirit will not be forgiven;' [17] or 'Father, into Your hands I commit My spirit;' [18] or 'Meanwhile the child grew up and His spirit matured;' [19] or 'Filled with the Holy Spirit, Jesus left the Jordan;' [20] or 'Jesus, with the power of the Spirit in Him, returned;' [21] or 'What is born of the Spirit is spirit;' [22] or 'I shall ask the Father, and He will give you another Comforter . . . , the Spirit of Truth;' [23] or ' "Why has Satan filled your heart,' " Peter asked Ananias. ' "You are lying against the Holy Spirit" ' [24] and afterwards, "You have not lied to men, but to God." [25] He is God from God and the Holy Spirit is God." So much from Epiphanius.

S: Although that transition seems to have gone quite far from the topic, it is useful for whoever wishes to understand sacred Scripture. It argued convincingly that the Godhead of the Word is exempt from suffering but suffered with Its human nature. It also proves that when

God said in the Gospel: "The spirit is willing, but the flesh is weak" [26] and "Father, into Your hands I commit My spirit," [27] He was talking specifically about the Holy Spirit. But we should go back to the main argument.

[4] *T:* "Let the earth produce a living soul." I.e., let the earth produce a living animal. See how beautifully, in the trope previously mentioned, he designated the whole from a part, i.e., the whole animal from his better half, namely his soul. And because the lesser half of the whole animal, the body, is taken from the earth, by the same trope the whole animal—i.e., body and soul—is ordered to be produced by the earth, although soul is not earth at all just as body is not soul. But since the soul clings to the body in the unity of the animal's nature, Scripture testifies that it is made at the same time from the earth. If anyone investigates this passage more deeply, however, he can understand it in a different way. By the word *earth,* the unchangeable solidity of the whole substantial nature of visible and invisible things is usually implied. We explained this point when examining what was produced on the third day. So it is that the Apostle says, "Mortify your limbs, which are upon the earth." [28] It is as if he were openly saying, "The limbs of evil, which are yours, since they were made from your disobedience and not from God; and from them you construct a kind of body of universal wickedness upon the earth, i.e., upon the solidity of the nature created by God. That the earth may be defiled by them no longer, mortify them and, destroying the limbs of evil, establish instead the limbs of justice, which are virtues. So just as you by your various sins have constructed upon the nature created by God a kind of abominable temple, worthy of being dwelt in by the Devil, you may reconstruct from the stones of virtues hewn by divine grace a precious house for the Creator of nature, when you have swept out and thoroughly removed all defilement." With this meaning the Psalmist concurs when he says, "May sinners and the wicked disappear from the earth so that they have no being." [29] There by a trope he signifies cause from effects, implying by sinners and the unjust the sins and iniquities which will so disappear from the earth of nature when it is

freed from all evil that they will no longer be. For sins and iniquities seem to have being, although they are nothing, as long as they are contained by nature which is subject to them. But when that nature has been cleansed and restored to its original wholeness, the sins and iniquities which cannot subsist by themselves will be so thoroughly reduced to nothing that they will not be. The Psalmist elsewhere says, in blessing all the just in the person of the man who lives justly, "They will be like a tree that is planted by streams of water;" [30] i.e., like the Word which was made Man at the end of all ages for us "who," as the Apostle says, "have come down to the ends of the ages." [31] He names in the plural the single End of all, i.e., Christ; for He is the "End of the ages" who is the fulfillment of all things. He added at once, "Not so are the ungodly. No, they are like dust which the wind has blown away from the face of the earth." [32] He calls "wind" the distinction of the just judgment by which He, whose winnow is in His hand, will cast forth the dust of all evil from the surface of the earth, i.e., from the substantial beauty of nature. About this earth he says in another Psalm, "His spirit will go out and return to its earth." [33] Whose spirit? Why, of course, the spirit of Him who, fixed on the cross for us, with bent head gave up His spirit. Where will it go out? It descends to Hell. For what purpose? To lead back from there the nature of man held captive there, "for He led back the captivity." [34] But since death could not hold Him captive because it had not found Him guilty. He returned to His earth, to His nature, which He made, redeemed, and accepted, into an immortal body, into the pristine state of human nature, and besides to the glory of resurrection. And that you may know that He, who promised that His spirit alone would emerge, will return not alone but with the whole of human nature, hear His words: "Unless a grain of wheat falls on the ground and dies, it alone remains; but if it dies, it bears a rich harvest." [35] "You will send out Your spirit and renew the face of the earth," [36] i.e., "You will restore the wholeness of nature." One may understand spirit in reference to the soul of Christ which, "with bent head," with His Godhead sharing the suffering, was handed over for the salvation of the world, and went out and returned to that nature which It had redeemed by Its mission; and was sent, also, to restore the beauty of that nature, which had been destroyed in

the first man. Or one may understand *spirit* in reference to the Holy
Spirit, which is the spirit of Christ which, with the head, that is Christ,
bent low, was handed over in a momentary death of the flesh to
universal creation, whose first-begotten He Himself is, whose spirit
He is. It will go out and return "to Its land," [37] i.e., to that nature
which It had deserted because of the sin of the first man. It had
belonged to It before it (the nature) abandoned the sinner; but because
of Him whose spirit it is, and who suffered for it, it (the spirit) returns
to it (the nature) and will return again at the time of resurrection, and
will be sent, so that, by its power, the appearance of universal nature
may be restored to its pristine beauty. Therefore since, in this land
common to all things, all animals were created causally and primordially in body and soul—for all things were made with honor—why is it
strange if the order is given by divine precept to produce "a living
soul," i.e., a living animal, so as to produce openly in genera and
species what it secretly possessed causally in causes and reasons? See
how the word of God reveals to us the natural sequence of things by
saying, "Let the earth produce a living soul in its genus." It put genus
first, since in it all species are contained and are one, and it is divided
and multiplied into them by general species and most specific species.
This point, too, it shows by saying, "Cattle, reptiles, and beasts of the
earth according to their species." [38] Hence it is understood that the art
of dialectic, which divides genera into species and resolves species into
genera, was not fashioned by human devices, but created in the nature
of things by the Author of all arts that are truly arts; and discovered by
wise men and, by skillful research, adapted to use.

[5] *S:* From what, if I am not mistaken, you have reasonably said,
whoever wishes can interpret in another way the passage: "Let the
waters abound with living creatures, and let birds fly above the
earth," [39] so as not merely to understand simply, as we discussed
above, that fish and flying creatures were made from this visible,
tractable, humid, cold element of the waters, but that also, in a deeper
sense, they were drawn into genera and species from the hidden,
profound recesses of nature, in which they had been made causally and

primordially. Nothing prevents us from understanding that just as the solidity and fertility of nature are indicated by the word *earth*, so the hidden depth of the same nature is signified by the waters; so that one and the same origin may be recognized for all the animals, whether we read that they are created from earth or from the waters, even though the speculation about them is divided. An account of the creation of some is given in the fifth speculation of the prophet, but of others in the sixth. Nor should I think that this was done without reason. It seems likely that terrestrial animals were ordered to be produced from the earth on the sixth day, when man too was made, because they appear to have a greater resemblance to man in their nature. In fact, the investigation of nature shows that everything in the nature of animate man except intellect and reason is naturally present in them too.

T: Not only, in my opinion, does nothing prevent us, but reason itself, when carefully examined, supports such an interpretation of the text which is consistent with the evidence of creation. The understanding of God's words is manifold and infinite. Why, in one and the same feather of a peacock, a remarkable, beautiful variety of countless colors is seen in one and the same spot of a small part of the same feather. And indeed the very nature of things attracts us to such an understanding. This sensible earth and water are bodies compounded from the qualities of the four elements. They generate nothing from themselves, and no species of nature is born from them, although it appears to be. But the force of seeds within them, through the operation of that life which is called nutritive, according to inherent laws and reasons, insofar as Divine Providence allows, through genera and species bursts forth from the hidden recesses of creation into different species of grasses, shoots, and animals. Hence that source from which visible and tractable earth and water have proceeded into their natural species, qualities, and quantities is the same source from which everything that appears to be born from them takes the origin of its generation. There is a most general and common nature of all, created by the one First Principle of all; and from It, as from a very copious fountain, corporeal creatures, like rivulets, are channeled through hidden passages and break forth into the different forms of individual things. That force, coming forth through different seeds from the secret recesses of nature and first emerging in the seeds themselves, then mixed with the different fluids, bursts out into the individual, sensible species.

S: That seems reasonable and plausible and in accord with the speculations of our discourse on nature. But since man, who was created on the sixth day, is established among the number of animals included under a single genus, I should like to hear from you whether in the divine precept in which the earth is ordered "to produce a living soul" man is to be understood or not.

T: Perhaps I could not answer this question easily if divine Scripture merely proclaimed: "Let the earth produce a living soul." But in adding "in its genus," it revealed very plainly that all animals are included in this precept; for there is no species which is not wholly placed within its genus. Since, however, the species of animal established in man surpasses the nature of the other animals in the same genus by the dignity of reason and intelligence, the prophetic view showed foresight in wishing to join it to the other animals, so as to relate its creation, in accord with the excellence of its nature, more fully and in greater detail at the end of everything which had been made by God. The greatest and most precious species of animal is therefore mentioned twice in the works of the sixth view of creation. First in its genus, namely animal, it is ordered to be produced from the earth; then, a little later, after a very brief division of the other animals has been given, the creation of man in God's image and likeness is introduced.

S: And so man is produced from the earth as a single species among the other animals; and soon after he is said to be made in God's image. This fact disturbs me, and rightly so. If the whole genus of animals with all its species were made "in God's image and likeness," perhaps I would not be disturbed by your teaching that man was, indeed, produced from earth among the other animals, and the later statement that he was fashioned in God's image and likeness. But since the divine account states that only man and no other animal was created in God's image, I am quite amazed at how man is produced from the earth and yet is the only one formed in God's image, incomparably far beyond all other animals; for as Scripture says, "Let us make man in Our image and likeness." [40] Still more puzzling is the way that man is produced from the earth among the things to which he is made superior and which he is ordered to rule; for Scripture has added: "and let him be master of the fish of the sea, the birds of heaven, the cattle, the reptiles that crawl upon the earth, and all creatures."

T: You have good reason to be disturbed, for these matters deserve the most careful and skillful investigation. First of all, to understand without any mist of ambiguity that man was created in the universal genus of animals, accept as the greatest proof the threefold division of this genus into cattle, reptiles, and beasts. This division was not made without cause, in my opinion. On the other days—i.e., the third and the fifth—when genera and species are mentioned, no division of genus into species is introduced but either simply the genus alone and its undifferentiated species, as on the third day, when the genera and species of grasses and shoots are ordered to rise from the earth; or the genus alone and one of its species, as on the fifth day, when the genus of fish is called *reptile* ("a crawling creature") and that of birds is called *volatile* ("a flying creature"), but neither is divided into species. For in saying "God created great sea-serpents," [41] we must understand that the species stands for the genus rather than that the genus is divided into species. It would be impossible for the division of a genus to be made into a single species, since every division involves at least two. On the sixth day, however, not only the creation of the genus but also its threefold division into species is related in the words: "God said: 'Let the earth produce a living soul in its genus, cattle, reptiles, and beasts of the earth according to their species.' " [42] Or according to the Septuagint: "God said: 'Let the earth bring forth a living soul according to its genus, quadrupeds, reptiles, and beasts according to their genus;' and it was so done." And so, in my opinion, the threefold division of all life which clings to an earthly body and produces an animate being by union with a body (for an animal is the joining together of body and soul with sense) implies a triple motion. That threefold motion is understood only in reference to man, who alone is a rational animal, subordinating to reason certain of his

motions which seem to be signified by the word *cattle* or *quadrupeds.*
E.g., by the arts he moves the fivefold sense of the body to recognize
sensible things with zealous care to understand them. This motion is
not unreasonably called *cattle,* for it furnishes no little aid to the
rational soul in its contemplation of the truth of all sensible things, with
all falsehood removed and with true and whole knowledge. The
motion of the senses subjected to reason is also like a quadruped, since
everything which we know through sense in the nature of sensible
things is compounded of the four elements or consists of the compound
itself. If you consider corporeal form (*species*), the form itself consists
of some matter made from the qualities of the four elements. If you
sense a sound or odor, it is from air compounded of the four elements.
Similarly if you experience the sense of taste or touch, you will have
no doubt that they come about from the joining together of water and
earth. Quite aptly, then, corporeal sense has received the name of
quadruped since everything which it perceives derives its origin solely
from the four elements. Certain ones drawn from lower nature and
improperly assigned to sensible creatures you would be right to call
irrational—i.e., opposed to reason—for example madness, greed, and
the disordered appetites of the corporeal senses. Since these motions
have been implanted in human nature from irrational animals, they are
not unfittingly designated by the name of beasts, especially since they
never cease struggling against the rational disciplines and can hardly, if
ever, be tamed by them. They always strive to tear the rational
motions to shreds with a fierce onslaught. Besides, a rational animal has
certain hidden motions by which in particular it governs the body
joined to it; and these motions are established in the part of the soul
that relates to growth and nutrition. Since they perform their functions
by their natural capacity and covertly, as it were—for they do not
upset or disturb the concentration of the soul in any way if the
soundness of nature survives unimpaired—as they penetrate the
harmony of the body in their silent course, they not unreasonably have
earned the name of *reptiles.* The other animals except for man have
only two of the three motions mentioned; one which is properly in the
senses and lacks the direction of reason and hence is bestial; the other,
like a reptile, which is assigned to nutritive life. These motions man

shares with the other animals and they with him. Do you see, then, that man is in all the animals and they in him, but that man is above them all? Whoever examines carefully the remarkable and altogether ineffable creation of nature itself will clearly find that the same man is a species in the genus of animals and yet subsists above every species of animal. Hence one can correctly speak of him both affirmatively and negatively by saying: "Man is an animal; man is not an animal." When one considers in him body, nutritive life, sense, memory of sensibles, and all irrational appetite, such as madness and greed, he is altogether an animal; for all of these he has in common with the other animals. But in the higher part of himself, where he consists of reason, intellect, the inner sense with all its rational motions called *virtues* and with the memory of things eternal and divine, he is *not* an animal in any respect. All of these latter attributes are the same in man as in celestial essences, which in some incomprehensible way, by the excellence of their substance surpass everything included in the nature of animals. As we said, then, it is correctly stated of man, "He is an animal; he is not an animal." We can confirm this point from the authority of divine Scripture, for the Apostle says: "An animal-like (*animalis*) person does not perceive the things which are God's." [43] And then: "A spiritual man judges everything, but he is not judged by anyone." [44] Observe how clearly, how openly, he virtually divides a man into two men. One of them is animal-like since he is like the nature of animals, which receives nothing spiritual into itself. The other is spiritual, since it communicates with eternal, spiritual, and divine subsistences and is wholly free from the nature of the animal. The part in which man is an animal belongs to the outer man; but that by which he surpasses other animals including himself, insofar as he is an animal, fittingly receives the designation of *inner man*. Among those who live spiritually, as the same Apostle says, "The outer man is subject to decay, but the inner man is renewed from day to day." [45] For whoever lives perfectly not only utterly despises his body and the life by which it is administered and all the corporeal senses along with the things which he apprehends through them, and all the irrational motions which he perceives in himself, along with the memory of all changeable things; he even crushes and destroys them, insofar as he can, lest they prevail in him in any way. He strives wholly to die to them and to have them die to him; but insofar as he participates in celestial Essence, he renews himself, rising from day to day, i.e., from virtue to virtue, with divine grace moving him, working with him, guiding him, and bringing fulfillment. The nature shared by man with animals is called *flesh*, but that which participates in celestial Essence is mind (*mens* and *animus*) or intellect. Hear these words of the Apostle: "With my mind I serve God's law, but with my flesh I serve the law of sin." ⁴⁶ And countless passages of divine Scripture prove this very point. Why is it strange, then, if there is understood to be a twofold creation of man since he himself is, in a way, twofold? What is like animals is created with the animals, but what is like the purely and absolutely spiritual is created with the spiritual. Therefore do not be disturbed by my statement that man was produced from the earth in one and the same genus with the other animals; and that beyond the nature of all animals he was made "in God's image and likeness."

S: Perhaps I would not be disturbed if I could clearly discern how, under one and the same genus as the other animals, man was so created that, in the better part of himself, he subsists above all nature of animals.

T: I wonder why you are bringing up the same point again. We have said that man, insofar as he is an animal, is among the animals in a single genus. Insofar as he is not an animal, he was made outside the whole genus of all animals.

S: Oh, now a greater and far more serious question has arisen, as I see it.

T: Please tell me what it is.

S: You seem to me to think that two souls subsist in one man. One governs the body, gives it life, nourishes it, and makes it grow, perceives sensible things through the corporeal senses, stores their *phantasiae* in its memory and does the other things which, as is very well known, the souls of the other animals perform in their bodies. The other subsists in the reason and intellect, and "is made in God's image and likeness." But this seems thoroughly ridiculous.

T: Neither reason nor divine authority allows me to believe that there are two souls in one man. Or rather, they actually prevent me, and it is not right for any true philosopher to entertain such a thought. I affirm that man is one and the same rational soul joined to a human body in some ineffable way; and that man himself, by a marvelous and intelligible division, in the part in which he was made in the Creator's image and likeness, does not participate at all in the nature of animals and is absolutely free from it; but in the part in which he does share the nature of animals, he was produced in the universal genus of animals from the earth, i.e., from the common nature of all.

S: Are we to say, then, that the human soul is a simple nature free from all compound, or must we believe that it is joined by some parts into a unity?

T: I maintain the former alternative very firmly—namely, that it is simple and free from all linking of parts; but I completely deny the latter, i.e., that it receives any compound of parts different from one another. All of it is everywhere present in it throughout the whole. As a whole it is life, intellect, reason, sense, and memory; as a whole it endows the body with life, nourishes it, holds it together, and causes it to grow; as a whole, with all the senses it perceives the appearances (species) of sensible things; as a whole, beyond any corporeal sense it treats, discerns, joins, and distinguishes the nature and reason of things; as a whole, outside and above all creation and itself (for it is included in the number of creatures) it revolves about its Creator in an intelligible and eternal motion when it is cleansed of all vices and *phantasiae*. And although it thus subsists as naturally simple, it receives the divisions of its intelligible and substantial differentiae as divisions of a whole into parts, according to the multiplicity of its motions. Hence it is called by many names. For example, when it is borne around Divine Essence, it is called *mind* (*mens, animus*) and *intellect*. When it considers the natures and causes of created things, it is called *reason*; when it takes in the forms (*species*) of sensible things by the corporeal senses, it is called *sense*; when it brings about its hidden motions in the body as irrational souls do, nourishing the body and causing it to grow, its usual proper designation is *vital motion*. But in all of these activities, the whole soul is everywhere present.

S: Then the whole soul was produced from the earth in the genus of animals, and the whole was made in God's image. That is my inference from the reasons that you have given.

T: You are right, and no true and devout philosopher may doubt this point lest he seem to split an altogether simple and individed nature, which would be a very impious act.

S: How one and the same man, then, according to the preceding argument, is both an animal and not an animal, or how he is like an animal and not like an animal, and is flesh and is not flesh, and is spiritual and not spiritual; and how these opposing and contradictory conditions can be understood in an altogether simple nature I do not see very well.

T: From what has already been said, anyone who examines the matter quite carefully will see with utter clarity that everything that seems to you contradictory in the simplicity of human nature is not only not contradictory, but even thoroughly suitable. Wise men agree that in man universal creation is contained. Man understands and reasons like an angel; he has sensation and governs his body like an animal; and hence all creation is understood in him. Of course, the division of all creation is fivefold. It is corporeal, vital, sensitive, rational, or intellectual. All of these aspects are contained in man in every respect. The lowest part of his nature is body; then comes the life contained in seed which governs the body and which is under the dominion of sense; next reason, which rules over the parts of nature beneath itself; and mind holds the highest place of all. Thus human nature as a whole, insofar as it has a share with animals, is rightly considered an animal. Moreover, it has a share with them insofar as it is a body, and a life governing the body, and sense and a memory of sensible things that deals with *phantasiae*. But insofar as it is a participant in Divine and Celestial Essence, it is not an animal, but participates in Celestial Essence by reason, intellect, and the memory of eternal things. There, consequently, it is wholly devoid of the nature of animal. It is made in God's image only in that part of itself which God addresses in the case of worthy men. As St. Augustine says in Book 11 (§2) of *The City of God*: "He speaks to that part of man which is better than the other parts of which man consists, and than which only God Himself is better. For since man was made in God's image, surely he is nearer to God who is above him in that part of himself by which he surpasses his baser parts, which he has in common even with beasts." We must note also that even in this life, before everything of animal nature in man is turned into the spiritual and everything compound is united into an ineffable simplicity, man as a whole can become both like an animal and spiritual. He can become like an animal merely by free choice; but he can become spiritual by free choice along with grace, without which the natural power of the will by no means suffices to move man to spirit. Man is therefore made and said to be like an animal when he abandons the motions which, according to reason and intellect, focus on the knowledge of Creator and creation, and by spontaneous appetite falls into the irrational motions by which brutish animals are aroused by the desires of the body. In this latter way man absorbs himself completely in the death-bearing delights of temporal and destructible things which tend toward non-being. The spiritual man, however, changing his whole way of life for the better, is wholly transformed into the likeness of celestial essences. Thus what is to be his in his changeless substance comes to him early in accord with the quality of his life, which is adorned with virtues. In two ways, then, man is recognized as like an animal; one, by his natural subsistence, the other from the irrational motion of his free will, which is inclined toward evil. Likewise, spiritual both according to nature and by his good will, anticipated by divine grace, cleansed by action and knowledge, and crowned with the ornaments of virtues, man is recalled to the original honor of the divine image.

S: I willingly accept this explanation, but I do not see very clearly how, when all species are one in genus, they can subsist in it as one although they are in opposition to one another. For example, the definition of man seems to contradict the definitions of the other animals; for man is a rational animal, while the others are irrational. Do you see how the rational and the irrational oppose each other?

T: Take a somewhat sharper look at the natures of things, and you will find that this statement, which serves as a differentia, involves differentiae under a single genus, not oppositions; e.g., every creature is either visible or invisible. This statement presents a differentia, not an opposition. Visibility and invisibility are two separate things, not mutually antagonistic. Likewise, every creature is either corporeal or incorporeal. A statement of differentiae also distinguishes the relationships of Divine Persons. The Father is unbegotten, the Son begotten, and the Spirit neither unbegotten nor begotten; and there are countless examples of this kind. And to recognize the distinction more clearly, note that every opposition is understood in reference to one and the same species or part, but a differentia relates to different species. Take as an example the following statement about the natural species designated in substance as man. Man is a rational animal; man is an irrational animal. The propositions will be contradictory, and one of them will necessarily be true and the other false. Contradictory propositions about the same subject, whether they relate to universals or particulars, cannot both be either true or false at the same time. When you say, however, "Man is a rational animal; horse is an irrational animal," no opposition is understood since you are revealing the substantial differentia of a rational and an irrational animal. When you assign reason to man and take it away from horse, you are signifying the difference between man and horse. For the differentia which distinguishes man from the other animals is the possession of reason, just as the differentia distinguishing the other animals from man is the non-possession of reason, since their state and privation are not discerned by this feature. The condition of man is to have reason, but the condition of horse is the absence of reason. Naturally, a horse is not deprived of the condition which it was never able to have. Where a condition does not precede, privation will not follow. Death would not befall an animal or whatever else participates' in life unless the condition of life were present first. For that reason, we never properly call an animal stupid except one in which we see that the condition of reason can be produced; nor do we call any insensitive unless the condition of feeling can be naturally present in it.

S: Why, then, did you say that about one and the same subject two contradictory propositions cannot both at the same time be either false or true; but that if one is true, the other will necessarily be false? An example would be a statement about one and the same creature,

"This animal is a horse; it is not a horse." Yet you seem to be affirming that opposing propositions can be true at the same time in man: e.g., "Man is an animal; man is not an animal." And you show that this contradiction is naturally inherent in him until the whole animal-like man is turned into the spiritual. Why is this true of man alone but not at all of other animals, of whom it is entirely true that they are animals and entirely false that they are not animals?

T: Do you think that another animal besides man has been made in God's image?

S: By no means.

T: Will you deny that two opposing propositions, when predicated of God, are true at the same time and by no means false, although both are not of the same force? Consider, for example, "God is Truth; God is not Truth."

S: I should not dare to deny it, for He says of Himself: "I am the Way, the Truth, and the Life." [47] But St. Dionysius the Areopagite says in his *Symbolic Theology* (5) that God "is neither Truth nor Life." He states: "He is neither Virtue nor Light nor Life;" and a little later: "Nor Knowledge nor Truth."

T: Is Dionysius perhaps contradicting Christ, who declares of Himself that He is Truth?

S: Far from it.

T: Both statements, then, are true. God is Truth; God is not Truth.

S: They are not only true, but the ultimate in truth. One statement is made as a metaphorical affirmation, since God is the Creator and Primordial Cause of truth, by participation in which all true things are true. The other is a statement by negation because of excellence, since He is More Than Truth. Hence the statement "God is Truth" is true, for He is the Cause of all true things; and the statement "God is not Truth" is true, because He surpasses everything which is said, understood, and has being. Nor am I unaware that you added "although they are not of the same force." For affirmation is less able to signify the ineffable Divine Essence than negation, since the former is transferred from creatures to Creator, but the latter is predicated of the Creator in Himself beyond all creation.

T: You see well the force of what I added. Why is it strange, then, if it can truly be predicated at the same time of man, who alone among animals was made in God's image, "Man is an animal; man is not an animal"? By that statement we may at least understand the special creation in God's image of that animal about whom propositions, contradictory in reference to other animals, are made truly at the same time. Besides, if affirmations and negations about the Divine Essence are compatible because It surpasses everything made by It and of which It is the Cause, who may not perceive that negations and affirmations are harmoniously united in reference to Its image and likeness, which is in man, since he surpasses the other animals among which he was created in a single genus, while they were created for his sake? What truly wise man would be unaware that this visible world with all its parts, from top to bottom, was made for the sake of man, that he might be over it and rule all visible things. St. Gregory imparts this teaching in his sermon *On the Image* in the following words: "All creation except man was established by Divine Power together with the giving of the command; but deliberation preceded the making of man. The Artificer planned in advance by the Word of Scripture what man was to be, of what nature, and to what archetypal exemplar he should bear a likeness; in what he should be made, what he should do when made, and what creatures he should rule. The Word considered all these matters first in order that he who was to hold dominion over existing things might be allotted greater dignity in his generation before his coming into essence. For God said, 'Let us make man in Our image and likeness, and let him rule over the fish of the sea, the beasts of the earth, the birds of heaven, cattle, and all the earth.' " [48] And this was granted to him whether or not he should sin, although he would not be ruling in the same way if he had not sinned as he does after sinning. And to make this point clearer, You surely do not think, do you, that man is an animal in that part of himself in which he was made in God's image? Or that God's image subsists in that part in which he was produced from the earth among the animals? Or that both aspects, i.e., image and animal, are not truly in him?

S: I should by no means agree with the last statement; for true reason proves that these things exist together in man. I should also utterly deny that the image is in the animal and the animal in the image if I were not disturbed by your previous determination that man is everywhere whole in himself. From this I believe we may understand that the whole image is in the whole animal, and the whole animal subsists in the whole image throughout the whole man.

T: I am surprised at your being disturbed by such considerations when you see that the image and likeness of God in man's nature can be recognized particularly in this way. God is both above everything and in everything, since He, who alone truly is, is the Essence of everything; and although He is whole in everything, He does not cease being whole outside of everything; whole in the world, whole around the world, whole in sensible creation; whole in intelligible creation; whole He makes the universe; whole He is made in the universe; whole in the whole of the universe, whole in its parts, because He Himself is both whole and part, and neither whole nor part. In the same way human nature is whole in itself in its world, in its universe, in its visible and invisible parts; whole in its whole, and whole in its parts; and its parts are whole in themselves, and whole in the whole. Even its lowest and meanest part, the body, according to its reasons is whole in the whole man, since body, insofar as it truly is body, subsists in its reasons, which were made at the first creation; and although human nature is such in itself, it exceeds its whole. It could not cling to its Creator without exceeding both everything under it and itself, since, as Augustine says: "No creature is interposed between our minds, with which we understand the Father, and Truth, through which we understand Him." The same point is well made as follows by Dionysius the Areopagite in the *Symbolic Theology* (1): "O my friend Timotheus, entering steadfastly upon the course of mystic speculations, abandon the senses and intellectual activities, things sensible and invisible, and all being and non-being. Then, unknowing, strive to restore yourself to unity with Him who is above all essence and knowledge. By this unity, in an immeasurable and absolute ecstasy of the mind you will go outside yourself and all things, abandoning them and freed from them; and you will ascend to the Superessential Radiance of Divine Shadows." And in the Gospel too the Lord says: "Where I am, there is my servant also." [49] He, moreover, is above all things. A man who clings to Him, then, is above all things and above himself insofar as He is in all things. Human nature, while involved in this mortal life, cannot actually cling to God. Yet, since clinging to its Creator is possible and natural for it, it is appropriately said to cling to Him by the grace of Him to whom it clings. Often potentiality is accepted as the experience, and what is certain to occur at some time in the future is accounted as a present deed actually performed. And why did I say "in his world, in his universe," when it would have been clearer to state "in the whole visible and invisible world"? For human nature is whole in the universe of created nature as a whole, since in it all creation has been established and joined, and will return to it and be saved through it. Hear its Creator saying: "Proclaim the Gospel to all creation," [50] i.e., to man, of course. Man has intellect, reason, sense, seminal life, and body, not this body corruptible after sin, but that body which man had before sin; not this compound and soluble body, but that simple and indivisible one; not this animal-like and earthly body, but that spiritual and celestial one; not this body begotten by seed from the carnal union of the two sexes, but the body produced from the simplicity of nature before the transgression, and the one that will have being at the Resurrection; not this body known to the corporeal sense, but the one still hidden in nature's secret recesses; not this body added because of sin, but that which was implanted in a nature still undefiled, the body to which this corruptible, mortal body will return. "It is sown," the Apostle says (i.e., it is born from seed) "in corruption, but it will rise in power (*virtute*)." In what kind of power? That of the body itself, which formerly was created naturally. "It is sown in dishonor, but it will rise in glory; it is sown as the body of an animal, but it will rise as a spiritual body." [51] Everything created naturally in man necessarily remains eternally whole and uncorrupted. For it did not seem good to Divine Justice for anything that It had created to perish, especially because sin was not committed by nature itself, but by perverse will which is irrationally set in motion against rational nature. There is a very cogent proof for this point. If man naturally has an inherent loathing of death, how could he fail to have a natural loathing for the cause of death, namely sin? It is common to all animals to avoid and fear death and its causes. Therefore, as no wise man wishes to make a mistake, so human nature did not wish to sin; and hence its Creator, since He is just, did not wish to punish it but wished to add to it something in which sin, which had resulted from perverse will and the persuasion of the serpent, could be cleansed so as not always to cling to it. For although rational and intellectual nature did not wish to be deceived, it was able to be beguiled, especially since it had not yet received the perfection of its form which it was to receive as a reward for obedience, namely deification. We should therefore not judge human nature according to what appears to the corporeal senses. As a punishment for transgression, it is born in this world in time and corruptibly like irrational animals through union of the sexes; and its end is death. But we should rather judge it according to its creation in God's image before it sinned. This human nature, in accord with its ineffable dignity, cannot be grasped but eludes all corporeal sense and all mortal thought. But it was beguiled and slipped, blinded by the darkness of its perverse will, and handed itself and its Creator over to oblivion. And this is its most wretched death, its deep submersion in the shade of ignorance, its vast distance from itself and its Creator, and its close and shameful likeness to irrational, mortal living creatures. From this death no one was able to redeem or recall it, to lead it back and to restore it to the pristine state from which it had fallen. But God's Wisdom, which had created it and received it into unity with Its own substance, freed it from all wretchedness that so It might save it. Do not be disturbed, therefore, by the statement that human nature is everywhere whole in itself, and that the image is whole in the animal and the animal whole in the image.

[6]   Everything which its Creator primordially created in it remains whole and intact, but it is still in hiding while it awaits the revelation of the sons of God.

S: Perhaps I would not be disturbed if you were to persuade me clearly of what I cannot perceive by myself. I am pondering whether man, if he had not sinned, would be an animal; or, to put it differently, whether man was an animal before his sin. If he was not, why did we expend so much effort in asking and, as I thought, finding that man was created in the universal genus of animals? If he was not created in that genus, either he was not an animal at all before his sin, or, if he was, he had been created in another genus of animals. But divine Scripture does not bring up such a point, nor does careful rational investigation of the nature of things discover it; for all animals subsist in one genus, from which they proceed by divisions. But if in the passage "Let the earth produce a living soul," [52] the creation of man among the other animals was brought up before man's sin, why does the Psalmist, as though heaping great reproach upon human nature after the fall, say "Man, when he was held in honor, lacked understanding and was like dumb cattle and made similar to them"? [53] Here the prophet seems openly to proclaim that man before the fall subsisted in the honor of spiritual substance beyond the nature of all animals; but that when he fell, since he did not understand the dignity of his nature, he plunged into the disgrace of likeness to cattle. But if man was an animal before his fall, why is he justly reproached for incurring likeness after his fall to the animals with which he was naturally created in a single genus?

T: You would be justified in pondering the matter if the prophet had simply said that man was like cattle and made similar to them. But by adding to the word *cattle* the adjective *dumb* (*insipientibus*), he made clear enough that the chief cause of reproach against man is that, though he was a spiritual and wise animal when first created in God's image and likeness, he foolishly and irrationally, by going against his Creator's command, drew upon himself likeness to dumb, i.e., brutish, animals; and by their motions, which are inappropriate for him, he dishonored the natural dignity of his own nature. He is not praised for being an animal, but for being the image of God; just as he is denounced for his willingness to disfigure not the animal, but the image, which he could not destroy. In other animals, irrational motions are not shameful since they are naturally inherent and since without them the animals cannot have being. But it is worthy of reproach and base in a rational animal to succumb, by the forbidden appetite of a perverse will, to the impulses of irrational creatures, to which they are natural, and willingly to remain fixed in them and to abandon the higher beauty of the divine image.

S: It is just to blame a rational creature for the impulses of irrational animals. Any man of honorable form who willingly clothed himself in the semblance of a beast would deserve reproach for casting himself down from the better to the vastly inferior.

[7] But I still ask why God created man in the genus of animals, when He wished to make him in His own image and likeness. To be free from all animal nature would surely seem more glorious for the creature chosen to participate in the mark of the Highest beyond all animals, and to share the lot of celestial beings, who may not have any substance in common with earthly animals. They are not weighted down by earthly bodies, and they make no use of corporeal senses to attain knowledge of sensible things; for they do not receive *phantasiae* from without, but within themselves they recognize the reasons of what they see. A soul does not receive its perceptions externally either, but through *phantasiae* within itself; but this process does not occur in angels. Although Plato defines an angel as a rational and immortal animal, we should not accept his definition among the sure observations about natures; for it would be rash to do so since we cannot prove it by the authority of holy Scripture or the holy fathers. Moreover, the fact that St. Augustine not only does not deny but even affirms that the highest angels have spiritual bodies in which they often appear by no means compels us to believe that celestial substances are animals, especially since it is not the harmony and inseparable union of celestial and incorruptible bodies with angelic spirits, but the connection through the mediation of senses of terrestrial and corruptible bodies with souls, whether rational or irrational, that produces an animal. For if outer sense is present in angelic bodies and intellects, what prevents us, as Plato would have it, from calling them animals compounded of body and soul through the mediation of sense and the endowment of life by intellect? And if so, why are they not reckoned in the genus of animals? Of course man, even if he had not sinned, would be an animal; for nature, not sin, made man an animal. But no authority records that even the angels who transgressed are animals. This point is proved in particular by an argument such as the following. The

future felicity promised to holy men is declared to be simply a perfect and complete equality with the nature of angels. What person of sound judgment would believe that the future transformation of man will be as though from a lower to a higher animal, from an earthly to a celestial one, from a temporal to an eternal one, from a mortal to an immortal, from a wretched to a blessed? Rather one would believe that everything perceived or understood as shared in this life by holy men with the other animals is transformed in some ineffable way into that essence which is celestial, incommunicable, and wholly free from the nature of an animal. Such a lot would have befallen man too if he had not sinned. Why, then, was man created in the genus of animals produced from the earth, since he will not always remain there? Of course, at the end of this world, of which man is an animate part, everything of animal nature in man will perish with it and in it. True reason does not grant that the whole suffers death while parts of it are rescued from death. Moreover, if the whole world with all its parts will perish, I do not see very well how, insofar as man is part of the world, he will remain after the world, or where or in what manner. I therefore beg you to loosen the knots of this problem.

T: You are demanding a very deep speculation on the nature of the human condition, and you are forcing our discussion to range quite far afield. To your question about why God created in the genus of animals the man whom He intended to make in His own image, I would be satisfied to give the brief answer that He wished to create him that way in order that there might be some animal in which He might show His image represented. Whoever asks why He wished it is asking about the causes of divine will, which it is excessively presumptuous and arrogant to question. "For who knows the Lord's thoughts?" [54] But if I make such a statement, you may be resentfully silent and think that I cannot complete any topic or make it clear. I shall not say why He wished it, then, because that surpasses every intellect; but I shall say, insofar as He allows, what He wished to accomplish. He made all visible and invisible creation in man, since the universe of created nature is understood as being in man. For although, because of the eclipse of the supernal light after the transgression, it is not yet revealed how noble was man's original condition, yet there is nothing naturally present in celestial essences which does not subsist essentially in man. There is intellect and reason; there is the natural inherent reason (*ratio*) of possessing a celestial and angelic body; and this reason will appear with perfect clarity after resurrection in both the good and the evil. It will be common to all human nature to rise again in eternal, incorruptible, and spiritual bodies. As the Apostle says, "It is sown as the body of an animal, but it will arise as a spiritual body." [55] This whole sensible world has been established in man; for there is no part of it, whether corporeal or incorporeal, which has not been created in man and which fails to perceive, live, and be incorporated in him. Do not think of the corporeal mass of a man, but rather consider the power of his nature; especially since you see in the human body itself the pupil of the eye which, although the smallest of all the members in size, is the greatest in potency. If, then, God had not created man in the genus of animals, or surely if He had not put the whole nature of all animals in man, how would visible and invisible universal creation be comprehended in him? We can therefore reasonably say that God wished to station man in the genus of animals since in him He wished to create all creation. If you ask me, moreover, why He wished to create all creation in him, my answer is that He wished to make him in His image and likeness in order that just as the Archetypal Example surpasses everything by the excellence of Its essence, so His image might surpass everything by the dignity of His creation and by grace. But I confess that I am wholly unaware of why God wished to make man in particular, rather than any other visible or invisible creature, in His own image.

S: I think that you have given a satisfactory and reasonable answer to my question about why God wished to make man in the genus of animals. But I still ask how all things were created in man and subsist in him. Is it only according to their essence, to their accidents, or everything observed in universal creation—i.e., essence, species, differentia, property, and everything understood in relation to them.

T: I do not readily see how I can solve this problem reasonably. If I say "only according to their essence," you will rightly answer that everything has being, then, only insofar as it subsists essentially; but that the other things understood in reference to essence or substance are not to be reckoned in the number of the universe of things, and do not completely possess being. In that case, you will ask me the source of what is understood in reference to (*circa*) the essence of things. If I say "They were made from God," you will say, "Why are they not included, then, in the reckoning (*numerus*) of the universe created in man?" On the other hand, if I say "They were not made by God," you will answer, "Then they have no being." For if they did, they would come simply from the Cause of all, namely God." And if I agree that the things understood in reference to essences are not in the number of things because they are not from God, you will say at once, "How, then, are they understood?" For everything which is not from God cannot be understood in any way since it has no being in any way. If I say that not only essences but everything naturally understood in reference to them is from God and is reckoned in the parts of the universe, I shall undoubtedly have to choose one of two alternatives; either that not the whole universe has been created in man if only the essences have been made in him; or that the whole universe, i.e., the essences and whatever is perceived in reference to and in them, was created in man. And if I say that not part of the universe, i.e., substances, but the whole was established in man, you will track me down with the very serious argument that, in such a case, irrationality was made in him along with bestiality, four-footedness, capacity for flight, and all the differentiae of the various animals and other things, as well as the species, properties, accidents, and the countless other things which seem so far removed from human nature that if it were agreed that they are present in man, he would rightly be judged to be not man but some exceedingly vile monster.

S: You have exaggerated the difficulty of the question and have deliberately brought up against yourself whatever opposition might be raised by someone else. So you will either find the key to the difficulty or pass it by as too obscure and go on to something else, which will seem highly inappropriate.

T: Let us try, then, to examine the question in some way in order not to abandon it for the time without touching upon it at all.

S: That is the only way that I shall be satisfied.

T: Do you think that everything known by intellect and reason or perceived in an image by corporeal sense can be created and produced in some way in him who understands and senses it?

S: Yes, I do. I think that the forms (*species*), quantities, and qualities of the sensible things which I touch by corporeal sense are created in me in some way. When I fix their *phantasiae* in my memory and, inside myself, deal with, divide, compare them and, as it were, collect them into a certain unity, I perceive that a certain knowledge of the things outside me is produced in me. Similarly I realize that some ideas (*notiones*) of intelligible things which I observe with my mind alone—e.g., the Liberal Arts—are born and made in me deeper within when I investigate them carefully. But I do not clearly see the difference between the awareness and the things which are the object of the awareness.

T: Do you think that things and the awareness of them produced in the soul are of the same or different natures?

S: Different, for how will there be a single nature of a corporeal species, such as an animal, grass, or tree, and of the awareness of it, which is produced in an incorporeal nature? According to the same principle, how can the intelligible species of any discipline and the awareness of it be made of a single nature?

T: If they are of a different genus or nature and not the same, tell me, please, which of them do you think must be put in the prior position? Are things of a loftier nature than the ideas of them or the ideas than the things?

S: I should have said that visible species are of a better nature than the ideas of them, if St. Augustine did not state in chapter 11 of the 9th book *On the Trinity* (9,11–16): "When we learn about bodies through the sense of the body, some likeness of them is made in our mind, which is a *phantasia* in the memory. For the bodies themselves are not at all in the mind when we think about them, but their likenesses are. Yet the representation of the body in the mind is better than that form (*species*) of the body insofar as it is in a better nature, i.e., in a vital substance, since the mind is a vital substance. I do not dare to say, moreover, that intelligible things are better than the idea of them which is in the soul." Reason teaches us that what understands is better than what is understood. If the knowledge of all things subsists in

Divine Wisdom, I should be justified in proclaiming it incomparably superior to all the things of which it is the knowledge. In that case, as I think, such an order proceeds from Divine Providence through universal creation, that not only is every nature which comprehends the knowledge of the nature next to it better and superior, but also the knowledge itself, because of the dignity of the nature in which it exists, far precedes that nature of which it is the knowledge. Hence I should more readily say that the knowledge of intelligible things is prior to (*antiquiorem*) the intelligible things themselves.

T: Perhaps you would be right in your statement if what is formed were more outstanding than what forms it.

S: Why are you making this point in opposition?

T: Because the knowledge of the arts, which is in the soul, seems to be formed from the arts themselves. But if you were to offer a very sure and persuasive argument that knowledge is not formed from the arts but the arts from knowledge, perhaps your reasoning would be on the right track.

S: Haven't we already agreed that everything which understands is superior to what is understood?

T: Yes, we have.

S: Tell me, then, whether the skill of the mind understands the discipline or the discipline understands the skill.

T: I am quite sure that the discipline is understood by the mind. But if I say that the same discipline is known from the skill itself just as by the mind to which the skill belongs, I am afraid that I may seem to be stating that the mind and its skill are two things possessing ideas of the discipline and not one and the same essence in which knowledge of the discipline is naturally inherent. But if true reason teaches that mind and its skill are not two, but one and the same thing, I am compelled to admit that everything understood by the mind is understood by its skill also; and the immediate consequence will be that mind and skill, or in any case a skilled mind, is of a nature superior to that art which it understands, if things which understand are prior to what is understood. If I say, however, that the discipline of the skilled mind is itself a skill, the result will be a confession that either the skilled mind and the skilled art are two things which understand and are understood by each other, and hence enjoy an equal dignity of nature, or that mind and its skill and the art which it understands and by which it is understood are of one and the same essence. But which of these views must be held is not yet clearly evident.

S: Perhaps it will be clear if we undertake a straight course of reasoning with God as our guide.

T: Let us inquire carefully. First I should like you to say whether the nature of mind, in which the skill of the discipline is present, is simple or not.

S: I think that it is simple, for it is incorporeal, intellectual, and hence must be wholly uncompounded.

T: You are right. Do you think, then, that it has any accident which is not naturally present in its essence?

S: Indeed I do, for I see that many things happen to it: e.g., it is moved in time, although it itself is not time; the skill of the discipline is accidental to it, for now it is discerned to be skilled, now unskilled, now disciplined in the arts, now undisciplined, now wise, now foolish, now going astray when it walks in circles irrationally, and now walking straight on the path of reason; and it has many other such experiences.

T: Then the skill of the discipline and the discipline itself are not naturally present in it, but come to it from accidents from outside.

S: I should not dare to make such a statement, for it is not likely that God created in His image and likeness a mind in which skill and art are not naturally inborn; otherwise it would not be mind, but some brutish and irrational life. No one would be correct in saying, I believe, that man was made in God's image accidentally and not substantially, especially since we see that intellect and reason are substantially present in him.

T: They are not, then, accidental to him, but naturally inherent.

S: That would be a judicious statement, I believe. For although the mind seems to be born unskilled and unwise, an accidental state resulting from transgression against the divine command by forgetting itself and its Creator, yet by the rules of learning it is formed again and can find in itself its God, itself, its skill and discipline, and everything which naturally subsists in it, for it is enlightened by the grace of its Redeemer.

T: It remains, then, to consider how skill and discipline are present in it, whether as natural qualities called virtues, such as the kinds of wisdom and knowledge which it receives when struck by Divine Radiance, or as the substantial parts of which it consists, so that there is a kind of trinity of one essence, namely mind, skill, discipline.

S: I am inclined to believe the latter. It seems to me a kind of substantial trinity of the same nature.

T: And so mind understands its skill and discipline, and its skill and discipline understand not *what* it is but *that* it is. Otherwise the trinity will not be coessential and coequal.

S: I should not deny that point either, for reason forces me to admit it.

T: Consider, then, whether they are formed by one another or by some nature superior to themselves.

S: If the Catholic faith did not persuade me that there is a Higher Nature by which this trinity is established, formed, and understood, and if truth did not confirm the teaching, perhaps I would not be rash in answering that it is formed by itself or surely that it is an archetypal form. But now since there is a Higher Nature from which all things are formed and begin to be formed, and turning to which all things that are or can be turned toward it are formed, I do not doubt that the trinity of mind is formed by that same Nature.

T: It would be very foolish to be in doubt on that point. Only the Divine Mind, then, has in Itself the true knowledge of the human mind, skilled and trained in the arts, formed by Itself and turned toward Itself.

S: That seems the truest belief.

T: Do you think that the human mind is one thing and that the idea of it in the mind of the One who forms and knows it is something else?

S: Far from it. I rather understand that the substance of man as a whole is simply the idea of him in the mind of the Artificer who knew all things in Himself before they were made. The knowledge itself is the true and only substance of things known, since in it they subsist perfectly made, eternally and changelessly.

T: We can therefore define man as follows: Man is a certain intellectual idea eternally made in the Divine Mind.

S: That is an altogether true and praiseworthy definition of man. In fact, not only of man, but of all things made in the Divine Wisdom. Nor do I fear those who define man not according to what he is understood to be, but from the qualities understood in reference to him; as for example: "Man is a rational, mortal animal, receptive to sense and discipline." What is more remarkable, they call this a definition of essence, although it deals not with substance but with qualities related to substance and is externally derived from what is accidental to substance through generation. Now the idea of man in the Mind of God is none of these things. There, of course, it is simple and it cannot be called one thing or another, for it surpasses all definition and collection of parts; for one can merely predicate *that* it is, but not *what* it is. The only true definition of essence states affirmatively only *that* it is and negatively *what* it is.

T: Do you think that there is a certain idea in man of all the sensible and intelligible things which the human mind can understand?

S: Indeed I do; and in fact, he is understood to be man especially through the fact that he has been allowed to have an idea of everything, whether it was created equally with him or he was ordered to have dominion over it. How would man be given dominion over things of which he had no idea? His dominion would go astray if he did not know what he was ruling. Divine Scripture indicates this point to us very clearly in the words: "When all the animals had been formed from the earth and all the birds of heaven, the Lord God led them to Adam to see what he would call them. Now, whatever Adam called a living creature is its name." [56] "To see," it says, i.e., to understand what he would call them. For if he did not understand, how could he call them correctly? "Now, whatever Adam called it is its name," i.e., it is the very idea of the living creature.

T: Why is it strange, then, if the idea of things which the human mind possesses, since the idea was created in it, is understood as the substance of the things of which it is the idea, similarly to the Divine

Mind, in which the idea of the created universe is the incommunicable substance of the universe itself? And why is it strange that, as we call the idea of all things understood in the universe and perceived by the corporeal sense the substance of what is subject to intellect or sense, so we also call the idea of differentiae, properties, and natural accidents, the differentiae themselves, the properties, and the accidents?

S: It is not strange.

T: There has been created in it, then, irrationality, and every species, every differentia, the property of irrationality itself, and everything naturally recognized in reference to it, since knowledge of all of these and of what is like them has been created in it. I mentioned "what is like them" because of the things besides animals which the universe contains—e.g., the cosmic elements, the genera and species of grasses and trees, quantities and qualities, and the other things multiplied by countless differentiae. True knowledge of them all is implanted in human nature, although it itself is still unaware of their presence until it is restored to its pristine wholeness in which it will understand very clearly the greatness and beauty of the image created in itself, and none of the things created in it will escape its notice. It will be enveloped by Divine Light and turned to God, in whom it will contemplate everything with utter clarity. Isn't that the meaning of the great Boethius when he says: "Wisdom is comprehension of truth about the things which have being and are allotted their changeless substance. Moreover, we say that those things have being which are not increased, diminished, or changed, but, supported by the resources of their own nature, always preserve themselves in their proper force. These resources are qualities, quantities, forms, magnitudes, smallnesses, equalities, conditions (*habitudines*), actions, dispositions, places, times, and whatever is found united in some way to bodies. Although themselves of incorporeal nature and thriving by reason of changeless substance, they are changed by their participation in body and, by contact with variable matter, they pass into changeable inconstancy." [57] Where do you understand that these things subsist except in the ideas of them in the soul of a wise man? For they have being where they are understood, or rather they *are* the understanding (*intellectus*) of themselves.

S: Finding a solution to this problem demands a many-sided explanation; and while the process is taking place, a countless host of different problems surrounding on all sides keeps pouring out as if from an infinite source, so that the fictitious image of Hercules' hydra becomes an appropriate analogy. As the hydra's heads were cut off, they kept growing at such a rate that a hundred teemed out of one that had been cut off. The implication is that human nature is a hydra, a manifold source of infinite depth; and no one except Hercules, i.e., Virtue, can perceive it clearly. For the passage says, "No one knows what is in a man except man's spirit within him." [58] And so if that inner idea of things, present in the human mind, is the substance of the things of which it is the idea, it follows that the very idea by which man knows himself is believed to be his substance.

T: That certainly does follow. We said that the human mind, the knowledge by which it knows itself, and the discipline by which it learns itself in order that it may recognize itself subsist as one and the same essence.

S: Did we not establish a clear definition of man a little while ago by saying that man is an intellectual idea eternally made in the Divine Mind? If that is so, and if the preceding definition has not been rashly established, how would that idea by which man knows himself be his substance?

T: It has not been rashly established. That definition is true which states that an idea eternally made in God's Mind is the substance of man. Nor are we unreasonable now in teaching that the awareness by which the human mind recognizes itself is substantially inherent in man. For every creature is considered one way in God's Word, in which all things have been made, and another way in itself. Hence St. Augustine says in his *Exemeron*: "Those things made by Him are under Him in one way, and the things which are Himself are in Him in another way. Indeed, the understanding (*intellectus*) of all things in the Divine Wisdom is the substance of all things, or rather it *is* all things. The knowledge by which intellectual and rational creation understands itself in itself is, as it were, a kind of second substance by which it merely knows that it has knowledge, being, and will, but does not know what it is. And that substance established in God's Wisdom is eternal and changeless, but the other is temporal and changeable. The one precedes, the other follows. The one is primordial and causal, the other proceeds and is caused; the one contains everything universally; the other, insofar as it is distributed by the superior, embraces particularly by knowledge what is subject to it. The latter is produced by the former and will return to it." Nor am I now speaking of that superessential Substance which, in Itself, is God and the unique Cause of everything, but of that which was primordially created causally in the Wisdom of God, whose effect is this substance which we, or rather the natural order of things, have established in second place.

S: We should therefore understand two substances of man, one generic in the primordial causes, the other specific in their effects.

T: I should not say two, but rather one understood in two ways. For human substance is perceived one way through creation in intellectual causes, and another way through generation in effects. In the former it is free from all changeability; in the latter, subject to it. In the former, simple and free from all accidents, it eludes all observation and understanding. In the latter, it receives a certain composition from quantities, qualities, and the other things understood in reference to it; and through this composition it is susceptible to mental observation. So one and the same thing is called virtually twofold, because of the twofold way of looking at it; but everywhere it preserves its incomprehensibility—I mean in causes and in effects— i.e., whether bare in its simplicity or clothed with accidents. In none of these is it subject to any created intellect or sense, and it does not itself understand what it is.

S: Why, then, did you say before that the human mind has an idea by which it knows itself and a discipline by which it learns itself; but now, on the other hand, you affirm that the mind cannot be discerned either by itself or by any other creature?

T: Reason teaches us that both statements are true; for the human mind both knows itself and does not know itself. It knows that it is, but it does not know what it is. This is the greatest source, as we showed in previous books, of our teaching that God's image is in man. As God is comprehensible, since from creation it is inferred that He has being, and He is incomprehensible because no intellect of man or angel can grasp what He is, nor can He Himself, since He is not something but is rather superessential, so the human mind is granted knowledge of its being merely to know that it is, but it is not allowed to know in any way what it is. What is more remarkable and splendid to those who consider themselves and their God is that the human mind is praised more for its ignorance than for its knowledge. It is more praiseworthy for the mind not to know what it is than to know that it is; just as negation is more closely and fittingly related than affirmation to the praise of Divine Nature, and it is wiser to be ignorant of It than to know It; for ignorance of It is true wisdom since It is known better by not knowing. Very evidently, then, the divine likeness is discerned in the human mind by the mere knowledge that it is, but the ignorance about what it is. Whatness, if I may use the term, is spoken of negatively in reference to it, and only being is attributed to it affirmatively. Nor is this without reason. If it were known to be a certain thing, it would surely be circumscribed in something, and hence would not altogether express in itself the image of its Creator, who is wholly uncircumscribed and understood in nothing, because He is infinite, superessential, above everything which is said and understood.

S: How, then, has all creation been made in the knowledge of man, when that knowledge does not even know what it is itself, and this ignorance is taken as very praiseworthy, as a mark of man's superiority, since his knowledge is bounded by no finite substance?

T: Indeed, this is the greatest proof by which we infer that all creation has been created substantially in man. The substance of all things endowed with being cannot be defined in any way, according to Gregory the Theologian, who argues about such matters against those who deny that the Word of God is superessential. They strive to enclose it in some substance, and hence, wishing to separate the substance of the Son from the substance of the Father, they hold that It is not above everything but is contained in the number of all things. Thus, just as Divine Essence is infinite, so human substance[59] made in Its image is bounded by no definite limit. From what is understood in reference to it, moreover, namely times, places, differentiae, properties, quantities, qualities, relations, conditions (*habitudines*), positions, actions, receptions of action (*passiones*), it is merely understood to have being, but what it is is not at all understood. Hence we may understand that the only subsistence of any creature is that reason according to which it was stationed in the primordial causes in God's Word; and so there can be no definition of what it is because it surpasses all substantial definition. But it is defined by its accidental circumstances, as it comes into its proper species by generation, whether intelligible or sensible.

[8]   *S:*   Both divine Scripture and reason itself assert that the nature of man and of angels is either the same or very similar. Both man and angel are called, and are, intellectual and rational creatures. And if they correspond so closely, one may appropriately ask why we read that every creature was created in man but not in an angel.

T: There is good cause, I believe. We see, of course, that quite a few things in man do not subsist in angels either according to the word of authority or the understanding of reason—e.g., this animal body, which Divine Scripture attests was joined to the human soul even before sin; the fivefold corporeal outer sense, the *phantasiae* of sensible things, which through that sense are borne in upon the human soul; the perplexity and the troublesome difficulty of the reasoning process in inquiring into the natures of things; also, the painstaking acuteness demanded for distinguishing between virtues and vices; and very many other things of the kind. It is quite clear that the essence of angels is free from them all, and yet no one of sound judgment will deny that they are in the nature of things. Although St. Augustine seems to have taught in Book 8, Chapter 7 of *The City of God* (8.6) that angels have perception when he praises the power of contemplation of great philosophers who "saw that in every changeable thing the whole species by which it is whatever it is and however and of whatever kind it is by nature, can have being only from Him who truly is because He is changelessly. Hence the body of this whole world, the figures, qualities, ordered motion, the elements arranged from heaven to earth, and whatever bodies are in them, or all life—whether the kind that nourishes and holds bodies together, such as is in trees; or the kind that also has sense perception, such as is in animals; or the kind that also has intelligence, such as is in men; or the kind that does not need the help of nutrition but merely holds bodies together and has sense perception and intelligence, such as is in angels—all can have being only, I say, from Him who simply is." But I should think that he was talking about the inner sense. Who is unaware that celestial essence is devoid of very many parts and motions of nature which are naturally present in human nature? Besides, true reason attests that celestial substance does not have awareness of the things which are not present in it either substantially or accidentally. For although angels are said to govern this world and all corporeal creation, we must not believe that they have any need of corporeal senses or of motions in place or time or of visible appearances in order to perform this task. All of these things which are accidental to us because of the deficiency of our nature, which is still subject to variations in place and time, are correctly judged not to be accidental to them because of any deficiency in their power. When they transform their spiritual and invisible bodies into visible forms so that they can appear visibly in place and time to the senses of mortals, this transformation is not accidental to them because of themselves, but because of men, over whom they are and to whom they proclaim divine mysteries. They do not have local sensory vision or accidental temporal knowledge of what they will do in governing affairs, for they are eternally above all time and place in the contemplation of Truth, in which they see together the causes of their government. Do not think that I am making such a statement about all celestial essences, but only about the superior orders which are always around God and which have within them no ignorance except that of the Divine Shadow, an ignorance which surpasses all understanding. But the lowest order properly called *angelic*—the one by which the higher orders govern whatever Divine Providence orders to be accomplished by divine revelations in human minds or in the other parts of this world—is not yet free from all ignorance. For this reason, as St. Dionysius the Areopagite very subtly discusses in the book *On the Celestial Hierarchy* (10.2), "it [i.e., the lowest order of angels] is taught by the higher orders and introduced to the knowledge of divine mysteries above it." So we are not unreasonably bidden to believe and understand that all creation, visible and invisible, was created in man alone, since no substance has been created which is not understood to be in him; and no species, differentia, property, or natural accident is found in the nature of things which is not naturally present in him, or of which he cannot possess knowledge and be inwardly aware. And the very knowledge of things inwardly contained is better than the objects of the knowledge in direct proportion to the superiority of the nature in which the knowledge has been established. Moreover, every rational nature is rightly put ahead of every irrational and sensible nature since it is closer to God. Therefore the objects of the knowledge present in human nature are fittingly understood as subsisting in their ideas. They should be judged as more truly existing where they are the objects of better knowledge. Moreover, if things subsist more truly in the ideas of them than in themselves, and if knowledge of them is naturally present in man, then they have been universally created in man. The return of all things to man will undoubtedly prove this point at the appropriate time. For how would they return to him if they did not have some natural kinship with him and if they did not proceed from him in some way? As for that return, I have promised to talk about it in the appropriate place.

S: Although these matters seem exceedingly difficult since they surpass the limit of simple doctrine, yet when they are regarded by the eye of reason they are quite fitting and extremely useful for an understanding of the greatness of man's created state; so that we may appropriately say not that man was produced from the earth in the genus of animals, but rather that the whole genus of animals was produced in man from the earth, i.e., from the solidity of nature. In fact, not only the whole genus of animals, but also the created universe was made in man, so that one can understand truly about man the statement of Truth: "Proclaim the Gospel to all creation." [60] Likewise the Apostle says: "All creation is groaning and even to this time is still giving birth." [61]

If these points seem too abstruse or utterly incredible to anyone if he is unskilled in all the natural disciplines called "liberal," he should either keep silent or learn, and not rashly oppose what he cannot understand. If he is learned, he will clearly see (to produce an example from one of the arts) that geometrical figures do not naturally subsist in themselves but in the reasons of the discipline of which they are the figures. For example, a triangle, which is perceived by corporeal sense in some matter, is surely a sensible representation of the triangle present in the mind. The educated man will understand the triangle itself which subsists in the mind trained in the art, and he will weigh with right judgment which is better, the figure of the triangle or the triangle itself which the figure represents. If I am not mistaken, he will find that that figure is truly a figure but that it is a false triangle, whereas the triangle which subsists in the art is the cause of that figure and is the true triangle. I am not talking about a *phantasia* of a triangle, which descends from the mind through the memory to the senses, and through the senses to sensible figures; nor am I talking of the one which, coming from a sensible figure, is fixed by the corporeal sense in the memory. I am rather talking about that very triangle which endures uniformly in the discipline itself, where line and angle are together, and there is no line in one place, angle in another, middle in another, end in another, point of inception (*signum*) in another, space of sides from point of inception in another, space of angles from point of inception in another, in another a point from which lines begin and in which angles are bounded by joining of the sides; but everything that I have mentioned is one in one and the same idea of the geometrical mind; and the whole is understood in the individuals and the individuals in the whole; and they are united in the intellect itself, because it is the substantial reason of all things which it understands, and from it the figures (*formulae*) of geometrical bodies are given specific form. What I have said about the triangle should be understood also about the other figures, angular, circular, or oblique, plane and solid. All of them subsist in the ideas of themselves according to one and the same reason in the skilled mind trained in the discipline. If geometrical bodies, then, whether in the *phantasiae* of memory or in some sensible matter, are formed in the rational ideas of themselves which are free from all *phantasia* and matter, they subsist above everything perceived by bodily sense or represented in the memory. Why is it remarkable, then, if natural bodies too, compounded from the qualities of the cosmic elements, subsist in that nature in which the knowledge of them is present, especially since all things perceived in reference to bodies are incorporeal? For example, the species in which they are contained are incorporeal. Similarly no wise man doubts that quantities and qualities are of intelligible nature and proceed from the intellectual reasons of vital substance.

[9] *T:* Whoever carefully examines the natures of things will immediately find that that is true.

S: And now that we have discussed these matters, it is appropriate to ask how every creature was created in man although he himself is said to have been made after the creation of everything else. If the whole visible and invisible creation was made before him, then, as Divine History records, and we read about the creation of nothing after him, by what reasoning can we perceive that all creation was made in man? If anyone should say, e.g., that universal creation occurred twice, first specifically in itself and secondly generically in man, I should not readily believe such a view compatible with reason; for if it is, man will not have any proper substance but will be, as it were, a compound of many things, or rather of all previously made creation, and a manifold conglomeration of various forms. An even more serious difficulty is that if all creation, visible or invisible, was made perfectly in itself—for since the Creator is perfect and more than perfect, we cannot believe that He created anything imperfect—how did it receive something like a second perfection of its creation in man, who was created last among the operations of God? And if that is so, God did not make man in His own image from nothing, but from the things which were made before him. But if anyone should say that the human body was created not from nothing but from something earthly, namely clay, what will he say about the better creation of man, which undoubtedly was established in the soul and the spiritual body at the first creation? We believe that this soul was created by the breath of God, or rather that it *is* the breath of God, created from nothing, not from something.

T: I realize that this question is enveloped by a thick mist of obscurity, and requires a many-sided skill to reveal it clearly. But to avoid passing over it untouched, we shall try to consider it in some way to the extent that the inner ray of Divine Light shines upon us. First, please tell me whether intelligibles or sensibles are prior to the mind which understands them or to the sense by which they are perceived.

S: Where one thing understands and another is understood, and what understands is of a better nature than what is understood, I should be justified in saying that what is understood or perceived is inferior to the understanding mind or the perceiving sense. But as for things which understand themselves insofar as they can, I should not say that they are superior to themselves. When a thing itself and the knowledge of it are one and the same, I do not see what kind of priority there can be. For example, I know that I have being, but the knowledge of myself is not prior to me because I am the same as the knowledge by which I know myself. And if I did not know that I have being, I would not be unaware of not knowing it. Hence, whether or not I know that I have being, I shall not lack knowledge, since I shall still have knowledge of my ignorance. And if everything which can know that it does not know itself cannot be unaware of its being—for if it had no being at all, it would not know that it did not know itself—the conclusion is that everything which knows that it has being or which knows that it does not know that it has being, actually has being. Whoever is buried in such ignorance that he does not know that he has being and does not perceive his ignorance, I should call not a man at all, or else wholly extinct. In our previous arguments we established clearly enough that knowledge and ignorance are present together, inseparably and at all times, in the human soul. It knows that it is a rational and intellectual nature, but it does not know what intellect and reason themselves are.

T: Didn't you have being, then, before your knowledge or ignorance about your having being?

S: No, along with my being I received knowledge that I am and understanding that I am ignorant of what I am.

T: Tell me, when does a man receive knowledge of himself? Is it at that creation in which all men were made universally in the primordial causes before the times of this world, or at the procreation by which, in the order of times predetermined and known only to God, he proceeds into this life?

S: At both, I think; in one generally and latently in the causes; but in the other specifically and openly in the effects. For in that primordial and general creation of all human nature, no one recognizes himself specifically or begins to have his own knowledge of himself. In that creation there is a single, general knowledge of all, known to God alone. There all men are one, that one, of course, who was made in God's image and in whom all men were created. Just as all species contained in one genus are not subject to intellect or sense by means of differentiae and properties, but subsist as a kind of undivided unity until each of them intelligibly or sensibly receives its property and differentia in its individual species, so each one in the community of human nature fails to distinguish himself or others of the same substance by proper knowledge before he proceeds into this world at his own time, according to what was established in the eternal reasons.

T: Why, then, does not everyone know himself as soon as he has come into this world by generation?

S: I should say, with good reason, that the penalty for man's transgression against nature is revealed in this way. If man had not sinned, he surely would not have fallen into such deep ignorance of himself. Likewise, he would not have suffered ignominious generation from the two sexes like irrational animals, as the wisest of the Greeks declare by the surest reasons. That Man who alone was born in the world without sin—namely, the Redeemer of the world—nowhere and never endured such ignorance, but as soon as He was conceived and born, He understood Himself and all things. And He was able to speak and to teach, not only because He was His Father's Wisdom, which nothing eludes, but also because He had received undefiled humanity in order to cleanse the defiled. Not that He received a humanity different from that which He restored, but He alone remained undefiled in it, preserved in the innermost reasons of violated nature for the purpose of healing its wound. Humanity perished wholly in all except Him, in whom alone it remained incorruptible. He Himself is the greatest example of grace, not because any remission was granted to Him from the guilt of human nature, but because alone of all, with no previous merits, He was joined by the Word of God to a unity of substance. In Him all the elect, receiving from the fullness of His grace, become sons of God and participants in the divine Substance.

T: Human nature had an inherent ability to know itself perfectly, then, if it had not sinned.

S: That is altogether probable. The greatest and saddest misfortune of human nature was to abandon the knowledge and wisdom implanted within it and to slip into deep ignorance of itself and its Creator, although it is understood that the yearning for its lost bliss remained in it even after the fall. Such yearning would not remain in human nature at all if it were completely ignorant of itself and its God.

T: Then an altogether perfect knowledge both of itself and of its Creator was naturally implanted in it before sin, insofar as the knowledge of a creature can comprehend both itself and its Cause?

S: That is my very opinion. For how would man be an image if he differed in some respect from that of which he is the image, except for the reason [*ratio,* principle] of the subject, about which we spoke in previous books when we were discussing the prototype—i.e., the archetypal example and its image—saying that God Himself is the Archetypal Example by Himself, from Himself, in Himself; and that He subsists not created, formed, or changed by anything; that His image, man, was created by Him and does not subsist through, from, or in himself, but has received being according to nature from Him whose image he is, and has received deification by grace? Everything else predicated of God can be predicated also of His image, but predicated of God essentially and of His image by participation. For the image is both goodness and a good image by participation in the Highest Good and the Highest Goodness, of which it is the reflection; it is eternal too and eternity by participating in that Eternal and Eternity by which it was formed; and the image is omnipotence by participation in that Omnipotence by which it was created and toward which it was turned when given specific form. For if human nature had not sinned and had clung without change to Him who had created it, it would certainly be omnipotent. Whatever in the universe it wished done would necessarily be done, since it would not wish anything to be done except what it understood that its Creator wished. It would completely understand, moreover, that its Creator's will is omnipotent and unchangeable if it had clung to Him completely, and had refrained from deserting Him in order to avoid being unlike itself. And all other examples would hold which can rightly be understood, thought, or predicated about God and His image.

T: Well, then, if perfect knowledge of self and Creator was inherent in human nature before sin, why is it strange, if we understand it reasonably, that it had the fullest knowledge of natures like itself, such as celestial essences, and of those inferior to itself, such as this world with its reasons subject to the intellect; and that it still has such knowledge potentially only, but even actually in the case of the best men?

S: For those of clear understanding it will not be strange, but true and likely.

T: That is great and true praise of human nature, or rather of Him who wished to create it that way. Therefore we must similarly accept the following point about its intellect and knowledge. As the creative Wisdom, God's Word, saw all things that were made in It before they were made, and the vision itself of the things seen before they were made is their true, changeless, and eternal essence, so created wisdom, which is human nature, knew all things in it before they were made; and the knowledge itself of the things known before they were made is their true and abiding essence. Thus the very knowledge of the creative Wisdom is correctly understood to be the first and causal Essence of all creation; and the knowledge of created wisdom is the second essence and the effect of the higher knowledge. And what we have said about the first and causal Essence established in the idea of the creative Wisdom, and about the second essence, which is its effect and which, as is appropriately asserted, subsists in the human soul, must similarly be understood without hesitation about all things discerned in relation to the essence of all creation. An accurate view of nature makes clear that everything established in human intelligence about the substances of things proceeds from the knowledge of the creative Wisdom through created wisdom. Established about these essences are sensible species, quantities, qualities, places, times, and the like without which essence cannot be understood to have being. We can therefore sum up our whole point briefly as follows: just as the Intellect of all things which the Father made in His only-begotten Word constitutes their Essence and the foundation of everything naturally understood about that Essence, so the knowledge of everything which the Father's Word created in the human soul is their essence and the foundation of everything naturally discerned about it. And just as Divine Intellect precedes everything and is everything, so the knowledge of the intellectual soul precedes everything which it knows and is everything of which it has foreknowledge. Thus everything subsists causally in Divine Intellect and in effect in human knowledge. Not, as we have often said, that the Essence of all is one thing in the Word and something else in man, but that the mind views one and the same Essence one way in eternal causes and another in their effects. In the former, It surpasses every intellect; in the latter, from what is observed about It, It is merely understood as having being. In both cases, however, no created intellect may know what It is. For if It could be known, It would not wholly express its Creator's image in itself; for the Creator is merely recognized as having being from the things of which He is Beginning, Cause, and Founder; but *what* He is eludes all sense and intellect.

S: No creature, then, visible or invisible, precedes the creation of man in place, time, dignity, origin, eternity, or, to put it simply, in any kind of priority. In knowledge and dignity, though not in place or time, it precedes what was created with it, in it, and below it; and it was created together with the celestial essences, with which it is equal in dignity of nature. For it too participates in celestial and intellectual essence, since it has been written about the essence and nature of angels and man: "Who made the heavens in intellect," [62] as if it were openly saying: "Who made the 'intellectual' heavens." It is therefore not easy to understand, if man was created together in substance with the essences of angels, how all things visible and invisible were created in him. It does not seem reasonable that man should have the beginning of his creation together with the celestial powers although they were created in him.

T: If you carefully examine the mutual bond and the unity of intellectual and rational natures, you will surely find the essence of angels established in the human and the essence of man in the angelic. Whenever, in fact, the pure intellect knows something perfectly, it is made in that thing and becomes one with it. So close had been the association of human and angelic nature, that if the first man had not sinned they would both have been made one. This union is beginning to be made in the best men, whose first fruits are among celestial beings. An angel is made in man through the intellect of the angel which is in man; and a man is made in an angel through the intellect of the man established in the angel. For as I said, whoever clearly understands is made in what he understands. So the intellectual and rational nature of an angel has been made in the intellectual and rational nature of man, just as that of a man has been made in the nature of angel through the mutual knowledge by which angel understands man and man, angel. Nor is it strange, for we too, while debating, are made in each other. When I understand what you understand, I become your understanding (*intellectus*), and in some ineffable way I am made in you. Similarly when you plainly understand what I plainly understand, you become my understanding and from two understandings there is made one, formed from what we both understand wholly and unhesitatingly. For example, to take an illustration from numbers: you understand that the number six is equal to its parts. I have the same understanding, and I understand that you understand it, just as you understand that I understand it. The understanding of both of us becomes one, formed by the number six; and hence, I am created in you and you in me. For we are not one thing and our understanding something else. Our true and highest essence is understanding given specific form by contemplation of the truth. That understanding can conform itself not only to natures of the same essence but also to lower ones when it understands or perceives them by love, we are taught by the words of the Apostle, who forbids the intellectual part of us to love visible forms when he says, "Do not conform yourselves to this world." [63] By this principle of mutual understanding, then, an angel is justifiably said to be created in man and man in an angel. Nor is it right to believe and understand that the angel precedes man by any law of creation or in any sense of priority, although according to the interpretation of many the Biblical account relates first the creation of angelic nature and later the creation of human nature.

Chapter 10 (Columns 781D–784D)

Still not satisfied, the Student asks why angels were made on the first day of Creation, but man not until the sixth. It would seem as if not only the angelic essence but that of sensible things preceded man's substance in dignity.

In his reply the Teacher argues that the Bible, properly understood, is always telling of man's creation while it talks of the creation of other things. Man's creation actually preceded the making of all other things in him. When we read, "God said 'Let there be light'," *light* stands not only for the angelic substance but also for the human. If, then, man partakes of the celestial essence symbolized by light, everything mentioned after the making of light must be made in man. One then sees that this sensible world was made on man's behalf. It was intended to be his kingdom. Had he not sinned, he would have ruled all things, not by means of his senses, to be sure, but by intellectual insight into their rational natures and interior causes. He would have governed the whole world and each of its parts eternally and infallibly. As punishment for his sin, he fell from the dignity of his nature and became simply one of the parts of the world.

Scripture introduces man explicitly as the last work of creation so that we might understand that everything described as created earlier actually subsists in him. Not only is the account of the making of light on the first day an allusion to the angelic nature created in man, but also the firmament of the second day, the dry earth, water, and vegetation of the third day, and the sun, moon, and stars of the fourth day are all references to him. The firmament, we recall, represents the universal elements which are undeniably found in human nature. Earth and water signify substance and accidents, and these are surely to be found in him, as is the life that nourishes the plants. Sun, moon, and stars symbolize the creation of our senses, which function in three ways. In the first way, like the sun, they present to the mind the species of sensible things so clearly that it can judge them with no difficulty. The second way, which is like the "smaller" light of the moon, is that whereby the mind errs most often. It is misled by shadows, as when it mistakes the straight stick as bent, misinterprets reversed images in a mirror, or misjudges the origin of sound through hearing echoes. As if in moonlight the mind must struggle to determine the real state of affairs. The third way whereby the senses function is in flooding the mind with forms as innumerable as the stars. It is then so confused that it almost always judges erroneously.

From Chapters 10 and 11 (Columns 784C–788A)

T: Do not be surprised that what is seen in human nature, I mean the corporeal senses, is signified by the greater things of the world, i.e., by celestial bodies. Completely sound reason informs us readily that man alone, and individually a single man, is greater than the visible universe, not in the mass of his parts, but in the dignity of his rational nature's harmony. "For if," as St. Augustine tells us, "the soul of a worm is better than the body of the sun which enlightens the whole world;"—for the lowest form of life, such as it is, is prior to the foremost and most precious body by the dignity of its essence—why is it strange if all the bodies of the whole world are ranked after human sense? First, according to the principle that a natural cause takes precedence over what is made naturally because of it. Of course, sensible things are made because of sense and not vice versa, as no wise man doubts. Next, whatever judges is reasonably prior in dignity of nature to what is judged; and no one with clear insight into the natures of things doubts that the senses judge about sensible things, not sensible things about senses. Besides, sense is established only in vital substance, in which there is very evident motion of life; but since sensible things, insofar as they are bodies, hold the last place among creatures, they do not always clearly show the motion of life. Of sensible things, some show vital motion rarely or never. Finally, nothing sensible is life, although it seems moved by life; whereas sense is not only alive but is substantially present in life, as nature itself teaches. And if the quantity and greatness of corporeal mass is praised in sensible things, the quantity and greatness of the power established in the senses is more praiseworthy. See how great is the power in the sense of the eyes to search out the lighted spaces to infinity, to form in itself the innumerable different kinds of bodies, colors, figures, and the other things of which the *phantasiae* enter the memory through this sense. What about the power of hearing? Hearing can take in and discriminate so many different voices, sounding at the same time. Whoever examines the other senses in this way will observe their remarkable and ineffable powers. Hence, we may understand how the intelligible reasons of the created universe, insofar as they can be understood, were created in the intellect of man. Likewise the sensible species, quantities, and qualities of the universe, insofar as they can be sensed, establish the causes of their creation in human sense and subsist there. But since sense is naturally present not only in man but in the other animals as well, it undergoes another distribution also. It is assigned to reptiles (crawling creatures) of the sea and flying creatures of the heaven in the prophet's consideration of the fifth day of creation. And rightly so, since the sense itself which was inserted into the nature of things on the fifth day consists of five parts. On the sixth day it was joined to earthly animals as well, intentionally, I believe, because they seem to have a closer relationship to man, who was made on the sixth day, than do the animals made from the nature of waters. And so man himself, whose creation is covertly implied in the individual accounts of the preceding considerations of the divine creative operation (since in him and with him everything previously mentioned was created, not through intervals of time but by an ordering of causes flowing into their effects), was openly formed at the end of the creation of the whole universe. The account of the prophet's speculation was completed on the sixth day to signify by the number *six* not only the perfection of human nature, but also the creation in it [viz., in human nature] of all things previously disclosed. According to Scripture: "God said, 'Let Us make man in Our own image and likeness, and let him rule the fish of the sea, the birds of heaven, the beasts and all creatures, including reptiles that move upon the earth.' And God created man in His image, in the image of God." [64] Here we should first note that at the creation of all things recounted from the beginning of creation in the previously mentioned five intelligible days, the superessential Unity of Divine Nature and the ineffable Trinity, or as St. Dionysius the Areopagite says, "The fruitfulness of the Highest Good" is not openly expressed. Nevertheless in the passage "In the beginning God created heaven and earth," it is appropriately understood that the persons of the Father and the Son are signified. By the term *God,* the Father is introduced, by *beginning* the Word; and a little later the Holy Spirit is introduced by the words: "And God's spirit hovered over the waters." Thus at the creation of the primordial causes, the proper character of the Holy Trinity is persuasively indicated. In the processions of those causes into their forms and species, Scripture is observed as calling to mind the same Trinity. For example, "God said, 'Let there be light'." [65] By the name *God* it alludes to the Father, by the sensible word *said* to His only-begotten and superintelligible Word, in which and by which He made everything with being. When it says "And God saw that the light was good," [66] it implies the Holy Spirit. Scripture does the same thing on the other days too, wherever it adds, "And God saw that it was good." On the sixth day when man was formed, both the Unity of divine Nature and the Trinity are quite openly declared: the Unity by saying "and He said" in order that *God* might be supplied (as subject); or, according to the clear Septuagint rendering of "and God said" with the plural verb "let us make," the three Substances of one Essence or, as it is usually designated in Latin, the three Persons of one Substance, are expressed. [67] And rightly so, for when the image is created, the Archetypal Example whose image it is is most openly revealed.

[11] But since man, although one, is composed, as it were, of many parts—for he consists of body, i.e., formed sensible matter, and of soul,

i.e., sense, reason, intellect, and vital motion—it is asked whether man was made in God's image in all his parts or only in those which are of a loftier or most excellent nature. Tell me your opinion on this subject if you will.

S: On this question practically all expounders of sacred Scripture speak out. First of all, they unanimously state that man, insofar as he is body, is not made in God's image. God is, of course, incorporeal and no corporeality is inherent in or accidental to Him. Whether man has been created in God's image in soul—i.e., in all the parts understood to be in soul or only in the most outstanding of them—has been questioned with the greatest care by spiritual men. Their conclusion is that the Divine image is expressed only in the soul's most excellent part, the intelligible. This part is understood as virtually threefold, consisting of intellect, reason, and inner sense, concerning which we exchanged many views in previous books. Of course, that life by which the body is governed and which the human soul seems to share with the life of nutrition and growth especially assigned to grasses and trees, and also the fivefold outer sense which man shares with irrational animals, even though they are understood as belonging to parts of the soul, are said by many wise men not to have within them the image of God. But when reason itself observes the human soul more carefully, it finds it of utterly simple nature and whole in itself throughout the whole, in no way unlike itself in any of its parts, or inferior or superior to itself in respect to any of those things understood to be in it essentially. The whole, as we have said, governs its body, nurtures it, and causes its growth; the whole perceives through the senses; the whole receives the *phantasiae* of sensible things; the whole is in reacting numbers, which first receive the *phantasiae* of sensible things; the whole is in advancing numbers, which introduce the *phantasiae;* the whole is in memorial numbers, which commend the *phantasiae* to memory.[68] The whole is in the whole memory, the whole is above the whole memory, whether of sensibles or of intelligibles. Hence, there is discerned not the diversity of its parts, if one should speak of parts in it, but the variety of tasks of supervision and of motions. Those parts of it are motions which bring about different intelligences in the soul. It itself, of course, is everywhere whole in itself and undivided; but its motions, which men also call animate numbers because they are in the soul, are designated by different terms. When it turns in contemplative motion about its Creator, above itself and above the intelligence of all creation, it is called *intellect* or *mind*. When it investigates the reasons of things as though by a second natural motion, it is termed *reason*; when it finds those reasons and distinguishes and defines them, it is the inner sense. When it receives the *phantasiae* of sensible things through the organs of the corporeal senses, it is the outer sense; not because the sense is substantially outside the soul, but because through that sense the soul perceives the forms and species of sensible things. There is a great difference between the nature of simple mind and the manifold variety of corporeal instruments. Since it governs the body by nurturing it and causing it to grow, it has earned the designation of 'vital motion,' although it is of utterly simple, indivisible, and unpartitioned essence. It is not lesser in its lesser duties, greater in the greater, or greatest in the greatest; but in all it is equal to itself, as the great Gregory of Nyssa declares in the sermon *On the Image*.

Hence we may understand that the whole human soul has been made in God's image, for the whole is intellect understanding, the whole is reason discoursing, the whole is sense in the inner sense and sentient, the whole is life and life-giving. In two ways in particular, moreover, we know that the human soul is made in God's image. First, because, like God, it is diffused through all things with being and can be comprehended by none of them. Soul thus penetrates the whole instrument of its body but cannot be confined by it. Second, because just as it is predicated of God only that He is without any definition of what He is, so the human soul is merely understood as having being, but neither it nor any other creature understands what it is.

Chapters 11–26 (Columns 788B–860B)

Eriugena now draws extensively from the writings of Gregory of Nyssa and others to support and amplify his doctrine of man. Gregory confirms his previous explanation of the soul as incomprehensible because it is made in the image of the incomprehensible God (788B–790B). From Gregory he also derives the concept of vital motion, the connecting link between mind and body.

Man has been made as a composite of three factors which have a natural order: mind (*animus*), vital motion, and matter. The whole virtue of the soul resides in mind; created by God without any intermediary, mind is the image of God. Vital motion is the image of mind, a mirror of a mirror, as it were. Since it centers around matter, it is also known as material life. While the image of God in the strict sense inheres in the mind alone, vital motion connects mind and body in such a manner that one may speak of the whole man, mind and body, as God's image. As image of an image, vital motion acts as that through which the mind displays a material aspect. Body, then, is in a sense derived from vital motion and obeys it, while it in turn is obedient to the mind. Vital motion does not belong to man's substance, for in a manner it belongs to body as well as mind. It is that through which the body is formed, made alive, and nourished. When body and mind are separated, that is, when the mind ceases to move its body, then vital motion disappears entirely (790B–791C). Gregory is cited again in support of a corollary of this theory: wherever an organ of the body is defective or corrupted, mind cannot manifest its power, not because the soul is defective, but because that part of the body is incapable of receiving the soul's power (791C–793B).

Eriugena adopts Gregory's doctrine that all men were simultaneously made in the one first man. Had Adam not sinned, he would have multiplied in the manner of the angels, spiritually and without sexual intercourse. Adam's fall was from unity into diversity, from a sexless state into a state of division into male and female (793B–799B). Here and later (846D–847A) Eriugena is careful to say that sexuality, though the result of sin, is not an evil. Since man could not multiply spiritually once he had taken on a corporeal body, God provided that human procreation be like that of the animals. Because He foreknew that Adam would sin, He made Eve before the fall. Man is both soul and body: hence both must have been created simultaneously. The original human body must have been spiritual and immortal, for the cause of materiality and corruption is sin. The entire human being, then, is immutable and eternal in its pristine state, while after the fall man is mutable and variable (800). Here again Gregory explains: the form is permanently unaltered and is like a seal imprinting itself on many things. At the resurrection it will receive back into itself everything that corresponds to the stamp of the form (801A–C). Eriugena interprets this to mean that whatever is immutable in man, whether soul or body, belongs to the first creation, while whatever is mutable is added as the result of the fall. The immaterial, spiritual body is the form that remains immutably the same in all human bodies. The innumerable individual differences among men are accidents of the form, consequent upon the changes in sensible matter. Everything pertaining to matter—that is, to the qualities and quantities of the four elements—is an addition to the original spiritual body. This external body is like a cloak that undergoes changes in size and shape, while the spiritual body which it clothes remains eternally the same. The material body will be dissolved into the elements from which it has been composed, and since its form remains, at the resurrection it will be fashioned again according to that interior body (801C–803B).

The Student notes a discrepancy between this account based on Gregory's and that given by Augustine. Augustine repeatedly and emphatically asserts that the body of the first man even before his sin was an animal body, earthly and mortal. He would not have died, however, had he not sinned, and his body would have been changed into an incorruptible spiritual body. He would never have grown old but would have enjoyed a life as free of cares as that of Enoch and Elijah (803B–804C).

The Teacher replies that it is not his task to choose between the best of the Greek authorities, Gregory, and the best of the Latins, Augustine. He does not dispute Augustine. It is legitimate to add details noted by others that had not occurred to Augustine. What Augustine called the animal body is the external body that Gregory said had been added by the divine foreknowledge because of Adam's future sin. Gregory has simply given a fuller account (804C–805B).

Dissatisfied, the Student asks how, if man had an animal body before he sinned, he could have become blessed like the angels. The Teacher replies that, as we have seen, God made everything in the temporal world at once, and therefore He knew beforehand that man would sin and fall into the irrational motions of an animal. At one and the same time God made spirit, reason, and inner sense in His image and those things which were the result of the sin that was yet to be. God foreknows many things which He does not cause, since they do not exist substantially. He is, moreover, the wise maker and orderer of the universe and does not permit these additions to harm its beauty. He alone can make good from the evil of our irrational will. Man's animal, earthly, corruptible body, his division into two sexes, his animal-like procreation, his need of food, drink, and clothing, his changes in physical stature, his need for alternate sleeping and waking—all these are the consequences of sin before sin, made in man by God as if external to him and added to his changeless, unitary nature. Had it not sinned, human nature would have remained free of all these encumbrances, as it will be free of them in the future (807A–808A).

In God's nature there is no before or after, no past, present, or future, but everything is all at once. When we think of a time before sin and a time after sin, we are really displaying the mutability of our own thought. We can thus make sense of Augustine's teaching that Adam would not have eaten the fruit had he not already possessed an evil will. Man has never been free from sin, for he can never be separated from the mutability of his free will (808A–809A).

The same point can be made if we reframe the question to ask how long Adam and Eve dwelt in paradise. The answer is, no time at all. Had there been any duration to his stay, man would have been able to acquire sufficient perfection to prevent sin from occurring. We conclude, then, that he never really was in the paradise of human nature. What is written as if describing the first man is really a reference to what is to come at the end of the world.

Augustine teaches that the devil and pride, the cause of his fall, were created simultaneously. As soon as the devil existed, he fell inwardly from the blessedness that would have been his had he desired, like the angels, to be subject to God. This, argues the Teacher, shows us that in the parallel case of man, what Scripture speaks of as in the past really refers to that future which might have been had not man and his pride been created together (809A–810C).

Additional evidence that Adam's stay in paradise is to be understood symbolically is furnished by the inconsistencies yielded by a literal reading. Why had Adam and Eve no children in Eden when they had been commanded to be fruitful and multiply? Why, if they ate the fruit of the tree of life, were they not protected against corruption? A spiritual interpretation is obviously needed, and Gregory, as we have seen, has supplied it (810C–812C).

Augustine himself has said that there are three legitimate ways of understanding paradise: as a physical place, as a spiritual state, or as both place and state; he himself prefers the third. The Teacher then proceeds to interpret a passage in which Augustine writes of man's fall from eternity and intellectual good to time and sensible goods as an indication that Augustine really believed that the spiritual paradise, man's inner state, is real and the earthly Eden only its sensible appearance (814B–815B). Appeal is made to Ambrose, who also finds a spiritual as well as a physical paradise, but then goes on to identify paradise with human nature itself. The Teacher agrees with the many details of Ambrose's spiritual reading: Adam signifies reason, Eve the senses, and the serpent pleasure. Christ is the river watering the garden, and its four streams are the cardinal virtues, prudence, temperance, courage, and justice (815B–D).

A halt is called, but only temporarily, to this mode of exegesis when the Student protests that in allegorizing too much his Teacher has forgotten the literal meaning that Ambrose also intended. A spatial, corporeal paradise seems to be denied. The Teacher, however, cannot agree that there is or was a geographical Eden. He refuses to argue the matter, claiming that his intention has been only to set forth the various opinions of the Fathers so that each reader can adopt the view that he wishes to follow. As for himself, Gregory is the most congenial: the inner man is made in paradise; the second, outer man, is made beneath paradise, that is from the dust of the earth outside eternity and in time. The integrity of the first is divided into the two sexes of the second. Eve's creation from Adam's rib is the introduction of sense into the unity of the rational human nature (816B–817).

The Teacher continues his account of man's dual nature, borrowing freely from Gregory. The inner man is paradise itself. The tree of life, or "every tree," is Christ Himself, planted in the midst of human nature. In this tree all good subsists, but in the tree of the knowledge of good and evil, or as Gregory calls it, the "mixed tree," all evil is concealed under the alluring guise of good. While Christ, the tree of life, dwells in the inner man, the "mixed tree" is found in the outer man; that is, its appeal is to the corporeal senses. The woman, Eve, represents the senses because the Greek word for sense (*aisthesis*) is feminine. Thus, through the appearance of good to the senses, reason and intellect are deceived, human nature receives falsity, and mankind falls (817A–827B).

God does not create evil, and Scripture does not state

clearly that He made the tree of the knowledge of good and evil. Evil is neither found in the substance of things nor caused by anything natural. In itself, evil is nothing at all but that irrational, disordered, perverse motion of the free will, originating in the corporeal senses that are beguiled by the goodness of the apparent beauty of the fruit (827B–829B). In the ensuing chapters (19–26) the Teacher completes his spiritual allegorizing of the Biblical account of creation with details again drawn from the interpretations of earlier commentators. Adam's sleep signifies the relaxation of that contemplative attention which man owes his Creator, and in that sleep, Eve, the outer senses, is added to his nature. The moment when Adam and Eve realize their nakedness is their recognition of the loss of their original virtues. The fig leaves represent man's obedience to the letter of God's law as opposed to its spirit. That God curses the serpent but not Adam and Eve is the occasion for the Teacher to emphasize that God never curses what He has made, and spirit and senses are God's creations. The serpent does not come from God, for it represents the unnatural irrational passions that seduce man from his true employment. After the fall, then, man loses nothing that God created as of the substance of human nature.

The ground that is accursed so that it bears brambles and thistles, the suffering that man must undergo as with sweat on his brow he toils for his daily bread, and his return to the dust from which he was made can indeed be understood, as Augustine would have it, as a literal description of human life on the physical earth. Again, however, as Maximus shows, there is a higher, spiritual meaning: man must labor in thought and action to purge himself from all diseases of body and soul until he returns to the earth, that is to the changeless stability of his source. "Dust you are and to dust you shall return" means that because the nature of the soul, made in God's image and likeness, originated in the primordial causes, it is destined to return to them.

Book IV closes appropriately with an anticipation of the end of all creation in God, that final aspect of nature which neither creates nor is created.

From Chapter 27 (Columns 860B–D Migne)

T: The Divine Nature is believed not to be created because It is the Primal Cause of all, beyond which there is no beginning by which It can be created. But since after the return of the created universe of visible and invisible things to their primordial causes contained in Divine Nature, no nature will be generated from It any more or multiplied into sensible or intelligible species; they will be one in It, just as they are one now and always in their causes. It is deservedly believed, therefore, and understood not to create anything; for what will It create when It alone will be all things in all things?

Notes

1. Gen. 3:19.
2. Ps. 132:5.
3. Acts 27:37.
4. Gen. 46.27.
5. John 1:14.
6. Mark 14:38, cf. Matthew 26:41.
7. Luke 23:46.
8. John 14:6.
9. 1 Peter 3:18.
10. 1 Peter 4:1.
11. 1 Cor. 2:8.
12. Acts 2:33.
13. Acts 1:4.
14. Luke 4:1.
15. Matthew 10:19–20.
16. Matthew 12:28.
17. Mark 3:29.
18. Luke 23:46.
19. Luke 1:80.
20. Luke 4:1.
21. Luke 4:14.
22. John 3:6.

23. John 14:16–17.
24. Acts 5:3.
25. Acts 5:4.
26. Matthew 26:41.
27. Luke 23:46.
28. Colos. 3:5.
29. Ps. 104:35.
30. Ps. 1:3.
31. 1 Cor. 10:11.
32. Ps. 1:4.
33. Ps. 146:4.
34. Ephes. 4:8.
35. John 12:24–25.
36. Ps. 104:30.
37. Ps. 146:4.
38. Gen. 1:24.
39. Gen. 1:20.
40. Gen. 1:26.
41. Gen. 1:21.
42. Gen. 1:24.
43. 1 Cor. 2:14.
44. 1 Cor. 2:15.
45. 2 Cor. 4:16.
46. Romans 7:25.
47. John 14:6.
48. Gen. 1:26.
49. John 12:26.
50. Mark 16:15.
51. 1 Cor. 15:42–44.
52. Gen. 1:24.
53. Ps. 49.13.
54. Romans 11:34.
55. 1 Cor. 15:44.
56. Gen. 2:19.
57. *De. Inst. Arith.*, ibid.
58. 1 Cor. 2:11.
59. Reading *substantia* for the *substitutio* of the text.
60. Mark 16:15.
61. Romans 8:22.
62. Ps. 136:5.
63. Rom. 12:2.
64. Gen. 1:26–27.
65. Gen. 1:3.
66. Gen. 1:4.
67. Gen. 1:26.
68. In my translation of *reacting, advancing,* and *memorial* for *occursoribus, progressoribus,* and *recordabilibus,* I follow R. C. Taliaferro's translation of Augustine, *On Music* 6.6 in *The Fathers of the Church* 2 (Cima Publishing Co., Inc., New York, 1947).

Book V

[1] *T:* "Now, then, *ne* he may by chance set his hand upon the tree of life and partake of it and eat and live forever." Before we contemplate the prophetic force of these words by which is most clearly promised the return of human nature to the same felicity which it had lost by sinning, the order of the whole chapter must be shown. Whoever observes keenly will find that the great prophet Moses spoke in it in transposed order. The order of the words is as follows: "And the Lord God made coats of skins for Adam and his wife and clothed them and said: 'See, Adam has become like one of Us.' And the Lord God expelled him from paradise to till the soil from which he had been taken. 'Now, then, *ne* he may by chance set his hand upon the tree of life and partake of it and eat and live forever.' He cast Adam out, and in front of the paradise of pleasure He posted Cherubim and a flaming, flashing sword to guard the way to the tree of life." [1] The passage "Now, then, *ne*[2] he may by chance set his hand upon it" and the rest to "and live forever" could involve ambiguity about whether the words are those of the prophet speaking for God or of the Lord Himself, if the point were not explicitly clarified in the Septuagint, where it is written: " 'And now,' God said, '*ne* he may at some time stretch out

271

his hand and partake of the tree of life'." But no one who examines the force of the words clearly will doubt, I believe, that these words, whatever their order, promise the return of human nature to its pristine state. I have little regard for the observation of those who believe that the particle *ne* denotes negation rather than interrogation or something like doubt in this passage, and that man was expelled from paradise in order that he might not be able to partake of the tree of life and to live forever. How, after sin, while not yet freed from sin and from death, the penalty of sin, could human nature possibly partake of the tree of life and eat and live forever, when even before sin it had not partaken or eaten of that tree, as we infer from careful investigation of divine Scripture? For if man had partaken and eaten, surely he would not have sinned and fallen but would have lived happily forever. Moreover, if that paradise from which man was expelled was local and earthly, and if the tree of life planted in its midst was earthly and sensible and produced fruit fit for the uses of the body, why did God not banish man merely from the tree of life and hedge him about in some part of paradise in order that he might not be able to touch that tree? If the only cause of living in paradise happily and eternally was the eating of the tree of life, which was granted only to rational creatures, why was man, wretched and mortal after sin, unable to spend his limited time in some part of paradise? We believe that the other animals, and especially that serpent by which the ancient adversary practiced his malice, were able to be in paradise without living eternally and happily, since they were not created for the eating of the tree of life. Why, then, would not delinquent man too be allowed to live among them, since true reason has taught that a rational creature, even though sinful, surpasses every irrational, sinless creature by the dignity of his nature? If irrational animals remained in paradise after the expulsion of man who excels the others, why was not he, too, even when a sinner, allowed to remain among them in paradise? Or were the other animals perhaps expelled from paradise with him? But if anyone should make such a statement, he should search in divine Scripture or the authority of the holy fathers or both for proof that the expulsion of the animals, upon which before his sin man in paradise had conferred names, occurred at the time of man's own expulsion from paradise when he sinned. But if this proof is unattainable, he should stop thinking about paradise and its animate creatures in carnal terms and should readily enter upon the spiritual interpretations taught by truth, the only path by which the inmost shrines of the mystic writings are penetrated. Come, then, and observe the force of the divine words more carefully.

S: Here I am, ready to understand whatever you say. Although these subjects are vital, only a few, I think, have dealt with them. In fact, I have not read or heard that anyone has yet written about the return of human nature and the return of the other things in it and because of it to the eternal reasons from which it proceeded, and about its restoration to its original dignity; although scattered here and there in the divine books and the teachings of the holy fathers the form of such a doctrine often appears in our support.

[2] *T:* The divine word implies such a return by the words "Now therefore [*Nunc ergo*]" or, as another version more openly proclaims, " 'And now [*Et nunc*],' God said." It is as if the divine mercy and infinite goodness, always most inclined to indulgence and pity, were sighing over what had befallen the divine image, and with pitying condescension, were patiently enduring man's arrogance. "Now therefore," i.e., "Now I see man expelled from paradise and transformed from blessed to miserable, from abundantly endowed to needy, from eternal to temporal, from full of life to mortal, from wise to foolish, from spiritual to animallike, from celestial to earthly, from new to aged, from happy to sad, from saved to lost, from the prudent son to the prodigal, straying from the flock of celestial virtues; and I share his grief, for he was not made for this purpose. He was rather created to possess eternal life and bliss; but now you, his neighbors and friends, see that he has been expelled from paradise to the region of death and wretchedness." God addressed these words to the celestial orders who, clinging to their Creator, remained in perpetual bliss but whose number was diminished by man's perdition. You see, then, how much this divine expression of pathos contains, although it is very brief and made up of a temporal adverb *now* and a causal conjunction *therefore*.

But just as if after a lament for man, the same divine mercy, turning to console itself and the celestial powers, promises the return of man to paradise in a form of speech which indicates doubt and interrogation. In saying "*Ne* he may by chance set his hand upon the tree of life and partake of it and eat and live forever," He is virtually saying, "We should not grieve and mourn so much about man's death and his fall from paradise, for hope of return has not been wholly withdrawn from him. Perhaps *ne* he may set his hand, i.e., through his virtues he may extend his zeal for good works so that he may be able to partake of the fruits of the tree of life (i.e., of the spiritual gifts of God's Word) and eat the food of pure contemplation, by virtue of which he will live forever and never return to the need for temporal things which will wholly perish with the world, but he will wholly cross over into God and be one in Him." This meaning is clearly indicated by the following words of Scripture which say: "He cast Adam out, and in front of the paradise of pleasure He posted Cherubim and a flaming, flashing sword to guard the way to the tree of life." I think that you have not forgotten how, in Book IV, we clearly inferred from the statements of the holy fathers who write either in Greek or in Latin that the paradise from which man was banished is human nature itself, created in God's image. When that very human nature scorned the divine precept, it fell from the dignity of that image. We therefore conclude that the banishment and casting out of man is simply his loss of the natural felicity which he was created to possess. Man did not destroy his nature which, made in the image and likeness of God, is necessarily incorruptible. Rather he destroyed the felicity which he would have acquired if he had not disdained obedience to God.

S: Not only have I not forgotten, but I have fixed the point firmly in my memory.

T: Why, then, does it say: "And He posted Cherubim in front of the paradise of pleasure," i.e., before the spiritual delights of human nature? What is it trying to signify by this name? Is it that celestial power placed third in the first hierarchy of angelic orders (for divine tradition counts the Seraphim, Cherubim, and Thrones in it), or merely the meaning of the name? Or is it trying by the name to convey something else of deeper significance? Because of this uncertainty, the interpretation of this name must first be made clear. *Cherubim* is interpreted as meaning "abundance of knowledge" or "outpouring of wisdom," as St. Dionysius the Areopagite writes in the book *On the Celestial Hierarchy* (7.1). His view is corroborated by Epiphanius who, in the book *On Hebrew Names*, says that *Cherubim* is interpreted as "full knowledge" or "the knowledge of many." But if divine Scripture wished celestial essence to be signified in this passage, we shall have to admit that paradise is of a spiritual nature. Reason does not allow us to believe that a nature spiritual and next to God, which always moves around Him, can be posted before a local and earthly paradise, unless we perhaps say that not a Cherubim himself but one of the lowest order of celestial powers, properly[3] called angelic, was posted before paradise and called *Cherubim* because it was ordered by a Cherubim to be posted before paradise. Whatever in the universe is accomplished by the lower orders of celestial beings is referred to the higher, since the lower do only what the higher instruct them to do. In the same way it is written that a Seraphim cleansed the prophet Isaiah, although as St. Dionysius the Areopagite explains, "The Seraphim himself did not cleanse the prophet by his own agency, but he did it through one of the angels of the lowest order of celestial essences," who deserved to be called by the name *Seraphim* because, as a Seraphim had ordered, he cleansed the prophet; and the cleansing is attributed not to the cleanser but to the one who ordered the prophet to be cleansed. But even with such a statement, will the same difficulty not remain? It is not likely that an angelic substance, although last in the order of celestial powers, can be posted in any earthly place. But if we understand only the meaning of the name but no celestial substance in this passage, we can say that God posted before the paradise of pleasure—i.e., before the view of human nature which was rational although banished from paradise (i.e., removed from the dignity of its primal condition)—Cherubim, viz., abundance of knowledge or outpouring of wisdom, by which human nature might recognize itself and wish and be able, when cleansed by action and by knowledge and when trained by the zealous pursuit of wisdom, to return to its original felicity, which it had abandoned by sinning. Hence we may understand that divine mercy rather than retribution was involved in the banishment of man from paradise. The Creator was unwilling wholly to condemn His image, but wanted to renew it, to train it with abundance of knowledge, and also to water and give light to it by an outpouring of wisdom; and to make it worthy both to approach again the tree of life from which it had been removed and to enjoy the tree of life in order not to die but to live forever. But if anyone wishes to perceive more deeply that by the name *Cherubim* God's very Word is signified, his understanding will be appropriate. God's Word, in which are hidden the treasures of knowledge and wisdom, is always and constantly accessible to observation by human nature. The Word cautions human nature, cleanses it, enlightens it, until It may lead it back to its unblemished perfection. Why is it strange if the Wisdom of God is designated by the name *Cherubim* since It is also called "Angel of Great Counsel" and Virtue [Power? *Virtus*]? Hear the Apostle speaking about God the Father: "From the creation of the world, His invisible things have been understood and perceived through what was made and so have His everlasting virtue and power." [4] In short, by a remarkable metaphor He is customarily alluded to in divine Scripture by the names of all the celestial essences. In the same way we fittingly understand that the flaming sword, too, signifies the very Word of God, for it burns and divides. It burns our sins, for "God is a consuming fire," [5] cleansing the irrational defilement of our nature; and It divides our nature and separates it from what it earned as recompense for transgression, the accretions tainting and deforming it which render it unlike its Creator. That Sword, the Father's Word, the only-begotten Son, Virtue, and Wisdom, is deservedly believed and understood to be flashing since, although unchangeable by nature, in His ineffable mercy and loving-kindness He moves Himself toward the salvation of human nature. So such a Cherubim and a flaming, flashing Sword is always posted before the eyes of our soul, i.e., our reason and intellect. The point, then, of "to guard the way to the Tree of Life" is that we should not forget the way of the Tree of Life but should constantly keep before the eyes of our souls the memory of the tree itself and of the way by which one may go to it. Do not be surprised that I used *Cherubim* as a singular although St. Jerome declared that such Hebrew names ending in "-im" are masculine plural. I have followed St. Dionysius the Areopagite, who uses the names *Seraphim* and *Cherubim* even in the singular, especially since it is the practice of Hebrews and Greeks to use singulars and plurals interchangeably.[6] But what is that way which leads to the tree of life? And what is that tree to which it leads? Is it not that same Son of God, who says of Himself: "I am the Way, the Truth, and the Life"?[7] That He Himself is the Tree of Life is found quite openly in many passages of divine Scripture, so that it needs no evidence. Thus in multiple fashion the symbolic names of God's Word have been heaped up in this passage of holy Scripture. He is called *Cherubim, flaming, flashing Sword, Way* and *Tree of Life* in order that we may understand that the Word never withdraws from the sight of our hearts and is always immediately present to enlighten us. In no place and at no time does it allow us to lose the memory of the bliss which we lost by transgression, but always wishes us to return to it. Until that end is achieved, it sighs while sharing our grief and goads us on as we take the road which leads there by mastering the steps of knowledge and action. "I have come to bring fire to the earth, and my sole desire is to see it blaze."[8] But before we deal with the actual return of our nature, I think, if you agree, that we should take up some highly persuasive arguments drawn from sensibles by which we are taught to believe unhesitatingly that the return will come.

[3] *S:* I certainly do agree. True reasoning, taking natural proofs derived from sensibles as its point of departure, can arrive at the pure knowledge of the spiritual.

T: Consider then whether or not those local and temporal returns of the parts of this visible world are free from a kind of mystery.

S: I should not readily say that they are free from mystery, for in my judgment there is nothing among visible and corporeal things which does not signify something incorporeal and intelligible. But I wish that you would briefly recall some of those returns from which you want to draw your arguments.

T: I think that everyone who considers the nature of things realizes with the utmost clarity both through the conception of the mind and through the judgment of the corporeal sense that the celestial, star-bearing sphere always revolves and returns to the same place within the space of twenty-four hours; that the sun likewise reaches the same point of the equinoctial diameter after four years at the same instant of time, namely its rising; that the moon, too, returns to the same place of the constellation-bearing heaven in which it was lighted in an interval slightly over twenty-seven days and eight hours. It will seem superfluous to speak about the return of other planets, for it is extremely well-known to all skilled in astrology [i.e., astronomy]. It sufficed to set down the natural laws and revolutions of the two greatest luminaries of the world in order to persuade you about what we are trying to assert. The moon is recalled to the beginnings of its circuit after nineteen years and the sun after twenty-eight. These two numbers multiplied together give a product of 532 years. When this period is completed, the two luminaries, bringing to fulfillment the whole harmony of their circuit and the whole reckoning of the Paschal cycle, are said to return to the same positions in the places of the heavens and the same numbers in the seasons of the great year. Is not the air also recalled to the same qualities of cold, heat, or moderation at definite seasons? What about the ocean, which in all respects follows the course of the moon and observes the fixed intervals of its return? Whether it brings about the daily flowing or ebbing or high tides,[9] it does not ignore the always varied and the fixed returns of nature. As for the animals of air[10] and earth and the shoots and the grasses, don't they likewise observe their seasons in which they burst forth with offspring, flowers, leaves, and fruits? To state it simply, there is no corporeal creature endowed with vital motion which does not return to the beginning of its motion. The end of the whole motion is its beginning, for it is bounded only by its beginning, from which its motion starts and to which it always strives to return in order to cease and rest in it. Besides, this very same point must be understood not only about the parts of the sensible world, but about the whole. Its end is its beginning, which it strives to attain; and when that beginning is found, it will cease, not with the perishing of its substance, but with its return to the reasons from which it set out. As the Apostle says, "The figure of this world passes away." [11] St. Augustine briefly commented on this statement by the Apostle as follows: "The figure, *not* the nature." I believe that he was using *nature* interchangeably with *essence* according to a very common practice of both Greek and Latin. The Greeks quite often substitute *physis* for *ousia* and *ousia* for *physis*. *Ousia* or "essence" is properly predicated of what cannot be corrupted, increased, or diminished in any creature, visible or intelligible. *Physis* or "nature" is properly predicated of the generation of essence in places and times in some matter which can be corrupted, increased, diminished, and affected by various accidents. *Ousia* is derived from the Greek verb *eimi* (the Latin *sum*, "be"), and its masculine participle is *ōn* and the feminine *ousa*, hence, *ousia*. *Physis*, however, comes from the Greek verb *phyomai*, i.e. *nascor*, "be born"; *plantor*, "be planted"; or *generor*, "be generated." Every creature, insofar as it subsists in its reasons, is *ousia;* but insofar as it is generated in some matter, it is *physis*. But, as we have said, just as the Greeks use *ousia* for *physis* and *physis* for *ousia*, so in Latin *essentia* is used interchangeably for *natura* and *natura* for *essentia*, although the proper individual significations are preserved. Thus true reasoning confidently affirms that the essence of sensible things, which St. Augustine designated by the term *nature*, will endure perpetually since it has been made unchangeable in the Divine Wisdom beyond all places, times, and changeability. No one instructed by the study of wisdom can doubt, however, that nature, generated in times and places and encompassed by the other accidents, will perish at an interval predetermined by the Creator of all things. By these and similar motions and returns of the sensible world both as a whole and in its parts, and by the firmly fixed restoration to the very beginning from which motions had proceeded (when the motion of things begins from it, it is usually called *beginning;* but when the motion ceases in it, it is called *end*. Among the Greeks too the beginning is called *telos*, i.e., "end", since they indiscriminately say *telos* for beginning and end), what is mystically intimated to us except the return of our nature to its beginning, from which it was made, in and through which it moves, and to which it always strives to return? Generally in all men, whether they are perfect or imperfect, pure or defiled, renewed in Christ and so aware of the truth or held fast in the shades of ignorance in the old man, there is a single, same natural striving for being, well-being, and being perpetually; and, as St. Augustine briefly summarizes it, of living blessedly and of avoiding wretchedness. That motion of living and subsisting happily comes from Him who is always and in a state of well-being and is present in all. And if every natural motion necessarily refrains from ceasing or resting until it reaches the end which it seeks, what can inhibit, check, or stop the necessary motion of human nature from being able to arrive at the goal of its natural striving? No creature wishes or strives to be nothing. Moreover, every creature flees from having non-being fall to its lot, especially since it is difficult for everything made by Him who truly is and is above being to return to nothing. In fact, if through some occurrence a nature like God is removed from its beginning by unlikeness, it always strives to return to its beginning in order to recover the likeness which it had marred. If visible fire, burning in some matter and raising the tongues of its flames, always stretches for the heights and does not seek the depths by any motion of its conflagration; how can one believe that the intelligible fire of substance created in God's image can permanently be detained in the depths of death and wretchedness so as to be unable to rise to the sublime heights of life and bliss by its natural striving and by the grace of its Creator? I am not saying that nature will be equally blessed in all, but that it will be free in all from death and wretchedness. For being, living, and being eternally will be common to all, both good and evil; but well-being and being in a state of bliss will be proper and special only to those perfect in action and knowledge. It certainly cannot be proved likely that the kindly Creator of rational nature prevents its rational motion from reaching Him. Examples both of sensibles and of the intelligibles observed only by the mind's eye attract us to the thought, belief, and understanding that all things, through the compelling force of natural law, return to the beginning of their motion and their primal causes. Among such intelligibles are the arts which philosophers call *liberal.* I see that I must present a few illustrations from them to establish my point, if you don't mind or consider it a waste of time.

Chapters 4 and 5 (Columns 868C–871B)

Each of the seven liberal arts also obeys the same cyclical law of nature exemplified by visible things: each proceeds from a principle and seeks to return to it. Dialectic begins with being as its principle and proceeds from the higher genera down to forms and the lowest species and then returns to being. Arithmetic begins with the monad, descends through all the kinds of numbers, and then returns. The point is the principle of geometry, which proceeds through lines and planes, returning ultimately to the point. Music originates in the tone and proceeds through simple and composite *symphoniae,* which are again resolved into the tone. Astrology begins with its principle, the atom, and returns to it.

Grammar and rhetoric, however, are special cases. Some treat them as branches of dialectic, the mother of the arts, but more important, they do not deal as do the others with the nature of things but with the rules of human speech, which are based on custom. Unlike the others, the art of writing well and the art of speaking well are matters of human invention at the service of dialectic. Even they, however, do have their principles—grammar its words and rhetoric its hypotheses— and are resolved into them. Hence in both the visible and the invisible things of this world we can find abundant analogies to the universal principle by which everything proceeds from and returns to God (868C–870C).

In response to the Student's request, the Teacher quotes Maximus the Confessor, who argues that whatever moves is caused to move and to exist by another, which is its principle. The same principle is also the end of its motion. There is one universal cause of motion and of existence (*causa essendi*), God, who is that being who does not exist through any cause. He must therefore be the end of all things as well (870C–871A).

The Student cannot see the connection between the return

of sensible and intelligible things to their principles and the cosmic return of all things to God (871A–B).

[6]   *T:*   I wonder why you are so slow that you don't clearly see the point of such illustrations. Don't all the proofs which we have brought in from the nature of sensibles and intelligibles aim at making us understand and believe unhesitatingly, through support from the surest kinds of arguments, that just as each and every thing, whether sensible or intelligible, is naturally compelled to return to its beginning, so human nature also will return to its beginning, which is nothing other than God's Word, in which it was made and unchangeably subsists and lives? For if God is the Beginning of all things with and without being—of those, I say, subject to the corporeal senses and the contemplation of the mind and of those which, because of the excessive subtlety and depth of their substance, elude the corporeal senses and mental insight—and if they strive for Him and their striving is not prevented in any way from reaching its goal, why is it strange if it is believed and understood about human nature, which was made specially in the image and likeness of the one common Beginning of all, that it will return to the place from which it set out? Especially since human nature did not depart in such a way as to desert its Beginning altogether? For, as the Apostle says, "In Him we live and move and have being." [12] But because it has been tainted by a certain unlikeness on account of sin, it is said to have withdrawn. Likeness made it very close, unlikeness distant; since it is not removed from God or brought close by the steps of the body but by the affects of the mind. One does not withdraw from the light of the sun by intervals of space, but by the loss of the eyes or by blinking or by the setting of the light itself. Health is not left behind because of space, but because of pain. Similarly life, bliss, wisdom, and all the virtues are abandoned only because of their respective states of privation, namely death, wretchedness, folly, and vices. Just as the skin of the human body is afflicted by the contagion and deformity of leprosy, so human nature was infected and corrupted by arrogant disobedience and made deformed and unlike its Creator. When it is freed from this leprosy by

the medicine of divine grace, it will be restored to its original fairness of form. In fact we should rather say that the nature itself, made in the image of God, by no means lost and cannot lose the vital force of its beauty and the wholeness of its essence. Of course, the divine form always remains unchangeable, but it was made receptive of the corruptible as a penalty for sin. We can prove this point by the words of St. Gregory of Nyssa who says in chapter 27 *On the Image*, when dealing with resurrection: "It is not incredible that in the case of the hidden and incorruptible body which will rise again a liberation from communion with the four general elements of the world to the proper state of nature, i.e., a return of rising bodies, takes place. For what is ours is not wholly in a state of flux and transformation. If it were, it would be utterly deserving of condemnation as having no fixed state by nature. But according to the more subtle account, of the things which are in us, some are stable but others come from a process of change. The body changes through increase and diminution, clad in succeeding periods of life as in garments. Through all change, however, the form remains unchangeable in itself, not leaving the marks once implanted in it by nature, but appearing with its inborn signs in the midst of all the corporeal transformations. But the change added to the form as a result of suffering is to be removed by God's Word. For just like a strange face, the deformity from disease takes hold of the form; and when this deformity has been taken away by God's Word, as in the case of Naaman the Syrian or of those lepers of whom the Gospel tells, the form (*species*) hidden beneath the suffering will clearly appear again in health with its features. So, in the godlike form of our soul, there is nothing that flows away in change and can be transformed; but what remains and is the same in our composition has been implanted within us." Note how clearly, how openly Gregory of Nyssa affirms that not only the form of the soul was made in God's image, but even the natural form of the body, which patterns itself after the image of the soul, always remains incorruptible and unchangeable. Whatever, on the other hand, has been added to the natural body from the accretions of the elements and to the soul from the defilement of irrational motions is always in a state of flux and corruption. This point, as he says, is very well implied by the figure of

Naaman the Syrian and the ten men who, as the Gospel relates, were cleansed by the Lord. The Syrian and those ten men had not lost their human appearance, but they were merely afflicted and covered with the swelling and ugliness of leprosy. From this exemplum we may understand that our nature has not been destroyed or changed but rather tainted by the deformity of vices. And note how immediately that Syrian assumed normal human form. *Naaman* means "handsome", and *Syria* means "contemplation of the celestial." Wouldn't human nature be handsome if it weren't arrogant? It was created beautiful and was intended to contemplate the celestial, but because of transgression it was afflicted with leprosy. After Naaman had gone down to Judea and returned to Syria, as the prophet Elisha had commanded, he laid aside his leprosy in the river Jordan, and the skin of his body was renewed. Will not our nature too, having recognized its illness and the ugliness of its vices, humble itself to confess its misery and be cleansed so as to return to itself? And who will cleanse it? Elisha, of course; i.e., the Savior or Salvation of God. Is not our Elisha God's Word, our Lord Jesus Christ, who is the Savior and Salvation of God? Upon our return to Syria, He will save our nature, commanding us to return to our original state, the contemplation of intelligible virtues. Where will He cleanse us? In the Jordan, which means "descent of the Lord" or "descent of judgment" or "power" or "farthermost land" or "the ascent of those." When do we believe and hope that the salvation and return of our nature to the Syria of celestial contemplation will come except when the Lord descends in His glory, descends to judge the living and the dead, to reveal His power in the farthermost land, i.e., at the outer limit of the world, when heaven and earth will pass away at the ascent of those, i.e., at the exaltation of the saints to eternal bliss, or surely at the common resurrection of all? Of course, the common resurrection of all is the ascent from death to life, from the animal and corruptible body to the spiritual and incorruptible. Moreover, the whole leprosy and corruption of human nature will be heaped up and turned upon Giezi. *Giezi* means "seeing the valley" or "separation from vision." Typologically, Giezi signifies the Devil who, since he is a worthless servant of our Savior, without whose orders or permission he may not exercise his wicked devices, constantly looks into the depth of perdition and eternal death and, separated by his arrogance, departs from the contemplation of truth. So our leprosy, which had contaminated the image of God because of his enmity, will be brought back upon him since, full of grief at our salvation and restoration, he will have his punishment increased. As for the ten lepers, they too bore the stamp of the same nature of ours which was redeemed by its Redeemer, is redeemed daily in individuals, and at the consummation of the world will be redeemed and freed universally in all.[13] Human nature, in fact, is customarily signified by the number ten, for it undoubtedly consists of soul and body. Now body is associated with the number five, viz., the four corporeal elements and form, which compounds those elements and gives them form. Soul too is in harmony with the number five, for it subsists in intellect, reason, the twofold sense, inner and outer, and vital motion, by which the body is governed. There you have man's number ten, I believe, which by the grace of his Creator and Redeemer will be freed from all wretchedness added to it like a kind of leprosy, and it will be reduced to one so as not to remain ten, but rather to be the single understanding (*intellectus*) of simple truth united with pure contemplation. I believe that this meaning is signified by the leprous man who alone returned to the Lord, rendering to God glory for his purification, and like a stranger returning from the distance of unlikeness, clung to his Liberator and Cleanser. The other nine have not yet been found, for the whole of human nature will be poured back into intellect alone, so that nothing will remain in it except the intellect alone by which it will contemplate its Creator. [7] But before we deal with the cleansing of human nature and its unification with itself and with its Creator, in whose image it was made, I think it appropriate for certain matters about the return itself to be discussed. Unless one first explains to what depths human nature fell, from what point the return of nature begins, through what steps it ascends, what it strives for, and in what it ends, he will not easily persuade his hearers about what he is affirming.

S: That is very true in my opinion. Who will find it easy to speak persuasively about the return of nature without first demonstrating, by clear methods of reasoning, where it fell and where and how it will return?

T: The place from which it fell and the place which it reached are unfamiliar to none of the faithful, for the Psalmist says: "When man was held in honor, he lacked understanding and was like the dumb cattle, made similar to them." [14] And so he abandoned the honor of the divine image and of equality with the celestial powers, and fell into the likeness of irrational animals. For the nature created to strive for and love the celestial naturally is overwhelmed by earthly desires and carnal longings. It is caught in a circle of irrational motion, although it was made to enjoy reason. There is no bestial motion which is not apprehended in man after his sin; and, as clear reason shows, what is praised in a beast is reproached in man. Why? Because in a beast irrational motion subsists naturally, but in man against nature. Moreover, whatever has been implanted by nature is good; but whatever has been added in opposition to nature, even though it is good in the substance of a beast, is unfitting and foreign to man. The sole source of irrational motions which have been added to human nature is the substantial impulse of beasts, which human nature has been made, by sin, to resemble. This point too is attested as follows by Gregory of Nyssa in chapter 18 *On the Image*: "I believe that from this beginning, viz., the likeness to irrational animals, even our individual passions, like a flood from some source, have been established in human life. This reasoning is confirmed by the kinship of the passions manifested equally in us and in irrational creatures. For it is not proper to attribute the beginnings of liability to passion to the human nature fashioned in the divine form. The likeness of man to God does not consist of madness, nor is the preeminent nature shaped by pleasure. Fear, too, and ferocity, longing for what is more, aversion from what is less, and all feelings of this kind are far from the true mark of divine beauty. So human nature has drawn them to itself from its irrational part. For those things by which irrational life was fortified for self-preservation became passions when transferred to human life." No wise man doubts that man fell into these irrational motions, which are present in bestial life naturally but in human life as passions; and that from them he suffered another downfall to the death and dissolution of the body. Nor could he have fallen more or to a lower state, since in the nature of things nothing is lower than what lacks life, reason, and

sensation. Lowest of all is the corruptible body, since no nature is
allowed to return to nothing. When it has set an end to its ruin, it
begins to return again from that state. Now the end of ruin is the
dissolution of the body, and so the return of nature sets out from the
dissolution of the body. Thus the death of the flesh has conferred
greater profit than punishment upon human nature, even though it has
been considered the penalty of sin. So true is that statement that the
dissolution of the flesh, usually called death, is more reasonably termed
the death of death than the death of the flesh. If human life in this
corruptible flesh is correctly called death by the wise, how would the
end of life itself be marked by the name of death, when it rather frees
from death than imposes death on the dying? Hence St. Maximus in
chapter 28 of his *Ambiguities* says: "It is unjust, I believe, to call the
end of this present life death rather than estrangement from death,
separation from corruption, freedom from slavery, rest from agitation,
cessation of wars, crossing over from confusion, return from shadows,
repose from griefs, quiet after inglorious pomp, tranquility after
instability, the veil of shame, refuge from passions, the abolition of sin,
and, in sum, the boundary of all evils." Thus the end of the present life
is the beginning of the future, and the death of the flesh is the
auspicious sign of nature's restoration and return to its pristine
soundness. [8] The first return of human nature occurs when the body
is dissolved and summoned back to the four elements of the sensible
world, from which it was compounded. The second will be fulfilled at
the resurrection, when each one will receive his own body again from
the common mass of the four elements; the third, when the body will
be changed to spirit; the fourth when the spirit, and to speak more
clearly, the whole nature of man returns to the primordial causes,
which have being always and unchangeably in God; the fifth when
nature itself with its causes is changed into God, just as air is changed
into light. God will be all in all, since there will be nothing except God
alone. By this statement I am not trying to affirm that the substance of
things will perish, but that it will return to a better state by the steps
just indicated. Indeed, how can something perish when it is proved to
return to a better state? The transformation of human nature into
God, therefore, must not be regarded as the perishing of substance, but

as the remarkable and ineffable return to the pristine condition which it had lost by transgression. Everything that clearly understands is made one with that which is understood. Our nature, in the case of the worthy, will contemplate God face to face to the extent of its capacity. Why is it strange, then, if it rises on clouds of speculation and can become one with God and in Him?

Chapters 8–13 (Columns 876C–884A)

The Teacher notes with scrupulous candor that not all authorities agree with his account of the stages of the return to God. While all agree that the body returns to the elements from which it came until it assumes its original form on the day of resurrection, some deny and others doubt the transformation of body into soul, soul into its causes, and causes into God. They do not want to say that the humanity of Christ is converted into His divinity. The Latin Fathers, Augustine and Boethius, hold this view, while Eriugena can again marshall the Greeks in support of his position. Lest it be thought that no Latin writer is sympathetic, he finds some indirect confirmation in Ambrose. While Ambrose says nothing of the transmutation of substances, he does teach a certain ineffable and unintelligible union of substances at the resurrection (876C–878D).

Everything in human nature is spiritual and intelligible, even the substance of the body. Intelligible substances can be united in such a way as to constitute a single thing while each retains its own distinct nature. Inferior substances are attracted by superior and absorbed in such a manner that their existence is preserved in the depths of the superior, there to subsist and be one unitary thing with it (879A).

Eriugena then proceeds to give a series of examples of union without loss of identity of the parts. Air does not lose its substance when it is changed into sunlight; nothing but light can be seen in it, and yet light is one thing and air another.

Iron, when it becomes incandescent in fire, appears to be changed into fire; yet the substance of the metal remains. In the same way, when the body passes into the soul and the soul into God, neither loses its substance but is saved in a better state (879A–B). The three factors present in all substances—essence, power, and operation—are a simple and uncompounded unity; but it is one thing to be, another to be able to effect something, and still another actually to effect that something (881A–B). Many individuals are one in a species, and many species one in a genus; all numbers are in the monad, all lines in the point (881B–882B).

The catalogue of illustrations of the union of natural things without loss of individuality is interrupted by a brief inquiry into the nature of light rays so that they too may be seen to exemplify the general principle. While rays of light are sensible like bodies, they do not have length, breadth, or depth, nor are they confined in space. Yet they are unlike the incorporeal, which exists apart from body, for they are found only in connection with bodies. A three-fold classification of creatures is proposed: bodies, incorporeal entities, and an intermediate class of corporeal (*corporale*) entities. Perhaps light rays, whether emanating from the sun or issuing from the eyes, belong along with color and shape to this third intermediate class (882C–883A).

Examples are drawn from the property of light to show that the many can be one while remaining a many. A golden globe on the spire of a tower can be seen simultaneously by many people. Everyone who sees it sees the rays shining from it, yet no one demands that another take away his glance so that he may see. Many rays flow together into one, but none is confused with another. Similarly, as Dionysius has pointed out, many lights may burn together in a church. Together they make one single light and yet the individual light of each, though not detectable by sight, is not destroyed (883A–C).

While listening to a harmony one cannot discriminate any distinct tone of the human voice or musical instrument, and yet each retains its own proper character. So many examples of union without loss of the integrity of the many render it quite credible that the whole of human nature will be brought together into an ineffable unity in which the uniqueness of body, soul, and intellect remains intact (883C–884A).

From Chapter 13 (*Columns 884A–885C*)

T: But since our discussion is about return, if the substance of body is always to endure unchangeably and without any transformation, we must ask what of the body will return to the soul to be made with it, as Gregory the Theologian says, "one and spirit and soul and God;" or "to be fermented into an uncompounded one" as St. Ambrose declares. The same St. Gregory resolves this question in the following few words: "The mortal and the fluid are absorbed by life." It is as if he were clearly saying, "When whatever is mortal and in flux in the body is absorbed by life. . . ." The Apostle teaches this very clearly by saying, "An animal-like body is sown, a spiritual body will arise." [15] The earthly, mortal, and fluid drawn and compounded from the different qualities of sensible elements under this form subject to the corporeal senses, as we have discussed in the preceding books, was added to the natural and substantial part of the body as recompense for sin. It will therefore be dissolved and changed for the better, and at the time of resurrection will return to spirit and stable substance which cannot flow away or die. In accord with the most sound and Catholic faith and steeped in the dogma of those godly men, Gregory the Theologian and Maximus, whose accounts of such matters are irrefutable, we believe that the Creator of human nature made the whole at once and did not create soul before body or body before soul. We therefore not irrationally hold that in that first creation, soul and body subsisted together without any capacity for corruptibility or death. It is incompatible with right reason to think that the Creator of the nature made at once, created part of it, the soul, immortal and incorruptible, but part, the body, mortal and corruptible. We therefore judge, fittingly in my opinion, that the whole nature of man, soul and body, was created immortal and incorruptible. Wise men hand down the tradition that angels too were created of such a nature. They do not doubt that the angels are incorporeal spirits and spiritual bodies free from all corruption. To men and angels who transgressed, however, as a penalty of sin corruptible bodies were added, earthly to men and aerial to angels. But what was added to us, since it was drawn from our Redeemer, who emptied Himself out and received the form of a servant, will be changed into spirit and into the very substance first created by God when "death will be swallowed up in victory" [16] and the whole man, the outer and the inner, the sensible and the intelligible, will be united into one. If it seems incredible to anyone that earthly body can be changed into spirit, let him see how the qualities of sensible things are transformed into one another, although the substances of which they are the qualities remain. Let him see how watery quality is turned into fiery; let him see how clouds, heaped into masses from air, are resolved into the purest air so that none of their density remains; let him see how the air itself, as we have often said, is consumed by the brilliance of the sun; let him see how smoke is turned into flame; let him see the exceedingly great force of reasoning. For if the qualities of visible things are incorporeal, as no one who argues correctly doubts, and if all earthly bodies are pressed into a mass from the piling up of these very qualities, why is it strange or incredible that what is made from incorporeal qualities can return to incorporeal things?

S: To those who clearly observe the substances and qualities of things, as well as their transformations and compositions, their unifications and progressions from the primordial causes and their return to those same causes, perhaps it will not seem strange or incredible. As for me, since I am not objecting to anyone's opinion or refuting it contentiously even if it differs on such matters, enough has been said. I need no further persuasion by sound arguments about the uniting of substances without any confusions or transformations of blendings or mixtures or compositions; and about the return and dissolution of the qualities from which all these sensible bodies have been compounded into the substances themselves, without which they cannot subsist. No quality, quantity, or any other accident can subsist by itself. Hence I should not be rash, I believe, in saying that the return with which we are now dealing will be not of substances, which remain unchangeably and indissolubly in themselves, but of qualities, quantities, and other accidents, which in themselves are both changeable and transitory, subject to places and times, and liable to generation and corruption.

Chapters 14–20 (*Columns 885D–893A*)

The point is emphasized by repeating that the substances as essences and reasons of created things never descend into the spatio-temporal world. What produces the temporal generation of particular things in this world is not the procession of substances but that of their accidents. Just as the causes of everything remain forever unchangeable in the Word which created them (for they could not subsist were they to be separated from their creator), so the substances remain perpetually unchanged in their causes. Only the accidents flow forth to create this visible world, and at its end they return to rest in their substances. Even the accidents or qualities never wholly desert those substances around which they revolve; for in an ineffable fashion they both remain permanently related to their substances and also constitute the visible world by their composition (885D–887A).

The distinction between causes and substances is amplified. While both are incorporeal and intelligible, causes are the most general reasons of everything and are constituted in the Word of God. Substances are constituted in causes and distribute them as individuals, particularizations of individuals, and the reasons of the most particularized individuals. That is, causes are the most general reasons of everything and are subdivided into those more and more particular reasons which are properly called the substances of individual things. This world, therefore, has proceeded from the causes and the substances by means of the binding together of the qualities of the latter, and when it is dissolved, it will return and pass over into them again (887A–B).

Surprisingly, perhaps, the causes and substances are not to be thought of as creatures. Creatures, strictly speaking, are those things, either visible or invisible, that come to be by generation in time. Only figuratively is the term to be applied to that ideal universe which comes "after" God but is made beyond all space and time (887B–888A).

What of space and time themselves? Are they parts of the physical universe and therefore subject to dissolution and return to their immutable causes? Or are they beyond change? Three chapters (17–19) are devoted to consideration of this question because there is general disagreement on the issue among both Catholic and secular thinkers. Some argue that both space and time are outside the physical world, containing and circumscribing it, and since the container is greater than the contained, places and times are not parts of the world and are therefore incorporeal. Others, and Eriugena sides with them, maintain that space and time are within the physical world and therefore were created simultaneously with it, issuing from the eternal reasons in the Word. In refutation of the first position, these thinkers argue that if space and time were before the world came to be, they would be eternal; but if eternal, then either they would be God or they would be primordial causes of things—but either is absurd. As Augustine says, men make two great errors: first, in thinking that space is above the heavens; and second, in thinking that time is before the world. The correct view, then, is that space and time are to be counted among those things which the world contains and that they too proceed from those general causes which are indeed beyond the world (888A–D).

A second question arises: is everything that moves temporally also moved locally? Again, authorities disagree. At issue is the motion of spiritual creatures, which some hold to occur in time alone, while others, maintaining that space and time are inseparable, conclude that such motion must also be local.

The first position is identified as that of Augustine, the second, that of Maximus and Gregory of Nyssa (888D–889B). In defense of the second position, Eriugena argues that if nothing preceded the world except eternity, and if space and time were made simultaneously with the world, then it follows that they will perish with it. If one part perishes, so does the whole, and with it, places and times. Of course, that place which is equivalent to definition always remains in the soul. What will pass away is that space by which the quantity of bodies is extended. As for time, time is the measure of motion. If, then, that which is measured ceases to be, so must its measure (889B–890B).

Furthermore, the end of the world is not just a matter of reason and natural necessity; the Bible confirms it. Even the wisest men of the secular world dare not teach that this world began through a temporal principle or that its end will occur through a temporal cause. Hence some of them have claimed either that the whole world—that is, both matter and form—are coeternal with God, or, alternatively, that formless matter alone is coeternal with Him, while the form and the actual formation of this world are attributed to God (890B–C). The Church teaches, however, that God gave both matter and form to the world when He willed it to be, and when He ordains, all will end. Only God was before the world came to be and the primordial causes in Him. After the world ceases to be, there will again be only God and the causes joined together (890C–892C). The end of the world is the eternal causes in the Word; since they are the principles of the world, they must also be its end. If the Word of God is the Cause of causes, the universal end of all creatures is the Word. All things that are in motion will find the end of their motion in the Word which they seek (892C–893A).

From Chapters 20–23 (Columns 893A–905D)

[20]   *T:* So the beginning and end of the world subsist in God's Word and, to speak more clearly, *are* the Word Itself, which is multiple End without end and Beginning without beginning (*anarchon*) except the Father. Hence we can also briefly summarize what we are trying to persuade you about by many courses of reasoning, and give the following definition. Everything comes from Him and goes toward Him, for He is Beginning and End. The Apostle summed this up very clearly in the words: "Since everything is from Him, through Him, in Him, and directed toward Him." [17] The fivefold division of all created natures, a division "handed down by apostolic authority," as Maximus writes in chapter 37 of his *Ambiguities*, illustrates this point very lucidly, and so do the return and unification of the same natures through the same divisions and collections of all creation into one and finally into God Himself. The first division of all natures separates the created from the uncreated, namely God. The second divides the created into the sensible and the intelligible. The third differentiates the sensible into heaven and earth. The fourth distinguishes paradise and the world. The fifth and final division separates man into male and female. In man every creature visible and invisible has been created, and so he is called the "workshop of all things," since in him all things after God are contained. Hence he is also customarily called the mean, since, consisting of body and soul, he comprehends within himself and collects into a unity the extremes, namely the spiritual and the corporeal, which are far distant from each other. For this reason the Divine History introduced him at the consummation of the fashioning of all things, thereby signifying that the whole of creation is contained within him. Accordingly, from the unification of man's division into two sexes, the ascent and unification of the previously mentioned divisions begins. At the resurrection, sex will be taken away and nature united, and there will be only man [*homo,* a human being], just as he would have been if he had not sinned. Then the world will be united with paradise and there will be only paradise. Next heaven and earth will be united, and there will be

only heaven. We should note that the lower are always transformed into the higher. Sex is changed to man since sex is lower than man. The world, which is lower, is changed to paradise. Earthly bodies, which are lower, will be changed to celestial. Then the unification of all sensible creation and the transformation into the intelligible follows, so that universal creation is made intelligible. Finally universal creation will be united with the Creator and will be one in Him and with Him. This point marks the end of all things visible and invisible, since all visible things will be transformed into intelligible and the intelligible into God Himself by a remarkable and ineffable unification, not, however, as we have often said, by a confusion or death of essences or substances. Our Lord and Savior Jesus Christ, by rising from the dead, brought this whole to completion in Himself and gave a prior example of all things to come. When rising, He had no sex; although to confirm the faith of His disciples, after the resurrection He appeared to them in the masculine form in which He had been born of a virgin and had dwelt among men until His passion. They would not have recognized Him if He had not revealed Himself in the condition known to them. But none of the faithful may believe or think in any sense that He was held fast by sex after the resurrection, "For in Jesus Christ there is neither male nor female," [18] but only the true and whole man, I mean body, soul, and intellect, without sex or comprehensible form, since these three things are one in Him and have become God without transformation or confusion of properties. He is wholly God and wholly man, one substance, or—to speak in more customary fashion— one person, without local and temporal motion since God-man is above all places and times; without any form, since He is the Form of all things and the mark of His Father's substance; without any likeness, since all things strive to be like Him. The humanity of Christ, made one with deity, is contained in no place, moved in no time, circumscribed by no form or sex because it is exalted above all these things; and not only above these, but also "above all virtues and powers" [19] and the other spiritual orders, because "He sits at the right hand of the Father," a position to which no creature can attain. Accordingly, those persons deserve to be refuted who try to establish the Lord's body after the resurrection in some part of the world, moved in place and time, and held fast within the world in that sex in which it appeared to the world. How can body be among all things when it has been exalted above them by union with the Divine? Next one must consider that upon rising from the dead, He returned to paradise. We must not believe that there was any temporal space between His return from the dead and His entry into paradise; or that paradise itself, which He entered upon rising from the dead, is local or contained in some part of this sensible world. We must not believe that when He revealed Himself to His disciples, He was outside paradise; but that He was in paradise at the same time that He revealed Himself to His disciples. He was already in paradise, because human nature had been restored in Him; but those to whom He revealed Himself were not yet in paradise, i.e., they were not yet in a restored nature. And when He vanished from their eyes, He did not withdraw from them locally; but He hid Himself in the subtlety of the spiritual body, which could not be perceived by the still carnal eyes of the Apostles. Hence, we may understand that the paradise which He entered when He arose is simply the wholeness of human nature, which He had restored in Himself and in which the first man would have remained in glory if he had not sinned. It is the very same paradise promised to the saints, which they have already entered in part, namely with the soul, but from which they are still partly excluded, I mean with the body. So in Himself He united the world with paradise. In fact, to Him the world was paradise; for in Himself He changed to a spiritual nature the whole which He had received from the world, His masculine form and His material flesh with its accidents except for sin. Not only did He exalt and restore to equality with the nature of angels the humanity which He had accepted and renewed in Himself, as was signified by His ascent to heaven when, within the sight of His disciples, He was raised up into the air as He was withdrawn from their eyes by a cloud symbolizing His glory and spirituality (for before the passion, He had said, "O Father, make Your Son glorious" [20]). He even raised that humanity above all the angels and celestial powers and, in short, above all things with and without being. What He fulfilled particularly in Himself, He will fulfill generally in human nature as a whole at the time of resurrection. This means that He will not only convert to spirit everything which human nature after sin had drawn from this material world, but He will bring it to equality with the celestial glory possessed by the angels. Do not be surprised that many points have already been dealt with about such matters in other books of our discussion and are now being recapitulated; for the order and necessity of finding what we are looking for demands that we repeat and turn over again in many ways the same statements and courses of argument and call them to mind again in a kind of recapitulation. I mention this point because in previous books we introduced and had as a foretaste many statements of St. Maximus about the return of nature, but now we should deal with them more fully. Not only in the *Ambiguities*, but also in chapter 48 of the *Scholia* about the unification of creatures, Maximus discusses the subject when expounding his speculation about the towers which Ozias built in Jerusalem.[21] "The language of Scripture may have used the term 'corners' for Christ's different unifications of separate creatures. He united man by mystically removing and transforming to spirit the distinction into male and female and by making natural reason free from the properties present in both as a result of the passions. He united the earth by banishing the separation into the sensible paradise and the world. He also united earth and heaven, revealing a single nature of visible things, one in itself. He united sensibles and intelligibles and revealed the single existing nature of created things, a nature fitted together in some mystical way. By some supernatural principle and method He united created nature with the uncreated."

S: Well, then, according to what reason or analogy should we believe that the Lord arose without any sensible and circumscribed form, especially without the one which He received when born from the Virgin? And since He was and is the example of the general resurrection to come, if He arose without any sex, it necessarily follows that mankind as a whole at the time of the Resurrection and afterwards will lack sex.

T: It is superfluous to inquire about this point, for in previous books we were persuaded about it reasonably and in many ways. Besides, we drew our conclusion in accord with views expressed by St.

Gregory and his interpreter, Maximus, that in the future life after resurrection the nature of mankind will wholly lack sex, i.e., masculine and feminine form, since it will return to the very form made in God's image. God's image, moreover, is not male or female, for that division of nature was made because of sin.

S: In the future life, then, there will be neither male nor female if the single simplicity of nature absorbs into itself the twofold sex which now exists.

T: Why do you hesitate about this matter when Truth says generally about men at the resurrection, "They will not marry or be given in marriage, but will be like the angels in heaven"? [22] Surely we believe that angels consist of intellectual and spiritual body, and we have no doubt that they lack all circumscribed form. When the Divine History relates that they often appeared in human likeness, we do not have to believe that they are naturally confined in such a likeness. Their human appearance was temporarily assumed, since otherwise it would have been difficult or impossible for them to appear to men and to speak with them. If angels, then, lack all circumscribed form, why is it remarkable if men, when equal to the angels, will be free from all sex and circumscription of forms? Otherwise men will not be equal to angels. Besides, this point does not seem incredible. Some bodies are liquid and spiritual and lack circumscribed forms. I do not see that what is liquid, spiritual, and of the purest substance can be contained by corporeal quantities and features or any circumscribed mass, since true reason does not allow me to think such thoughts. Of course, the four simple cosmic elements are not confined by any forms. They are everywhere in the world, no part of which lacks a combination of them. And how can whatever is everywhere ' in the world be circumscribed by any form? There are, therefore, bodies which lack sensible forms. What about the rays of the eyes? Aren't they too corporeal but lacking in all form? If you should say, however, that angels have intelligible forms, I grant the point completely; and not only do I not deny that men too at the resurrection will similarly have intelligible forms, but I even affirm it. I confess, though, that I am wholly ignorant of the nature and quality of the forms which angels have now and men will have in the future "until," as Augustine says, "my body crosses over into the affect of my will." Yet I am aware of many great sages who have a completely different opinion about human bodies after the resurrection. In the course of this book, I shall make a point of bringing in their statements to show that I neither disdain them nor have failed to read them.

S: The following order of discussion indicates that you should tell what each of the wise theologians whom you have read (I believe that you have not read all of them, since that would be impossible for anyone) has thought about such matters. This procedure will allow the reader to judge whom he wishes to follow. Now my question is why something that will return to the primordial causes or, in fact, to God Himself is said to perish. Shouldn't it rather be declared to be alive and enduring than to die and pass away?

[21]   *T:* I can answer this question of yours briefly and easily, considering the prophetic statement of St. Dionysius the Areopagite as he expounded the meaning of: "Precious in the sight of the Lord is the death of His saints." [23] He states that the Prophet, in speaking of the death of the saints in this verse, meant simply their crossing over into God through the sublimity of contemplation by rising above all things visible and invisible even when still in the body. Had not Peter, that highest of Apostles, died to all creation and crossed over into God when he answered the Lord's question about who he would say He was with the words, "You are the Christ, the Son of the living God"? [24] Had not John the Evangelist similarly died to all creation when he rose above all things by the height of his speculation and proclaimed: "In the beginning was the Word and the Word was with God, and the Word was God," [25] and the whole remarkable and ineffable speculation of this theologian? Hear the Apostle, although still held fast by the mortal body, proclaiming himself dead and crucified: "The world is crucified to me and I to the world." [26] Such, then, is the death of the saints who, by the power of contemplation, cross over into God Himself and rise above everything endowed with being, including themselves, when deified by the height of divine grace. And as those who, filled with virtue and knowledge, die in mind alone while

still in this life, so the whole world will die when it is brought to an end. It will return to Him who is called *Nothing* because of the superessentiality of His nature, not so as to be wholly deified or made one with God, like the celestial powers and human minds that are illuminated, cleansed, and perfected; but so that each of its component elements, as we have often said, will return to its own cause. That the causes of all things are stationed in God none of the faithful doubts. In fact, whoever does doubt it is an infidel or a fool. Why, then, should it be doubted that everything restored to its cause returns to God? And lest you think that rashly and unsupported by authority I called God *Nothing,* hear St. Dionysius the Areopagite in chapter one (1.5) *On Divine Names:* "We said, when expounding the divine characteristics, that it is impossible to say or to understand what is the One, the Unknown, the Superessential, the inherently Best (I mean the triune Unity, which possesses the same divinity and goodness, *homotheon* and *homoagathon*). But the angelic unities of the holy powers, whether one should call them speculative or receptive of the Goodness beyond knowledge and light, are mysterious and unknown; and they subsist only in those angels who, beyond angelic knowledge, are worthy of them. Human minds, godly through imitation of angels and having ceased all intellectual activity, are united with the angels as far as they may be. Such is the union of deified minds with the highest light, God. They praise Him most effectively by asserting His freedom from all things with being. Truly and supernaturally illuminated in this from their most blessed unity with Him, a unity which is the causal force of all things with being, they praise Him Himself as Nothing because He is superessentially exalted above all existing things." Note how this theologian unhesitatingly alludes to the highest light, God, who illumines all intellectual and rational creation, by the name *Nothing.* He also has added the reason for calling Him *Nothing.* "Because He is superessentially exalted above all things with being." It is common, then, for all created things to return, as though at a kind of death, to the causes subsisting in God. It is proper to intellectual and rational substance to become one with God by the power of contemplation and to become God by grace.

S: I perceive clearly that dying to the world is simply returning to one's causes and being changed for the better. But since the greatest part of the sensible world is the human body—greatest not in mass but through the dignity of the rational soul, by which it is informed, given life, ruled, and held together—I believe that the order of topics and the sequence of discussion demands that we treat of its return.

[22]   *T:*   You are quite right. We must set right out on that course now.

S: Begin then.

T: The whole Church commonly confesses that the second return of the human body—for the first is its dissolution into the elements—is its resurrection.

S: The common confession of all who believe properly and correctly is that the second return of bodies is simply their resurrection and their restoration from the four cosmic elements into which they are dissolved. We must inquire, though, whether the resurrection of bodies occurs by grace, nature, or both jointly, for I have found relatively few authors who deal with this point.

[23]   *T:*   I, like you, am unable to recall having read about this question in Latin books, although I believe it may have been dealt with by someone still unknown to me. We should not think that writers in the Roman tongue have passed by this important question and left it untouched or have failed to deal with it once they have noted it. I should rather think that any definite statement on the subject has not come into my hands. While I was reflecting about this subject for a long time, my only thought was that the resurrection of the dead generally, of the good and the evil, will occur solely by the grace of the Redeemer of the world, without constraint of any natural power. In fact, if God the Word had not been made flesh, dwelt among men, and received the whole of human nature, in which He suffered and rose, I believed that there would be no resurrection of the dead. I had been drawn to such an understanding by His words: "I am the Resurrection and the Life," [27] as if only through His incarnation the

human race, without exception, had received the general gift of resurrection from the dead, i.e., restoration and redintegration of human nature as a whole, which consists of body and soul. But if God's Word had not taken up human nature and risen in it from the dead, no one at all would have the grace of resurrection; but human bodies, like the corpses of the other animals, would perpetually remain in the dust of the earth. This was also my thought when I heard the Apostle saying that "God the Word is the firstfruits of the dead." [28] This was my opinion about the resurrection of the dead. After reading the sermon *Ancoratus,* "On Faith," by St. Epiphanius, Bishop of Constantia in Cyprus, and the discourse of the great Gregory the Theologian, *On the Image,* I changed my view. Agreeing with their authority and depreciating my own opinion, I granted that the resurrection of the dead will occur by natural power. I have therefore judged it appropriate to insert their words into our present discussion. Epiphanius, discussing resurrection and convicting of error the Greeks who wholly deny resurrection, says the following (83,2–84,6): "The Greeks, indeed, utterly deny resurrection in their ignorance of God and His commandments. But they will rise again even against their will. Creation itself plainly refutes them, by daily revealing the form of resurrection. For the day sets and imitates[29] the way of the dead. When night is removed, day rises, inspiring us and suggesting a symbol of resurrection. Fruits are gathered and the state of present things is destroyed in a clear likeness of our transformation from our present state. The earth is sown and produces, because the seeds deposited after the harvest [i.e., after the gathering of crops] will rise again. When a locust is dead and buried, what has been cast off from it is taken up in the earth, and after a time earth gives back what has been entrusted to it. The seeds of sprouts are sown and first die; for if they do not die, they are not brought to life. God has made in us symbols of resurrection in our two sets of ten nails, providing evidence about our hope. But also by the crown of the head, our hair, He proclaims our resurrection. For what seems in us dead body, i.e., hair daily cut and nails, grow again and symbolize the hope of resurrection. Nor is it a waste of breath to cite examples from nature for the benefit of the skeptical. Doves, animals which do not fly together swiftly, die after six months and after forty days immediately come to life again. Beetles, feeling their imminent death, hide themselves in a sphere of dung, burying the sphere in the earth and covering it up. And so from their own excrement they are found again, coming to life from their remains. It is superfluous for me to speak of the phoenix, an Arabian bird, for it is already known to many of the faithful and the infidel. The cause is as follows. When five hundred years old, it has foreknowledge that the time of its death is impending. It makes a sepulchre with spices, and carrying it into the Egyptian city of Heliopolis, i.e., City of the Sun, and striking its breast hard with its claws and producing fire from its body, it kindles the fuel laid in the place of the sepulchre; and so it burns its whole self, flesh and bones. By divine governance, however, a cloud is sent and pours rain and extinguishes the flame consuming the bird's body after the bird is already dead. When the flame is extinguished, the remains of its consumed flesh are left and, failing to appear for a single day, produce a worm, which grows plumage, becomes new, and on the third day becomes solid; and in that state it reveals itself to those seeking the place and tending it. Then it swiftly returns to its own country from which it had come and, though burned, grows young." Such are the words of Epiphanius. Natural force is operative, then, in restoring things, including parts of the human body and in reviving irrational animals, as is proved by the examples of the author just cited. Why is it strange, therefore, if the vital natural force which never deserts the substance of human bodies is so strong that by its operation the bodies themselves are restored to life and to the integrity of human nature as a whole? The different, specific bodies of the other animals and of all sensible things (since in them, too, vital motion flourishes and moves while they are contained within their forms and, when they are dissolved, lies still without deserting their substance) will generally be transformed with the world in the kind of transformation with which we dealt at greater length above. And since all sensible and intelligible things have been created in the fullness of human nature, is it not reasonable to consider that the whole world with all its parts will rise in a kind of general resurrection when that nature is restored in which the whole is contained? Especially since the nature of all sensible things, considered in itself, is perceived to be one and the same; and true reason considers in this world not the size of the corporeal mass but the union of incorporeal substances without any mass and heaping up of parts and without composition; just as in the monad and in the center it perceives not the quantity or quality of numbers and lines, but only the force circumscribed by no mass, no space, no quantity and quality. It is wholly in itself throughout the whole, encompassed by no place, moved in no time. Accordingly, if in the universe of sensible things human nature is outstanding, and if superior things always attract inferior things to themselves—for reason does not grant that superior things are consumed by the inferior, but gives absolute approval to the crossing over of the inferior into the superior—is it not plausible to think that human nature at the end of all things will link and unite to itself everything created within and below it? Furthermore, I believe that we should not pass over Epiphanius' statement (91,1–3) about the spiritual subtlety of human bodies after the resurrection. He made the following statement in a discussion about Christ's body after resurrection, for in Him there was a perfect precedent and example of human resurrection as a whole: "He entered the closed doors, for His carnal body arose as spiritual and not other than what it is. And what it is, adorned with the subtlety of spirit, He united to Godhead. For if there was no subtlety of spirit, He received a heavy body. But to show that this corruptible body of ours will put on incorruptibility in truth—for if it is mortal, it will put on immortality —He entered the closed doors to show that the grossly-limbed is the subtly-limbed, the mortal immortal, and the corruptible incorruptible. Moreover, to refute all disbelievers in our salvation—I mean resurrection—transforming body into subtle spirit, He produced resurrection by blending spirit with spirit." Observe how unhesitatingly he declares the resurrection of spiritual bodies and the incomprehensible return to subtlety, with absorption by the spirit of all slowness, earthliness, and the whole weight subject to the corporeal senses and circumscribed by local spaces. He understood very clearly the words of the Apostle: "An animal-like body is sown, but a spiritual body will rise." [30]

S: I do observe the point and embrace the great man's authority. In fact, I was already persuaded about the spirituality and the non-locality of all human bodies in general after the resurrection, since human nature, consisting of body and soul, will be equal to the angels. My persuasion is based both on the authority of the holy fathers and on my own inner rational perception that it is most plausible and likely for bodies which are changed to a celestial quality and which strip themselves wholly of everything earthly to be regarded as free from all circumscription in place. The simple elements of this corruptible world, as we have often said, penetrate everything contained within its circuit, and their diffusion everywhere into everything is not prevented by the density of any circumscribed body. Anyone carefully discussing the nature of this visible mechanism and investigating with insight the subtlety and virtual incorporeality of its cosmic elements would readily assert that the thinnest air penetrates all celestial and terrestrial things, as well as things of air and sea, without being delayed by any obstacle; that the spirit of fire, more marvelous yet and closer to the rareness of spirit, simple, pure, and removed from every corporeal sense, not only fills and encompasses all the spaces of the world, but even passes through the very thinnest air because of its exceeding subtlety and likeness to incorporeal natures, for it is the innermost of all elements. The same opinion must be formed about simple water and earth. They too are everywhere present in all bodies in due proportion. Why is it strange, then, if bodies at resurrection, ascending beyond all sensible quality, freed from all mass and locality and, so to speak, wholly converted into spirit and very like life, are exalted by their ineffable spiritual subtlety above all that the corporeal sense can reach? I am just now beginning to reflect about the point that the resurrection of bodies will occur with the cooperation of natural force and not solely through the grace of the Word incarnate. Where I first stumbled over the problem of whether the operation of nature brings about resurrection—for, just as you once did, I attributed the redintegration of the human body solely to the Redeemer's grace, I am now certain because reason is my guide. We read that God has produced no miracle in this world contrary to nature, but the Divine History relates that by the governance and effect of natural causes, all theophanies of powers have been produced when set into motion by God's command. The miracle of miracles is the general resurrection of the dead, the greatest example and precedent of which was Christ, so that virtually all other natural proofs are correctly understood as having been made to prefigure Him. Wouldn't it therefore seem consistent with truth for us to think that resurrection will result from the effective power of natural causes, a power subject to divine will?

T: In that case resurrection will be achieved through the cooperation of both, nature and grace.

S: I should think so. But I do not see very well what part is properly played by grace and what part by nature in bringing about resurrection. Of course, no one who carefully searches out the secrets of wisdom will say that there is no difference between them.

T: On the contrary, there is a great difference, worthy of careful investigation and clear discovery. In this part of our speculation, we should observe three things: the first, the inexhaustible and infinite diffusion of Divine Goodness through and into what has been created; next, the general and twofold streaming of the division into things which are granted (by nature) and those which are given (by grace). Three things, then, must be considered: Goodness, Its grants, and Its gifts. The keenness of reason distinguishes these from one another and joins to each thing what properly belongs to it. So a grant of the Divine Goodness is the establishment of the universe and the distribution of all creatures according to general and special reasons, a distribution which the Superessential Goodness, God, lavishes universally upon all from the highest down, i.e., from intellectual nature, the highest of all creatures, to corporeal, which holds the last and lowest place in the universe. The Highest Goodness, then, grants being to all created nature, since It has brought it from the nonexistent to the existent. Hence St. Dionysius in chapter four *On the Celestial Hierarchy* says: "First of all it is true to say that by universal goodness Superessential Divinity has established the essences of existing things and brought them to being. For it is the property of the Cause of all things and the Goodness above all things to call everything with being to a common sharing, such as is defined for each in its own proportionate measure. Everything with being, then, participates in the providence flowing from the Superessential Divinity, the greatest Cause. Perhaps there would not be essences of things with being unless they took them from the Beginning. So all existing things participate in His being, for the being of all things is Superbeing, Divinity." So much from Dionysius. And Superessential Goodness grants not only being, but also eternal being to all things. Every essence and substance has being and subsistence only from the Superessential and Supersubstantial Goodness, which truly has being and subsists by Itself. No substantial or essential good has being through itself except only the One which grants goodness to all Its participants, but gives the gift of grace, deification, only to the elect. No essence or substance has been created by Divine Goodness which does not remain eternally and unchangeably. Whatever things cannot endure perpetually are accidents added to substances, massed around them, and destined to return to them. It follows that every nature brought into essence and perpetually guarded from perishing is the grant of Divine Goodness. But since between being and being eternally there is established a mean called *well-being,* without which those extremes (viz., being and being eternally) do not truly have being and are not correctly said to be, even though they have being—for when well-being is removed, being and always being are not truly being and always being; for that truly and always is which subsists well and blessedly—that inserted mean, namely well-being, is the gift of Divine Goodness, joined with the free and good motion of the will belonging to an intellectual and rational creature. By these two things, namely free will and a divine gift, which sacred Scripture calls *grace,* well-being is brought about. But that gift is not distributed generally to all. Deification is given only to the nature of angels and men, and not to all of them, but only to the angels who, burning with the love of their Creator, remain fixed in the contemplation of truth, and only to men called according to the (divine) plan. Besides, the gift of grace is not contained within the limits of created nature and does not operate according to natural power, but achieves its effects superessentially and beyond all natural, created reasons. If the resurrection of the dead should occur only through divine grace, therefore, natural power will be wholly eliminated, as will vital motion, which never deserts the substances of things, whether dormant in potentiality, as numbers are in the monad, or actively revealed, like numbers proceeding from the monad, and the other things which, from hidden causes, emerge into open effects. On the other hand, if natural power brings about resurrection without the help of grace, how is it possible to believe that the power of the Redeemer of mankind prevails at the resurrection of the dead, even though He Himself has said, "I am the Resurrection and the Life"?[31] We should not interpret this statement by the Lord as relating merely to the resurrection of souls from the death of injustice and impiety to the life of justice and piety—that is, to the contemplation of truth—but also as relating to resurrection of bodies, the primal example of which He first showed in His own flesh. With sound faith, then, we can attribute the power of resurrection both to the natural efficacious potency granted by Divine Goodness and to the grace surpassing all natures, the grace given by that same Goodness. The Apostle James also differentiated these two things, namely a grant (*datum*) and a gift (*donum*), in the words: "Every good grant and every perfect gift is from above, descending from the Father of lights."[32] It is as if he were openly saying, "Every granted establishment and restoration of natures jointly formed from a grant and a gift, and every perfect deification (which the Greeks call *theosis*) of those worthy of eternal bliss flows from a single source, i.e., from above, from the Father of lights." Hence we should understand *grant,* as we said before, in reference to the establishment of creatures universally in substance, but *gift* specifically in reference to the superessential deification of the elect. For Divine Providence wished to establish in this way the order of the universe which it created (and indeed no other way was proper or possible) by first granting essences and substances to which It would later distribute ornaments—i.e., would give powers according to the dignity of angels and men about whom It foreknew and predestined that they would share the form of God, the only-begotten Word.[33] To sum up briefly, then, a grant is conferred by nature, a gift by grace. Nature leads things from nonexistence to existence, but a gift brings out some existing things beyond all other existing things to God Himself. True reason does not allow those who participate in communion with the Divine above all other things to be numbered among all things. Concerning Itself, Truth says, "Wherever I am, my servant will be there too."[34] We unhesitatingly believe that God is above all things; therefore, His servants are above all things. But the others, who do not attain the power of pure contemplation, gain possession of the lower orders, whether in theophanies or in the heights of lower natures. I have spoken of theophanies in the plural, since neither intellectual nor rational natures will contemplate Truth in the same way, but the height of speculation is distributed and defined for each of them proportionally. This the Lord says about the nature of angels and men, which hold the loftiest place in the created universe. We do not make this statement because any creature except the Word in human form can rise beyond all theophanies and attain to Him "who alone is immortal, whose home is in inaccessible light;" [35] but because some theophanies are so sublime that they are understood to be exalted above all creatures in a very close contemplation of God and are believed to be, as it were, theophanies of theophanies. For God in Himself is not wholly visible to any creature, but is seen and will be seen in the clouds of speculation. As the Apostle says: "We shall be taken up in the clouds to meet Christ, and so we shall always be with Him." [36]

Chapters 24–25 (*Columns 907B–913B*)

Teacher and Student then undertake to consider the manner in which all things are to be in God. Everything can be understood in two ways, as within Him or outside Him. Within Him they are termed the causes and reasons of things, and outside Him they are called effects. In the Word, the Wisdom of God, every creature is and lives and cannot perish, for if the container not only persists in being and lives but is Himself eternal life, that which He contains is necessarily eternally and is eternal life. Outside Him, however, things are nothing in themselves. They are said to be outside because without Him they cannot exist. These effects are dispersed in space and time, and are discriminable in genera and species, properties and accidents (907B–908B).

As Augustine teaches, God is not only the eternal Creator

but He is also the eternal Lord. But if He is always both Creator and Lord, there must always be a creature and servant, not as coeternal with Him but as inseparable from Him. The Creator and Lord precedes the creature and servant not in time but as their principle (908B–909A).

The Teacher then suggests that the primordial causes alone are created in God and are His servants, but not their effects which compose the sensible world. This, however, raises the question whether only the causes are eternal, while the effects perish. The Student replies that while he was once of that opinion, he has changed his mind; he is now convinced that the effects too will endure perpetually, not in their own right as proceeding from the causes, but as returning into their causes. Still, the matter requires clarification: the world is said to perish. Can it be, then, that the effects will not remain as do their causes, but will return into the nothing from which they were made and perish absolutely (909B–910B)?

The Student is perplexed by the apparent contradiction: how can the effects both perish and endure forever? In reply the Teacher explains how the Incarnation and Resurrection effected the salvation of the world. The Word of God, in whom, by whom, and for whom everything was made, as considered in His Divinity, descended into the effects of the primary causes insofar as He was man. The Word went out from the Father and took on the whole of human nature in which all creation is contained. He descended in order to save in His humanity the effects of those causes which are present to Him as God eternally and immutable. He calls them back to union with their causes so that both causes and effects might be saved. If the Wisdom of God were not to descend, the causes themselves could not endure. Just as no effect could remain if its cause were to perish, so no cause could remain were its effects to perish. Cause and effect are correlative, either arising and disappearing together or abiding together always (910B–912B).

Christ wholly redeemed the whole of human nature which

He had wholly assumed, but it does not follow that the whole of human nature is to share the unity of substance which the Word shares with the Father. The whole human race is saved, indeed, but for some men this is restoration to the original natural state of mankind while for others it is deification, the granting of a supernatural excellence. Through deification, mankind is thus enabled to participate in the divine nature, but for Himself, Christ, the head of the Church, reserves more than participation: the substantial unity of His manhood with Deity. To this height no one but He ascends or will ever ascend (911B–C).

Everything is made perfect, not human nature alone. For in assuming human nature, the Word also assumed every creature that is made in human nature; therefore, in saving and restoring man, He also saved and restored every creature, whether visible or invisible. Angels, too, benefitted from the Incarnation, for they were enabled to know the Word. Before the Incarnation the Word was above all that is and is not and therefore surpassed all that can be said and known. As Incarnate, He proceeds as a theophany into the knowledge of angels and men, revealing the Father and the Holy Spirit as well. The inaccessible light is made accessible to all intellectual and rational creatures (912B–913A).

From Chapters 25–26 (Columns 913B–916D)

S: Shall we say that irrational animals, as well as trees, grasses, and all parts of this world from the highest down, were restored in the incarnate Word of God?

T: I wonder why you repeat the same thing so often. Didn't the Word, when assuming humanity, receive all creation, visible and invisible, and save the whole which He received in man? If He received all creation by receiving human nature, surely He saved all creation and will do so for eternity.

S: Then corporeal masses, extended in local space and composed of many different parts, and the visible species in which the masses are contained and kept from flowing into one, will arise at the general resurrection of men. Hence, if the parts themselves rise again into their masses, forms, and species with which the visible world is adorned and of which it is composed, it follows that the whole world will not perish but return to the same state. For if the parts are restored, why not the whole also?

T: We do not say that the masses and species of visible and sensible bodies will rise again but that, as we have often agreed, at the resurrection of man they will, along with man and in man, return to their causes and reasons, which have been made in man. All animals are rather to be called animals in these causes and reasons than in the corporeal and sensible effects, for where they subsist, there the animals truly are. A similar understanding should be applied to all sensibles, whether celestial or terrestrial. Indeed all things varying in place and time and subject to the corporeal senses must be considered not the substantial and truly existing things themselves, but certain transitory images and reflections of them. An example of this principle is the voice and its image, called *echo* by the Greeks, or bodies and their reflected shadows, whether formed in the pure air, from the waters or from anything at all from which they are customarily reflected. All of these are proved to be not things but the false images of things. Therefore, just as the images of voices and the shadows of bodies do not subsist by themselves because they are not substance, so those sensible bodies are, as it were, likenesses of subsisting things and cannot subsist by themselves. For natural reason teaches that human bodies too, which now are extended in space and varied with increases and diminutions and move, and their species too, whether those general species in which all human bodies participate or the special ones by which the quantity of individual bodies is circumscribed, will not be at the resurrection to come; but they will pass into spiritual nature, which cannot be circumscribed by places, times, and proper species taken from quality and quantity. I say this without objecting to the views of those who argue altogether differently about the resurrection of bodies. They affirm that human bodies will be in the quantity and species in which each has fallen, and declare that their sex, masculine and feminine, will remain. I shall call them to mind again afterwards. But we can argue unhesitatingly from the words of St. Dionysius that animals will have being again according to the principle already mentioned, i.e., in their causes. In chapter six (6.1) *On Divine Names*, when discussing Divine Life, he says: "The life and immortality of the immortal angels and that indestructible quality of constant angelic motion has being and subsistence from it [namely Divine Life] and through it. They are therefore called ever-living and immortal, and yet not immortal; because not from themselves do they have immortal being and eternal life, but from the life-producing cause which makes and continues all life. And just as we say in regard to the *on* [i.e., when dealing with essence, for the Greeks call Divine Essence *on* as well as *ousia*] that it is also the cause of the same being, so we say again in this respect [viz., in regard to life] that through Itself Divine Life is life, vital and substantial; that It is all life and vital motion from Life Itself, which is above all life and every beginning of life as a whole. From It, too, souls have their indestructibility, and all animals and plants have life on the lowest level of soul. When it is taken away [i.e., general life as well as special and individual life], as Scripture says, all life passes away and when things that pass away turn again to participate in it, they are again endowed with spirit." By these words of the theologian, we do not understand a future resurrection of irrational animals or restoration of things deprived of sense to their original species and quantities with which this world is filled, but the future return to their causes, from which they proceed and in which they subsist. For he did not say that Divine Life is the cause only of angelic and human, i.e., intellectual and rational life, but of life as a whole. As we discussed at length in previous books, all life is rational or irrational or nutritive of bodies and the cause of growth, i.e., belonging to angel, man, animal, or senseless creatures such as trees, grasses, and other similar things in which only vital motion operates. Hence divine Scripture proclaims, not only about human life but about all these species of life, and not only about human bodies but about all endowed with activity by the spirit of life: "You will take away their spirit and they will pass away and return to dust." [37] For no life, whether rational, animal, or nutritive, can enliven and govern corruptible, mortal bodies long, not to say forever. It therefore abandons them, and at the same time the bodies pass away and return to their dust. That is the meaning of "And they [i.e., animals and plants] will pass away through failure to share in life because of their weakness." They cannot always participate in life because of the weakness and frailty of corruptible earthly bodies. The natural operation of life in bodies, whether ruling or abandoning them, is referred to the Creator of all things. The Psalmist therefore says, "You will take away their spirit," not because God takes away the spirit of any body, but because He allows the spirits, weighted down by corruptible bodies, to fail them for a time; but turning again to the same incorruptibility and spirituality, they will return by their natural motion. What has been born with them into this world they cannot abandon forever, but at some time, at the end of the world, they will receive it again, since in the causes what rules and what is ruled will be an inseparable one by a marvelous harmony. The Psalm therefore says, "Send out Your spirit and they will be created." [38] As if it were saying, "Send out the vital spirit which You made," i.e., allow it to be sent out and to return to bodies which it has temporarily deserted, since it wishes by a natural striving to return. "And You will renew the face of the earth," [39] i.e., by inseparably uniting bodies with their vital species, you will restore the wholeness of nature, mystically signified by the name *earth*. But if it seems to anyone incredible and contrary to natural reason for irrational and senseless beings to cross over into human nature, let him first intently observe that the lower parts of human nature—I mean corporeal sense, the nutritive life, and the body itself—are very like creatures that are irrational, senseless, and with earthly bodies. If that is so, why is it strange or incredible if likes pass into likes, so that from many like things, a single one like itself is produced, but even so the lower pass into the higher things which they are like? For natural reason does not allow the higher to be changed to the lower, but the lower naturally strive for the higher and wish to be united with them. One should perceive too that the passions of irrational creatures which, after the fall of man from the dignity of the divine image, human nature had drawn to itself and added as a kind of penalty for sin, and which were not naturally implanted before the fall—that these passions, I say, can be changed into natural virtues in those who are perfect. By passions I mean pleasure and sadness, concupiscence and fear, and whatever springs from them, which can undoubtedly be changed to virtues. For example, concupiscence brings about the motion of the intellectual striving for godliness by those who long for it; pleasure causes the harmless joy of the nutritive operation of the soul; fear, too, arouses the care which provides against future retribution for faults; and sadness evokes penance, a corrective of evils in the present. If the passions derived by rational nature from the irrational can so be changed to the natural virtues of the soul, why should it be incredible that irrationality itself is transformed into the sublimity of rationality? Pride, too, which is said to be virtually the source of all evil, is changed in good men into love of celestial excellence and scorn of earthly weakness; for the Apostle says: "Let your thoughts be on heavenly things, not on the things that are on the earth." [40] In short, there is no vice which cannot be changed into a virtue in the wise through the operation in them of divine grace. And so goodness is customarily made from evil, but not evil from good; for the power of goodness consumes its opposite though the ugliness of evil cannot taint the beauty of goodness. In sum, we do not deny that vices are changed to virtues, although they are opposites. Why, then, should we deny that lower natures are transformed, by a remarkable union, into higher natures, which they do not at all oppose?

Chapters 26–33 (Columns 916D–952B)

The defeat of wickedness is certain, and evil must cease to be. Gregory of Nyssa argues that this follows necessarily from the very nature of things, and Teacher and Student concur. Gregory reasons that our rational nature as mutable is always in motion either toward or away from God, the Good. If it moves toward Him, the motion will never terminate, for the distance is infinite. If it moves away from Him, it reaches the limit of evil but cannot stop its motion and turns back in the direction of God. The Teacher adds a further reason that evil must be limited: if the divine Goodness, which always works good not only in the good but also in the evil, is eternal and infinite, its contrary by necessity cannot be eternal and infinite or it would not be its contrary. Human wickedness, then, must eventually be changed into goodness (916D–918C). All rational beings, even sinful ones, seek God, the highest Good, for all seek their cause. They never desire evil, but since they are often mistaken and deceived, they take the wrong path to their goal. When the perverse motions of the irrational soul are corrected, it is moved to seek its cause and to enter into paradise. Because the ultimate object of desire and longing is unattainable by any creature, the longing and the motion are eternal. The soul forever seeks and in a marvelous way finds what it seeks; it does not find what it cannot find. That is, the soul finds God through theophanies, but God as He is in Himself it cannot find, for He is beyond the contemplation of any creature. The inaccessible light in which God dwells is, as Dionysius rightly names it, the "divine darkness", for it is incomprehensible. The ascended Christ, whose humanity is one with His divinity, is for the same reason incomprehensible by any creature (919A–921B).

A dilemma is encountered. Christ, it is held, ascended in His manhood as well as in His divinity, thereby redeeming the whole human race. But if the elect are only part of mankind while the others are to suffer forever in the fires of hell, can it be said that the whole nature of man ascends? If not, if only part ascends while part is punished, then one would have to say that the divine Word had not assumed the whole of human nature but only a part and that therefore He did not wish to save, nor did He in fact save the whole human race. But this is absurd (921B–922A).

The simplicity of human nature cannot be divided into parts as if it were a composite of similars and dissimilars. It is one, free of all composition, dissimilitude, and multiplicity of parts. If the Deity is one and undivided, then necessarily humanity as made in His image must be one and undivided, and all men must be one in the image. Gregory of Nyssa has taught that *Adam* is not a proper name but a universal name for all mankind, for all are equally God's one image. If, then, the Word of God took humanity upon Himself, He took it all, and if He has thereby redeemed all, there can be no one left to suffer punishment for sin. How, then, can there be eternal damnation (922A–923C)?

What is clear is that the Divine Mind which creates all things in knowing them knows no evil or wickedness. Were He to know them, they would have a cause and would exist substantially. He cannot know, then, impious men and angels. He knows their substances which He made but not the perverse motions of their wills (925D–926A).

Everything God knows and makes participates in Him and is eternal. Nothing contrary to the divine nature can be coeternal with it. Thus the divine Goodness will consume evil, eternal life will destroy death, and blessedness overcome sorrow (926A–927A). Human nature will be released from the chains of wickedness, death, and misery when it returns into its causes.

But what of the demons? Is wickedness to be abolished in every creature or in humanity alone? The answer can be gleaned from the writings of Augustine, Ambrose, and Origen: no nature, not even that of the demons, is evil, for they participate in goodness or they could not exist at all. The substance of the Devil will not be destroyed in the sense of ceasing to exist, but his hostile will shall no longer be an enemy of the highest Good (927A–931A).

Eriugena now embarks on an exploration of the problem of evil and its consequences. Evil cannot be anything substantial, for it is unthinkable that God who creates all substances should have made it. What is it, then, and where? And what are we to make of its punishment in hell? If God is to be all in all, how can punishment be eternal? Borrowing freely from Gregory, Augustine, Ambrose, and Dionysius, Teacher and Student examine many facets of the issue, beginning with an analysis of evil as corruption.

What men call corruption is nothing substantial but is either a privation of the good or the natural decay of mutable things. Natural changes of growth and decay are the conversion of accidents into one another while the essences remain unaltered. There is no evil in this. The evil of corrupt demons is a privation, that weakness whereby they failed to remain obedient to their principle, the highest Good. Those angels who fell sought what is not, and this is all that is evil and wicked in them. But evil will vanish. Only what God has made will remain and will in no way be punished (931B–935A).

What is true of wickedness is also true of death and sorrow. They will be abolished, and the general resurrection of the whole of creation will be its purgation of all filth, liberation from all the corruption of death, and the renewal of the mystical earth, that is, the restoration of human nature (935A–B).

If this reasoning is valid, however, there remains the problem of interpreting the punishments described in Holy Scripture as an eternal fire, a burning pool of sulphur, a canker worm, and all the torments of the damned. If they are to take place at some time in the future and in some sensible place, everything will not return to God and He will not be all in all. Even more serious, what is left to be punished if no substantial subject capable of punishment remains (935B–D)?

To the first question, where punishment will take place, the answer is no *where*. The torments of hell will not occur in any part of God's creation or in any place in the visible universe. They are nowhere save in the perverse motions of evil wills, in corrupt consciences, and in repentance which is too late and futile. Punishment will not be physical. Rather, it will lie in the taking away of all ability to do evil. Just as faith without works is dead, so is sin without the possibility of sinning, evil-doing without the possibility of doing evil, and impiety without the cult of idols. Although the desire to act perversely remains in evil wills, it accomplishes nothing, and so the malevolent desire continues to burn only in itself. The severest torture that evil men and angels can undergo now and after the judgment is to desire to do evil and to be unable to accomplish it (935D–9368).

Judas was punished in his polluted conscience, forever consumed by his useless repentance. The rich man in hell suffers the loss of those splendid banquets that he enjoyed in this life. Herod is consumed by the very fury with which he slaughtered the innocents. Since Christ's descent into hell, the devil has been bound in chains, awaiting the judgment after which all creation shall be freed from bondage to him. His torture is his envy, foreknowing as he does that there will remain nothing captive to his power (937A–938B).

Now satisfied as to *where* future punishment is to take place, the Student raises the more difficult question *how* it can take place at all. Although the punishments cannot be corporeal, since after the consummation of the world there will be no bodies or time and space, how can they occur? Punishments are accidents of a subject which exists per se. But since all subjects are created by God, one is led to the monstrous conclusion that God punishes what He has made. Of course, the soul must be purged of earthly passions by the spiritual fire of the divine grace before it returns to its causes, but this is not punishment, this is not the torment of the impious, which is the matter at hand.

The Teacher replies that there are only three possible answers: either one admits the subsistence of "nothing" as the subject of punishment—which is nonsense, for "nothing" cannot exist to be punished; or one holds that punishment is inflicted on some existing nature—which is even more contrary to reason and the teaching of the Fathers; or one holds that the pains of hell punish what is not in some existing subject who is himself untouched by the punishment. Teacher and Student agree that only the third is probable: God punishes vice, which in itself is nothing, in something real which is itself unable to suffer punishment (938B–940D).

As for the demons, we know little of their fate, whether

their substance returns to its principle when it is purged or whether in its perversity it eternally flees the contemplation of truth. We can be certain, however, that their substance is never punished since God created it and that their wickedness will be completely destroyed since it cannot be coeternal with divine Goodness (941A–C). Rather than speculate on the future of the demons, however, we ought to concentrate on knowing ourselves.

Humanity is both one and many: one in its cause, the highest Good, and indefinitely multiple in the effects of that cause. Since the highest Good is wholly present everywhere, so is its image. Humanity, therefore, is diffused wholly in all men and is wholly present in each. There is no more humanity in the good man than in the evil (942B–D).

Light provides a helpful analogy: the sunbeam illuminates the unclean as well as the clean without itself becoming contaminated. There is no darkness within light itself, yet the cause of darkness is within it. All darkness is contained and circumscribed by light. Darkness is a privation, and all privation has its cause from that of which it is the privation. A thing and its privation belong to the same genus; for example, sound and silence, form and formlessness. In like manner the darkness of ignorance in spiritual beings is encompassed by the brightness of wisdom (942D–943A).

Even the similarity of human bodies shows the equality of human nature in every man. No man is any less human than another even if he is deformed. All differences are accidents. One fivefold bodily sense is common to all, though the organs of some may be defective. Reason and intellect are universally in all men, although not all use them correctly, and the abuses of these natural goods are the causes of damnation (943A–C).

The irrational motion of the evil will is punished in beings who share a rational nature that is both good and impassible. The evil will does not defile the good, and therefore its torture does not torment the natural subject of which it is an accident and in which it is contained. Human nature, inasmuch as it is always free from sin, is also free of the penalty of sin. If the judges of this world punish the fault of the criminal but not his nature, how much more rightly does the just Judge, Creator of all natures, punish in them only the wrongdoing that they have committed (943C–D).

Sin is not natural although it is voluntary. It is uncaused in the sense that it lacks all natural causes. It is caused in that it, along with its punishment, is the result of the evil will. The evil of the will, however, is inexplicable. Its beginning is pride, but pride cannot be a cause, for it is nothing real at all, rather a defect of virtue. Pride is the first step forward in that primordial sinning in which all have sinned (944A–B).

When at the end of the world all things rest in their causes and wickedness is no more, only the forbidden wills of evil men and angels will remain to be tormented in themselves. They will remember all that they desired in this life and expected to be theirs in the future, but all these things they shall never find. They will be tortured forever by *phantasiae,* the dreamlike images of those corporeal things which they loved insanely that will no longer exist when this world passes away. Evil will disappear from all human nature, but the *phantasiae* will abide forever as punishment in the consciousness of those who have sinned (944B–945B).

There are two kinds of passions and two corresponding kinds of *phantasiae.* By one kind of passion the deified are rapt in pure contemplation of their Maker; by the other the wicked are submerged in the deepest ignorance of truth. The just who undergo deification of the mind will experience the vision of God, not, to be sure, as He is in Himself, but in His theophanies. Each of the saints will experience God for himself according to his own capacity or degree of contemplation. What for the just are theophanies of God are for the unjust the delusive *phantasiae* of what can never be theirs (945B–946A).

For both just and unjust, however, the spiritual body will be the same, purified of all animality, equally incorruptible, equally beautiful, equally eternal. Human nature retains its integrity in all. It is capable of contraries, just as air is receptive indifferently to light and darkness, hot and cold, without change of its own substance. It shines in ethereal brilliance above and is found below in the thick clouds gathered from the earth and water beneath, but it remains one and the same air. So on the day of resurrection all humanity will be recalled to its former status, some men will shine in their deification, while others will retain in their memory clouds of *phantasiae* of earthly, mortal things (946A–949A).

Finally, however, we must confess that we cannot grasp the reason that the evil which God does not make is contained within those things which He does make or that it can be considered as outside human nature yet punished within it. God's thoughts are past finding out. The cause of evil and its punishment belong with those other inexplicable mysteries: the creation of the world from nothing and its dissolution and return to its causes, and the change of our mortal bodies not only into spiritual bodies but into our souls. Above all, we cannot comprehend how without exceeding the limits of their human nature the saints receive gifts of grace which surpass that nature. Neither angels nor men can understand these wonders. Yet we can say that all that is made is created to show forth and praise the Goodness that made it. We do not know how, but we do know why (950D–952B).

From Chapters 34–35 (Columns 952B–953B)

T: The following account is given, moreover, about why this world will be dissolved and return to its causes. All things which proceed from the Cause of all things and from the primordial causes established in It always strive, by a natural motion, for their beginning, outside which they cannot rest. Another account. All things flowing from the Source of all things would become worthless and utterly perish unless they were able to return to their Source and actually did return. But if the return of visible things to their invisible causes were prevented, it would be not only contrary to the quite natural desire of all things, but also harmful. Our mortal bodies will be transformed not only into spiritual bodies but actually into our souls, because natural necessity prescribes that just as a rational soul made in God's image is to return to Him whose image and likeness it is, so the body too, made in the image of the soul and, as it were, the image of the image, will, when freed from all earthly weight and corporeality, be turned into its cause, the soul; and through it as a kind of mean it will be turned into the unique Cause of all things. The clearest examples can be given as analogies for such change. We see moisture changing into smoke, smoke into flame, and hence moisture into flame and flame into the fiery element. Physicists say that the ray of the sun draws moisture to itself from the sea, from rivers, from all collections of water and from the dampness of the earth, and absorbs it into its own nature as though it were a kind of nourishment.

[35]   Next, the following explanation accounts for the fact that we, who in this life are a compound, will be united into a kind of simplicity. It was necessary for the image of the one and highest Trinity, inseparable, simple, and uncompounded in Itself, to be restored to a unity and an inseparable simplicity. Otherwise it would lose the greatness of its dignity and would deform its beauty; but the divine mercy does not allow such a result. For the Archetypal Example does not permit the image similar to It and made by and according to Itself to be removed from Itself permanently by any deformity and dissimilarity or any composition that would take away its simplicity. The same reason accounts for the return of mortal men, in whatever way they are called mortal; whether because they do not subsist from themselves or in themselves, or because, as a penalty for original sin, they were absorbed by mortality into their God, who alone is immortal. For it would not suit the goodness of the immortal Creator for His image to be held fast by eternal death. The fact that God had allowed man to become mortal and to die because of his perverse will in refusing to obey God shows God's mercy rather than his

retribution. He wanted to correct His image and so to recall it to Himself, but not to have it uncorrected and always banished and removed for infinity.

Chapters 35–36 (Columns 953B–972A)

It is one thing to consider the parts of the universe separately and another to view it as a whole. Evil, misery, and punishment take on a different aspect when seen within the whole context. What appears ugly by itself as a part is not only beautiful in the whole because it has been ordered beautifully; it is also a cause of the beauty of the universe. Wisdom, knowledge, life and light are first recognized and praised through comparison with their opposites. Virtues would receive no praise were there no contrast between them and vices. As Augustine says, the dark color in a picture contributes to the beauty of the whole. What is better than that from the comparison and contrast of opposites the universe and its Creator should be praised (953C–954C)?

The Greeks knew that hell is not a place beneath the earth and named it well, for *Hades* means sadness or loss of pleasure. Sadness is evil to evil beings who burn with desire for what they cannot have, but when it is seen within the beautiful order of the universe, it is a good to good men who repent their sins, and pain is a benefit to those who make slow headway toward the blessedness promised them. Not only does sadness manifest the eternal justice of the righteous Judge, it increases the praise due the beauty of blessed men and angels (954C–955C).

The pain and death of the visible body are in no way to be reckoned as punishments. They do not occur because of man's sin but belong to the order of nature. While we speak of them as corruptions, there are, as we saw, two kinds of corruption: that of the visible body and that of the perverse will. Only the latter is really corruption. In all things, we must remember, the natural integrity of substances remains unaltered. When their accidents, that is, visible bodies, dissolve into the universal elements, this is rather the death of corruption than corruption, and it ought to receive another name, *transmutation*, perhaps. We are not commanded to hold our so-called corruptible bodies in contempt because they are evil but because they are mutable and are awaiting their transmutation into something better, in comparison with which everything is contemptible. Neither the death of the visible body, then, nor sensible pain is a punishment. Both are ordained for our instruction, to recall our human nature to its Creator (957D–959A).

Only the second kind of corruption, that of the perverse will, deserves the name. The only place for corruption and punishment is the illicit desire of the rational creature, which springs neither from God nor from created nature. As the defect and privation of the natural will, it is causeless. This indeed is what is punished, not by the death of the body but by *phantasiae* of natural things in the memory. What is substantial remains necessarily incapable of punishment, but by its power what is punished undergoes punishment. Thus we have explained the paradox that what is cannot be punished, while only what is not can be punished (959A–960A).

Yet, the Student objects, what can it mean to say that there will be eternal punishment when nothing is left that merits punishment? If the substance of the sinner is purified of its wickedness, what is there to suffer torment at the end of this life? Again the answer is that while indeed the substance or nature is purged, the false *phantasiae* of temporal things will continue forever in the souls of the wicked. Their repentance which came too late will burn in them like an inextinguishable fire attacking asbestos (960A–961B).

It appears to the Student that this implies that truth will be eternally opposed by falsehood, for the *phantasiae* that endure forever are unreal and false. The Teacher then proceeds to explain the difference between what is false and a *phantasia*. That is false which is not real but tries to be; that is, it wishes to seem other than it is. Certain tales, for example, that of Daedalus, are not true or even likely, but they can deceive the unwise. Falsehood involves deceit. A *phantasia*, on the other hand, is a kind of image of something visible or invisible impressed upon the memory. While the senses do not perceive anything real at the time, *phantasiae* are similitudes of some natural thing and therefore do belong in a way to the nature of things. Outer sense perceives them as images of sensible and intelligible things, two rivers flow into the memory, and everything made from these memories is a *phantasia*. Though not themselves substantial goods, *phantasiae* are good because they are found in what is real and good and have their origin in what is real and good. Nor are they turned into punishments. Rather, in them the irrational motions of evil wills undergo eternal punishment. One must note further that in good men *phantasiae* are those theophanies in which Truth manifests itself. They can hardly be called falsehoods, therefore, for when Truth is all in all, there will be no falsehood for no one will be deceived (963A–963D).

Everything, then, is ordered justly and providentially as a perfect harmony without any discord. Nothing is more pleasing to the soul than the blending of different voices to produce sweet music. The sounds alone are not enough. They must be properly arranged in the right relation to one another. These relations, proportions, and proportionalities, are not heard by the corporeal senses but are perceived by the soul within and considered as if above the nature of things and therefore to be reckoned among the things that are not. If, then, from things which are substantial and their accidents and from that which is not, there should arise a harmony, it is no wonder that from the punishment of the evil will and from the rewards of the good the most beautiful harmony will ensue. The punishments are good because they are just, and the rewards are good because they are gratuitous, beyond what has been earned (965C–966B).

One cannot argue that perverse wills are evil and that therefore evil remains forever to detract from the beauty of the restoration of nature. The perversity of the will is not evil but illicit. Who can say that what proceeds from the free will of a rational creature is evil? Freedom is bestowed by God, for His image ought not to be coerced or bound by any law. It is given, not so that man can sin by it but so that he can serve his Creator rationally. If, however, its motions are irrational and he is attracted to things forbidden him, it will be corrected by divine justice and recalled to obedience by divine mercy. If, however, inflated with pride, the will persists in its perverse motions, they will be continued and it will never obtain what it desires. There will be no end of its cupidity. This and this alone is the punishment of the perverse free will (966C–967A).

There is no vice in a rational creature that is not a good in some irrational creature. Ferocity is good in a lion; it is a quality of his nature without which he would not be a lion. The ferocity in the nature of a rational being is a vice and is forbidden. Filth is a property of swine but counter to human and angelic nature. These things are vices and against human nature, but they are not evil (967B–C).

Since evil is not in the whole of things, it cannot be in the part, although it seems to be something forbidden that should be purged and restrained. Few people understand this now, but all will know it, just and unjust alike, when truth illumines all. All will see the glory of God, although the impious man who prefers shadows to the hated light will not rejoice in that glory. He will be like the rich man in the parable who was in hell and lifted his eyes to see Lazarus the beggar in Abraham's arms. He saw them in glory but he was deprived of the joy of that glory for he had repented too late (967C–968B).

There is no evil, ugliness, or injustice in the universe. Empty meanings and false arguments pretend that what is really nothing exists. They express the blasphemous claim that everything which frustrates perverted desire or is prohibited is evil and harmful. Men complain of the divine ordering of providence, saying that the striving of the free will should never be restrained or frustrated, not recognizing that the divine mercy has provided in this way for the will lest it destroy itself. The same blasphemy is spoken of the divine justice. Men rail against the unequal distribution of earthly goods. But such earthly goods are not really good, for they vanish and, like shadows, deceive those who love them. In His wisdom God gives to each His grants and His gifts. The natural goods are distributed equally to all, goods which cannot appear in the sensible and transitory things of this world but are hidden in the inmost depths of human nature until they are made manifest in the return (968C–972A).

From Chapter 36 (Columns 972A–975C)

S: This reasoning teaches that vices are not wholly evil, but illicit. For if they were evil, they could by no means be changed into virtues. Other similar things also seem to arise against nature from perverse motions abusing the free will of a rational nature which voluntarily makes itself captive. Yet they are not allowed to harm the orderings of the universe, but are rather compelled to adorn them, encompassed as they are by the eternal laws of Divine Providence and Judgment. Since this is so, without any uncertainty or deliberation I see with absolute clarity that the fullness of the created universe will return to its causes and to God Himself in whom all things subsist; also that the completely just penalties for irrational desires imposed by the sentences of the fairest of Judges, or permitted to be imposed and inflexibly defined, will endure perpetually within that very fullness, since not only will they do no harm in any instance, but they will even provide occasions for Him to display His praiseworthiness and His ineffable beauty.[41] Hence one would not be rash in saying that penalties and rewards are separated not by intervals in space, but by differences of qualities so that they both exist together, since the commonwealth of all creation is ordered from the two of them, and yet they do not exist together because of their different effects. The effects of sins are mourning, groaning, sadness, late repentance, the insatiable heat of desire which will find no rest in anything, the teeming putrefaction and infestation of wrongdoing, the deepest obscurity of profound ignorance, in which there is no knowledge of true things or of the truth itself, i.e., no bliss in enjoying that truth. By bound feet the difficulty of walking in the divine laws is symbolically implied, and by bound hands the difficulty of performing the good acts which must be done according to the virtues. There are other, similar things also, which are too lengthy and, in fact, impossible to enumerate. The effects of merits are happiness, joy, peace, bliss, felicity, glory, equality with the most blessed angels, and, in short, *theosis*, i.e., deification, by which "God has prepared for those who love Him what no eye has seen and no ear heard, what exceeds the mind of man." [42] Moreover, where the effects of causes are contrary, the causes themselves must differ. And if anyone should ask how things far different from one another can be united at one time and in one thing, i.e., how virtues and vices can be united within the bounds of nature, let him see that in a great royal house constructed with various ornaments the sound and the weak, the blind and the sighted, the happy and the sad, the carefree and the anxious, the rich and the needy, one beaten with lashes like a slave and one exalted with honors like a lord, one enclosed in a prison like a defendant and one freed from all bonds as innocent and freed from every charge, and others likewise can be held together in the same place and at the same time. If this example holds and is evident almost equally to everyone, why is it strange if we believe and understand that in the single harmony of a universe restored and about to return to its causes, the whole rational creation, through the grace of its Redeemer, who received it all, will be sound, and that the languid weakness of perverse will, which had clung to nature from the outside, is to be arranged in its fitting orders and will suffer retributions worthy of its works? Why is it strange if, when nature itself is not only healed but also enlightened, the blindness of evil wills should itself be overcome by the perpetual shadows caused by the absence of Him who restores natures? Why is it strange if, when the nature created in God's image is not only healed and illuminated but also led back to paradise (which wise men interpret as the place of spiritual delights), the leprosy which had deformed it because of sin should be deprived of all delights and burn with eternal lusts? Why (should it be strange) if everything else in which there is a distinction between nature and guilt should receive reward and punishment when nature, wholly free in a remarkable and ineffable way, would withstand the *phantasiae* by which guilt would atone for its wrongdoing?

T: These points all seem likely and reached by plausible arguments. But at this point we come across some who deal with spiritual matters carnally. They ask what disadvantage the pagans will have for their impiety in worshipping idols and not knowing the true God. What disadvantage will the Jews have for their treachery in denying that God's incarnate Word, our Lord Jesus Christ, is consubstantial and coeternal with His Father and equal to Him in all respects in His divinity? What harm will befall all the other nations who reject the truth because of their superstitious and utterly false devisings, if in the future life their whole nature will be saved so that neither body nor soul nor any natural part is left to be tortured by eternal penalties? It is difficult or impossible to persuade such persons that it is not part of God's justice but wholly alien from it to inflict penalties upon what He has made in everything. It is rather His practice to punish what He has not made, since all things found reprehensible in all evil things and judged worthy of eternal punishments have flowed not from nature, but from the utterly perverse motions of the private will of each of the evil ones. The speculation which distinguishes among things usually and not undeservedly calls these motions the vices of nature, because they struggle against the natural affections. Evils have flowed, too, from original sin, through which generally, except for the Redeemer of mankind, all men have sinned. This evil also is attributed to nature and called its sin, not because the very nature made in God's image committed it, but because irrational abuse of the rational good of free will given by God and the turning to the love of sensible things concealed the beauty of the nature in which it had been placed from the beginning of its creation, and hid its original dignity. For if you should refer the guilt to nature, you would seem to be referring it to the Creator of nature. If the cause of guilt is assigned to nature, nature's sin will necessarily be attributed to the cause of that nature, namely God. Of course, nature made in God's image is not wholly like its Archetypal Example if it admits the cause of sin into itself. As the Archetypal Example is the cause of no sin or evil, so too the nature made in Its image and likeness. It is completely ridiculous to say that human nature first lost the image and likeness of its Creator and then took into itself the causes of sin. Whoever says this will be forced to ask by what sin nature lost the image and likeness of its Creator, since it would not have lost it if it had not sinned in some respect. Besides, if human nature never lost the image and likeness of its Creator (for the image and likeness are reckoned among the natural goods and grants in no way subject to removal, diminution, or increase in the case either of human nature or of anything else made by the Lavisher and Establisher of all good things), who but a madman would say that natural goods can be receptive of the causes of sinning or that sin arises from them? If they are so receptive, then their natural beauty is corrupted, their dignity diminished, their changelessness wavers, their order totters. Hence the conclusion that no rational nature is receptive of the causes of guilt, or it would be convicted of unlikeness to its Creator. But the following question deserves to be asked: if we refrain from attributing the cause of sin to nature to keep it from being attributed in turn to the Creator—since nothing from Him is receptive of sin or cause of sinning, why should someone not say that by the same reasoning the occasion for sinning should not be attributed to free will or else the cause of guilt would be assigned to Him who conferred it upon nature? For the giver of nature created free will in it. Just as nature is a good and an incorruptible good, so is free judgment of will. The necessary consequence is that the causes of guilt, just as they are not established in nature, are not established in free will. For the cause of evil must not be established in any good. Accordingly, if no sin rises from natural causes, we must ask the source of its occasion for arising. Anyone who gives an answer that is true, likely, and approved by plausible arguments, namely that sin derives its origin simply from the irrational motions of rational nature and from abuse of the good of free will, will immediately seem to be establishing rational nature as the occasion of irrational motion. Such a person will be judged as proclaiming relatively that rational nature provides the occasion for the irrational motion which belongs to it. In that case, he will be forced to confess also that the causes of irrational motions preceded in God; for if every natural cause of rational nature has been established in God, whatever is referred to that nature will necessarily be referred to its Cause. But if true reason maintains that irrational motion is not relatively referrable to rational nature but is diametrically opposed to it as the irrational to the rational, we are left with the inquiry about the origin of the irrational motion in which the cause of sin is established. Here no likelier explanation occurs for understanding the cause of irrational motion than the abuse of natural goods, forbidden by divine laws. Such abuse characterizes the perverse and illicit desire of everyone's free judgment when he uses a good badly. Examples (of such abuse) are so widespread and obvious that virtually everyone can confirm them amply in himself. But we must note that no one can use the highest goods of our nature badly. Natural virtue does not allow the abuse of essence, power (*virtus*), and operation or of wisdom, intellect, and reason, since these hold the first place in our nature. But the possibility is granted to make good or bad use of the middle goods of nature, such as native intelligence (*ingenium*) and corporeal sense, as well as of the body itself and the lowest goods, such as those outside us established in the orders of sensible things. Native intelligence is a natural good, granted by God to men to reflect upon and discover what is useful and honorable. Yet perverse will abuses it, seeking harmful and deadly occasions for deceiving and destroying whomever it wishes.

Chapter 36 (Columns 975C–978D)

It is better to speak of the lustful appetite than the evil will as the cause of punishment. There are not two wills in human nature, one good and one evil. There is only the single will, found in good men as well as bad (976B).
Evildoers fall into two classes: those who have not fallen

into the depths of wickedness and repent, and those whose lives have been wholly perverse. The first group may even after death petition the saints for aid, to be delivered entirely or partially from their sufferings. They ask in vain, however, who in this life have accomplished no good by which to merit mercy in the next. This is the lesson of the parable of the rich man and Lazarus (977A–B).

There is a further punishment awaiting all who have committed all kinds of vice and have never repented in this life: there will appear to them in the shape of fierce, wild animals all that in this life they found so delightful. What they pursue illicitly now they shall then try to flee in terror, but they will be unable to escape (977B–C).

Just as there are two classes of the wicked so there are two of the just, and again the rewards of each will be different. While all the just will be given good *phantasiae*, those who lived well here, though not as the holiest of men, will have *phantasiae* of natural goods, while the saints will arise to God and enjoy theophanies of the divine power. For it is one thing to remain within the goods of nature and another to surpass all nature and its goods and to arrive at God Himself whose property is grace (977D–978A).

From Chapter 36 (Columns 978C–983A)

T: We have told about the general return of all sensible creation to its causes at the end of the world. Now again we should tell specifically about the return of human nature. The whole of humanity will return to its pristine state in Him who assumed it wholly, namely in God's incarnate Word. This return is considered in two ways, one of which tells us about the restoration of human nature as a whole in Christ, and the other generally perceives not only that single restoration itself but also the bliss and deification of those who are to ascend to God Himself. For it is one thing to return to paradise and another to eat of the tree of life. We read, of course, that the first man was made in God's image and likeness and placed in paradise, but we do not read that he ate of the tree of life. When man was caught after eating of the forbidden tree, he was banished from the sweetness of the tree of life.[43] He would have been able to eat of the tree of life if he had been willing to obey the divine precepts. He would even have lived happily before eating of the tree of life if he had not sinned immediately after his creation. Hence we may understand that our whole nature, which generally is designated by the name of man made in the image and likeness of God, will return to paradise, i.e., to the pristine dignity of its creation, but only in those worthy of deification will it participate in the fruit of the tree of life. Moreover, the fruit of the Tree of Life, Christ, is a blessed life, eternal peace in the contemplation of truth, which is properly called deification. As St. Augustine says, "A blessed life is happiness in the Truth, which is Christ." [44] Perhaps this is what the Apostle means, too, when he says, "We shall all rise, but we shall not all be transformed." [45] Many, almost all, have so translated this passage of the Apostle as if he were openly saying: "All of us men, without exception, shall rise again in spiritual bodies and with the wholeness of natural goods, and shall return to the ancient condition in which we were first created; but not all will be transformed into the glory of deification, which surpasses all nature and paradise." Therefore, just as general resurrection is one thing and special transformation another, so return to paradise is one thing and eating of the tree of life another. In one, of course, the restoration of nature is signified; in the other, the deification of the elect. I make this statement with full awareness that this passage by the Apostle has been differently rendered by various translators. Some have interpreted it as "All of us shall sleep, but not all will be transformed." Others, including John Chrysostom, have interpreted it as "All of us will be transformed, but not all will sleep." But I do not believe that their interpretations are pertinent to the subject at hand.

S: I don't see why not. Isn't anyone who discusses the return of sensible creation dealing with the resurrection of bodies? He must be, for rising again is not one thing and returning another. Isn't resurrection from the dead simply a return to one's natural state? Please give me a brief and quick explanation, therefore, of the interpretations which you wished to pass by wholly untouched.

T: Those who have interpreted "All of us shall sleep, but not all will be transformed" seem to me to have understood the Apostle's words as if he were saying, "We shall all die (for what living person will not see death?), but we shall not all be transformed. For those who, from the beginning of the world to the Lord's second coming—i.e., to the end of this world—have died, are dying, and will die, anticipate the common resurrection of bodies not at once and without any delay, but.after intervals of time. The exceptions are those who rose with Christ. But those whom the end of the world and the coming of the Lord will find alive in the flesh not only will sleep but will also be transformed. Without any interval of time, they will at once sleep and wake up, i.e., die and arise, just as the Apostle himself says "in a moment, in the blinking of an eye;" [46] so that transformation rather than death will be achieved in their case. For how can death be understood when there is no interval between departure from this life and crossing into the other? Those, however, who have translated "All of us will be transformed, but not all will sleep" seem to mean simply that all men will be transformed at the future resurrection from the present to the future life, some with the death of the body interposed, others without it. "When," as the same Apostle says, "this corruptible nature [namely the body] puts on incorruptibility and this mortal nature puts on immortality. Death will be swallowed up in victory," [47] and the last enemy, Death, will be destroyed. But we shall not all sleep; i.e., not all will suffer the death of the flesh before being admitted from the temporal life to the eternal. For those whom the coming of the Son of Man finds still alive in the flesh will not be dissolved by the death of the body, nor will they suffer the separation of body and soul; but only in a moment, in the blinking of an eye, will they be transformed. Therefore they will not sleep, but will always be alive without any death of the flesh interposed. This meaning is wholly favored by St. Augustine and John Chrysostom. Moreover, it seems to have the approval of the Catholic faith, which unhesitatingly believes that our Lord Jesus Christ will come to judge the living and the dead; the living, whom the coming of the Judge will find still in the flesh; the dead, who have already endured the separation of body and soul.

S: Then not all who will return to paradise, i.e., to the pristine condition of human nature, will share in the fruit of the tree of life?

T: Clearly not all, but only those who have conquered the world and the flesh, as is written in *Revelation:* "I shall allow the victor to eat of the tree of life which is in my God's paradise." [48] By grace and nature, as we have discussed previously, all men in common are permitted to return to paradise, but only by grace the deified alone may eat of the tree of life.

S: Why, then, does Scripture attest that the tree of life is in the middle of paradise, if it is not permitted and accorded to all who are to return to paradise to eat of its fruit?

T: Observe that divine Scripture does not simply attest that the tree of life is in paradise, but says more explicitly "in the middle of paradise," [49] so that by the term *paradise* you may understand the whole of human nature, in which all men, good and evil, participate; but by the designation of its middle, you are to understand the most secret and the inmost retreats of that nature, in which the image and likeness of God has been expressed, where the tree of life, our Lord Jesus Christ, has been planted. None but the purest in faith and action, the most enlightened in knowledge, the most perfect in wisdom and understanding of the divine mysteries is permitted to enjoy contemplation of it. In my opinion, this interpretation has been prefigured in the mystic construction of Solomon's temple. All without exception, good and evil, circumcised and uncircumcised, male and female, and all the nations of the whole world, whether they converged there from everywhere for prayer or for business, entered into the outermost porticoes and were allowed to transact their business there. But only the priests and the Levites entered the portico of the priests and Solomon's portico. Then the priests, bathed and cleansed in the brazen sea in Solomon's portico, entered the outer sanctuary, where were the loaves of offering and the candelabra. But none except the High Priest was permitted to go beyond the veil into the Holy of Holies, where was the Ark and the altar of incense, the place of atonement, and two Cherubim. From this prefiguration we may understand that all men within the bounds of the natural paradise, as though within a temple, are kept in their order; but that only those sanctified in Christ will enter the inner part. And further, those who are in the High Priest, Christ, and are one with Him and have been made in Him will be introduced into the Holy of Holies, as into the inmost of the inmost places. There is Christ, represented by the altar, since by His solidity He upholds all things, and not only is He the altar, but the altar of incense, for His fragrance, i.e., His praise and glory, suffuses everything. He Himself is the Ark in which are hidden all treasures of wisdom and knowledge. He is the rod because He rules and measures all things; and the manna, because He feeds all. He is the place of atonement because He always intercedes for us with the Father, showing Him the general sacrifice and the price of the world, namely His humanity, which He sacrificed and handed over for the purification and redemption of all mankind without exception. For just as He found in no one anything except sin which he refrained from taking upon himself, so He left in no man anything which He did not redeem; and by redemption He saved and sanctified, since He Himself is the redemption and salvation, the cleansing and illumination, and the perfection of all humanity as a whole and singly. About Him the Cherubim, i.e., orders of angels, move quickly, for through them He orders and arranges things visible and invisible. Perhaps two Cherubim are described around the Ark, i.e., Christ, because angelic nature governs the sensible and the intelligible world; although not unreasonably one of the Cherubim is understood in the form of intellectual nature among angels, the other in the type of rational nature among men. Of course, no wise man doubts that intelligible and rational substances are closest to Christ. Do you see, then, how deep and supernatural it is to approach such a tree planted in the midst of paradise (i.e., human nature) and to enjoy it? To this tree, removed from all and granted only to the deified, Paul was carried away into the third heaven of our nature—i.e., above all body and vital spirit to the intellect itself, in which God's Word, the Tree of Life, dwells in an ineffable manner above all essence, power, and operation in the inaccessible light, beyond and within the nature made in God's image. And so all men will enter into paradise itself as into a very ample and secret temple, each according to his own degree. And He will dwell within them who said "I shall be in their midst." Hence the Prophet said: "I shall pay my vows within the sight of His whole people, in the halls of the Lord's house, in your midst, Jerusalem." [50] *Jerusalem* is interpreted as "vision of peace" or "temple of peace," and it is the house of the Lord built on the mountain of supernal contemplation. To it the prophet, in the following words, encourages all men to ascend by the steps of virtues and the heights of speculation. "Come, let us go up to the mountain of the Lord, to the house of the God of Jacob." [51] For God dwells only in human and angelic nature, since to men and angels alone is given the contemplation of truth. Nor should we understand these two natures as two houses but as one and the same house constructed from two intelligible materials. It is presumably of this house that the Lord said, "There are many rooms in my Father's house." [52] In the halls of this house all men will possess rooms when they return to their causes, whether they have lived well or ill in the flesh. For no one can corrupt its beauty or taint its fairness, or increase or diminish its amplitude. What could be outside it; what could be unable to be within it? In it no one's baseness is base; evil does no harm, error does not err; and the worthlessness of unclean spirits and the irrational motions of impious men not only do not contaminate its beauty, but even increase it. No beauty is produced except by the joining together of likes and unlikes, contraries and opposites, nor would good be so praiseworthy without comparison from denunciation of the evil. Therefore, what is called evil when considered by itself is denounced; but when good is praised by comparison with it, it does not seem wholly worthy of being denounced. For what heaps up the praise of the good is not wholly without praise. Would the Creator of all goods, the arranger of evils, permit evil in the universe which He created if it provided no use? This inference is quite easily made from comparisons with sensible things or from human customs. From a barren tree, for example, the praise of a fruitful one is increased; from a lustful man, the praise of a chaste. So in the paradise of human nature, everyone will have his place in proportion to his conduct in this life. Some will be farther out as in the outermost porticoes; others closer within, as in the nearer halls of divine contemplation; others in the spacious temples of divine mysteries; and still others in the inmost theophanies above all nature in and with Him who is superessential and supernatural. Blessed are those who enter the inner shrines of Wisdom, which is Christ.

Chapters 36–38 (Columns 983A–1010B)

No intervals of space or time separate the good from the evil; the distance is a spiritual one. There is one nature or substance common to all men, but it is different in its affects in each. The rich man and Abraham were alike in spiritual substance, but there was a great gulf between their spiritual qualities and between the sorrow or joy each merited. Peter and Judas were physically in the same room with Christ at the Last Supper, but in reality one was next to him and the other far away. This is the distance between joy and sorrow even in this life, and it will be even greater in the next (983B–984A).

There are those who deny that this sensible world will perish and return to its causes. They contend that it will endure but with its qualities changed for the better. It will still be composed of many bodies, with separate places and distinct times, and in its lowest part the impious will suffer in the fires of hell. The body of every impious man, they say, will retain just that sex and shape he possessed in this life. Its only change will be from mortality to immortality, from time to eternity, from animality to spirituality. This change is attributed not to the powers of nature and divine grace but to the severity of a harsh and vindictive judge (984B–985A).

Confronted with such opinions, reason would prefer to laugh than to argue. Scripture teaches plainly that all men will have the same resurrected bodies. Christ said, "I am the Resurrection," not "I am the Resurrection of the just alone." As He gave men being equally, so they will arise equally, and all will resemble the nature of the angels (985B–986A).

A literal heaven between the moon and the sphere of the

fixed stars, where each will have his appointed place, is equally ludicrous. One is dumbfounded to read such things in some of the books of the Fathers. The readiest explanation is that they hoped thereby to elevate the thoughts of simple believers by giving them the rudiments of the faith. In learning that at the end of this world there will be no time, space, or body, the simple would be alarmed, thinking that then there would be nothing at all. It is easier for them to think that bodies will change from earthly to ethereal than that there should be no body of any kind (986A–987A).

Passages in Scripture that seem to teach the eternity of the corporeal world are easily interpreted allegorically. The promise that there will be a new heaven and a new earth refers especially to the renewal of human nature. Our present duality of body and soul will be simplified into unity when we put off the old man and put on the new. The "new earth" of our bodies will be made one with the "new heaven" of our souls (990A). Other passages in Scripture are to be understood in similar ways. One must note too that intelligible creatures as well as sensible things will pass over into their causes and be made one with them, for the knower becomes what is known (989D).

Augustine would appear to advocate a literal interpretation when in *The City of God* he claims that this corporeal world merely acquires the qualities of spirituality and immortality. Elsewhere he even writes that the body of the Lord after His Resurrection is located in heaven in the same shape and fleshly substance in which He appeared on earth, having added immortality only. He concludes that Christ is not now everywhere, as God is, nor is He changed into Divinity. From some place He will descend visible and corporeally to judge the living and the dead (990D–991A).

A careful reading of the last part of *The City of God*, however, shows that Augustine cannot really hold such views without contradicting himself: the corporeal heaven cannot pass away if the flesh of Christ is to be located there after His

Resurrection. It is far more credible to suppose that he writes according to the capacity of his readers than that he dissents from the views of his predecessors Ambrose and Gregory (991C–992A).

Christ's words, "I and my Father are one," refer not only to His divinity but to His entire substance as man and as God. He cannot, then, either as a whole or in part be bound by spatial limitations (992A–C). The body in which Christ appeared to His disciples after His Resurrection was like those spiritual bodies which angels assume temporarily when they appear to men. Every man possesses within himself the hidden ground (*ratio*) of such a body into which he will be transformed in the general resurrection and in which he will be like the angels (993D–994A).

When Paul writes, "Till we all come in the unity of faith, and of the knowledge of the Son of God, unto a perfect man, unto the measure of the stature of the fulness of Christ," he is not saying, as some foolishly think, that we shall all have the same kind of body that Christ had when He was thirty. Paul is talking about the Church as Christ's Body which has begun here on earth in faith and will grow into perfection of knowledge of the Son of God (994B–995A).

When the Creed says, "He shall come again to judge the living and the dead," it does not mean that Christ will return corporeally to some place at the end of time. The last judgment is not an event perceptible to bodily eyes. Rather, Christ's advent will be perceived by each man within his own enlightened conscience, where the books will be opened, God will reveal what is hidden, and each man will be the judge of his own thoughts and actions (997B).

A query from the Student about the correct interpretation of the account of the saints ascending to meet Christ in the clouds prompts a discussion of the many passages in both Old and New Testaments in which clouds are mentioned. All refer to that knowledge of God in His theophanies which will be man's on his return to his causes. When the Lord ascended in clouds, He was not using them as a vehicle to mount to some ethereal space; rather He wished to reveal Himself as a visible symbol of the way in which He ascends into the hearts of His faithful followers. He ascends into those ascending into Him in contemplation, for none can ascend to Him without Him (998B–999B).

There are three ways in which the saints contemplate God: as they are now, confined to their bodies; as released from their bodies; and as receiving spiritual bodies. All three modes are illustrated in the Transfiguration: Elijah represents the first, Moses the second, and the Lord Himself the third. Elijah did not come down out of some spatial paradise in the body he had when alive, nor did Moses come from some dwelling place of souls. They came from Christ Himself—that is, from the highest spiritual vision, nor did they really depart from that vision when they appeared to the corporeal vision of the disciples, for when the disciples raised their eyes, they saw only Christ (999C–1000A).

Like the clouds of the Ascension and Transfiguration, the clouds in which the Son of Man will return at the end of the world are theophanies in which the celestial substances see God. They will accompany Him so as to declare to both the good and the evil the greatness of His majesty. Their motion is spiritual, neither local nor temporal, for while Augustine holds that spirits can move in time without moving from place to place, the Greeks hold the sounder view: everything moving locally also moves temporally, and everything lacking local motion also lacks temporal motion. Either both space and time are or both are not; one cannot be without the other (1000B–1001A).

The return of all things into their causes when the sensible world is dissolved and the intelligible world is enfolded into Christ is to be understood in two ways: there is the general return when all come back to the principle that made them and the special return of those who are not only recalled to their primordial nature but to an end beyond all nature, God

Himself (1001A–B). Scripture is full of allusions to both kinds of return: the return of the people of God to the Promised Land (1001B–1002B), the parables of the prodigal son (1004C–1005C), the lost drachma (1005C–D), the lost sheep (1005D–1006)—all refer to the return of mankind to the Heavenly Jerusalem.

Most writers say that there will be exactly the number of men who return to the heavenly city as there were angels who fell. The reason seems to be that if more men are born than the number of fallen angels, there will not be room for them all and some men will not return. One cannot speak as if the matter were clearly settled, but Augustine writes that many more will be given life by the passion of Christ than died through Adam's sin. Whether the number of fallen men and angels is the same or larger than that of the redeemed, one thing is certain: the whole human race is redeemed in Christ and it will be brought back as a whole to the heavenly Jerusalem (1006C–1007C).

One point in the Teacher's account has troubled the Student. The parable of the prodigal son had been interpreted as teaching the return of all mankind to God the Father, the elder brother representing the angels, and the fatted calf, Christ as sacrificed for mankind. The Student finds it puzzling that the elder son should be depicted as jealous, for surely the angels will rejoice at man's return. The question affords the Teacher the opportunity to explain that not all parables make the same point throughout; many shift from one lesson to another in the course of the story. In the case of this parable there is such a shift at the point of the prodigal's return. The whole story may be taken as signifying the general return of all mankind, or it may have reference to the return of the Gentiles through faith in Christ. In this second interpretation the elder son represents the Jews, jealous because they think their loyalty ignored, while the Gentiles are forgiven their former idolatry and are rewarded bounteously. The Jews do not realize that in denying Christ, they have thereby denied His

Father. The Gentiles' sin of ignorance is more tolerable than
the Jews' sin of pride. Ignorance has been banished by the
light of truth and the Gentiles have been received by God,
while the Jews are left in ignominy and pain until the end of
the world when by the ineffable magnanimity of the divine
Goodness they will be received and will accept willingly the
Catholic faith (1008A–1009D).

From Chapters 38–40 (Columns 1010B–1022B)

S: Very often for those following one and the same kind of
exposition without any transition into different modes of speech, either
error or the greatest difficulty of interpretation arises. The fabric of
divine Scripture is intricately woven and entwined with turns and
obliquities. The Holy Spirit did not desire to make it so because It
grudged our understanding, a possibility about which we should not
even think, but because It was eager to exercise our intelligence and to
reward hard toil and discovery. The reward of those toiling over
sacred Scripture is pure and perfect understanding. O Lord Jesus, I ask
of You no other reward, no other bliss, no other joy than that I may be
free from the error of false speculation and may clearly understand
Your words, which were inspired by Your Holy Spirit. This is the
height of my felicity and the end of perfect contemplation, since the
rational and utterly pure soul will find nothing beyond, for there is
nothing beyond. As You are nowhere more fittingly sought than in
Your words, so You are nowhere more openly found than in them.
There You dwell, and there You lead those who seek and love You.
There You prepare the spiritual banquets of true knowledge for Your
elect, and there, passing through, You minister to them. O Lord, what
is that crossing of Yours except the ascent through the infinite steps of
contemplating You? You always pass through in the intellects of those
who seek and find You. You are always sought by them and always
found, and yet You are not always found. You are found in Your
theophanies, in which, in many ways as in mirrors, You are reflected
in the minds of those who understand You, as You allow Yourself to

be understood. You allow men to understand not what You are but what You are not, and that You are. But You are not found in the superessentiality with which You go beyond and surpass every intellect that wishes and rises to comprehend You. You administer Your presence to Your people, then, by the ineffable manner of Your appearance. You go beyond them by the incomprehensible loftiness and infinity of Your essence. I request, therefore, that we turn quickly to a consideration of the special return of man, in order that we may set it as a limit to our discussion. We should not linger longer over these matters, which have been gone over in many ways to make them clearer and more convincing. Otherwise we may seem to have filled our discussion with words rather than with understanding.

T: In the Gospel the Lord Himself likened to ten virgins the whole of rational creation, which was created specially in man and which naturally has within it a desire for bliss and a capacity for knowledge of the Highest Good—i.e., of the most sublime Trinity, from which flows all good. These virgins, taking up their lamps, i.e., the capacity for knowing the eternal light, went out to meet the bridegroom and the bride, i.e., Christ and the Church, which now is in heaven, consisting partly of the holy angels, partly of the purest souls of men. In them the firstfruits of human nature, which still is in the captivity of mortal life and frail limbs, are added to the citizens of the celestial country. But why to meet them? Because the Redeemer and Bridegroom of rational nature, with the ineffable condescension and readiness of His clemency, moved by regard for our salvation, always has come to receive us spiritually, accompanied by celestial powers and holy spirits. That Bridegroom generally shouts in the ear of all mankind: "Come to Me, all you who labor and are burdened, and I will refresh you. Take up my.yoke and learn from Me, for I am gentle and humble in heart, and you will find rest for your souls." [53] Therefore He came to meet all with His bride, the celestial Jerusalem, He who was dedicated to receiving all to a share in His city. Note that all humanity is compared to the number ten, for it holds the tenth region in the building of the city above. So the ten virgins—i.e., the whole throng of human nature—with a natural striving go out to meet their Beloved, who is coming to them. They go not with the steps of the body but with the affections of the mind. But although the motion of rational nature toward its end, Christ, is equal and although the striving for the eternal light signified by the lamps is equal, yet it does not participate equally in that Light which enlightens every man coming into this world. As St. Dionysius says, "There is one thing which all things naturally strive to participate in, but not all things equally participate in the One," [54] although no part of creation is wholly deprived of participation in It. The virgins, then, will not go out on equal terms to meet the Bridegroom and the bride. Those who have not only the capacity for the true Light, but also the Light Itself which the oil kindles will reach the Bridegroom Himself, and will enter with Him into spiritual marriage. Those who have only the capacity for Light but are not enlightened and adorned by the Light Itself will go forth to meet Christ, i.e., not only by a naturally implanted striving but by an actual attempt they will ascend to the sole natural goods of humanity, which subsist in Christ; but they will not arrive at the supernatural grace and joy of deification in Him. Such is the implication of the division into ten. The text says, "Five of them were foolish," i.e., imprudent, "and five wise." [55] The foolish ones took only the lamps without the oil. The wise took not only the lamps, but also the oil in their lamps. So the vessels are like the wise and foolish virgins, since reason, which is, as it were, the natural seat of Divine Light, has uniformly been distributed to the wholeness, as though to the virginity of incorruptible nature, which is neither increased nor diminished in any one; but that nature does not all receive the Divine Light in the same way. This inequality does not come about through the fault, envy, or inadequacy of the Light Itself, since It is present to all, shines with equal brightness upon all, and flows out equally for all with an inexhaustible outpouring. But since not all have the same power of vision by which the Light of minds is perceived, it follows that some enjoy It more, others less, and still others are wholly excluded from It. Examples are the unclean spirits unwilling to turn toward It. Even their exclusion from participation in the truly existing Light does not result from the intellectual substance of which they were created by the Highest Good—for otherwise they would be wholly reduced to nothing, since everything wholly deprived of participation in It lacks being. But insofar as they are contaminated by the irrational motions of their perverse will, they are excluded from participation in the true Light. They turn not to It but to themselves, i.e., to their worthlessness. If they considered their nature and its Creator, they would surely be blessed. Now if anyone should ask, "Why is the possibility of gazing at the Divine Light not given equally to rational nature as a whole; and why have the power and action of gazing at It not been given equally whether in this or the future life?" Let him question that man who, dumbfounded and struck by the inaccessible light, proclaimed: "How deep is the wealth of God's knowledge and wisdom! How inscrutable are His judgments and how trackless His ways at all times! Who knows God's thoughts, or who has been His counsellor? Who has lent Him anything that can be reclaimed? Indeed, all things come from Him, through Him, in Him, and directed toward Him." [56] Let him also ask why the Lavisher of all goods did not distribute equally to all orders of angels the power of contemplating Him. Of course, the Seraphim, Cherubim, and Thrones contemplate Him more deeply, clearly, and closely than the Virtues, Powers, and Dominations. They, in turn, see Him better and in a brighter light than the Principalities, the Archangels, and the Angels. Who will answer this question? No one except one reflecting within himself on the passage "God made all things by measure, number, weight." [57] What would be the beauty of the created universe if God had established everything on terms of equality? For the sweetness and beauty of sensible harmony is set in order not from like, but from different sounds arranged in fixed proportions. Someone might likewise propose the question: "If the first man had not sinned (for as punishment for his sin the human race is multiplied by male and female), man would not be propagated by male and female, but from the inmost bosom of nature either all men would proceed together into their own species and numbers, as all the angels did from their causes, or, in a set order of time, everyone would proceed into this world without any corruption and generation like that of beasts. In that case, would all men be of equal or the same power and order or, like the angels, would men, too, be arranged in their orders according to Divine Providence and Wisdom? Christ will answer him, I believe,

He who promises men that after the resurrection they "will be like the angels in heaven." [58] Angels, moreover, are arranged in their own orders. Men too, therefore, will be arranged according to the different rankings of virtues. But if they are to be so even after sin, surely they would have been so if they had not sinned, i.e., they would not have enjoyed the contemplation of truth in the same way. As St. Augustine says, moreover, the first man at his creation, before sinning, was neither wise nor foolish—for if he had been wise, he would not have deserted God to consent to his wife and would not have acted without caution for fear of imitating the pride of the Devil's cunning; because he was not seduced, but was puffed up with pride; but if he had been foolish, who would believe that God made a foolish man in His image and likeness? Surely, then, he was created in a balance between wisdom and folly and would have become wise had he preserved God's commandment. Scripture does not say "Let Us make man Our image and likeness" but "according to Our image and likeness." It is as though it were clearly saying, "Let us make man to become Our image and likeness if he guards Our precept." Man, then, was made not wise, but receptive of wisdom if he should wish to be. He could have received wisdom and arrived at its state if he had been unwilling to scorn God's advice. Since he did not raise himself up to wisdom by guarding the commandment, but by his own will fell prone through his transgression into the lust for temporal and sensible things, he must rather be regarded as foolish and imprudent even before he sinned, than as a striver for wisdom and prudence. For folly and imprudence preceded sin. Nor did he receive these qualities from the causes of his creation, but from the changeability of his own will, which by no means arises from natural causes. He became foolish and imprudent by himself, then, before his transgression of the command. Had he not transgressed the command, perhaps he would not have been banished from paradise, but would have enjoyed only the goods of his nature, which he had received at his creation, and would have rejoiced in them to a degree although deprived, because of his folly and lack of judgment, of participation in the highest wisdom and prudence. We see that many, in fact practically all improvident and foolish persons are happy and contented with their nobility of lineage, with their many kinsmen, with fairness, strength, and health of body, with cleverness of mind, with charm of words, with a beautiful and compatible wife, with abundance of offspring, with affluence in worldly affairs, not to mention dignities, honors, and the other things with which the world favors them. They are so contented, in fact, that they would wish to live forever in such a manner, without any desire to hear or reflect upon spiritual delights. To this status of the first men before sin, i.e., to solely natural goods without the ornaments of virtues, one part of the human race, typically represented by the five foolish virgins, will return. But to the loftiness to which man would have ascended by grace if he had not sinned—i.e., to participation in the highest wisdom and all virtues, the participation followed by deification and contemplation of truth—we must fittingly think that the other part of the number of mankind, whose symbol is the five wise virgins, will be elevated above all natural goods and will enter upon spiritual marriage with their Bridegroom. To their number none is admitted unless he is resplendent with the light of wisdom and glowing with the flames of divine love, the wisdom and love nourished by richness of knowledge and action. To this marriage no one lacking in knowledge and action, no matter how fully and fairly he has flourished with natural goods, is permitted to ascend, but he is wholly excluded from it. Not nature but grace raises the human mind to that height; and the merit of obedience to the commands of God and of the purest knowledge of God afforded in this life by books and by creation lifts one up. Observe the heart of this parable and how it makes a transition from genus to species, just as happens also in the previous parable about the two sons dividing their father's substance. In that parable is represented first the general return of the whole human race, then the special return of the gentiles. In this parable similarly by the ten virgins going out to meet the bridegroom is represented the return of all mankind to its pristine natural state. But the special return of all the saints is represented by the five wise virgins. The species is the number of the elect of the human race. There is implied, then, not only the return for mankind as a whole to the original, natural beginning, but an ascent of ineffable deification beyond nature to God Himself for a special group. All, as we have said, are to return to paradise, but not all are to enjoy the tree of life. Or surely all are to receive of the tree of life, but not equally. For that man is a fool who is unaware that natural goods too, in which all will equally participate, are the fruit of the tree of life. *Pan xylon*, i.e., "every tree," as we said before, is called Christ. Of course, the tree is productive of all goods for it itself is all good and the lavisher of all goods. So all men generally will enjoy its fruit by participation in natural goods. The elect specifically will enjoy the sublimity of deifications beyond all nature. Deifications, in which only the just will participate, are therefore symbolized by spiritual marriage, into which the wise virgins entered. Not all will enjoy supernatural goods, but only those "to whom" as Gregory the Theologian says "it is permitted, after overcoming matter and flesh, as though by rising above clouds and veils, to be made with God through reason and contemplation and to be held by the purest light, insofar as that is possible for human nature." Those are the blessed, by ascent from here, by deification there. The word *deification* is very rarely used in Latin books, but its meaning is found in many authors, especially Ambrose. I do not understand very well the reason for this rare usage. Perhaps it is that the meaning of the word *theosis*, commonly used by the Greeks to designate the passing of the saints into God not only in soul but also in body, so that they are one in Him and with Him when nothing animal, corporeal, human, or natural remains in them—perhaps, I say, to those unable to rise beyond carnal thoughts it seems too lofty, incomprehensible, and incredible and hence not to be proclaimed in public. But this point must be dealt with by wise men. Many divine mysteries have been passed over untouched by the holy fathers on this account, for weak eyes cannot bear the brightness of light. I believe that these few examples, taken from divine parables, suffice to show convincingly the general and specific return of mankind to his beginning, his primordial condition, and to God Himself in the case of those worthy to enjoy the most complete participation in Him. They are also convincing about the return of all sensible creation, made in and because of man, to its causes when there will be not only a general Sabbath of all divine works, but a special Sabbath of Sabbaths among the holy angels and holy men. The house of God will be filled, and in it everyone established in the order fitting to him, some lower, some higher, some at the height of nature, others above all natural power about God Himself. Thus that great banquet will be arranged and celebrated from which the substance of none will be rejected, for it was made by God, but the fault of none will be introduced because it was not made by God. Nature will be cleansed, vice will be winnowed away, the grains of substance will be buried, the straw of misdeeds will burn with the flame of the divine sentence, the hidden things of the shadows will be enlightened, and God will be seen as all things in all things.

S: What you have said is enough, but I beg you to explain the rest of the parable briefly.

T: What is that?

S: The delay of the bridegroom, the sleep and the sleepiness of all the virgins, and the other points which you left untouched.

T: The delay of the bridegroom is, I believe, the interval of time between the first and the second coming of the Lord, or from the beginning of the world to its end. For no time has passed or will pass through the six ages of the world in which virginity, i.e. the wholeness of human nature utterly destroyed in none although contaminated in all except Christ, does not wish to rise to meet its Bridegroom. In some persons that virginity is foolish, in others wise, but in all it strives to attain its Creator and the supernal homeland which it had deserted. Indeed, the striving for bliss is commonly and naturally present in all the wise and foolish, the good and evil. In this interval of the world's course through times ordained, some sleep, some are drowsy. Those sleep who are already dead or are destined to die in the future; but they are said to be drowsy whom the end of the world will find alive in the flesh. They are said not to be asleep but to be drowsy since, when death has run its course, they will not die or be detained by death for any period of time; but as though weighted down but not felled by sleep, without any intervening death they will be transported into another life. In the following passage from chapter twenty-one of Book 20 of *The City of God*, St. Augustine seems to agree with those who say that death will be extremely brief at the swift snatching away of those who will be alive at the end of the world. "If we believe that the holy ones who will be found alive when Christ comes and will be carried off to meet Him will, at that carrying off, depart from their mortal bodies and soon return to the same bodies made immortal, we shall find no difficulties in the words of the Apostle either when he says: 'Whatever you sow is given life only if it first dies';[59] or when he says 'We shall all rise again or all sleep, for they will not be brought to life through immortality unless they die for a short time first by some death; and hence they will not be estranged from resurrection, which they precede by a falling asleep, no matter how brief'." Midnight, when the shouting occurred and the Bridegroom came, implies the uncertain end of the world, and the coming of the spiritual Bridegroom without the knowledge of any. As He Himself said: "About that day and hour no one has knowledge, not the angels of heaven or the Son of Man; only the Father knows it." [60] And at the end of this parable, it says: "So stay awake, because you do not know either the day or the hour." [61] That shout signifies the very clear signs which will precede the destruction of the world and the coming of the Lord, concerning which He Himself, sitting on the Mt. of Olives, prophesied to His disciples. Moreover, the rising of all the virgins presages the regeneration of all mankind. The wise virgins adorn their lamps, i.e., their rational motions, with the fuel of good action and the brightness of a pure conscience. The foolish virgins, however, lack such action and knowledge. The refusal of the wise virgins to share their oil with the foolish ones probably indicates symbolically, I believe, that to the wise, merits will appear cheap and insufficient on that day of understanding when each one will scrutinize the depths of his conscience; and the merits will seem not at all to be compared to eternal felicity, as the Apostle says: "Our suffering at this time is not comparable to the coming glory which will be revealed in us." [62] Hence the Lord Himself said, "Happy are the poor in spirit," [63] i.e., happy are those who consider themselves and their merits nothing, and judge themselves wholly deficient in the wealth of virtues, "since theirs is the kingdom of heaven." Hence the virgins are to say to those who ask them for help, "*Ne forte* there be enough for us and for you." [64] This passage can be understood two ways: for *ne* is put either negatively (with a long $\bar{e}$) or to show uncertainty (with a short $\breve{e}$), as in the book of *Genesis*: "*Ne* perhaps he may put out his hand and partake of the tree of life." And lest perchance they might seem, through a kind of envy, to have been unwilling to share their own meager supply of merits with the foolish virgins when they refused the oil, they answered with the advice, "Go instead to those who sell it and buy some for yourselves," [65] i.e., go to those who not only have enough for themselves because of the excellence and abundance of their merits but who could also furnish help and the merit of future bliss to those able to honor them in this life. In this interval of slowness and negligence, the Bridegroom came and took the virgins who were ready and adorned for His coming; and He led them to marriage with Him, i.e., to the deification by which He glorifies the souls closest to perfection with the supernatural grace of contemplating Him. The others were left in the fullness of natural goods, but excluded from the height of ineffable deification, "which eye has not seen or ear heard; which has never arisen in a man's heart." [66] Such is the meaning of "and the door was closed," [67] i.e., the entry to contemplation of the Divine face to face. This door will not be entered by those who live heedlessly in this life, without pouring the oil of action and knowledge into the receptacle of their reason even if, touched by a late penitence, they shout and say, "Lord, Lord, open the door for us." [68] That doubling of the Lord's name signifies either how those human beings who have lived this life unsupported by any help of good conduct constantly strive to contemplate their Creator without any cloud of ignorance between, or the slothfulness of simple believers who do not sufficiently consider the depth of the Catholic faith. They think that our Lord Jesus Christ is composed of two substances, although He is one substance in two natures; and they seek what is not fitting for them. For this reason they are given the answer, "You pray but do not have your petition answered because you do not pray well." [69] How many there are who are either wholly unaware or wholly deny that the Divine Essence is in three Substances and the three Substances in one Essence. By their false reflections and carnal opinions they demand to enter upon the intimate marriage of divine and pure contemplation. How many there are who so divide the Lord Jesus Christ that they neither believe nor understand that His divinity is united to His humanity and His humanity to His divinity in a unity of substance—

or, as it is more customarily expressed in Latin, in a unity of person. Actually, though, His humanity and divinity are one and inseparable, with the reason of each of His natures unimpaired. To those who double Christ's substance, therefore, and say "Lord, Lord, open the door for us," the correct and appropriate answer is given, "I say to you, I do not know you," [70] i.e., I shall allow you to be ignorant of the inmost, secret marriage of My divinity and humanity, which I prepared before the creation of the world for my people who most clearly understand, and to which I have admitted them now at the end of the world. While you were still alive in the flesh, you did not make yourselves worthy of the joy of that marriage. I permit you, however, to stay within the limits of the natural goods which I have created in you." He promises that He will respond similarly to those who, at the Day of Judgment, will call out: "Lord, Lord, did we not perform many acts of prowess in your name?" [71] And elsewhere, "Not everyone who says to me, 'Lord, Lord' will enter into the kingdom of heaven." [72] The Word united to the flesh and the flesh united to the Word in an inseparable unity of one and the same substance from two natures, divine and human, receives only those who gaze at the unity of its substance with the simple eye of perfect contemplation. So, as man in the Word is truly the Son of God, and the Word in man is truly the Son of Man without any transformation of natures, our Lord Jesus Christ is understood as one and the same Son of God and Lord of man. Here you have a plausible, quick explanation of the parable as I view it.

S: Indeed I do.

T: What is left, then, and what is keeping us from bringing the work to an end?

S: Nothing except to add a recapitulation of the whole subject, i.e., of the division of universal nature.

[39] *T:* We have made a fourfold division of universal nature, which is understood as consisting of God and creation. The first species is that which considers and distinguishes nature creative but not created; the second, nature created and creative; the third, created and

not creating; the fourth, neither created nor creative. The first and the fourth forms are predicated of God alone, not because His nature, which is simple and more than simple, is divisible, but because it is the object of two kinds of speculation. When I observe that it is the Beginning and Cause of all things, there occurs to me the true reason which confidently suggests that Divine Essence or Substance, Goodness, Virtue, Wisdom, and the other things predicated of God are created by none, because nothing higher precedes Divine Nature. Moreover, all things with and without being are created by It, through It, in It, and directed toward It. When I perceive that all things have the same end and the same impassable boundary, for which they strive and in which they establish the limit of their natural motion, I find that it is neither created nor creating. Of course, the Nature which is from Itself cannot be created by anyone. Nor does It create anything. For since all things which have proceeded from It by intelligible or sensible generation will return to It by a remarkable and ineffable regeneration, and all things will rest in It since nothing will flow from It any more through generation, It is said to create nothing. What will It create, when It will be all things in all things and will not appear in anything except Itself? About the two middle species we have dealt sufficiently in the preceding books, and they have been so clearly explained that they are readily evident to those who search for them. One of them is perceived in primordial causes, the other in their effects. The one established in causes is created in the only-begotten Son of God, in whom and through whom all things were made; and He creates all things which flow from it, i.e., all its effects, whether intelligible or sensible. But the form established in the effects of causes is merely created by its causes and does not in turn create anything, for nothing in the nature of things is lower than it. For that reason especially it has been ranked among sensible things. Nor is any obstacle presented by the fact that angels or men, whether good or evil, are often thought to create in this world something new and unknown to human uses. Actually, they do not create anything, but, in obedience to divine laws and orders if they are good, they produce something from the material creation made by God in its effects through the causes. If they are evil, they do so moved and deceived by the wiles and devices of the Devil's cunning. Yet all things are set in order by Divine Providence, so that nothing substantially evil is found in the nature of things, or anything which may confound the commonwealth and civil arrangement of all things.

After the fourfold speculation about universal nature in these four species, of which we observed two in Divine Nature as the principles of Beginning and End, two in created nature as the principles of causes and effects, we saw fit to add some speculations about the return of effects to causes, i.e., to the reasons in which they subsist. Moreover, the mode of this return occurred to us as threefold. The first is noted generally in the transformation of all sensible creation contained within the circuit of this world—i.e., of all bodies, whether they are subject to the corporeal senses or elude them because of their excessive subtlety; so that there is no body within the fabric of corporeal nature, whether it flourishes only with vital motion, secretly or openly, or whether it has an irrational soul and corporeal sense, that does not return to its hidden causes after passing through its life. For nothing will be reduced to nothing among those things which have been established in substance by the Cause of all things. The second mode deals, in its speculation, with the general return of all human nature saved in Christ to the pristine state of its creation, and, as into a kind of paradise, to the dignity of the divine image by the merit of that One whose blood was shed for the salvation of all humanity in common. Thus no man is deprived of the natural goods with which he was created, whether he lived well or ill in this life. And thus the ineffable and incomprehensible diffusion of divine goodness and bounty into all human nature will appear, since what flows down from the Highest Good is not punished in anyone. The third mode of speculation about return involves those who not only will ascend to the sublimity of the nature established in them, but also, through the abundance of divine grace transmitted by Christ and in Christ to His elect, will cross superessentially above all the laws and boundaries of nature into God Himself, and will be one in Him and with Him. Their return is marked, in effect, by seven steps. First will be the change of the earthly body into vital motion; second, of vital motion into sense; third, of sense into reason; next, of reason into mind, in which the end of all rational creation is established. After this virtual fivefold union of the parts of our nature—namely of body, vital motion, sense, reason, and intellect—so that they are not five but one, with the lower always consumed by the higher, not so that they cease to be but so that they are one; there will follow three other steps of ascent, of which one will be the crossing of the soul into the knowledge of all things which are after God; the second, of knowledge into wisdom, i.e. intimate contemplation of truth, insofar as it is granted to creatures; the third and highest step is the supernatural falling of the most purified souls into God Himself and, as it were, into the shadows[73] of the incomprehensible and inaccessible light, the shadows in which the causes of all things are hidden. Then night will be enlightened as day—i.e., the most secret divine mysteries will be revealed in an ineffable manner to blessed and enlightened intellects. Then the perfect solidity of the number eight as a supernatural cube will be achieved. Foreshadowing it, the sixth Psalm is entitled "Psalm of David for the octave." The resurrection of the Lord too occurred on the eighth day for the very purpose of signifying mystically that blessed life which will come after the sevenfold revolution of this life through seven days, after the consummation of the world, since human nature, as we have said, will return to its beginning by an eightfold ascent: five parts within the bounds of nature, three supernaturally and superessentially within God Himself, for the pentad of creation will be united with the triad of Creator, so that God alone appears in everything just as only light shines bright in the clearest air.

[40]   These subjects comprise the whole matter of this work, which is made up of five books. If anyone finds that we have written anything still unknown or superfluous, let him impute the fault to our intemperance and carelessness; and with kindly heart, may the observer be humbly indulgent to human intelligence still weighed down by the dwellingplace of the flesh. I believe that in this murky life nothing has yet been achieved by human endeavors wholly without error. Even the just are not so called because they are just while still living in the flesh, but because they wish to be just, and, striving for

perfect future justice, are named from what their mind longs for. I should not believe that anyone except Christ while weighted down with mortal limbs and carnal senses has arrived at a perfect state of virtue and the height of true contemplation. As John the Evangelist attests: "If we say that we have no sin, we are deceiving ourselves and there is no truth in us." [74] Likewise the Apostle: "Now we see dimly in a mirror;" [75] and elsewhere "We know only in part and we prophesy only in part." [76] But if anything useful and relevant to the structure of the Catholic faith appears, it should be attributed only to God, who alone unlocks the hidden places of the shadows and leads to Himself those who seek Him, undeceived and freed from their errors. Let the reader, harmonious in charity of spirit, give thanks with us to the universal Cause of all goods, without whom we can do nothing. Let him be drawn by no desire for reproach and kindled by no torches of envy which, more than other faults, tries to break the bond of charity and brotherhood.

With the leave of all who receive our conclusions with good will and regard them with the clear sight of the mind, or harshly reject them and prejudge them before knowing their nature and quality, I offer this work to be examined and entrust it to be corrected first of all by God, who said "Ask and it will be given to you; seek and you will find; knock and the door will be opened to you." [77] Next I commend it to you for examination and correction, most beloved brother in Christ, Wulfad, fellow-worker in studies of wisdom. It was undertaken with your encouragement, and it has been brought to a conclusion, such as it is, through your expert knowledge. If constraint resulting from the weight of the subject and the amount of material to be explained has caused me to pass over any points in the context of this work, and if I promised to give some account of those points at some time, you should carefully exact payment of my promises. After my work has been reread and all the promises discovered and collected, I shall treat them in cursory and summary fashion to the best of my ability.

Meanwhile I ask that readers be content with the topics already discussed and that they consider, not the trifling or virtually nonexistent power of my poor wit, but the readiness of my humble but devout endeavors to track down these matters relating to God. I hope that you may be zealous in my defense, if not with rivals, at least with friends who search out the truth, and that your defense may rest as much on the force of your very keen intelligence as on the results eked out in wakeful nights by the dull visions of my mind. You will find this project no heavy task, I believe; for as soon as such a work reaches the hands of true philosophers, if it is suitable for discussions they will not only accept it willingly, but will embrace it as their own. But if it reaches those who are more ready to find fault than to be sympathetic, one should not engage in much conflict with such men. Let every man be lavishly endowed with his own interpretation until the coming of that Light which converts to darkness the light of false philosophers and changes into light the darkness of those who rightly know.

Notes

1. Gen. 3:21–24.
2. This version of *Genesis* 3:22 is taken from St. Jerome's Latin Vulgate. The word *ne* discussed by Eriugena does, indeed, have different meanings in different contexts. In the verse cited, however, it is clearly negative in force, a view that is supported by both the Hellenistic Greek Septuagint version and the original Hebrew text, both of which St. Jerome used in making his translation. As a negative, the *ne* would either mean *lest* (i.e., God would implicitly be expressing a fear that man might exceed his natural limits) or would introduce a negative command ("Let man not set his hand . . ."). Since such interpretations would attribute either fear or imperfect generosity to God, John the Scot finds it necessary to reject them.
3. Reading *proprie* for *prope*.
4. Romans 1:20.
5. Deut. 4:24.
6. St. Jerome is correct and Pseudo-Dionysius in error about the Hebrew forms.
7. John 14:6.
8. Luke 12:49.
9. I have omitted the "or *ledones*", which is evidently a textual corruption.
10. Reading *aeris* with the *Editio Princeps*.
11. 1 Cor. 7:31.
12. Acts 17:28.
13. Luke 17:12–19.
14. Psalm 49:13.
15. 1 Cor. 15:44.
16. 1 Cor. 15:54.
17. Romans 11:36.
18. Gal. 3:28.

19. Eph. 1:21.
20. John 17:1.
21. 2 Chron. 26:9.
22. Matt. 12:25.
23. Psalm 116:15.
24. Matt. 16:16.
25. John 1:1.
26. Gal. 6:14.
27. John 11:25.
28. 1 Cor. 15:20.
29. Reading *imitatur* with the *Editio Princeps*.
30. 1 Cor. 15:44.
31. John 11:25.
32. James 1:17.
33. Romans 8:29.
34. John 12:26.
35. 1 Tim. 6:16.
36. 1 Thess. 4:17.
37. Psalm 104:29.
38. Psalm 104:30.
39. *Loc. cit.*
40. Colos. 3:2.
41. Reading *ineffabilis* with the *Editio Princeps*.
42. 1 Cor. 2:9.
43. This sentence is my version of the probable meaning of the corrupt passage in the text.
44. Conf. 10.23.
45. 1 Cor. 15:51.
46. 1 Cor. 15:52.
47. 1 Cor. 15:54.
48. Rev. 2:7.
49. Gen. 2:9.
50. Psalm 116:18–19.
51. Isa. 2:3.
52. John 14:2.
53. Matt. 11:28–29.
54. Eccles. Hier. 1.2.
55. Matt. 25:2.
56. Rom. 11:33–36.
57. Wisd. 11:21.
58. Matt. 22:30.
59. 1 Cor. 15:36.
60. Matt. 24:36.
61. Matt. 25:13.
62. Romans 8:18.
63. Matt. 5:3.
64. Matt. 25:9.
65. Matt. 25:9.

66. 1 Cor. 2:9.
67. Matt. 25:10.
68. Matt. 25:11.
69. James 4:3.
70. Matt. 25:12.
71. Matt. 7:22.
72. Matt. 7:21.
73. Reading *tenebras* with manuscript F.
74. 1 John 1:8.
75. 1 Cor. 13:12.
76. 1 Cor. 13:9.
77. Luke 11:9.

Made in the USA
Las Vegas, NV
27 March 2022

46388114R10226